DUTCH
BY DESIGN

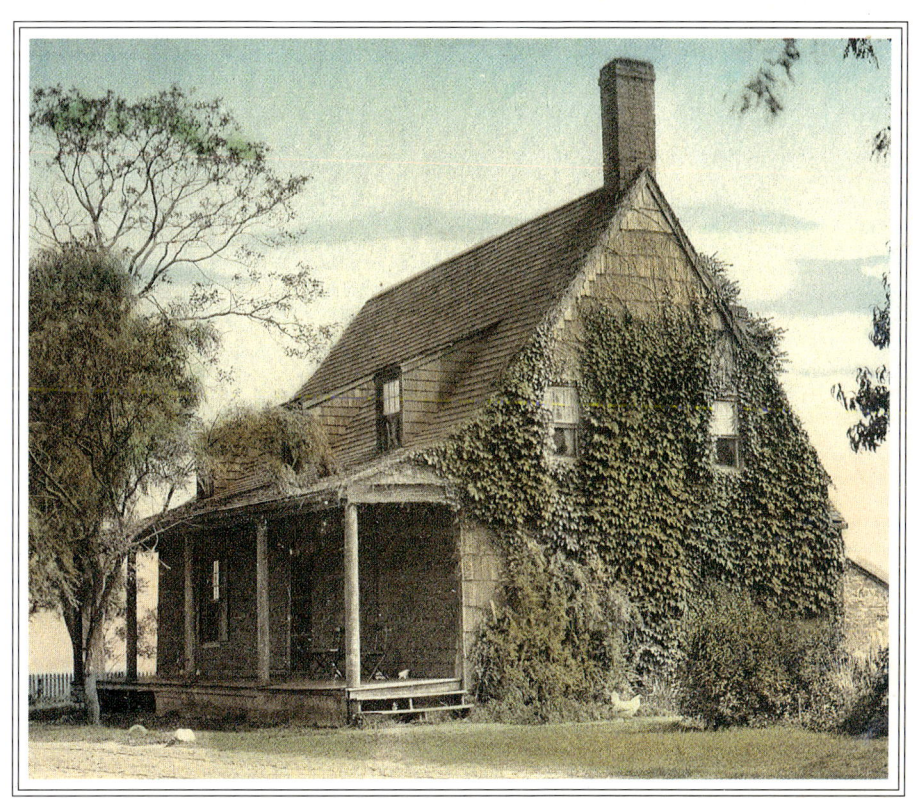

DUTCH
BY DESIGN

TRADITION AND CHANGE IN
TWO HISTORIC BROOKLYN HOUSES

The Schenck Houses at The Brooklyn Museum

KEVIN L. STAYTON

The Brooklyn Museum in association with
Phaidon Universe, New York

Front cover and frontispiece: Hand-tinted photograph of Jan Martense Schenck House from Charles Andrew Ditmas, *Historic Homesteads of Kings County* (Brooklyn: Charles A. Ditmas, 1909)

Back cover: Nicholas Schenck House, 1903

This publication has been made possible with generous support from The J. M. Kaplan Fund, the Surdna Foundation, Inc., and the National Endowment for the Arts, a federal agency.

Vice Director for Marketing: Rena Zurofsky
Assistant Director for Publications: Elaine Koss
Editor: John Antonides
Designer: Christina Bliss

Published in the United States of America in 1990 by Phaidon Universe
381 Park Avenue South, New York, NY 10016

© 1990 The Brooklyn Museum

All rights reserved. No part of this publication may be reproduced, stored in a retrieval system, or transmitted, in any form or by any means, electronic, mechanical, photocopying, recording, or otherwise, without prior permission of the publishers.

90 91 92 93 94 / 10 9 8 7 6 5 4 3 2 1

Printed in Hong Kong

Library of Congress Cataloging-in-Publication Data

Stayton, Kevin.
    Dutch by design : tradition and change in two historic Brooklyn houses / Kevin L. Stayton.
      p.   cm
   ISBN 0-87663-776-4
    1. Nicholas Schenck House (New York, N.Y.) 2. Jan Martense Schenck House (New York, N.Y.) 3. Brooklyn (New York, N.Y.) – Social life and customs. 4. Brooklyn (New York, N.Y.) – History. 5. Dutch Americans – New York (N.Y.) – History – 17th century. 6. Dutch Americans – New York (N.Y.) – History – 18th century. 7. Dutch Americans – New York (N.Y.) – Social life and customs. 8. New York (N.Y.) – History – Colonial period, ca. 1600–1775. 9. New York (N.Y.) – Social life and customs. 10. Brooklyn Museum. I. Title.
F129.B7S77   1990
974.7'1–dc20   90-34090
                                                                      CIP

CONTENTS

Foreword 7

Preface 9

Chapter One:
The Venerable Forefather 11

Chapter Two:
Of Cupboard Beds and Hearths without Jambs 27

Chapter Three:
From Dutch to Dutch American 53

Chapter Four:
A New Identity, A New Style 75

Chapter Five:
Consumer Goods and Family Heirlooms, or The Morn of Independence 89

Notes 121

Appendix 128

FOREWORD

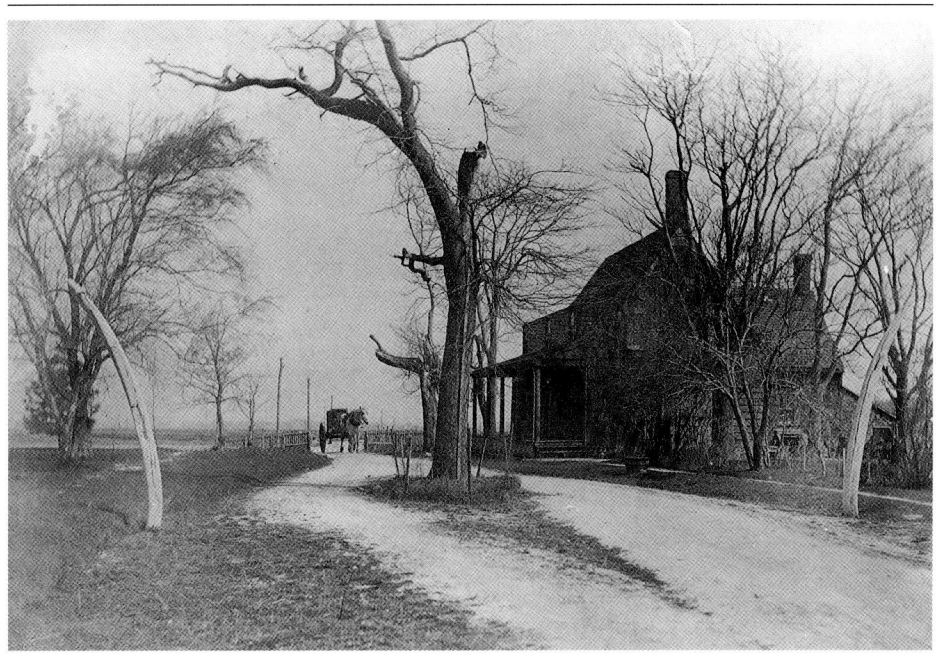

In 1976 The Brooklyn Museum initiated an ambitious program to renovate one of its most popular and critically acclaimed exhibits—a group of nineteen American period rooms first opened to the public in 1929. This display, assembled by Luke Vincent Lockwood (1872–1951), an early collector of Americana and a noted author on the decorative arts who joined the Museum's Board of Trustees in 1914, had long been known among museum professionals for three remarkable features: a high degree of architectural accuracy, the arrangement of the rooms by geographical origin so that comparisons could be made between the architecture of different regions, and the inclusion of entire ground floors so that wherever possible a visitor would have the impression of being in a house instead of in a room isolated from its original context.

The aim of the renovation was to continue the Lockwood precedent of approximating the past as accurately as possible. Throughout, an attempt was made to illustrate the range of choices—in fabrics, window and floor treatments, furniture, and accessories—available during the seventeenth, the eighteenth, or the nineteenth century in a room's given location. Care was also taken to reflect the standing of the rooms' original occupants in their respective communities. The goal was to appreciate the art and artifacts of early Americans while at the same time gaining some insight into the way they lived.

This project, which was coordinated by then-Curator of Decorative Arts Dianne H. Pilgrim, took eight years to complete and was accomplished in two stages. The first stage was achieved in 1980, when the New England and Southern rooms reopened. Reinstalled by Donald C. Peirce, then an Associate Curator of Decorative Arts, and Hope Alswang, then a Cura-

The Jan Martense Schenck House after 1891.

torial Assistant, these rooms were documented by the same scholars in *American Interiors: New England and the South*, published in 1983.

In like manner, the present book is an outgrowth of the completion of the second stage, which was accomplished in 1984 with the reopening of the Middle Atlantic rooms—four rooms and a stair hall from the Nicholas Schenck House of Flatlands, Brooklyn, built probably in the early 1770s, and a parlor and a dining room from the Abraham Harrison House of Irvington, New Jersey, built circa 1818. These reinstallations were carried out by then-Associate Curator of Decorative Arts Kevin L. Stayton with the assistance of intern Shelley Mills and consultant Hope Alswang, who had left the Museum by that time to become Curator of The Society for the Preservation of Long Island Antiquities.

Although precedent suggested that the Schenck and Harrison rooms be documented together in a publication similar to *American Interiors: New England and the South*, it was obvious that an even more interesting book could be had by examining the newly renovated Nicholas Schenck House in tandem with another Flatlands house built about a century earlier by Nicholas Schenck's grandfather Jan Martense Schenck—a house the Museum had acquired by fortunate circumstance in 1952. Though Curator of Decorative Arts Marvin D. Schwartz had published a book on this other Schenck house when he installed its two rooms in 1964, that book was long out of print and thanks to new scholarship somewhat out-of-date. Moreover, no one had ever done a comparative study of the two houses.

Such a study seemed especially promising in light of the Schencks' Dutch heritage. Jan Martense Schenck had immigrated to America when the eighty-one square miles that today comprise the borough of Brooklyn were still a part of the Dutch colony of New Netherland. His grandson Nicholas had lived to see the birth of a new nation. Together, their houses illustrate the gradual absorption of Dutch culture into the fabric of American life.

This book, then, does much more than serve as a guide to, and documentation of, the Schenck houses at The Brooklyn Museum. It also tells something of the history of Brooklyn—and by extension America—through an analysis of the life of a typical Dutch-American family living on Long Island from the time of its first colonization by Europeans to its emergence as part of a new republic. This family was neither rich nor poor; they were neither important people nor figures who changed the course of great events. We remember them by an accident of fate—because their houses have been preserved. And a lucky accident it is, for it allows us to study a classic case of American assimilation.

For their assistance over the many years it took to complete the reinstallation of the Nicholas Schenck House and the other period rooms and to publish this book and *American Interiors: New England and the South*, the Museum is indebted to many individuals and institutions. While seconding the acknowledgments Kevin Stayton makes in his preface, I would like to add my own special thanks to Mr. Stayton himself, first for his brilliant reinstallation of the Nicholas Schenck House. He has infused these rooms with the sensibilities of the middle-class farm family that occupied this house for three generations. One can feel that family's presence, their attachment to certain aspects of the past, and their desires for the future.

Second, I want to express my gratitude and admiration for this insightful book. Building on the work of Marvin Schwartz and his publication on the Jan Martense Schenck House, it not only illuminates both that house and the house of Nicholas Schenck but also weaves a fascinating history of the Dutch in Brooklyn through an enlightening examination of their architecture, artifacts, and customs.

ROBERT T. BUCK
Director
The Brooklyn Museum

PREFACE

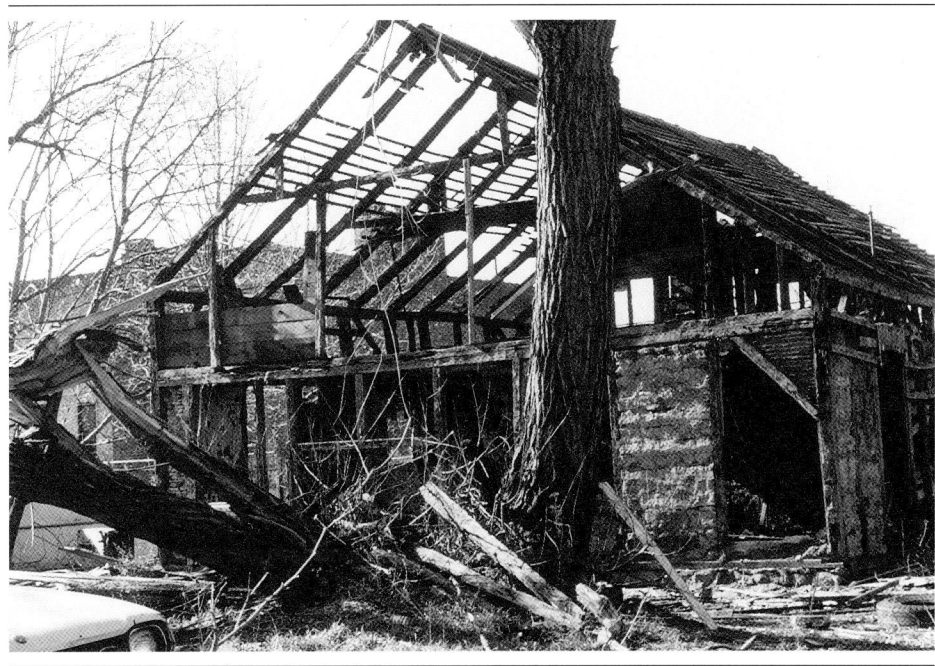

In November 1989, while this book was in preparation, one of New York City's last surviving eighteenth-century farmhouses—a one-and-a-half-story wooden house in the East New York section of Brooklyn built about 1787 by a Huguenot (or French Protestant) American named Christian Duryea—was destroyed by arson (see accompanying photograph). Sadly, this destruction came as no surprise. Abandoned for years, the house had become what some in the area described as "the oldest crackhouse in America." Addicts had moved in, littering the floor with their crack vials, burning doors and window frames for heat, and scrawling graffiti on the walls. Reportedly, concerned residents of the neighborhood—one of New York's poorest—had tried to enlist the help of both government and private organizations in order to preserve the house. But the owner (who died in 1982) had thwarted an attempt to designate it a landmark, and litigation over his estate had hampered private efforts to buy it. In the aftermath of the fire, charges were leveled that the city had dragged its feet while the house fell further into disrepair.

This tragic event brought home to us—in an all too real way—how important it is for this book to encourage, among other things, a greater appreciation of New York's architectural heritage. The pair of early Brooklyn houses chronicled here—named for the Dutch Americans Jan Martense Schenck and his grandson Nicholas—illustrate well two of the greatest pressures facing historical properties in New York City. One was threatened by "progress" (the creation of a middle-class urban neighborhood whose developers capitalized on the house's bay-front location) and the other by poverty (in this case the city's). Though we are pleased that both houses have been saved by their reconstruction in The Brooklyn Museum, we realize

Ruins of the Duryea House, 562 Jerome Street, East New York, Brooklyn, February 1990. Photograph by Kevin L. Stayton.

that such a solution has serious limits. At least fourteen old Dutch farmhouses still exist in the borough of Brooklyn, and the Museum clearly cannot save them all. In fact, of the few that now appear in danger from either development or neglect, the Museum would be hard pressed to accommodate even one. It is critical, therefore, that the appreciation of these houses already in the Museum's care be extended to their counterparts still standing on site. With the loss of any one of these tangible connections to the past, we would lose more than just a house; we would lose—as we did in the case of the Duryea House—part of our spirit and history as well.

If anything gives us hope in this cause, it is the many committed organizations and individuals that have contributed both to the publication of this book and to the maintenance of the houses it concerns. This book alone has received funding from three different sectors: the government, foundations, and private individuals. We are especially grateful for the generosity of the National Endowment for the Arts, the Surdna Foundation, and The J. M. Kaplan Fund, all of which provided major support. And our thanks go as well to Donald Schenck and Mrs. E. Dean Schooler, both of whom also donated funds for the publication of this volume.

For financial assistance with the recent renovation of the Nicholas Schenck House (see Foreword for a brief history of that project) we are indebted once again to the National Endowment, the Surdna Foundation, and The J. M. Kaplan Fund as well as to the Sack Foundation, the Wunsch Foundation, Mr. and Mrs. Richard Manney, Mrs. Carl L. Selden, Mr. and Mrs. Erving Wolf, and the firm Brunschwig & Fils. And for support in maintaining the Jan Martense Schenck House we wish to acknowledge the Lilian Pitkin Schenck Fund, which has given generously over the years to that end.

Numerous independent scholars and colleagues from other institutions have contributed to the solving of the many puzzles presented by the two Schenck houses and to the research involved in renovating the Nicholas Schenck House and preparing this book. As the curator responsible for the Nicholas Schenck House renovation, I would like to thank the countless people who gave their time, energy, and ideas to that project, especially Samuel Dornsife, Jane Nylander, Albert Wadsworth, and Michael Bishop and Murray Douglas of Brunschwig & Fils. As the author of this volume, I also owe thanks to Roderic Blackburn, David S. Cohen, Carol Day, Heidi Fried, Charles Gehring, Alan J. Lipsky, William McMillen, Roger Mohovich, Eric Nooter, John R. Stevens, and Henk J. Zantkuyl. The tremendously valuable research done by Judith Margles and Lee Roberts is particularly appreciated, and thanks are due as well to Lynn Warshow for many helpful editorial suggestions.

With regard to the illustrations in this book, I am indebted to all the institutions that have allowed us to publish works in their collections. Special acknowledgment goes to the following individuals for their assistance in locating photographs: Patricia Kane of the Yale University Art Gallery; Leslie Keno of Sotheby's, New York; Ellen Snyder, Lucy Eldridge, and David Moore of The Brooklyn Historical Society; and Elizabeth White of the Brooklyn Public Library.

For bringing to my attention—and in some cases into The Brooklyn Museum's collection—new material related to this volume, I would like to thank George T. Griswold, Mrs. Erastus V. Corning IV, and Norman S. Rice.

Many Brooklyn Museum colleagues, both past and present, have been of tremendous help in the course of this project. First and foremost I wish to thank former Curator of Decorative Arts Dianne H. Pilgrim, now Director of New York's Cooper-Hewitt Museum, The Smithsonian Institution's National Museum of Design. Her vision and direction were responsible for the genesis of this work, and her enthusiastic support, encouragement, and assistance were indispensable throughout its preparation.

Special thanks are likewise due to the former members of the Department of Decorative Arts whose past work forms the foundation of this study: Donald C. Peirce, Hope Alswang, and Marvin D. Schwartz.

Nor can I forget the other members of the department who have also contributed time, effort, and support. For their long-standing encouragement, I am indebted especially to Christopher Wilk, Celestina Ucciferri, and Caroline Mortimer as well as to Barry R. Harwood, Jim Hayes, Marianne L. Loggia, and Diane Quero.

In addition, numerous interns and research volunteers in the department have provided useful aid, among them Leslie Blacksburg, Kate Carmel, Brenda Hureau, Kirsten Rohrs, Larry Weinberg, Karen Zukowski, and last, but hardly least, Shelley Mills, whose work during the renovation of the Nicholas Schenck House proved invaluable.

I am also grateful for the assistance of Elizabeth Ann Coleman, the Museum's Curator of Costumes and Textiles; Paulette Willman, formerly Restorer in the Department of Costumes and Textiles; Ken Moser and Ellen Pearlstein, Chief Conservator and Conservator of Objects, respectively, in the Conservation Department; Deirdre Lawrence, the Museum's Principal Librarian; Patrick Cardon, formerly Deputy Director; and others too numerous to mention whose contributions have been essential to the completion of the project.

Finally, I would like to express my gratitude to Museum Editor John Antonides, whose interest in this work went far beyond editing it. He has generously and enthusiastically contributed ideas and helped me to formulate my own. Without his input this would have been a very different book. For his part, Mr. Antonides would like to dedicate his efforts to the memory of his father, Lloyd B. Antonides, who instilled in him an appreciation of his own family's Dutch Brooklyn heritage.

KEVIN L. STAYTON
Curator of Decorative Arts
The Brooklyn Museum
Brooklyn, February 1990

CHAPTER
ONE

THE VENERABLE FOREFATHER

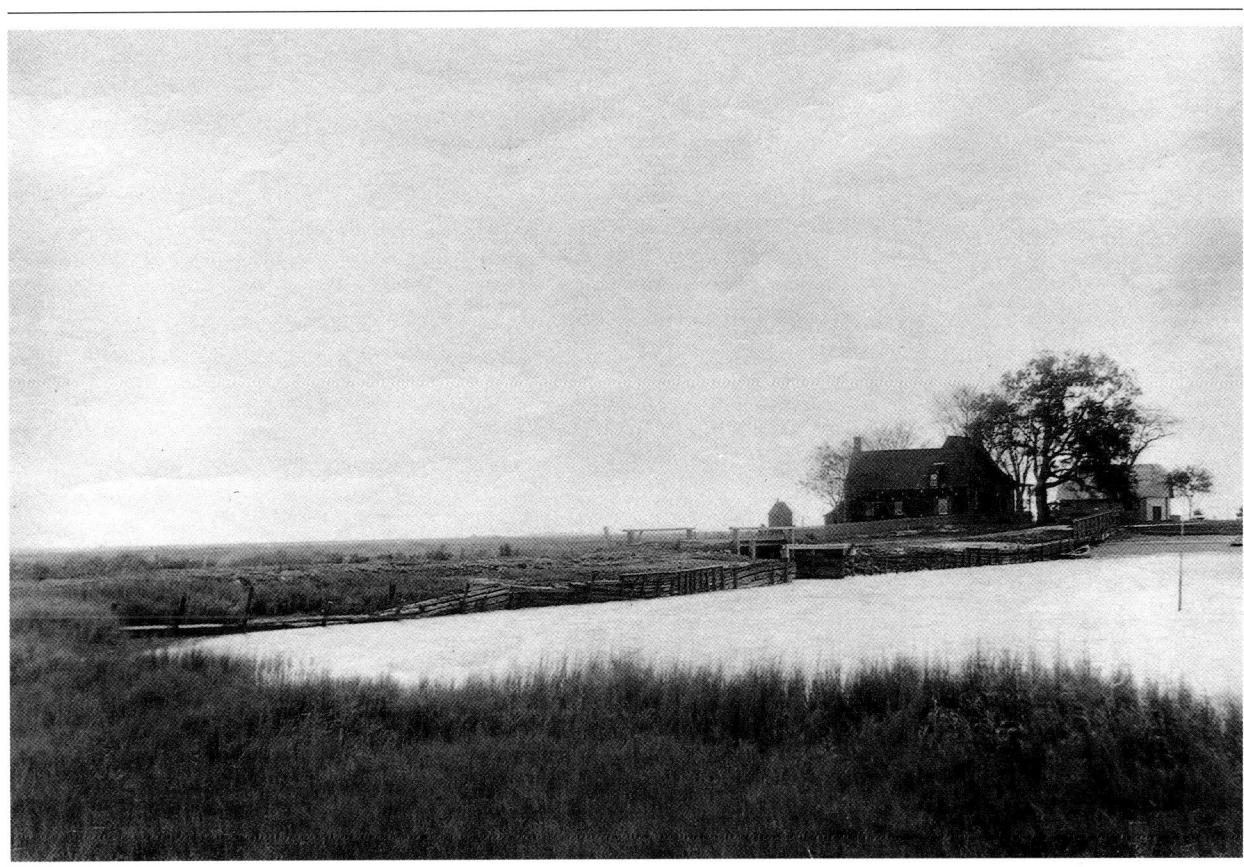

In early October 1891 the Reverend William Edward Schenck (pronounced Skenk) of Princeton, New Jersey, made a pilgrimage to Flatlands, Long Island, then a sleepy farming town about two miles southeast of Brooklyn, to visit a seventeenth-century house built by his Dutch ancestor Jan Martense Schenck. Arriving in Manhattan around 9:30 on a Friday morning, he crossed what he called the High Bridge to Brooklyn in a cable car, took a horse car to Flatbush Avenue, and then boarded a train to Flatlands, where the pastor of the local Dutch Reformed church met him with a horse and carriage. After lunch at the parsonage, he set out again with the pastor and, after traveling almost a mile and a half on a road lined with fields of corn and hay, neared, with great anticipation, his goal:

> We rode on about half a mile, then turned a rectangular corner to the right where there was a sudden and surprising change of view. Level meadowlands stretched out before us to the edge of the horizon, where the ocean was

1.1. The Jan Martense Schenck House, 1891. Photograph by the Reverend William Edward Schenck.

just visible, a mile or so away. Through these meadows, one or two tidal streams meandered. A little distance in front of us stood, on an island formed by one of those streams—an island containing from 50 to 100 acres—the venerable Schenck home of our forefather [*fig. 1.1*]...[1]

The stream that made the Schenck homestead an island has long since been filled in, the meadows and fields paved, and the town of Flatlands annexed to Brooklyn, creating one great urban expanse from the shores of Jamaica Bay to the cliffs of Brooklyn Heights. The house of Jan Martense Schenck, however, has survived, having been carefully dismantled in 1952 and reconstructed in The Brooklyn Museum in 1963–64 (*see fig. 1.2*). There, together with another house from Flatlands built about a century later by his grandson Nicholas, it provides a unique view of the evolution of Dutch-American culture. People are still drawn to it, and though they may not be Schencks—or even of Dutch descent—they discover within its walls what the Reverend Schenck also found: a romantic vision of a time very distant and different.

To step into the dark, low-ceilinged interior of the Jan Martense Schenck House is to be transported, in a sense, to the Long Island of 1730—the date to which the house has been restored. The area now occupied by the borough of Brooklyn (coextensive with Kings County) was then a patchwork of wilderness and farmland dotted with six scattered rural towns established under the Dutch colony of New Netherland, which had surrendered to the English and become New York in 1664. One of these towns, Gravesend, had been settled by English Anabaptist exiles from Puritan Massachusetts at the consent of the Dutch authorities. But the other five were peopled largely by Dutch or Dutch-speaking folk and were commonly referred to as "the five Dutch towns of Long Island" well into the eighteenth century. In addition to Flatlands, then probably still better known to its inhabitants as New Amersfoort, after Amersfoort in the Dutch province of Utrecht, they included the towns of Breukelen ("the broken land," named after another town in Utrecht), New Utrecht (named after Utrecht itself), Boswyck ("the town of the woods," called Bushwick by the English), and 't Vlacke Bos ("the wooded plain," anglicized to Flatbush and also known as Midwout or Midwood).

New Amersfoort, one of the first (if not the first) of these Dutch settlements on Long Island, had developed on a tract of land called Keskateuw by the Canarsie Indians. In 1636 several thousand acres of this land were divided up, by purchase from the Canarsie, among four men: Jacobus van Corlaer, an official in the Dutch West India Company, the firm that administered New Netherland for the Dutch government; Andries Hudde, a former member of the Council of New Netherland, the body established by the West India Company to exercise authority in the colony; Wolfert Gerritsen van Kouwenhoven, a onetime manager of a farm for Kiliaen van Rensselaer, a founder-member of the West India Company and New Netherland's largest private landowner; and Wouter van Twiller, the colony's Director General and a nephew of van Rensselaer. Probably none of these prominent men ever actually lived in New Amersfoort except van Kouwenhoven, who is thought to have named the town because he is said to have hailed from the old Amersfoort. In any event, settlement of the place happened slowly, led by a handful of Dutch families, including—in addition to van Kouwenhoven's descendants—the Gerritsens, the Stoothoffs, the Wyckoffs, the van Voorhees, and the Schencks. As late as 1790, the year of the first United States census, the entire population was only 423.

The earliest recorded evidence of Jan Martense Schenck's living in New Amersfoort dates to August 20, 1660, when Director General Peter Stuyvesant and the Council of New Netherland granted him two parcels of land totaling about 46½ acres near the local mill lane.[2] (He sold one parcel, encompassing a little more than 25 acres, to a man by the name of Pieter Claesen Wyckoff eight days later but did not dispose of the other until February 15, 1677.[3]) Details of his life before then are in the realm of family myth, though in some cases the myths do ring true. In 1687, for instance, when he took the oath of allegiance to the King of England, he stated that he had been in America for thirty-seven years[4]—a statement that seems to support in part the legend that he and his brother Roeloff and their sister

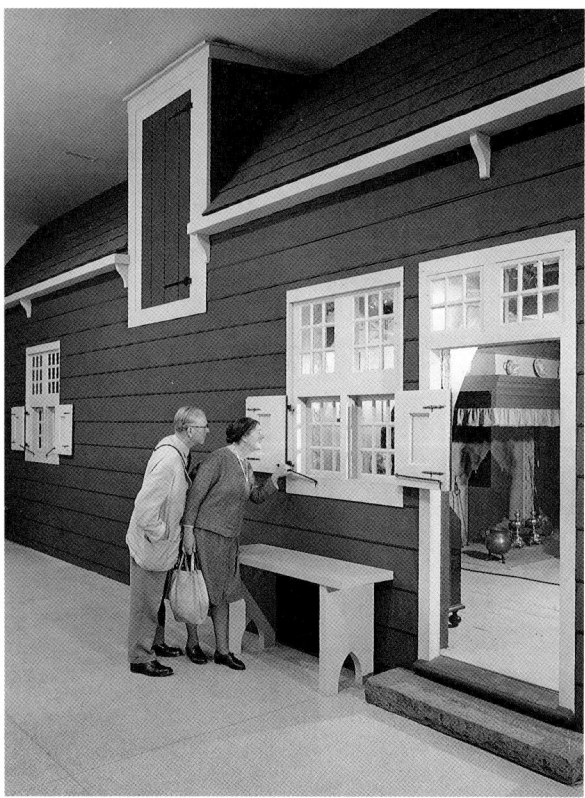

1.2. The Jan Martense Schenck House, as installed in The Brooklyn Museum, 1964.

THE VENERABLE FOREFATHER

Anetje came to New Netherland in 1650 on board the ship *de Valkenier* ("The Falconer"), which arrived in New Amsterdam harbor on June 28 of that year.[5]

Since the nineteenth century, genealogists have traced Jan and Roeloff Martense Schenck's ancestry through a Marten Schenck who was born in the Netherlands in 1584 (and supposedly died en route to America with his children) to the ancient family Schenck van Nydeck (or Nydeggen), a branch of the family Schenck, Barons van Toutenberg.[6] In the sixteenth century the members of the Schenck van Nydeck family were knights-landholders and soldiers of high social standing. But although the suffix "se" on the end of their middle names indicates, in the Dutch way, that Jan and Roeloff Schenck were sons of a man named Marten, there is no documentation to link them to the Marten Schenck of the Schenck van Nydeck line.[7]

In fact, although there is no doubt the Schenck brothers were Dutch, there is no convincing indication of where in the Netherlands they came from. Family legend has it that they were born in the town of Amersfoort, but as with their connection to the Schencks van Nydeck there is no documentation to support the assertion. The historian Rosalie Fellows Bailey speculated in 1964 that the story might have originated in the nineteenth century, when the place name of New Amersfoort, which had been discarded by then in favor of Flatlands, might have been confused with Amersfoort in the Netherlands. Strangely, though, Bailey offered her own, no more plausible, estimation of the Schenck brothers' origin, pointing to a document of 1662 signed by Roeloff Martense "van Breuckelen" as evidence they came from the Old World town of that name.[8]

Whatever the case, by the 1670s Jan Martense Schenck had set his roots down firmly in America. Although the exact date is not known, he is believed to have married Jannetje van Voorhees early that decade, for their eldest daughter, Jannetjie, is said to have been born about 1673 and their eldest son, Martin, in 1675. The latter may have been a twin, for the account book of the Flatlands Dutch Reformed Church contains the following entry: "In the year 1675 the 1st of November...Shroud and for the grave for Jan Martense's child."[9] The couple would lose at least two other children, in 1682 and 1688, but at least three others survived: Willemtjie, Neeltjie, and Stephen, who were born, respectively, about 1677, 1683, and 1685.

Undoubtedly, it was in order to provide both a

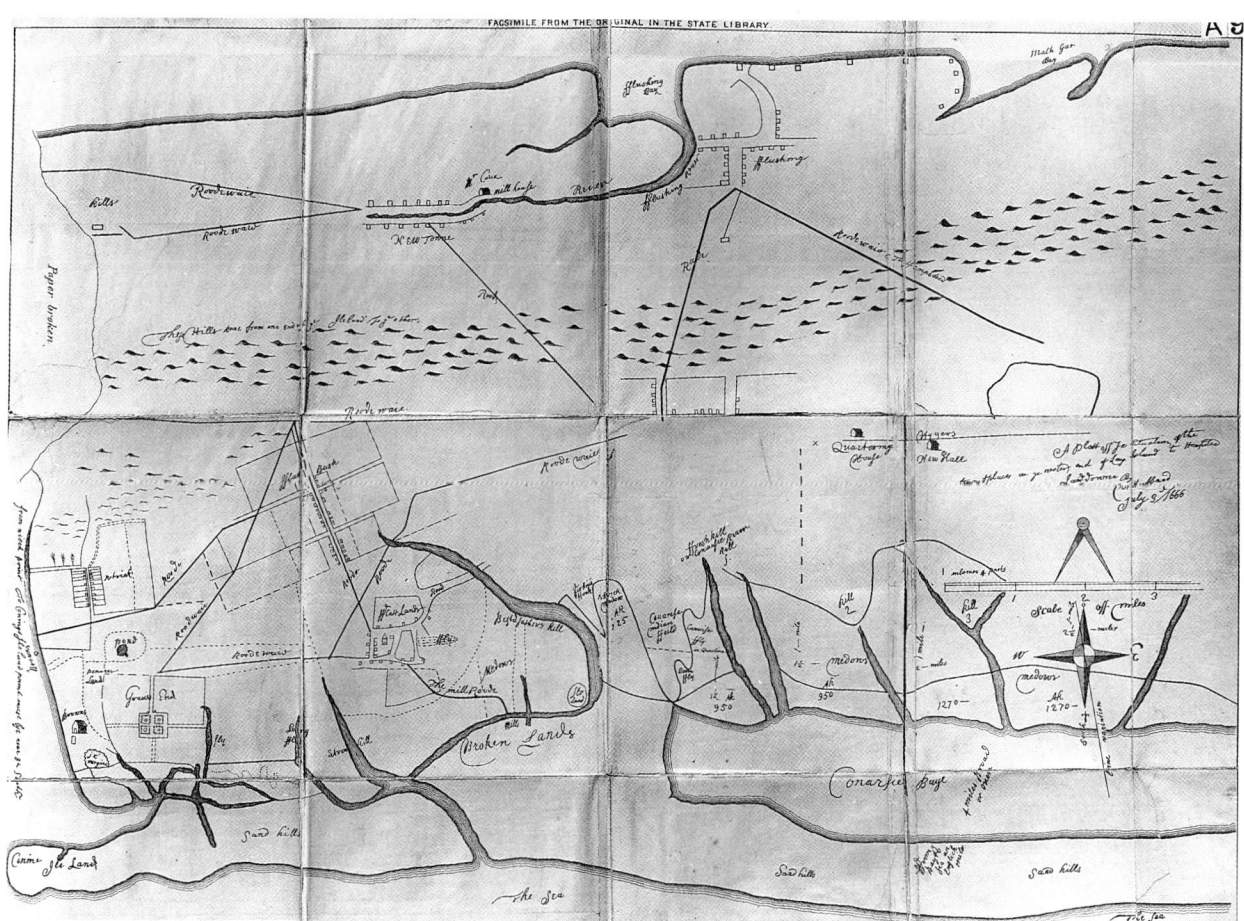

1.3. *Facsimile of a map of western Long Island by Cornelius Hubbard. Original dated July 3, 1666. Courtesy of The Brooklyn Historical Society.*

home and a living for his family that Schenck bought from a merchant named Elbert Elbertsen (Stoothoff) on December 29, 1675, the local island on which he would build his house, together with a half share of the tidal gristmill that gave the place its name—Mill Island.[10] The island and the wetlands around it, called Equandito, or "broken lands," by the Canarsie Indians, had been deeded by the Canarsie to John Tilton, Sr., and Samuel Spicer of Gravesend on May 13, 1664.[11] These two Englishmen may have acted as agents for Elbertsen, for although they did not officially convey the land to him until May 2, 1681, he was clearly in possession of the island and at least a half share of its mill when he dealt with Schenck. Indeed it was probably he who built the mill, which as evidenced by a seventeenth-century map of the area, was standing as early as 1666 (see fig. 1.3). Perhaps for a time he operated it in conjunction with Schenck. Unfortunately, however, the records do not indicate from whom, or even when, Schenck acquired the other half interest, though the will he wrote on his deathbed in 1689 suggests he was sole owner when he died.[12]

The best early description of Schenck's property and its environs is provided by Jasper Danckaerts and Peter Sluyter, two members of a Dutch religious sect called the Labadists who visited New Amersfoort in October 1679:

> There is towards the sea, a large piece of low flat land which is overflown at every tide, like the *Schor* [marsh] with us, miry and muddy at the bottom, and which produces a species of hard salt grass or reed grass. Such a place they call *valey* and mow it for hay, which cattle would rather eat than fresh hay or grass. It is so hard that they cannot mow it with a common scythe, like ours, but must have the English scythe for the purpose. Their adjoining corn lands are dry and barren for the most part. Some of them were now entirely covered with clover in blossom, which diffused a sweet odor in the air for a great distance, and which we

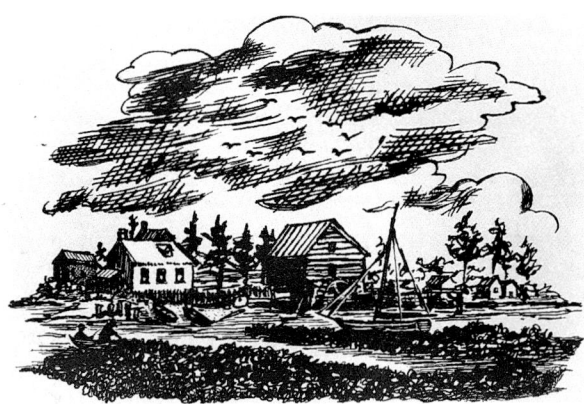

1.4. *The Jan Martense Schenck House and mill, 1833. Woodcut first published in* David Baldwin, or The Miller's Son, *no. 282 of* Publications of the American Tract Society, *vol. 9 (New York, 1833).*

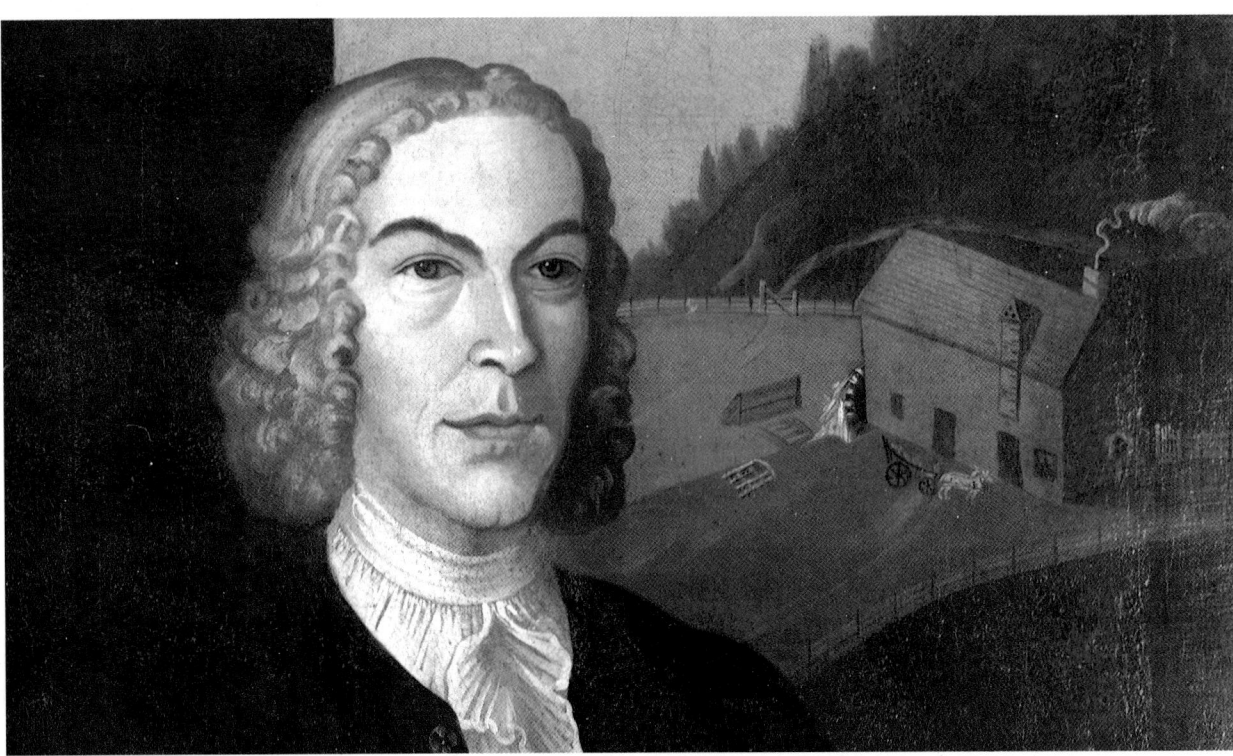

1.5. *Attributed to John Heaten (Anglo-American, active 1730–mid-1740s). Portrait of Abraham Wendell (1715–1753) (detail), circa 1737. Oil on ticking, 35½ × 29⅝ inches. Albany Institute of History and Art.*

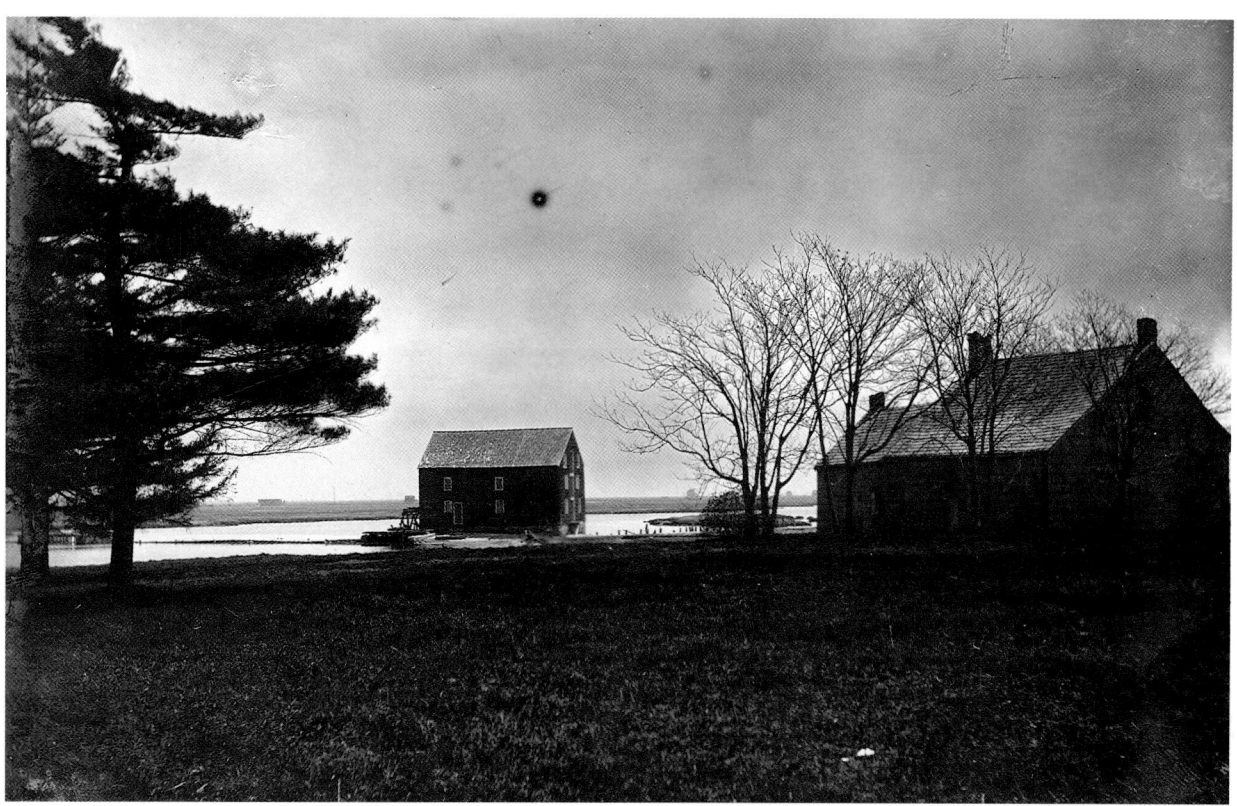

1.6. The Gerritsen mill, Gravesend-Flatlands border, circa 1900. Photograph courtesy of the Brooklyn Public Library.

discovered in the atmosphere, before we saw the fields. Behind the village, inland, are their meadows, but they also were now arid. All the land from the bay to *'t Vlacke Bos* is low and level, without the least elevation. There is also a tract which is somewhat large, of a kind of heath on which sheep could graze, though we saw none upon it. This meadow, like all the others, is well provided with good creeks which are navigable and very serviceable for fisheries. There is here a grist-mill driven by the water which they dam up in the creek; and it is hereabouts they go mostly to shoot snipe and wild geese.[13]

Regrettably, although the mill that gave the Schenck property its name stood for some two hundred years, we can only speculate about its appearance. A tax assessment of 1796 describes it as being twenty-eight feet square, and a woodcut of the Schenck homestead published in 1833 (*fig. 1.4*)—the earliest known representation of the place—provides a generalized view of a square, steeply roofed structure with a waterwheel on the side and a large loft for storage above. Perhaps it resembled the mill seen in the background of an early eighteenth-century portrait of Abraham Wendell of Albany (*fig. 1.5*) or the one owned by the Schencks' Long Island neighbors the Gerritsens (built before 1757), which is recorded in a turn-of-the-century photograph (*fig. 1.6*). At any rate,

it would have provided a steady income to its owner, for the rich farms of western Long Island produced an abundance of corn, wheat, and other grains.

To supplement this income, Schenck himself engaged in farming, as is evidenced by the grain and tobacco he is credited with in the merchant accounts of Elbert Elbertsen.[14] Together, these two trades of miller and farmer seem to have made him a man of comfortable affluence, though not of great wealth. Of the thirty-eight households taxed in New Amersfoort in 1683, the value of his property ranked thirteenth.[15] Although he was not nearly as well off as his brother, whose property led the same list (possibly because he married a daughter of the van Kouwenhovens, a land-rich family),[16] his will reveals that he accumulated fairly substantial cash assets for the period. In addition to two cows and a bed, he left to each of his three daughters one hundred pieces-of-eight, and to the child his wife was carrying as he lay dying he bequeathed, provided it were a son, "ye monny standing out att New Yorke the summ off Sixteen hundred gildens" (whether this child was even born is not clear).[17] Unlike his brother, who was a magistrate of the five Dutch towns as well as a patentee of New Amersfoort when its rights were renewed by the English governor, Richard Nicolls, in 1667,[18] he seems never to have held public office.[19] But as a prosperous farmer who contributed to the town's stability and also milled a good part of its grain, he was undoubtedly a well-respected member of the community.

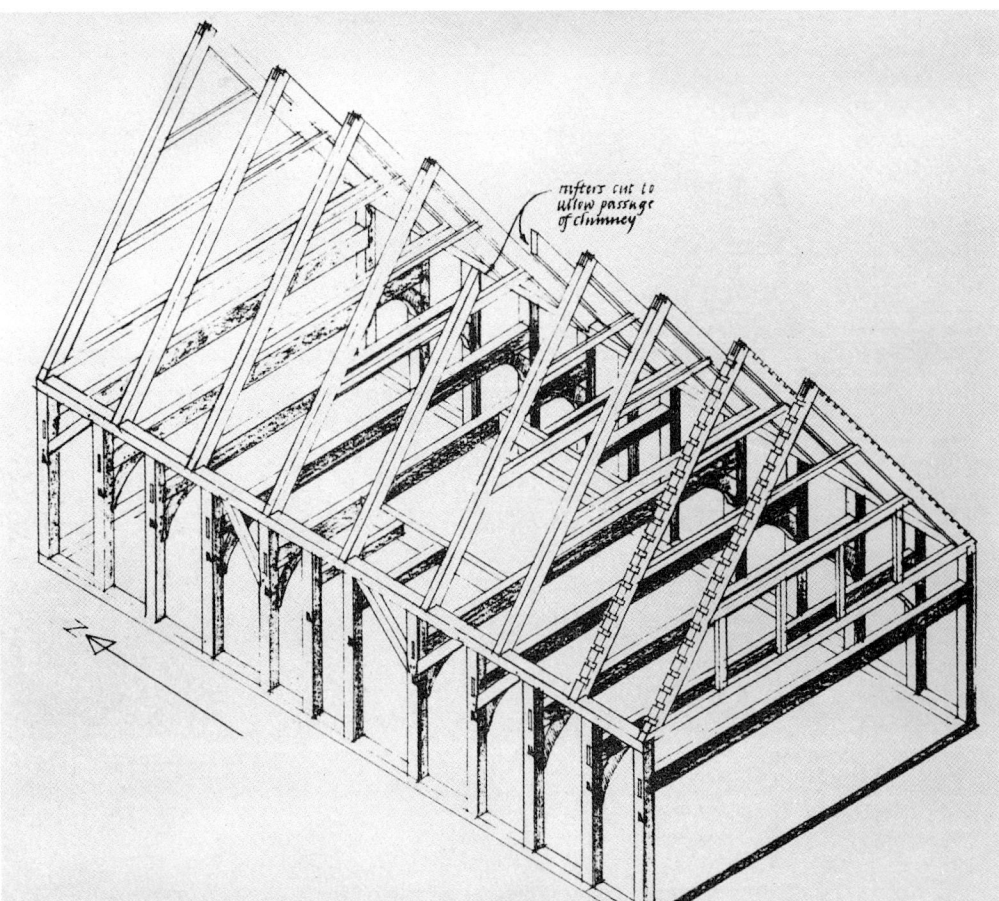

1.7. Isometric projection of framework, the Jan Martense Schenck House. Drawing by Ian Smith, 1963.

1.8. Structural elements of the Jan Martense Schenck House during dismantling, 1952, showing Roman numeral markings.

The house Schenck built on Mill Island (probably in the thirteen months between his purchase of the island in late December 1675 and his disposal of his remaining land near the local mill lane in mid-February 1677)[20] confirms in a number of ways the image of the man that legend and history have given us, reflecting as it does his immigrant sense of industry, his modest means, and his Dutch roots. A simple but well-crafted two-room wooden structure organized around a central chimney with a loft for storage above, it is constructed along a typical Dutch (or, more generally, Continental) framing plan (*see fig. 1.7*).

This plan, so different from the one seen in seventeenth-century New England frame houses (which follow an English example), represents the survival of a medieval tradition widespread throughout northern Europe. The historian David Steven Cohen describes it well:

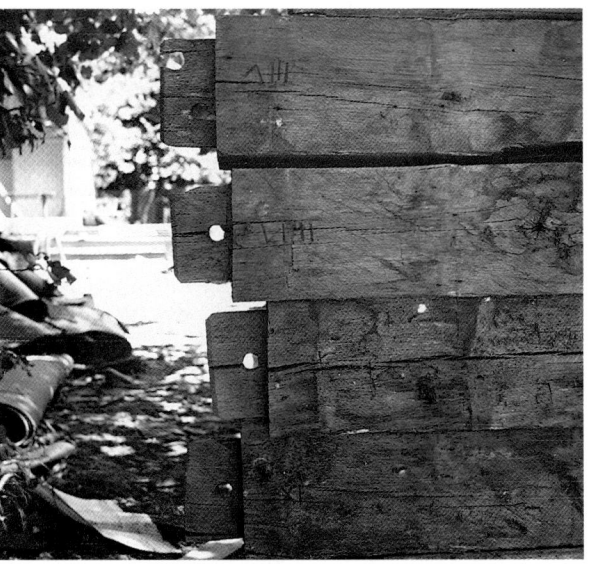

> Unlike the boxlike English frame, the continental frame resembles a series of goal posts, known as H-bents, each consisting of two vertical posts connected by a large anchor beam and reinforced by diagonal corner braces. Atop the posts on either side of the H-bents run horizontal plates, which support the widely spaced rafters of the pitched roof. The paired rafters are reinforced by collar beams and joined at the peak by mortise and tenon joints;...there is no ridgepole.[21]

This system, then, gives the Jan Martense Schenck House what is perhaps its most distinctive interior feature: the diagonal corner braces connecting the anchor beams to the vertical posts (*see, for example, fig. 2.35*), which like all the framing elements are inscribed with Roman numerals where they join with other members (*see fig. 1.8*). The area between the posts was originally filled with an insulation of brick nogging (*see fig. 1.9*), rather than the mud and straw Nicholas Schenck would use a century later in the building of his home.[22]

On the exterior, the house is covered with clapboards. Although few clapboard houses survive in New York from the seventeenth century, such buildings were probably common, especially in rural areas, where the danger of sweeping conflagrations was less than in towns, and particularly on Long Island, where there was a shortage of building stone in the sandy coastal soil.[23] In 1646 the French Jesuit missionary Isaac Jogues wrote of the colonists of Rensselaerswyck, Kiliaen van Rensselaer's 700,000-acre estate around Fort Orange (present-day Albany), "Their houses are merely of boards and thatched, with no mason work except the chimneys. The forest furnishing many large pines, they make boards by means of their mills, which they have here for the purpose."[24] And in New Amersfoort in the 1670s, around the time Schenck built his house, Elbert Elbertsen accepted for credit from one of his customers clapboards and shingles.[25]

Many details of the Jan Martense Schenck House as it is installed in The Brooklyn Museum are necessarily the result of informed conjecture, for during the three centuries that it stood on Mill Island it changed significantly, as houses do during the passage of time and successive generations. Nonetheless, evidence carefully gathered by Museum curator Marvin Schwartz and consultants Daniel M. C. Hopping and Ian Smith during the dismantling and reconstruction of the house (see Appendix for a summary of their findings) has allowed us to re-create, with some assurance of accuracy, its appearance in 1730.

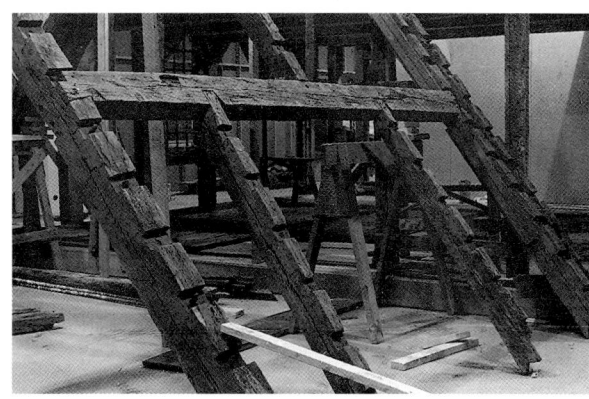

1.10. Rafters showing opening for loft door. The Jan Martense Schenck House during reconstruction in The Brooklyn Museum, 1963.

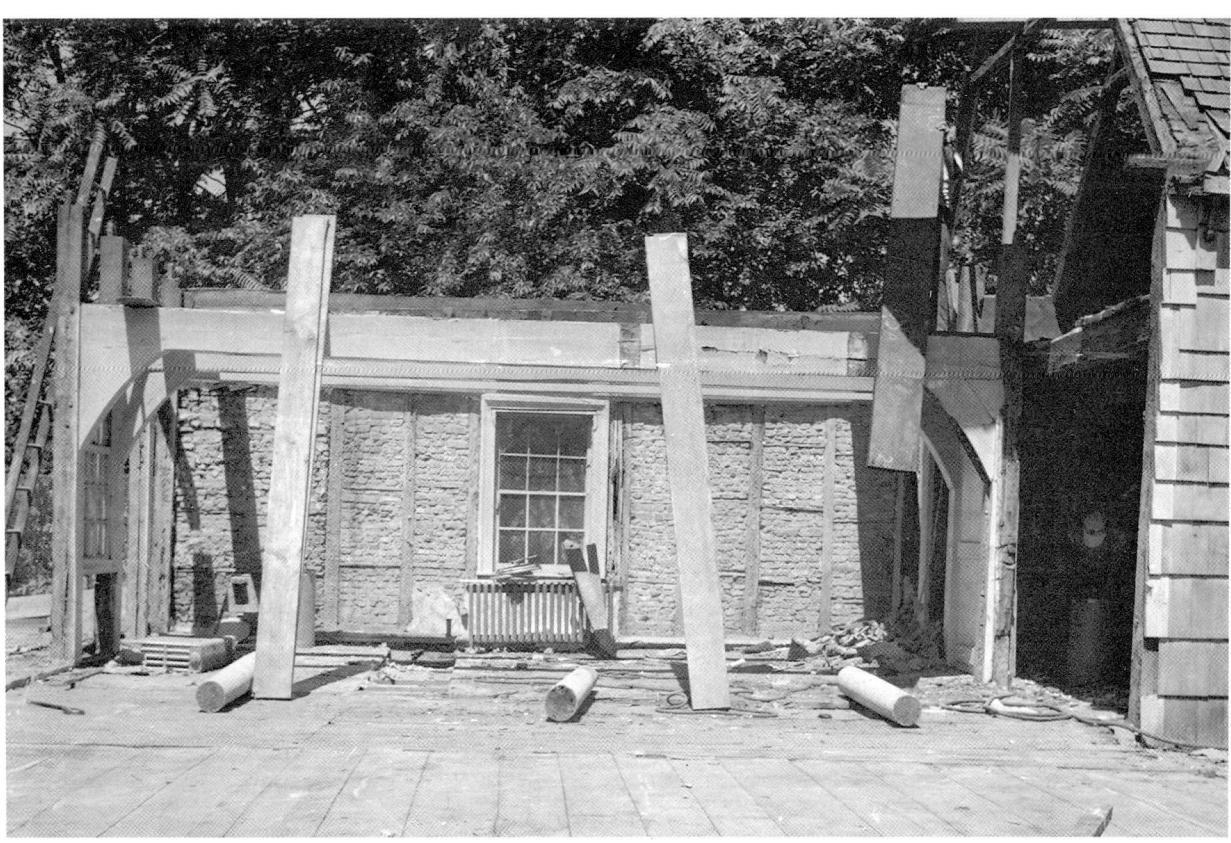

1.9. Interior of the Jan Martense Schenck House during dismantling, 1952, showing insulation of brick nogging.

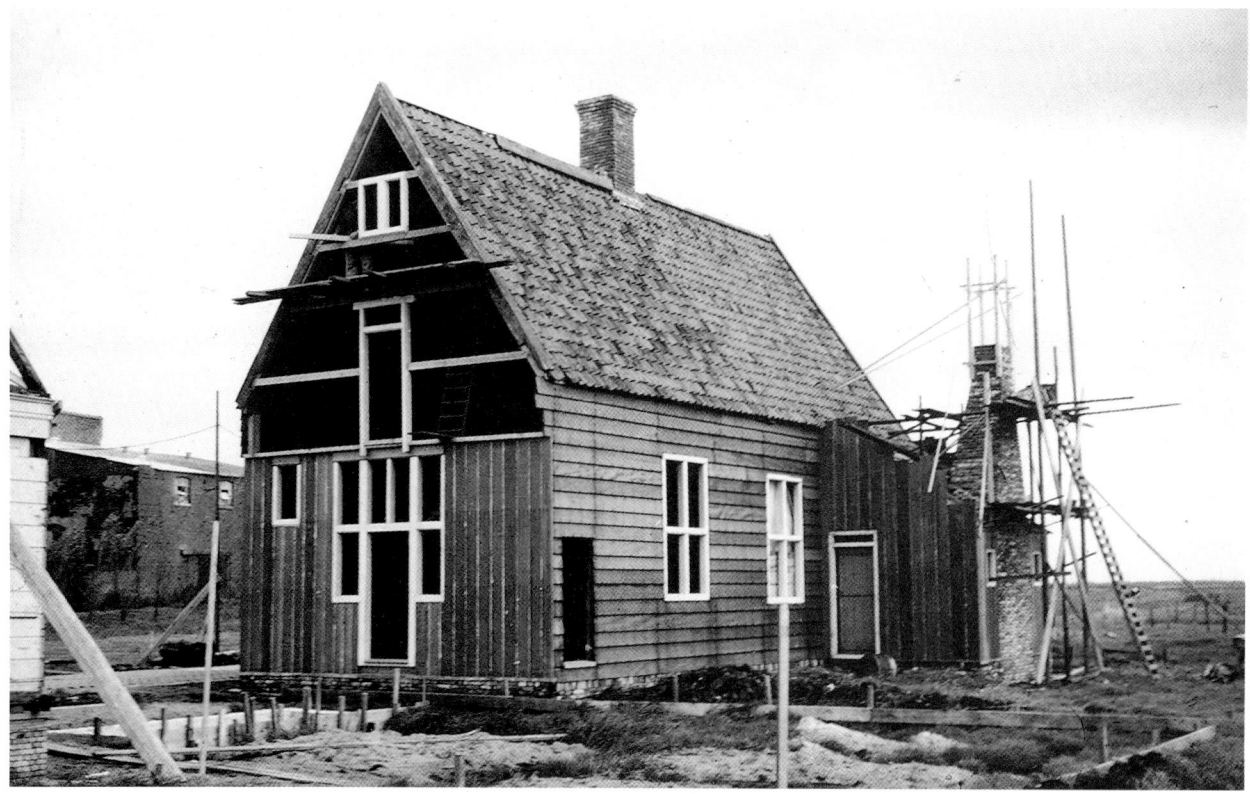

1.11. *House in Zaandam, the Netherlands. Built circa 1740. Photographed during reconstruction, 1963.*

The clapboards, for instance, were painted gray after microscopic analysis of the remaining original boards revealed that color.[26] Likewise, a dormer door providing access to the loft from the outside was included in the eastern (front) roof because the spacing of the beams there suggested it (*see fig. 1.10 and again 1.2*). Dutch prototypes typically had a loft door only in the gable end, especially in urban areas, where the gable was turned toward the street or canal to economize on space (*see fig. 1.11*).

Other evidence gathered during the dismantling of the house indicated that it had originally had doors in the east wall of the north room and the south wall of the south room; evidence for windows was found in both the east and south walls (*see fig. 1.12*). Though there was no indication of original doors or windows in the west wall, there were mortise holes in the original posts of that wall indicating that it had been built with a projecting shelter, or aisle (*see fig. 1.13*). This aisle, however, was omitted in the installation because it was believed to have been removed around 1730.

Although the house had long had a fireplace in the

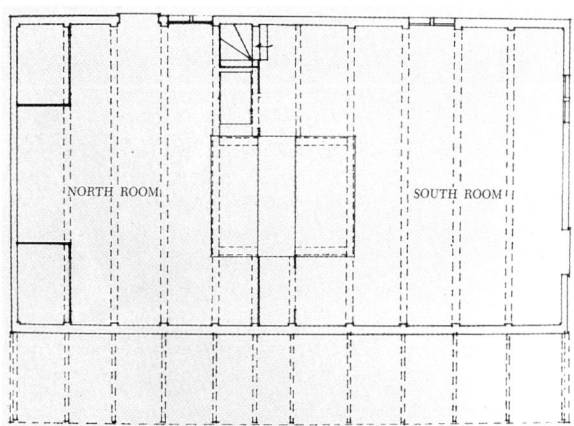

1.12. *Original floor plan of the Jan Martense Schenck House as proposed by Marvin Schwartz, 1964.*

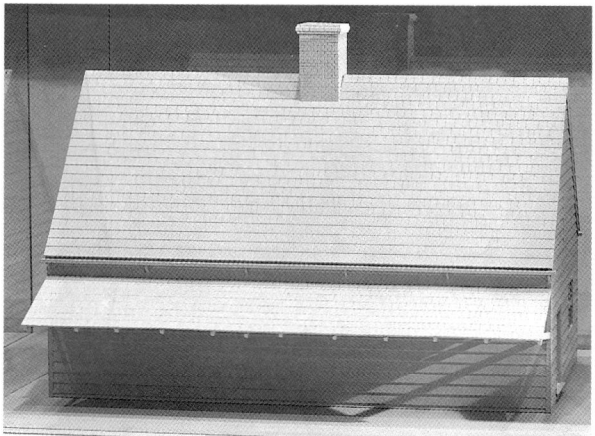

1.13. *Model of the Jan Martense Schenck House showing shelter along west wall.*

THE VENERABLE FOREFATHER

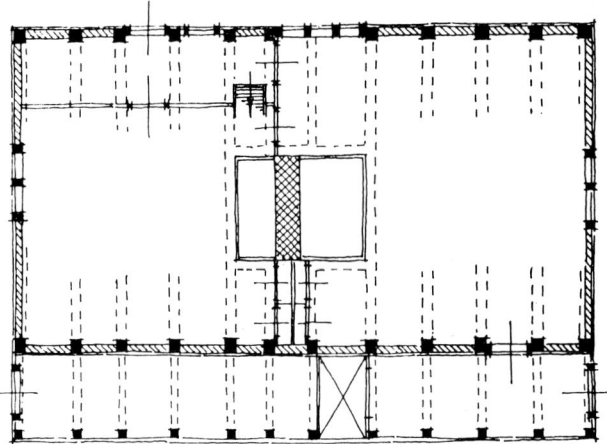

1.14. Original floor plan of the Jan Martense Schenck House as proposed by Henk J. Zantkuyl, 1985.

gable wall of the south room, a number of things confirmed that it originally had a central chimney. As Marvin Schwartz said of the central area of the roof:

> Here, the beams were the least convincing and, when the walls were taken down, proved to be nearly all replacements. Two original beams were uncovered; one was charred, and the other had traces of plaster indicating the chimney's previous position. An opening in the center rafter above added further proof [*see again fig. 1.7*].[27]

Recently, Henk J. Zantkuyl of the Dutch architectural preservation agency Bureau Monumentenzorg Amsterdam has proposed a slightly different version of the original appearance of the house than the one envisioned by Messrs. Schwartz, Hopping, and Smith (*see figs. 1.14 and 1.15*). Zantkuyl believes that the aisle on the west side of the house was more substantial than they imagined. Pointing to evidence on the original beams, he also holds, with some justification, that the entrance on the east wall was screened from the north room by a thin partition. The staircase to the loft, he thinks, was entered from this partitioned portion of the north room, rather than from the south room as in the Museum. Moreover, he contends, the window in the east wall of the south room was located nearer the fireplace, where light for working would have been essential.[28]

The impossibility of settling such matters helps explain why the installation is dated to 1730, an admittedly arbitrary date based on an estimate of when the removal of the western aisle—probably the first major alteration—occurred. Given so many unanswered questions about the house's original state, dating the installation to the 1670s would have been misleading. Dated to 1730, however, the house as installed pretends to be no more than it would have been then: a house that, though altered, still retains most of its original look.

In 1730 the house belonged to Jan Schenck's eldest son, Martin, who might have had to wait until 1710 to take possession of the "old land with ye small island and mill and dependencies," since, as stipulated by his father's will, he was not to do so until his youngest sibling (possibly the child his mother was carrying when his father died) came of age or was married.[29] He himself had married Cornelia van Wesselen, widow of the Dutch Reformed dominie, or pastor, Wilhemus Lupardus, on December 2, 1703, and had one son—John, born two years later on December 13, 1705. The alterations we suppose he made to the house could well have coincided with his son's marriage to Femmetje Hegeman on November 15, 1728.[30] Besides removing the western aisle, it is thought that he installed new windows about that time and put a door in the west wall of the south room opposite the fireplace.[31]

After these alterations, the house probably changed little until the late eighteenth or the early nineteenth century. Meanwhile, the Mill Island homestead passed from Martin Schenck to his son John, who in turn divided it by will among his heirs, including his son Martin, his daughters Margarieta and Femmetie, and the heirs of his deceased daughters Maria and Cornelia (these included Femmetie Hooglant and the Dutch Reformed dominie Ulpianus van Sinderen and his wife Femmetje).[32] On April 15, 1784, these heirs sold the property, which was described as including sixty-six acres of upland and six acres of woodland and salt meadows,[33] to Joris Martense of Flatbush for £2,300.[34] Members of the Schenck family, however, apparently continued to live in the house, for the tax assessment of 1796 lists it as being occupied by another John Schenck though owned by Jane Martense, the widow of Joris, who himself died in 1791.[35] In addition to the house, the assessment lists a barn measuring 44 x 42 feet and, as noted earlier, a mill 28 x 28, appraising the total value of the property as $5,600. The house itself, appraised at

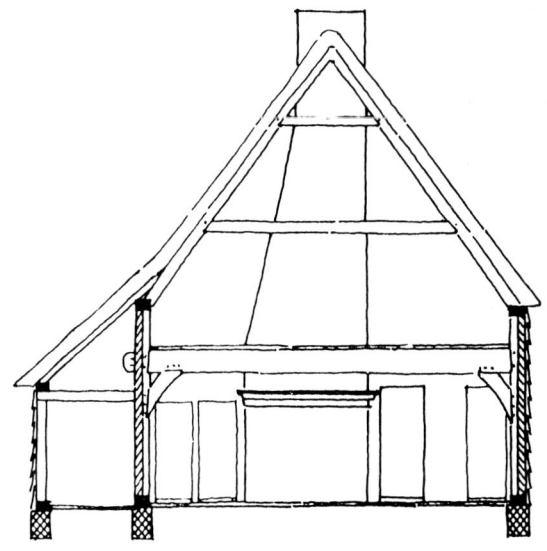

1.15. Original cross section of the Jan Martense Schenck House as proposed by Henk J. Zantkuyl, 1985.

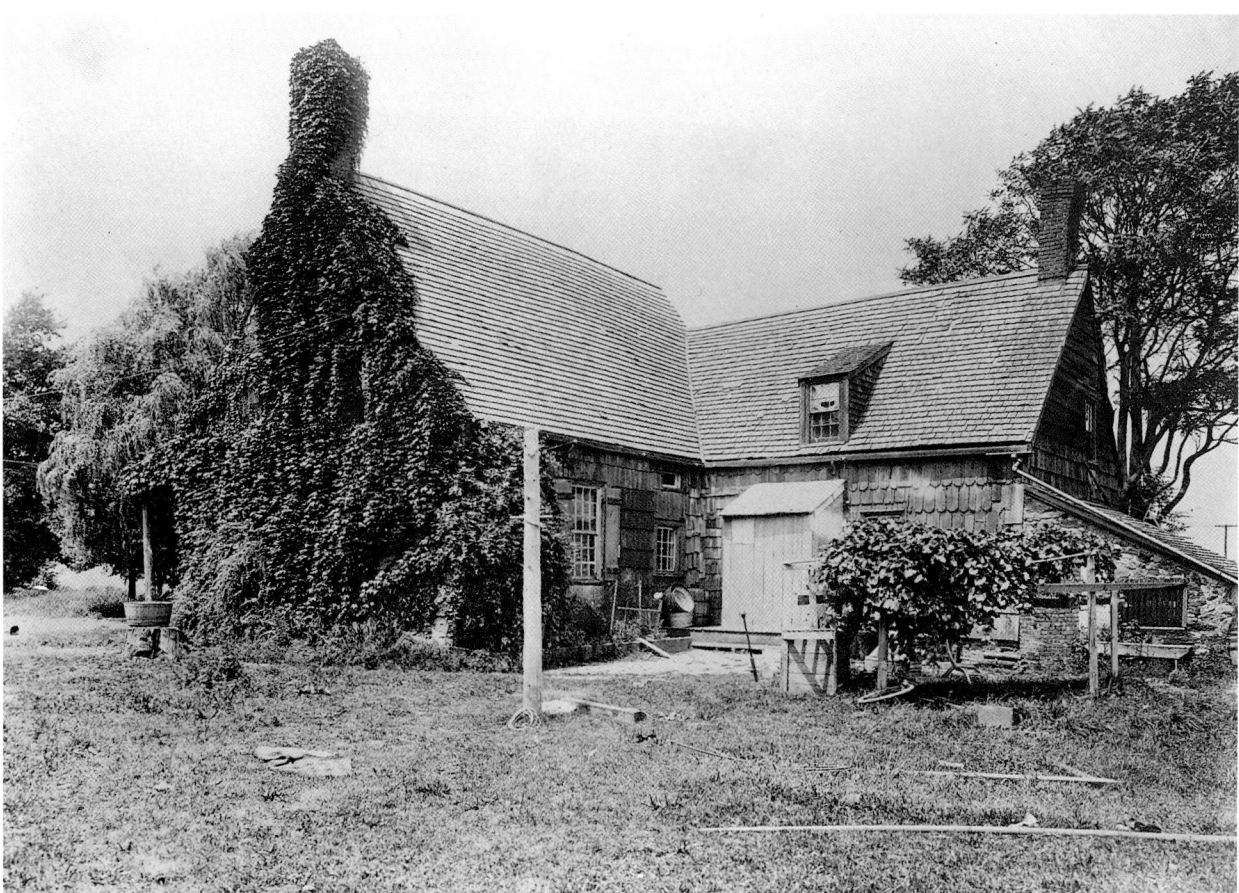

1.16. The Jan Martense Schenck House showing later wing at right, circa 1900.

$650 and described as being in good condition, is recorded as measuring 41 x 22—a measurement that does not include the kitchen wing that made the house L-shaped in later years (*see fig. 1.16*).³⁶

It would be hasty to conclude from this alone that the wing did not yet exist, because wings were sometimes excluded from survey measurements. But whether the wing existed in 1796 or not, it was probably added around that time, since its addition most likely coincided with the removal of the central chimney and fireplaces, a change that gave the original structure a central hallway and a room configuration approximating a more formal English Georgian plan (*see fig. 1.17*). As indicated by the appearance of the fireplace mantel found in the gable end of the south room when the house was taken down, this alteration occurred around 1800. If the wing was not added then, it was clearly in place by 1833, for it is the side from which the house is pictured in the woodcut of that date mentioned earlier (*see again fig. 1.4*).

Unfortunately, this woodcut shows only the upper gable of the original structure rising over the wing's roofline at the right, so that we cannot know for certain whether the overhanging porch roof with rounded columns seen in later photographs also existed then. It is likely, however, that it did, for the use of columns is in keeping with the Greek Revival style of the time.

The only other major change in the exterior of the house—the addition of dormers that necessitated a slightly lower porch roof—probably occurred at the end of the nineteenth century. A photograph taken by the Reverend Schenck during his visit to the house in 1891 (*fig. 1.18*) shows an uninterrupted roofline, but a photograph of no more than a few years later (with the same twig chairs on the porch) reveals the dormers' addition (*see fig. 1.19*).

By then, ownership of the house had passed through the daughter of Joris Martense into the Cowenhoven and Caton families and in 1837, through one of her daughters, into the Crooke family.³⁷ When the Reverend Schenck visited, it was owned by a Robert L. Crooke, who, according to the reverend, occupied it only in summer, closing it up and moving to Manhattan when winter came.

"The road by which we approached it," the Reverend Schenck wrote, "had formed the old milldam. A bridge about 20 feet long, over a rapidly flowing tidal stream which had moved the mill wheel, showed us where the mill had stood. We were afterwards told that the water wheel had lain there until a comparatively recent period. No trace of the mill or its wheel now remains."³⁸ Apparently the mill had been torn down before 1881, for Teunis G. Bergen's *Early Settlers of Kings County*, published that year, mentions a mill

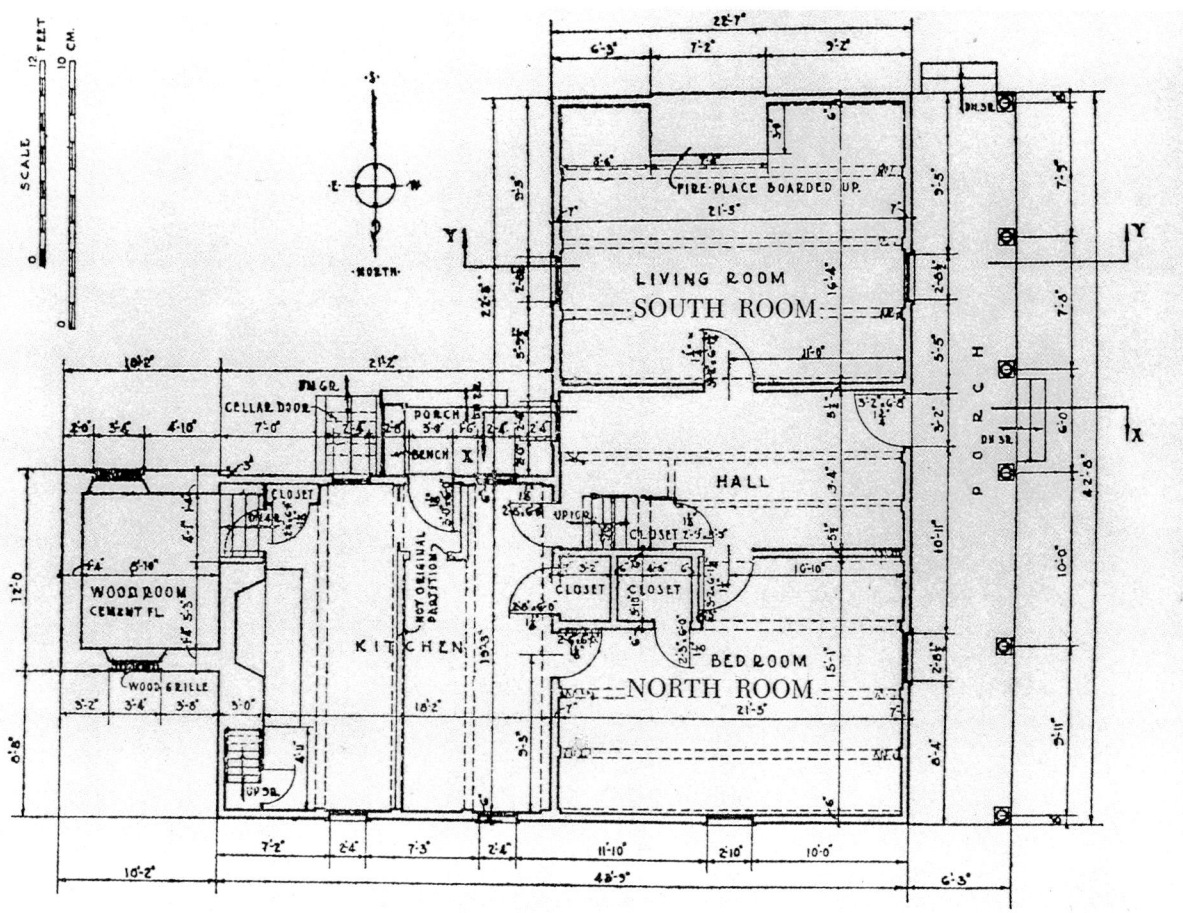

1.17. *Floor plan of the Jan Martense Schenck House in situ, 1934.*

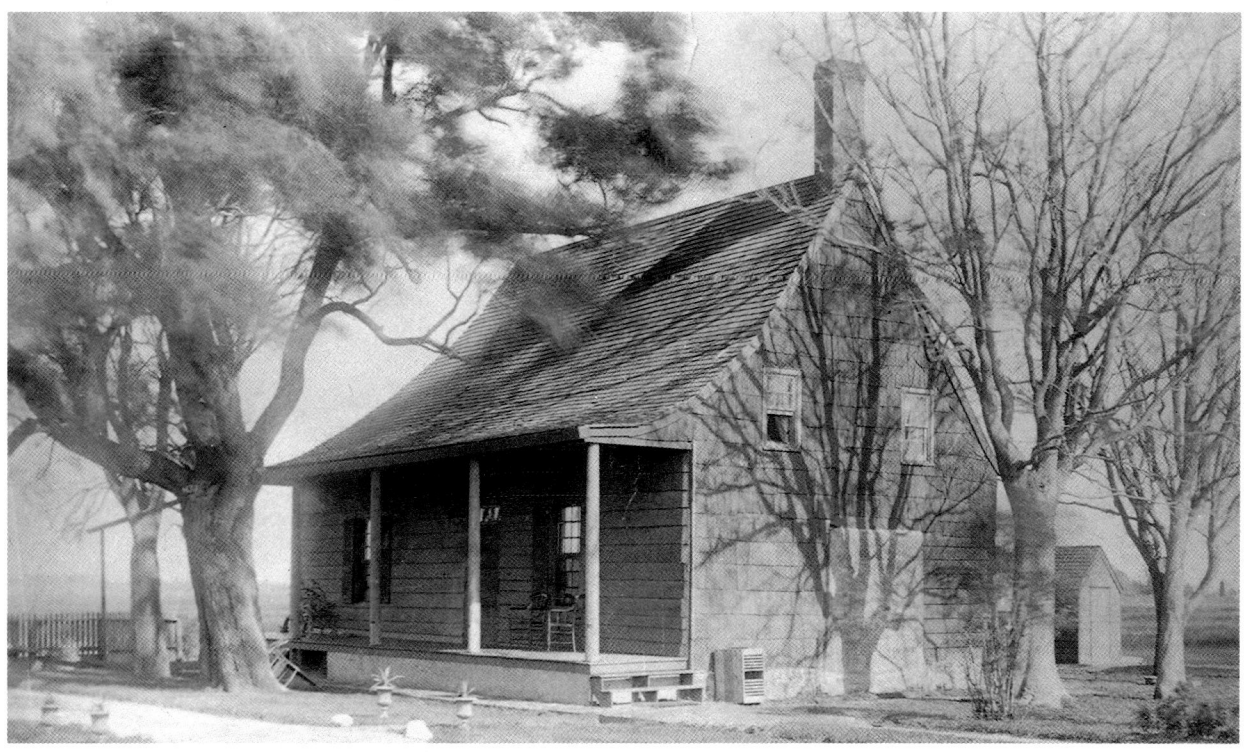

1.18. *The Jan Martense Schenck House, 1891. Photograph by the Reverend William Edward Schenck.*

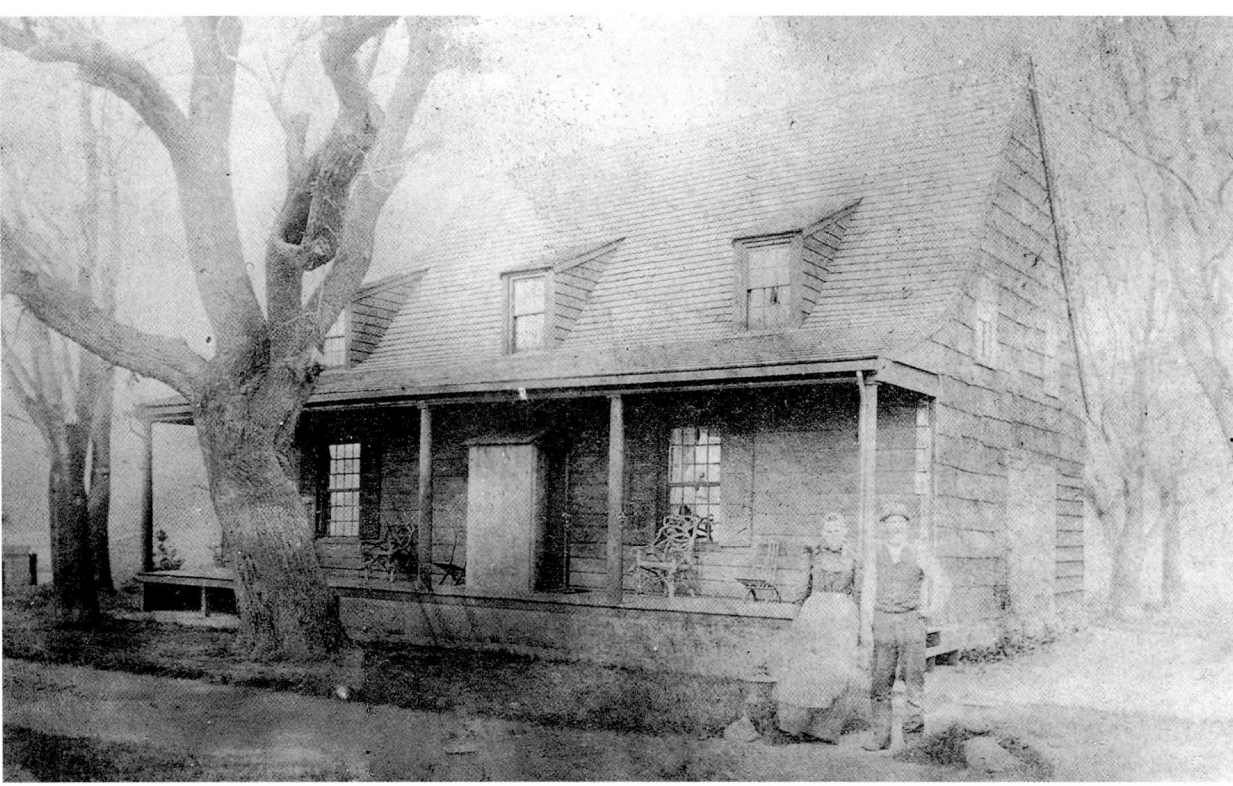

1.19. The Jan Martense Schenck House after 1891.

"lately known as Crooke's Mill, but now demolished."[39]

Pausing to survey the island, the reverend was infused with nostalgia:

> Beyond the house, towards the ocean, was a slightly elevated hillock on which were growing a few cedar trees. Nearer the house, one huge and venerable cedar stood, which had been trimmed nearly to the top—only a conical tuft of its evergreen foliage remaining. Away beyond, towards the sea, were some long dykes. We were told that by building these (Holland fashion) very many acres had been rescued from the dominions of the sea. It was a place every way suited to be the home of a Hollander & to make him feel that he was still in his own country.[40]

Kindly received by Crooke's sister, the Reverend Schenck was then shown throughout the house. "It might have been built by a *ship-builder*," he wrote, "and evidently showed it had been built by some one familiar with ships and with the sea. The timbers were all rough-hewn with the axe, & the marks of the axe were every where very plain. Where each rafter was united to the plate-beam, heavy knees of timber were mortised in, precisely as they are in a ship."[41]

The Reverend Schenck was not the first to display an ignorance of Dutch building methods and associate the construction with a ship's interior. During his visit, Crooke's sister showed him a recent newspaper article whose author, having witnessed the oaken beams resting on "regular ship's knees" and the joiner work "all of naval form," related a legend of how the house had been built by a notorious pirate-sorcerer named Captain Schenck whose apparition was said to haunt the place still. Besides installing the stairway from his pirate's craft in the house and burying a pot of gold on the island that was later accidentally dug up, this Captain Schenck, the story went, often used his home for strange, Faustian rites:

> [S]hrieks and infernal noises were frequently heard there at midnight. It became positively known that witches, ghosts and hobgoblins were in constant attendance there. . . .
> Horrible to tell, the captain's wife was one night dragged screaming from the house, and tortured beneath [a] tree. Soon after she died, but was never seen buried, although when it became known on what night she had died several remembered that on that occasion the flashes of lightning were continuous, while it thundered incessantly. Strange to say after this things took a more mysterious turn still. It was known for certain that Captain Schenck worshipped the Devil.[42]

For all his romanticism, the Reverend Schenck knew apocrypha when he saw it. "Such," he wrote, "was the product of a newspaper reporter's brain."[43]

Fifteen years after the reverend's visit, on January

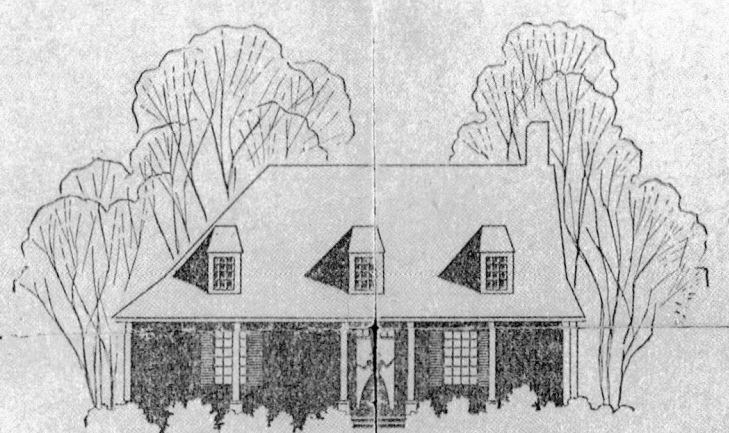

1.20. Advertisement. *New York* Herald Tribune, *July 27, 1941.*

12, 1906, Crooke and his wife Elizabeth sold the Mill Island property to one Florence C. Smith. She in turn deeded it the following day to a real estate company named Flatbush East, which transferred it on December 31, 1906, to a development firm called the Flatbush Improvement Company. On account of financial difficulties caused by the Panic of 1907, that firm was forced to turn the property over, on January 14, 1909, to the Atlantic, Gulf and Pacific Company as payment for the company's work in dredging and filling the marshy land surrounding the island—work that turned the island into a peninsula and hastened the creation of the neighborhood now known as Mill Basin.[44]

In the 1920s, as development of the area boomed, more and more people came to appreciate the house for its historical value, and a movement to preserve it began. *The New York Times,* calling it "the oldest house in habitable condition in New York State," reported in 1924 that a proposal had been put forward to purchase it by popular subscription and present it to the City of New York.[45] Deputy City Dock Commissioner Henry A. Meyer wrote the first check, for $100, but the idea eventually died for lack of money.

Later, in 1933, the small but ambitious Kings County Historical Society announced plans to restore the house on site. "A Dutch farmhouse built by Jan Martense Schenck of pine timber in 1675," the *Times* reported, "has been selected by the Kings County Historical Society as the central unit of a popular museum to hold valuable documents and relics of interest to Brooklyn." The members of the society were expected to raise $10,000 for the purchase of the property, $100,000 for the building of a fireproof exhibition hall, a library, and a caretaker's house, and $50,000 for an endowment to cover the institution's future needs.[46] As with the earlier plan, however, sufficient funds were never received, and in 1940 the society itself disbanded, leaving its collection to The Long Island, now The Brooklyn, Historical Society.

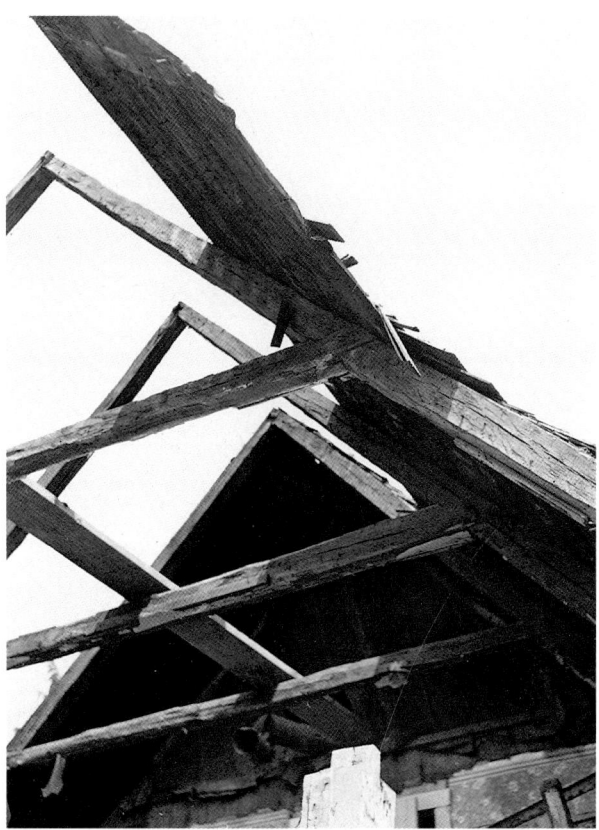

1.22. The Jan Martense Schenck House during dismantling, 1952.

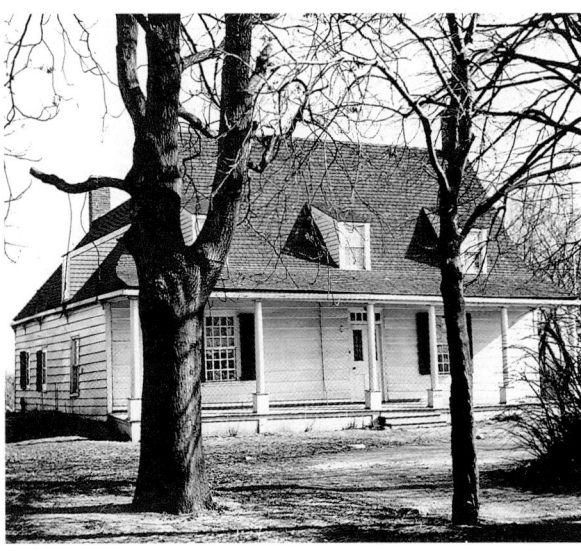

1.21. The Jan Martense Schenck House, circa 1950.

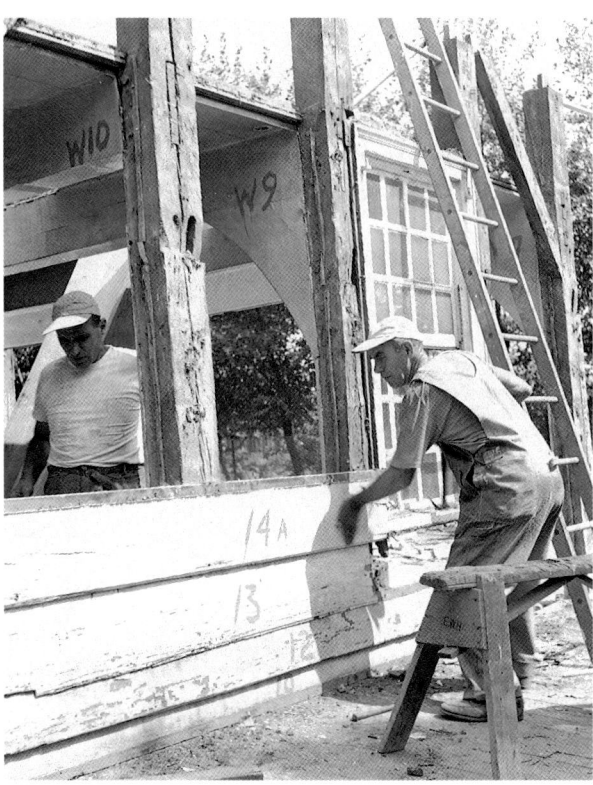

1.23. The Jan Martense Schenck House during dismantling, 1952.

THE VENERABLE FOREFATHER

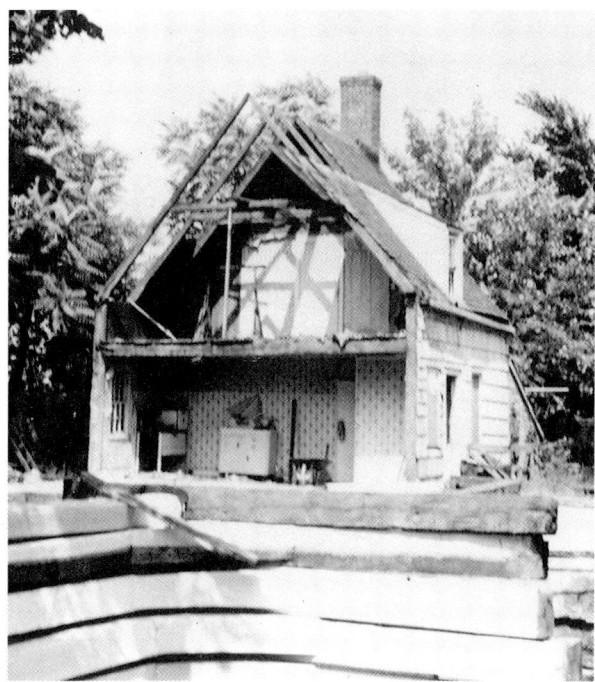

1.24. Later wing of the Jan Martense Schenck House after dismantling of original structure, 1952.

By 1941 interest in the house had developed to the point that the Williams-Harter Corporation decided to re-create it at its New Salem "colonial village" subdivision in Port Washington, Long Island. For $10,990 the re-creation offered "documented authenticity" and a "magnificently complete 'futura' kitchen" (*see fig. 1.20*).

Meanwhile, the house itself, which had acquired an address (2133 East Sixty-third Street) and now stood behind a school (P.S. 236), faced greater pressures than ever from commercial development. Indeed it might well have succumbed to the wrecker's ball had not The Brooklyn Museum agreed to remove it from the property.

In 1952, though lacking both funds and space for the house's reconstruction, the Museum enlisted the services of the E. W. Howell Company for the purpose of dismantling the structure (*see figs. 1.21–1.24*). The pieces were stored in a warehouse under the Interborough Parkway until 1962, when serious preparations for the installation of the house began. During 1963, after an extensive survey of the building's elements, Schwartz, Hopping, Smith, and others—with the aid once again of the Howell Company—reconstructed it piece by piece on the Museum's fourth floor (*see figs. 1.25–1.29*).

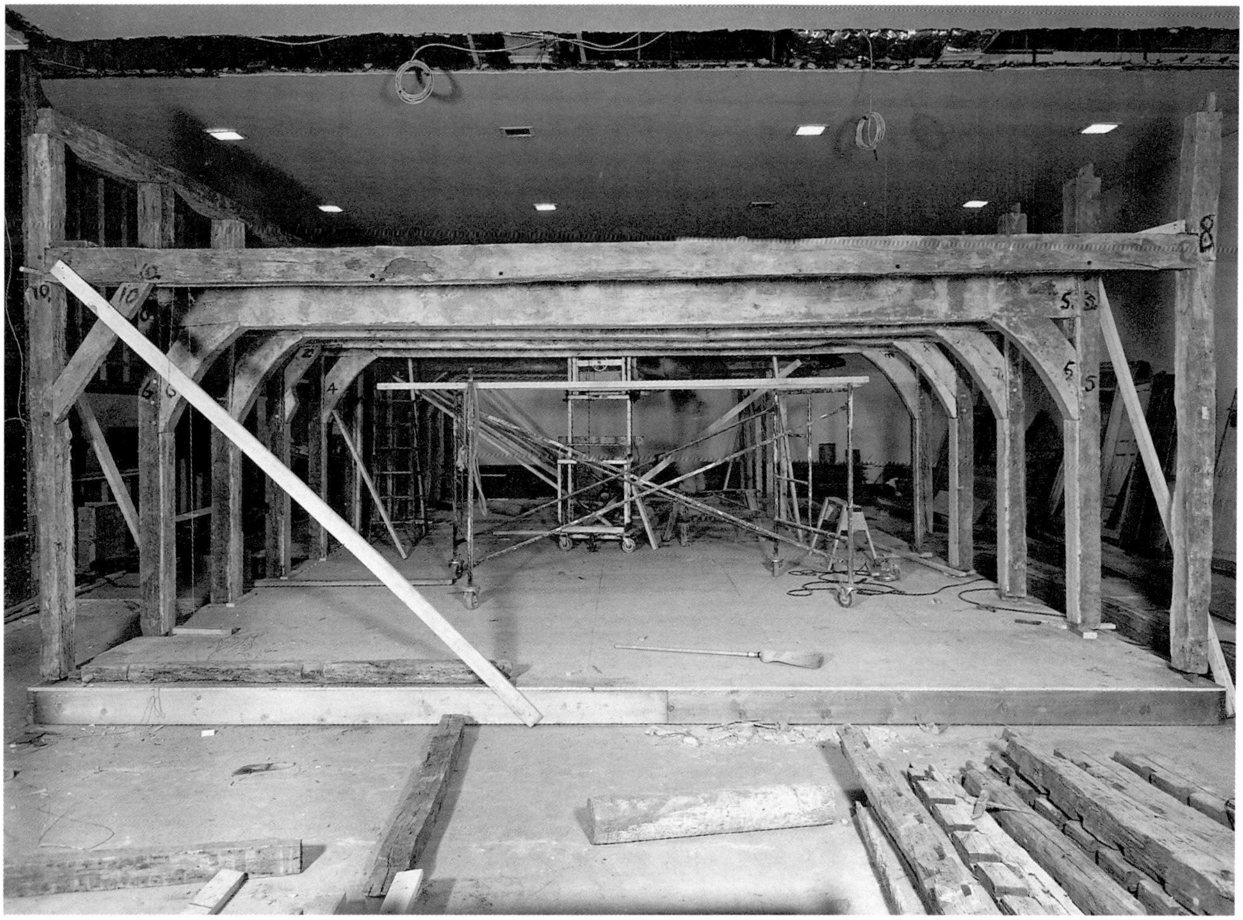

1.25. The Jan Martense Schenck House during reconstruction in The Brooklyn Museum, 1963.

Finally, on April 26, 1964, the Jan Martense Schenck House opened to the public. Since that time, it has had a special significance at The Brooklyn Museum, representing as it does the earliest period of European settlement on Long Island and providing a view of life in New York at a time when the colony was still more Dutch than English. In addition, by serving as an antecedent to the Nicholas Schenck House, itself installed in the Museum in 1929, it allows us to examine in a novel, tangible way how the Dutch in New York came to be Americans.

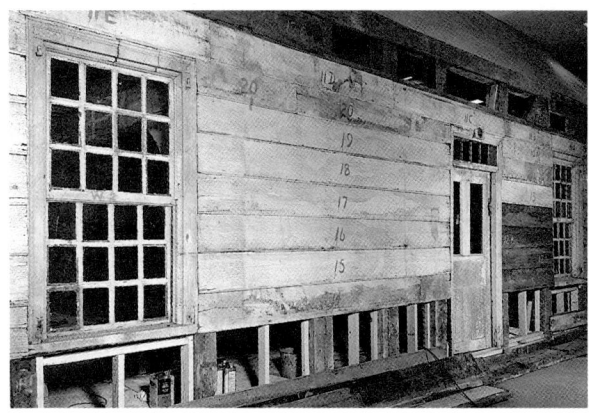

1.27.

1.28.

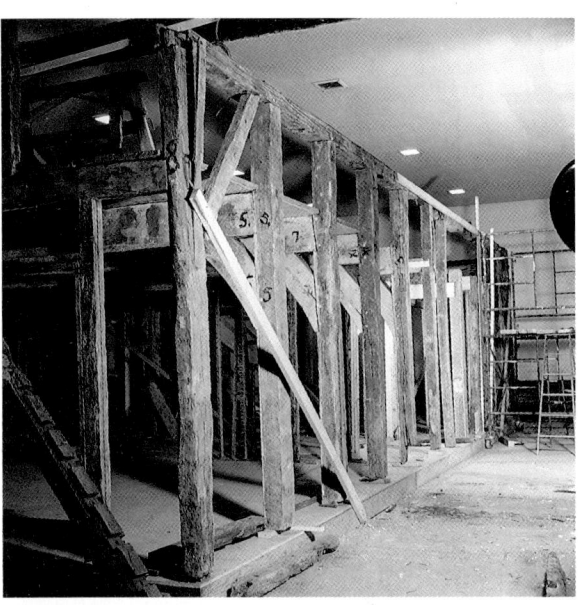

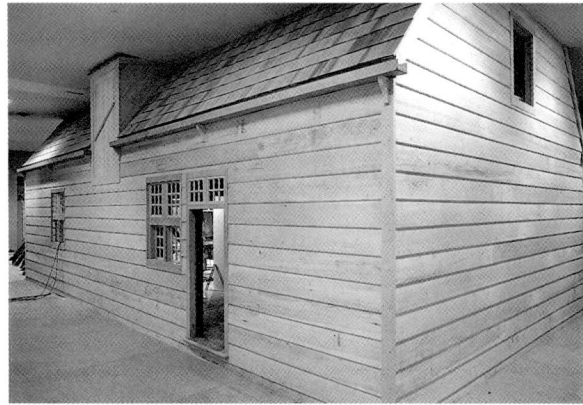

1.26–1.29. The Jan Martense Schenck House during reconstruction in The Brooklyn Museum, 1963.

1.26.

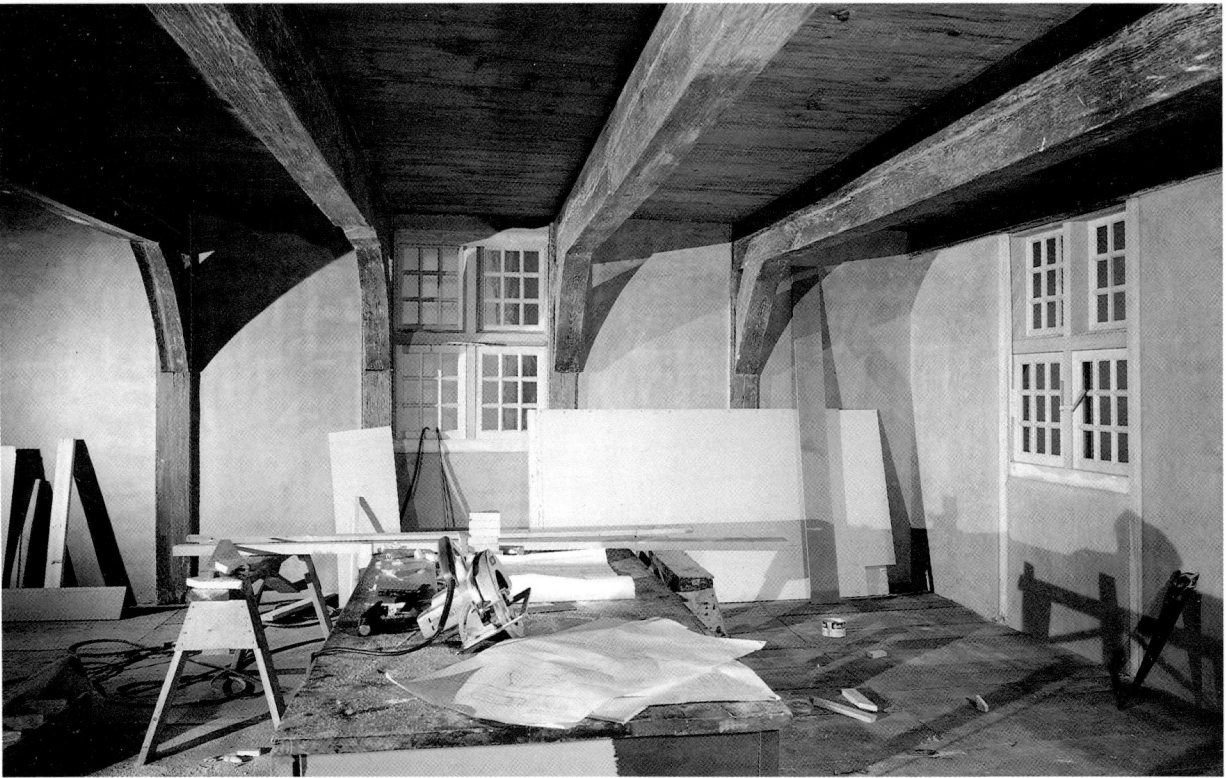

1.29.

CHAPTER
TWO

OF CUPBOARD BEDS AND HEARTHS WITHOUT JAMBS

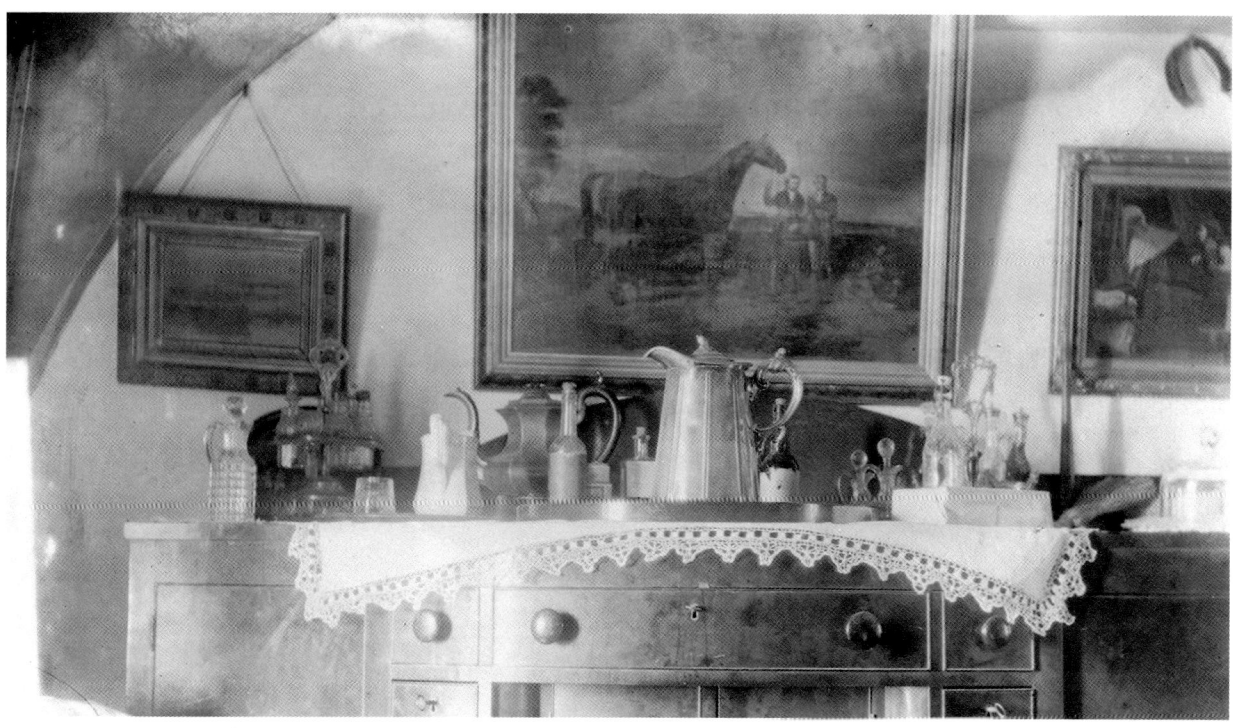

The choice and arrangement of furnishings in a museum period room present a daunting challenge, for one starts with the knowledge that it is never really possible to re-create the living dynamics of a specific room as they existed in the past when the room was in use. From our distant vantage point, we can only begin to guess how a room was touched by the complex human lives lived out in it. Our conclusions are but the vaguest of generalizations, blurred outlines of ghosts. Yet fantasy can play no part in the attempt at re-creation. The invention of an artificial past with no basis in truth would do justice neither to ourselves nor to those whose world we wish to understand rather than recast to suit our own version of it.

Of course the earlier the period we seek to re-create, the more difficult is the task. In the case of the two rooms of the Jan Martense Schenck House installed at The Brooklyn Museum, not even photography — that great mirror of history — can help us much. Consider, for instance, the turn-of-the-century photograph of the Schenck House interior reproduced here (*fig. 2.1*). It provides a fine impression of the way the rooms were furnished during the last years of the Crooke family's ownership, but it tells us nothing of how they looked around 1730 — the era we hope to imitate.

2.1. Interior, Jan Martense Schenck House, in situ, 1905.

Fortunately, however, there are other tools we can use to open windows, if not on the way things were, at least on the way they might have been. Objects with a history of ownership by a room's occupants or their family, estate inventories of the occupants or their contemporaries, physical evidence found in a room at the time of its removal from its original context, similar interiors still surviving or recorded in written descriptions, paintings, or prints—all these and more can allow us to accumulate knowledge bit by bit until our glimpses of the past begin to form a unified view, interpreted to be sure from a distance of decades or centuries but based nonetheless on facts.

With the aid of such tools, the Jan Martense Schenck rooms have been furnished in a manner intended to reflect the way in which a comfortably established Dutch-American family might have lived in a rather uncomfortable environment—isolated, rural Mill Island—in the early eighteenth century. For all their inherent imperfections, they illustrate how the customs and traditions of the Dutch were transferred to the Dutch settlements of the New World.

One of the first things one realizes in looking at these rooms is that life in this house in 1730 would have revolved quite literally around the hearth, for the central chimney split the interior in two and provided each half with a fireplace. In either room family members could cook a meal, heat water for washing, find light for reading or handiwork, or settle down in the winter for a comfortable night's sleep. Although the need for order dictated that certain related activities be confined generally to one room or the other, neither room served a single function in the same sense that say the parlor or bedrooms would a century later in the house of Jan Schenck's grandson Nicholas. Thus they are referred to simply as the north room and the south room. One can keep one's bearings by remembering that at the front of the house, which faced east on Mill Island, the north room is on the right and the south room on the left. Inside the rooms, the prominent beams run east to west.

THE NORTH ROOM

Photographs of the north room taken shortly before the house was dismantled in 1952 show how much the room had changed since the house was built around 1675. In one picture (*fig. 2.2*) we see a view toward what was originally the front of the house but with the addition of the kitchen wing to the northeast wall around 1800 became the rear. The door on the left leads into the wing, while the door on the right leads into the stair hall that replaced the central chimney about the same time. A view of the opposite, northwest, corner (*fig. 2.3*) reveals the installation of radiators and the addition of windows in the west and north walls.

When this room was installed at the Museum in 1964, many of its supposed original features were recreated on the basis of information gathered during the dismantling of the house and in the study of surviving examples of related interiors. The room was furnished as a combination parlor, dining area, and sleeping room (*see figs. 2.4 and 2.5*). Except for the removal of the

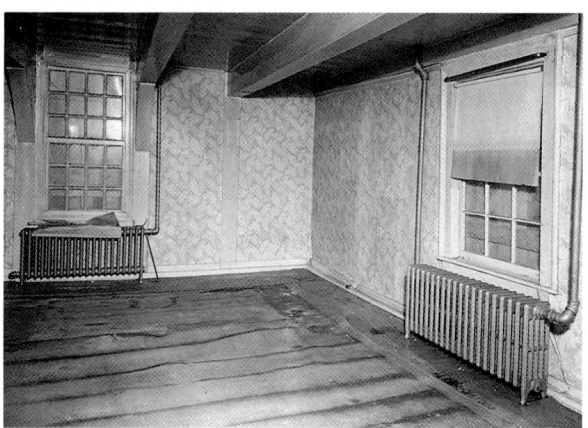

2.3. *North Room, Jan Martense Schenck House, in situ, circa 1952.*

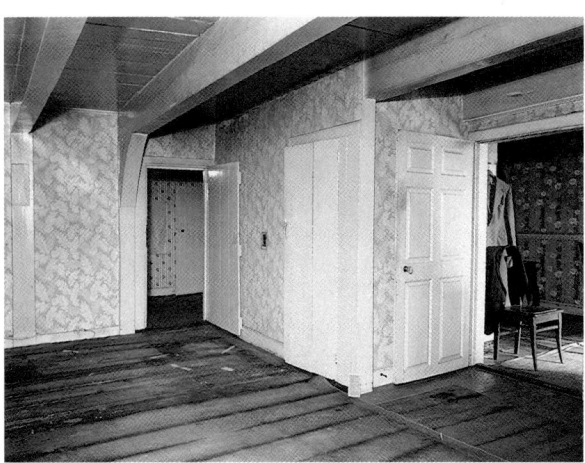

2.2. *North Room, Jan Martense Schenck House, in situ, circa 1952.*

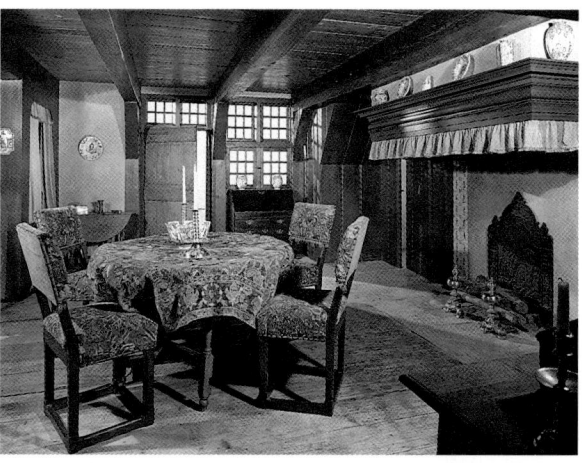

2.4. *North Room, Jan Martense Schenck House, as installed in The Brooklyn Museum, circa 1964.*

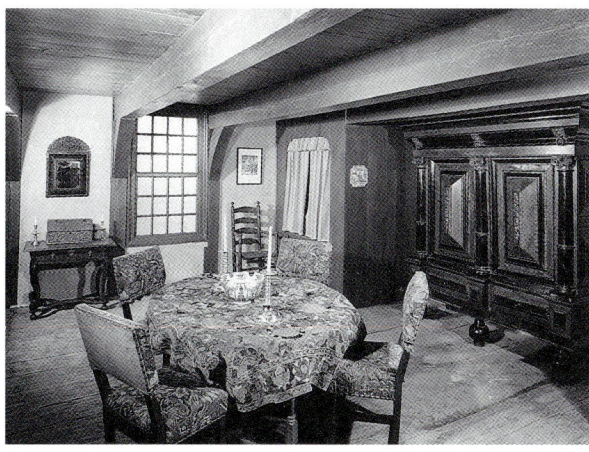

2.5. North Room, Jan Martense Schenck House, as installed in The Brooklyn Museum, circa 1964.

2.6. North Room, Jan Martense Schenck House, as installed in The Brooklyn Museum, 1985. Photograph by Paul Warchol.

western window, which was included in 1964 in the belief that it might have been added around 1730, it has changed little since its installation (*see figs. 2.6 and 2.7*).

The most notable feature of the restoration is the large hooded, or jambless, fireplace (*fig. 2.8*). Such fireplaces, favored in the seventeenth-century Netherlands (*see figs. 2.9 and 2.10*), were also the norm in Dutch-American houses built then. But to many Americans of the time they probably seemed as peculiar as they do to us today. A woman from Boston named Sarah Kemble Knight, who visited New York in 1704, found them curious indeed:

> The fire places have no jambs (as ours have) But the Backs run flush with the walls, and the Hearth is of Tyles and is as farr out into the Room as the Ends as before the fires, wch is Generally Five foot n the Low'r rooms, and the peice over where the mantle tree should be is made as ours with Joyners work, and as I supose is fasten'd to iron rodds inside.[1]

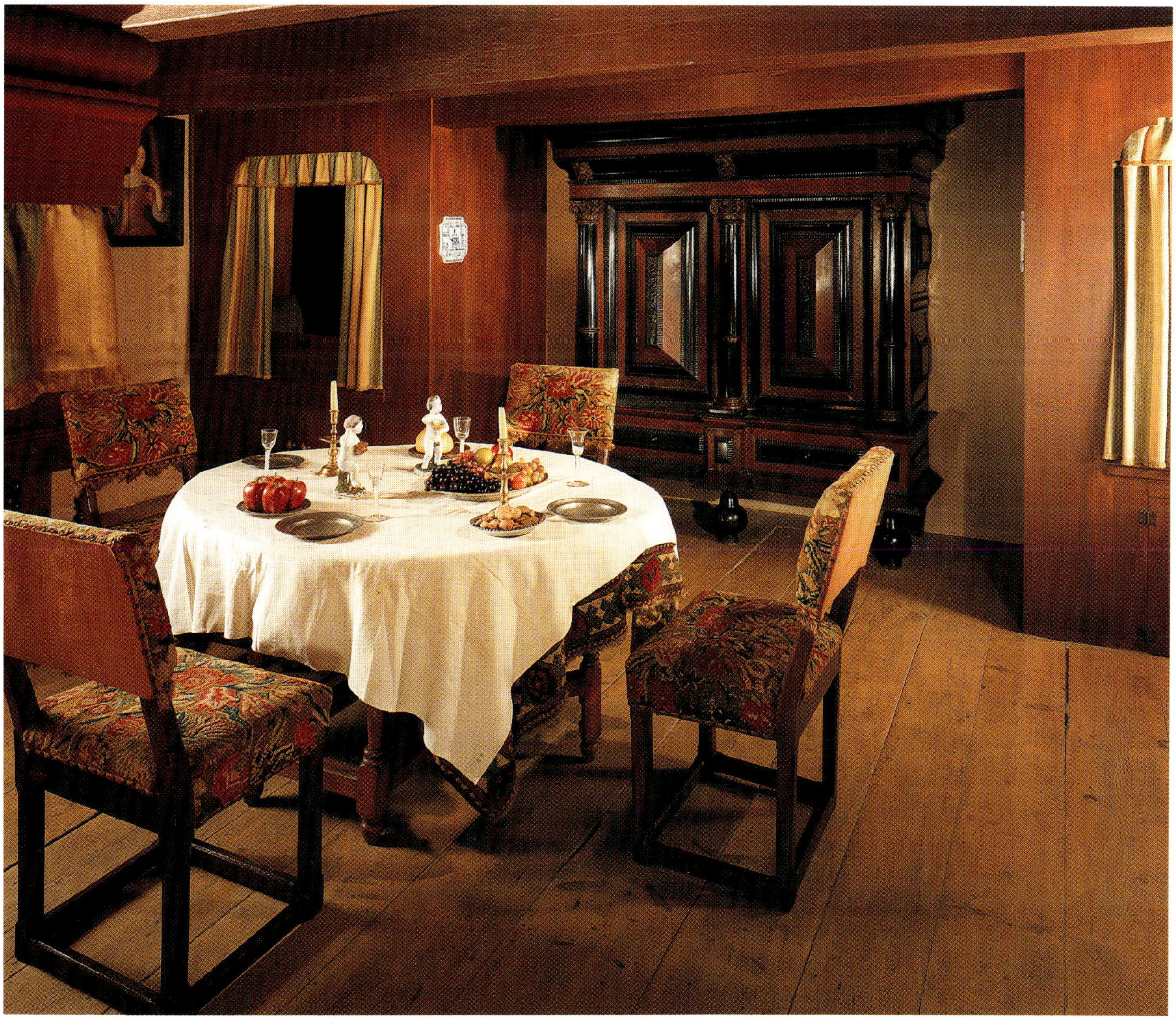

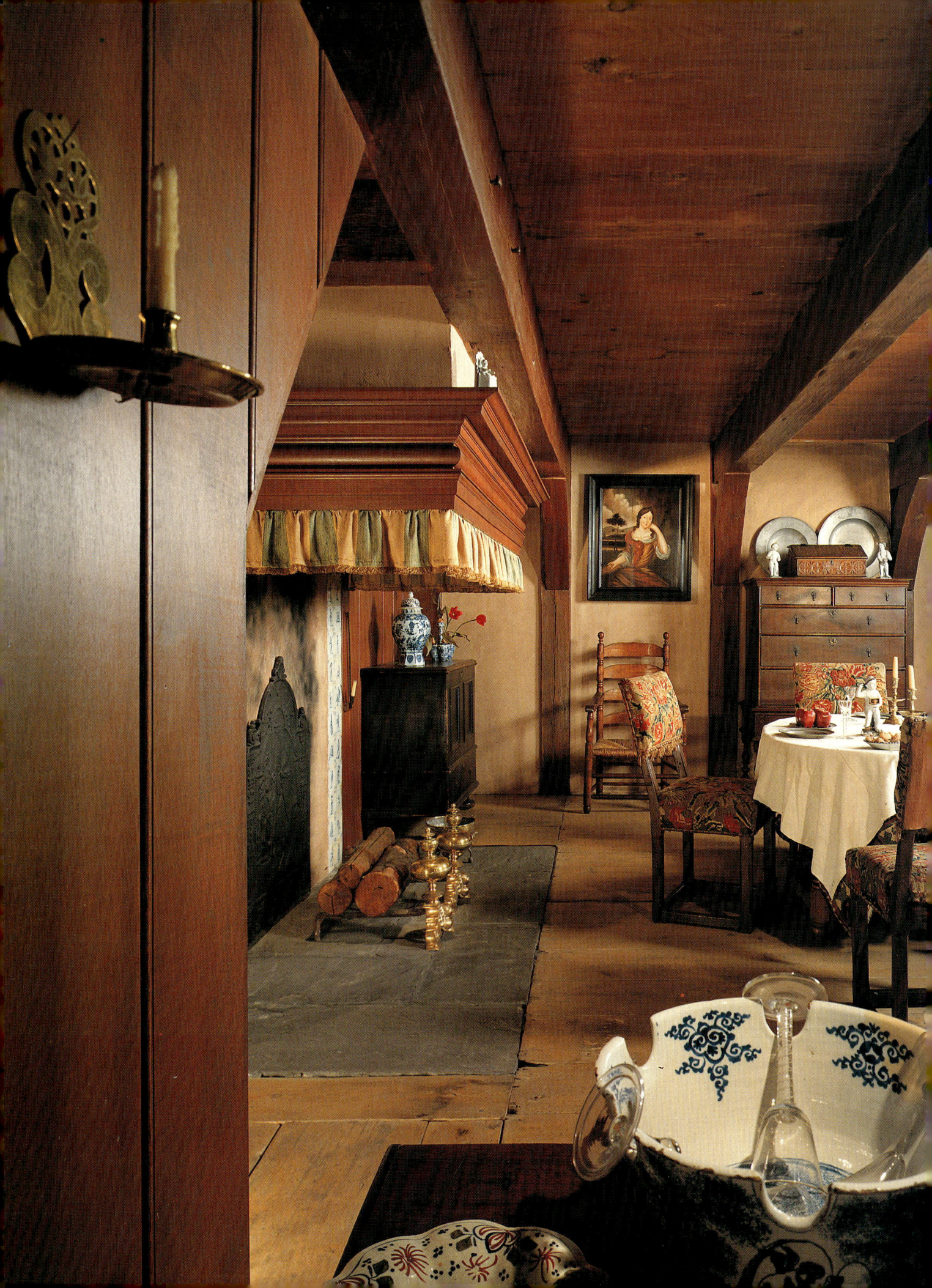

OF CUPBOARD BEDS AND HEARTHS WITHOUT JAMBS

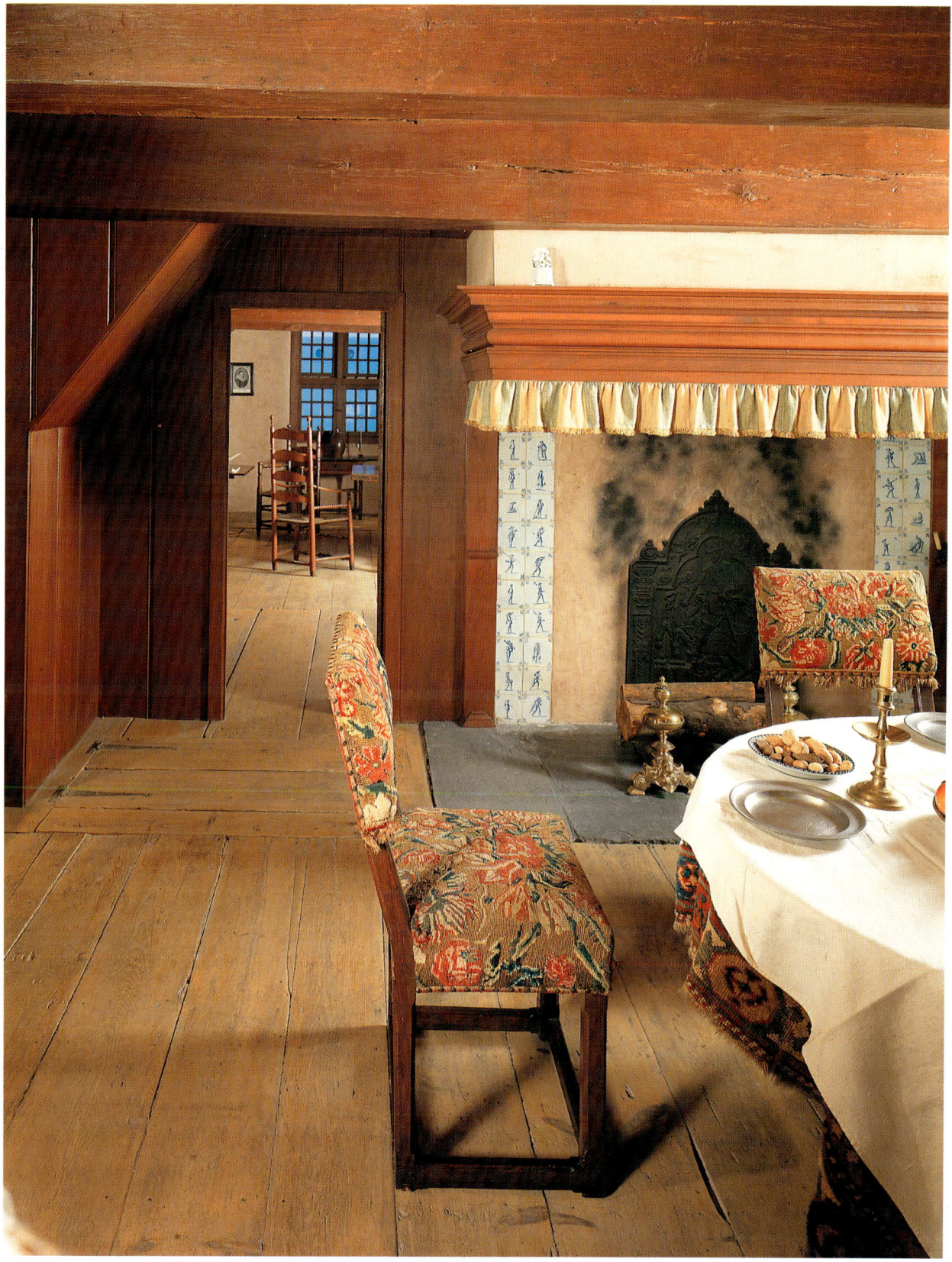

2.7. *North Room, Jan Martense Schenck House, as installed in The Brooklyn Museum, 1985. Photograph by Paul Warchol.*

2.8. *View through inside door, North and South Rooms, Jan Martense Schenck House, as installed in The Brooklyn Museum, 1985. Photograph by Paul Warchol.*

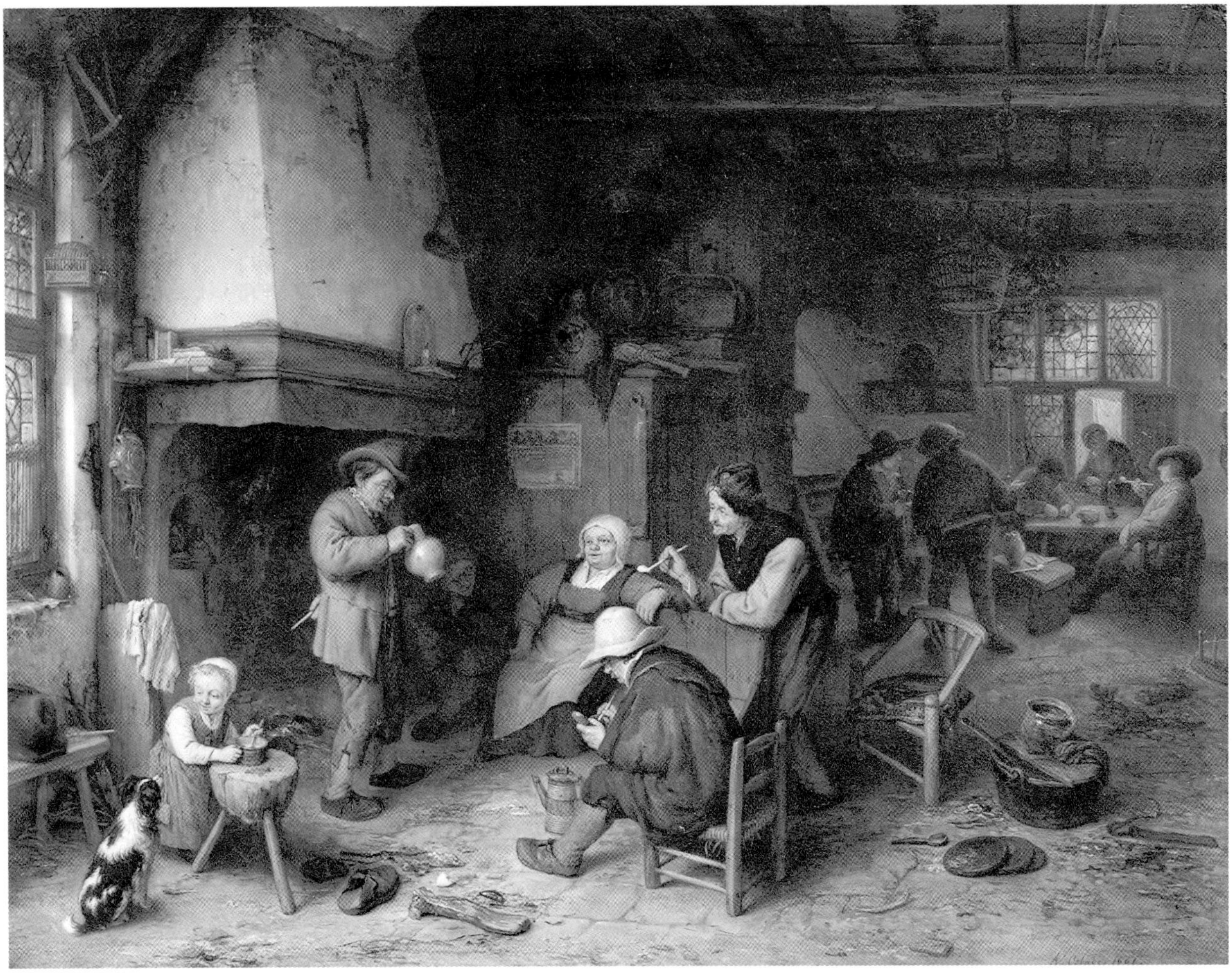

2.9. Adriaen van Ostade (Dutch, 1610–1685). Peasants in an Interior, 1661. Oil on copper, 14½ × 18½ inches. Rijksmuseum Amsterdam.

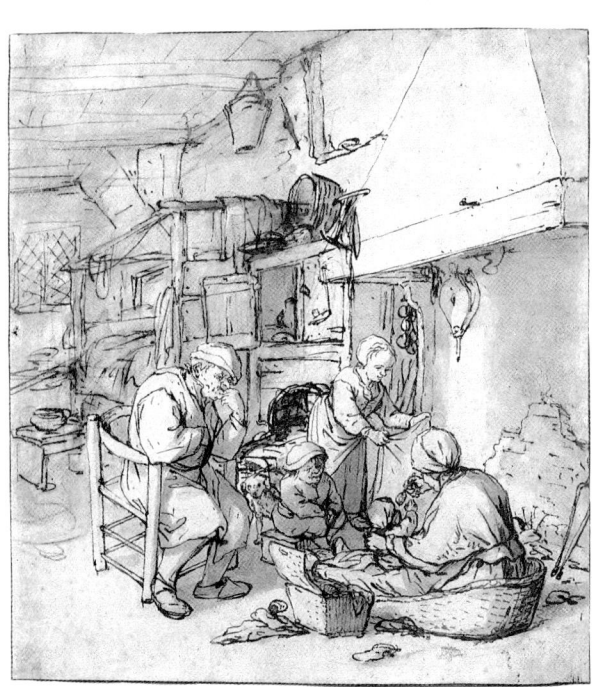

For the molding of the north room's fireplace the curators designed a re-creation based on the surviving seventeenth-century manteltree of a jambless fireplace now enclosed in an eighteenth-century paneled wall in the de Windt House of Tappan, New York (see fig. 2.11). For the fireplace tiles they used tin-glazed earthenware tile of the sort Madame Knight probably had in mind when she wrote of "the finest tile that I ever see."[2] Along with the elaborate seventeenth-century Baroque-style andirons and cast-iron fireback, the latter of which held the heat of the fire, such tiles would have been imported from the Netherlands.

The striped chimney cloth, or valance, under the mantel is based on chimney cloths seen in many seventeenth-century Dutch paintings, such as Pieter de Hooch's *A Woman Peeling Apples* (fig. 2.12). Although no examples known to have been used in

2.10. Adriaen van Ostade (Dutch, 1610–1685). A Family at the Hearth, circa 1650. Black chalk, pen and brown ink, and gray wash, 9½ × 8¾ inches. Rijksmuseum Amsterdam.

America still survive, their use here is well documented in seventeenth-century inventories. The 1685 inventory of the estate of a wealthy New York doctor named Jacob de Lange, for instance, lists no fewer than a dozen such cloths in a variety of fabrics, colors, and patterns:

> One white valion before a chimney, one redd chimney cloth, two ozenbrig [coarse linen] chimney valance, one blue calico mixed checkard valance, one redd ditto, one ditto white with red pointed lace, one ditto red flowered calico valance, one ditto flowered with red lining one blue say fringed valance and two valance carpet work.[3]

Like tiles, andirons, and firebacks, many chimney cloths were probably imported from the Netherlands. In 1660, for example, Jeremias van Rensselaer, who had inherited his father's estate around Fort Orange, or present-day Albany, wrote to his mother in the old country asking that she send him, among other things, a hanging for the fireplace.[4]

In many New York houses of the period, the mantel itself, as well as the rest of the woodwork, was left unfinished. "[O]nly the walls are plastered," Madame Knight wrote in 1704, "and the Sumers and Girt [horizontal beams] are plained and kept very white scowr'd as so is all the partitions made of Bords."[5]

In the Jan Martense Schenck House, however, all the woodwork—including the fireplace moldings—is stained reddish brown, a kind of walnut color determined to be original by analysis of the vertical posts in 1964.[6] The walls, in contrast, have a pinkish cast, from the mixture of local sands used in their plaster.[7]

We can only guess what sort of floor the house had, for the original did not survive. There is a good chance, though, that it was made of planks of tulip poplar. "The Indians frequently make their canoes of this wood," the Dutch lawyer Adriaen van der Donck wrote in his *Description of the New Netherlands,* published in 1655, "hence we name it *Canoe-wood*; we use it for flooring because it is bright and free of knots."[8] If the house did in fact possess such a floor, it was undoubtedly scrubbed white.

Because the original door and windows of the north room were removed along with the original staircase when the east wing was added, these details, too, had to be re-created. A door and windows, accordingly, were arranged along the east wall between the beams and vertical posts in a typically Dutch manner, while a narrow, winding stair to the upper floor was placed in the enclosure beside them with an opening in the next room.

It is here, along the east wall, that Henk J. Zantkuyl has recently suggested there would have been a wooden partition to create an antechamber to the room, a partition that would have kept the cold air of

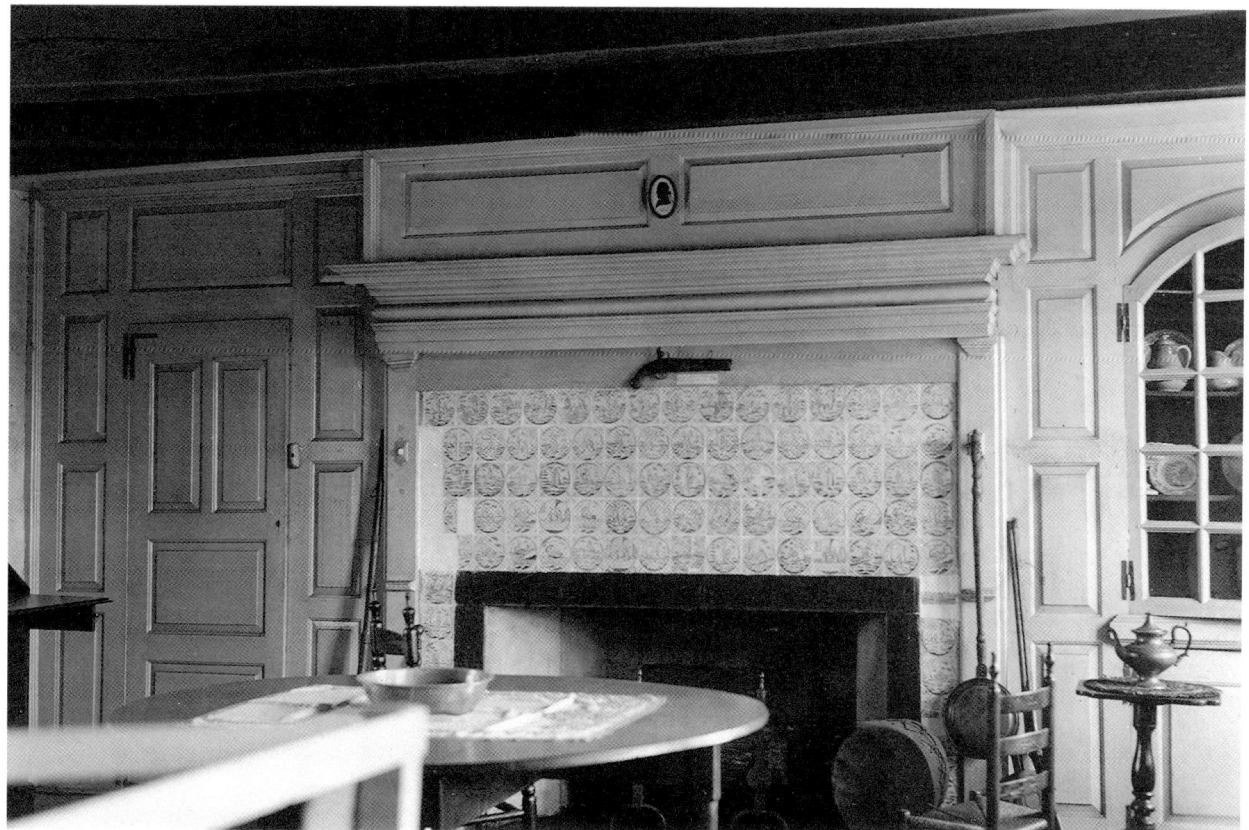

2.11. Seventeenth-century manteltree embedded in eighteenth-century paneled wall, de Windt House, Tappan, New York.

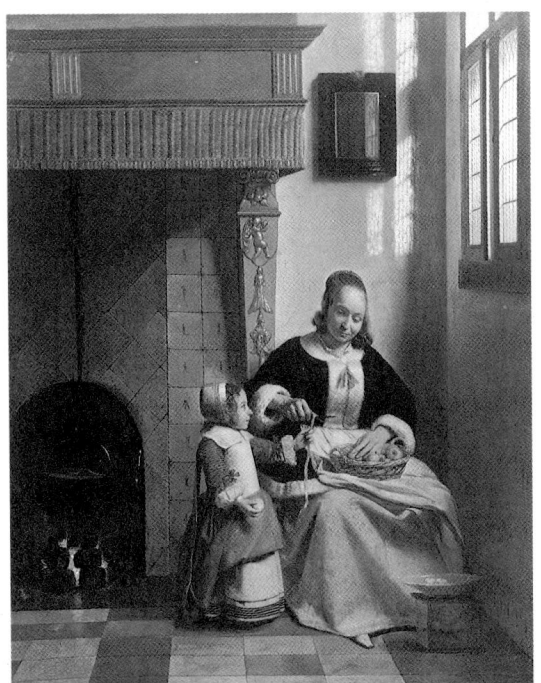

2.12. Pieter de Hooch (Dutch, 1629–after 1683). A Woman Peeling Apples, 1663. Oil on canvas, 27¾ × 21⅜ inches. The Wallace Collection, London.

harsh winters out of the room itself (*see again fig. 1.14*).[9] Zantkuyl cited markings on the original beams as proof such a partition existed, but when Curator Marvin Schwartz considered the possibility in 1963 he decided these markings were not enough to support a re-creation.[10]

Schwartz did, however, add one of the room's most distinctive architectural features—the two flanking cupboard beds on the north wall—almost entirely on the basis of speculation alone, for there is no undisputed physical evidence of the use of such beds in American houses. Since none remain to be copied, these beds are based primarily on seventeenth-century Dutch paintings, such as Pieter de Hooch's *Mother Delousing Her Child's Hair* (*fig. 2.13*). If bed boxes did indeed exist in this room, it is perhaps more likely that they were located nearer the fireplace for warmth, as in a mid-seventeenth-century painting by Esaias Boursse (*fig. 2.14*).

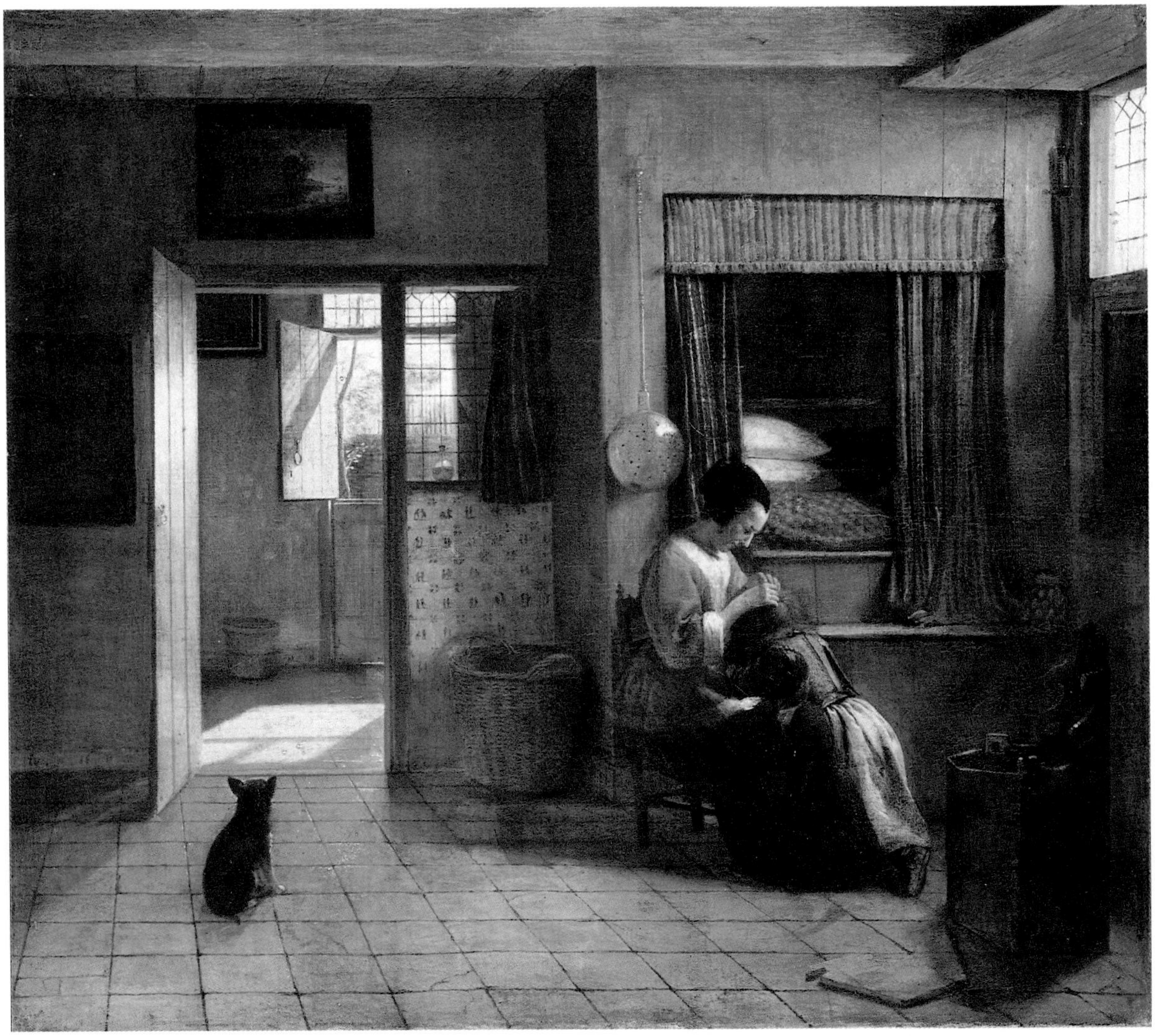

OF CUPBOARD BEDS AND HEARTHS WITHOUT JAMBS

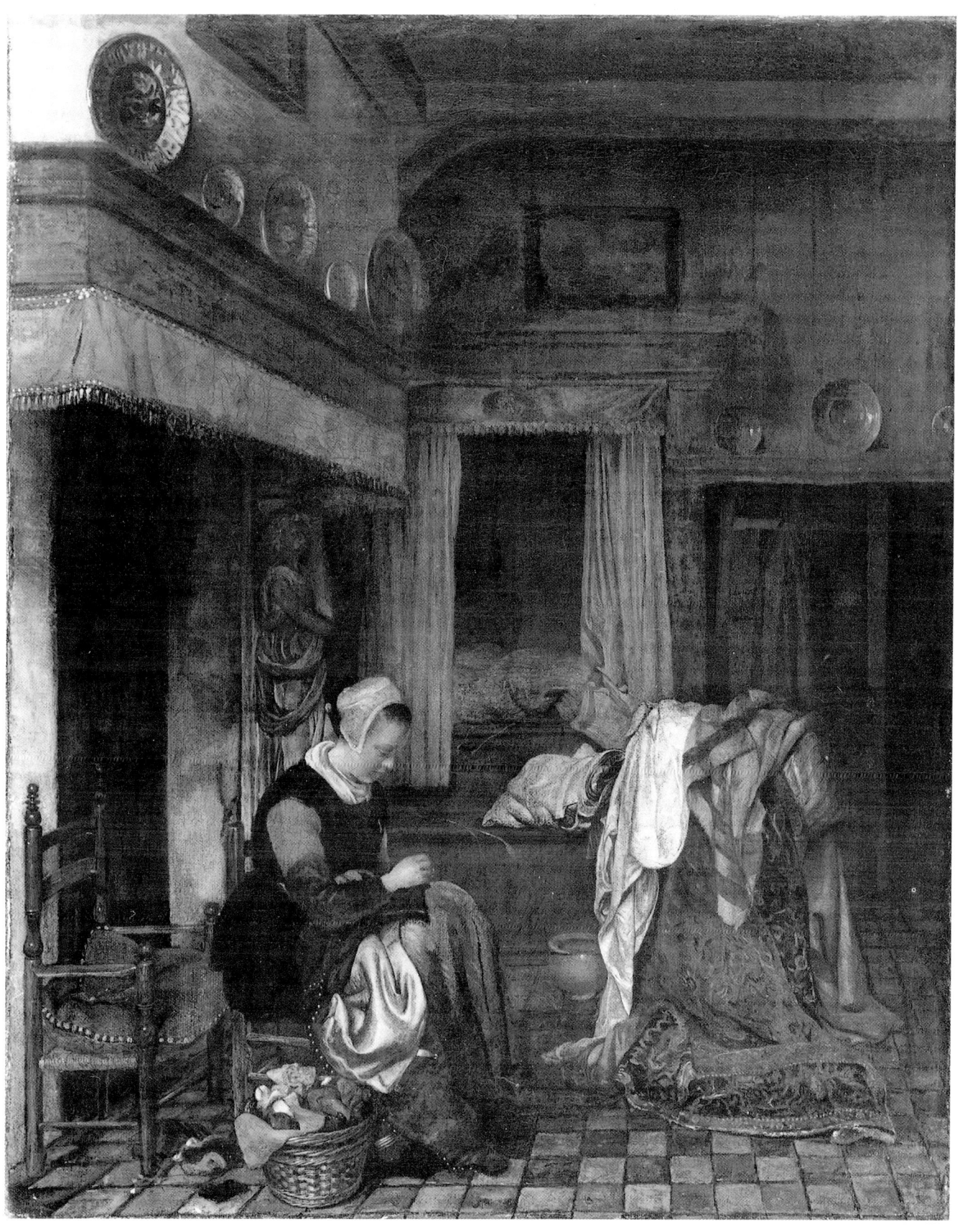

2.13. Left: Pieter de Hooch (Dutch, 1629–after 1683). *Mother Delousing Her Child's Hair,* 1660. Oil on canvas, 20⅝ × 24 inches. Rijksmuseum Amsterdam.

2.14. Esaias Boursse (Dutch, 1631–1672). *The Seamstress at the Fireside, circa* 1650. Oil on canvas, 24¾ × 19¼ inches. Rheinisches Landesmuseum, Bonn.

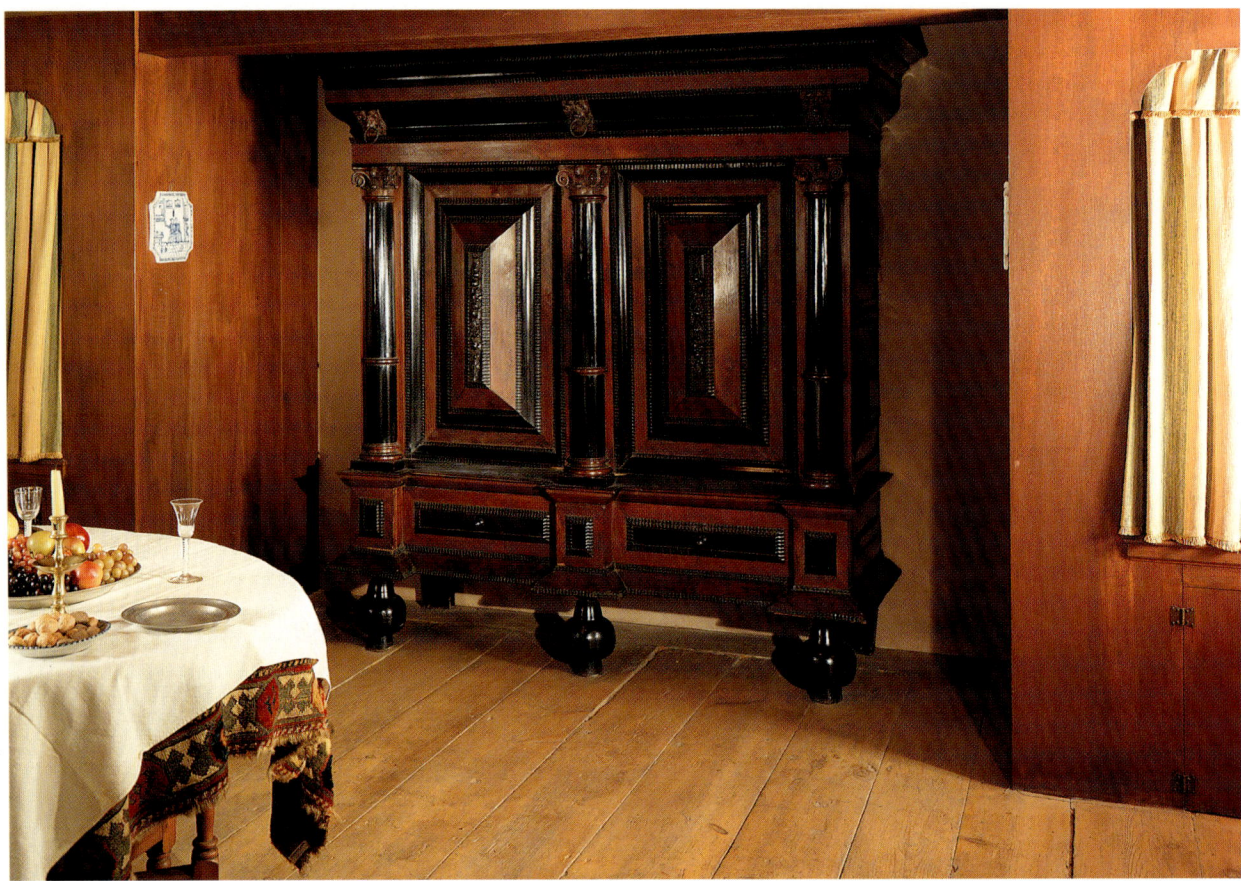

2.15. Kas, circa 1675. Dutch. Rosewood, ebony, and walnut, 83 × 75½ × 25⅝ inches. The Brooklyn Museum 51.157.1, Gift of Miss Mary van Kleeck in memory of Charles M. van Kleeck. Photograph by Paul Warchol.

Despite the lack of physical proof of the building of such beds in American homes, there is no doubt that the Dutch brought this tradition with them to the New World. In fact, if we accept the testimony of an elderly woman who remembered in 1964 that her mother had spoken of there having been a cupboard bed in the home of *Nicholas* Schenck in the late nineteenth century (see Chapter 5), then the tradition was revived long after it died out. For the purpose at hand, however, it is enough to cite a contract that the carpenters Jan Cornelisen, Abram Jacobsen, and Jan Hendricksen made with the ferry master Egbert van Borsum in 1655 for the building of a ferry-house, or tavern, at Brooklyn. Among other things, the carpenters agreed to "wainscot the east side the whole length of the house, and in the recess [build] two bedsteads, one in the front room and one in the inside room, with a pantry at the end of the bedstead."[11]

A comparison of de Hooch's *Mother Delousing Her Child's Hair* (*fig. 2.13*) with his *Woman Peeling Apples* (*fig. 2.12*) indicates that the hangings for cupboard beds included valances quite similar in character to chimney cloths. No doubt such curtains also came in a variety of fabrics, colors, and patterns. The inventory of the estate that a man named William Cox left his wife Sarah in 1689 lists a set described as "1 suite sage curtains and vallons wth silk fringe."[12]

Such hangings and other related textiles are the sort of thing that would have been stored in the large Dutch *kas,* or cupboard, between the beds. This *kas,* by far the most impressive piece of furniture in the entire house, is closely related to a *kas* seen in another painting by de Hooch (*compare figs. 2.15 and 2.16*). Such *kassen* provided a model for simpler eighteenth-century American *kassen* like the one to be found in the Nicholas Schenck House (*fig. 5.58*). The continued popularity of their form is a prime example of the prolonged influence of Dutch culture in New York.

Although this particular *kas* is probably more elaborate than anything that would have been seen in the house of a family of the Schencks' social standing, it is nonetheless believed to have been in New York in the seventeenth century. Moreover, it descended in the Brett and van Kleeck families of the Brett Homestead in Beacon, New York—families that number among their ancestors Jan Martense Schenck, François Rombout, and Barent Balthus (who immigrated to New Netherland between 1647 and 1654). Though it could have descended from any of these progenitors, family legend maintains that Rombout was the original owner. An immigrant from a Walloon (or culturally French) area of what is now Belgium, Rombout became a citizen of New Netherland in 1658 and later played a leading role in New York City government under the

English, serving frequently as an alderman in the 1670s and 1680s and becoming Mayor of New York by appointment of Governor Edmund Andros on November 21, 1679. At his death in 1691, leading the list of his possessions was a "Holland Cubbert furnished with earthenware and porcelain" and valued at £15. Since his daughter married Roger Brett, it is possible this object was in fact the *kas* now seen in the north room.[13] Although the inventory of his estate used the term "cubbert," we know that the English and Dutch words were interchangeable, for in 1714 a certain Jan Hendrickse Prevoost left to his daughter a no doubt similar piece described as "my new cupboard commonly called kass."[14]

Among the many articles kept in such *kassen* was the household linen, which included some of the most costly and important items in any seventeenth- or eighteenth-century home. Although Rombout was a much wealthier man than Jan Schenck or his son Martin, the inventory of his estate gives an idea of the sort of linen they might have owned. Listed there are fifty-six diaper (or soft white linen) napkins, forty-two coarse napkins and towels, thirteen tablecloths of linen and diaper, thirty sheets, four bolster covers, and sixty-one pillowbeers (or cases), including ten checked ones.[15] A linen tablecloth is seen, accordingly, in the Schenck House north room, covering a Turkey (i.e., Middle Eastern) carpet draped over a gateleg table set for a meal. Such a use of tablecloth and carpet together is documented by Jan Steen's seventeenth-century painting *Easy Come, Easy Go* (fig. 2.17). The tablecloth would have protected the carpet while the meal was in progress, but it would have been removed after the meal while the carpet would have stayed as the table was folded down to save space.

Seventeenth-century estate inventories of both

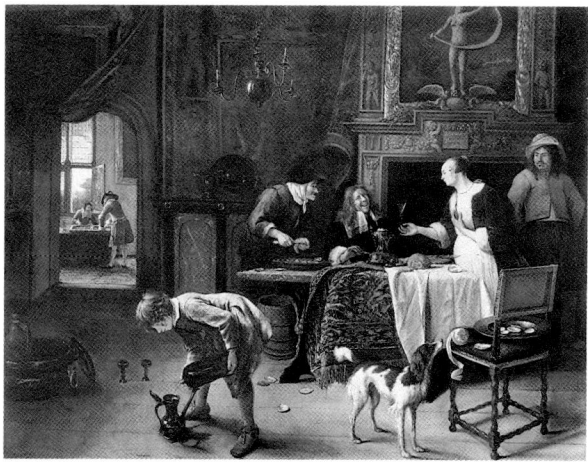

2.17. Jan Steen (Dutch, 1626–1679). Easy Come, Easy Go, circa 1660. Oil on canvas, 31⅛ × 41 inches. Museum Boymans-van Beuningen, Rotterdam.

New York and New England often list tables together with carpets, indicating that the Turkey carpet was a constant fixture on the properly dressed table. The 1676 inventory of the estate of a man named Cornelius van Dyck, for instance, lists an "oak table with a carpet,"[16] while the inventory of the estate William Cox left his wife Sarah in 1689 includes several tables with carpets.[17] In addition, the chairs around such tables were frequently upholstered with Turkey work, a needlework of woven woolen pile made in imitation of Turkey carpets. A man by the name of John Winder who died in 1672 had a dozen such chairs,[18] and Sarah Cox, at her death in 1692, had eighteen.[19] The four Turkey-work chairs around the north room's table are of English origin, but they are very similar in character to Dutch examples used in America.[20]

The table itself is simply set with dishes of turned wood and pewter, the most common wares in early eighteenth-century New York. Wooden plates were cheap and widely used in colonial America, while pewter ones—more expensive but still cheaper than porcelain—were also popular. Although the Schencks would not have owned the prodigious amount of pewter accumulated by wealthy individuals like the New Yorker Pieter Jacob Marius, whose estate inventory of 1702 lists a collection of pewter weighing more than 1,500 pounds,[21] they surely would have had enough for daily use.

The Schencks no doubt had ceramic dishes, too, though it is not likely they would have had expensive "china" plates to use on the table every day. Porcelain, Rhenish salt-glazed stoneware, lead-glazed earthenware, and the tin-glazed earthenware known as delftware (represented in the north room by a monteith, or wine glass rinser) have all been found in large quantities in a number of seventeenth-century New York archaeological sites and are listed in estate inventories of the time as well.[22] François Rombout, as we have seen, owned a *kas* stocked with earthenware and porcelain,[23] and the wealthy seventeenth-century

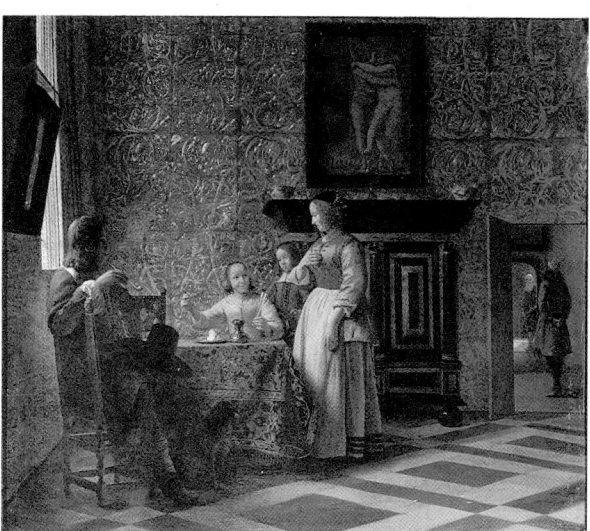

2.16. Pieter de Hooch (Dutch, 1629–after 1683). Interior with Figures, 1665. Oil on canvas, 23 × 27 inches. The Metropolitan Museum of Art, New York, Robert Lehmann Collection.

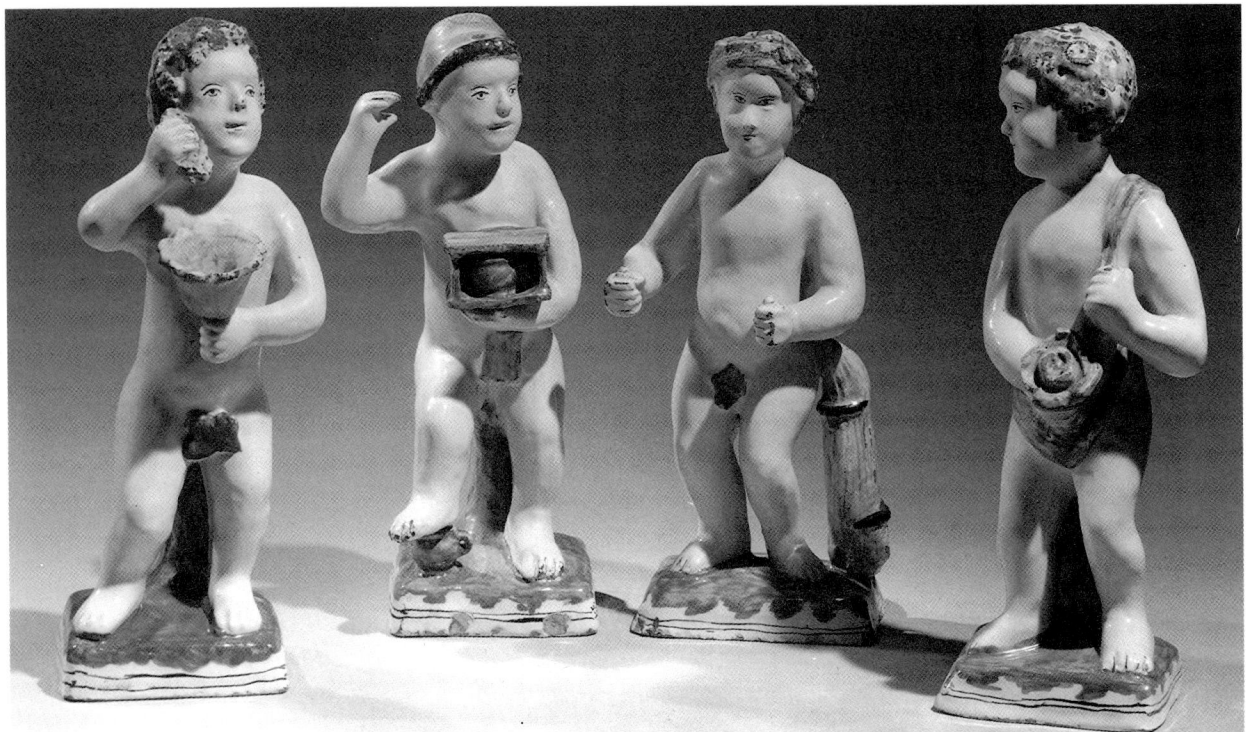

2.18. Attributed to Johannes Kruyck (Dutch, active 1662–1705). Figures Representing the Four Seasons, circa 1690. Tin-glazed earthenware, 9¼ to 9¾ inches high. The Brooklyn Museum 64.46.2a–d, The Gamble Fund.

New York City merchant Cornelis Steenwyck, according to an inventory of his house, kept "five earthen china" dishes in his "withdrawing room" and "nineteen china, or porcelain, dishes" in his "great chamber."[24] But true porcelain, imported from China through the Netherlands, was apparently difficult to obtain even for the rich. When Jeremias van Rensselaer ordered china through his sister Susanna in Amsterdam, for instance, she replied, "I had much trouble procuring the small table plates as not many are being made."[25]

Nonetheless, even purely decorative ceramic objects sometimes found their way to New York in the late seventeenth and the early eighteenth century, such as the small china dog, duck, two swans, and six white figures of men listed in the 1685 inventory of the estate of Dr. Jacob de Lange.[26] Thus the Schenck House north room has been furnished with a set of delftware figures representing the four seasons (*fig. 2.18*), a delft figure of a baby in a walker (*fig. 2.19*), and a Chinese-porcelain bulb pot (*fig. 2.20*)—all indications of the wide and complex trade network of which colonial New York was a part.

Like ceramics, most glassware of the time was imported as well. In 1656, for example, Jeremias van Rensselaer shipped 739 varied items of glass from Amsterdam on board the vessel *den Otter* for sale at his establishment in Beverwyck (i.e., "Beavertown," the village that grew up around Fort Orange and eventually became Albany).[27] Around 1730 the Schencks might have used eighteenth-century English glass of the type seen on the table and in the delftware monteith. Earlier,

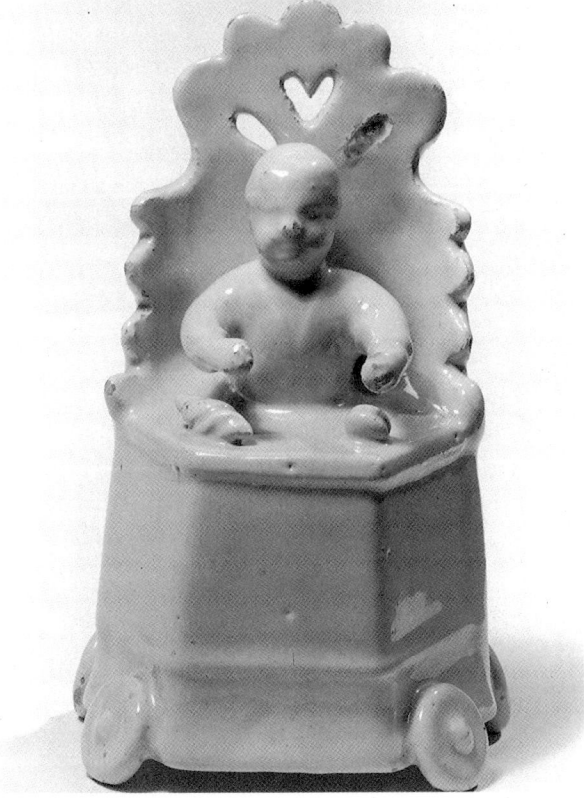

2.19. Figure of a Baby in a Walker, circa 1700. Dutch. White tin-glazed earthenware, 6½ × 3½ inches. The Brooklyn Museum 64.3.2, The Gamble Fund.

OF CUPBOARD BEDS AND HEARTHS WITHOUT JAMBS

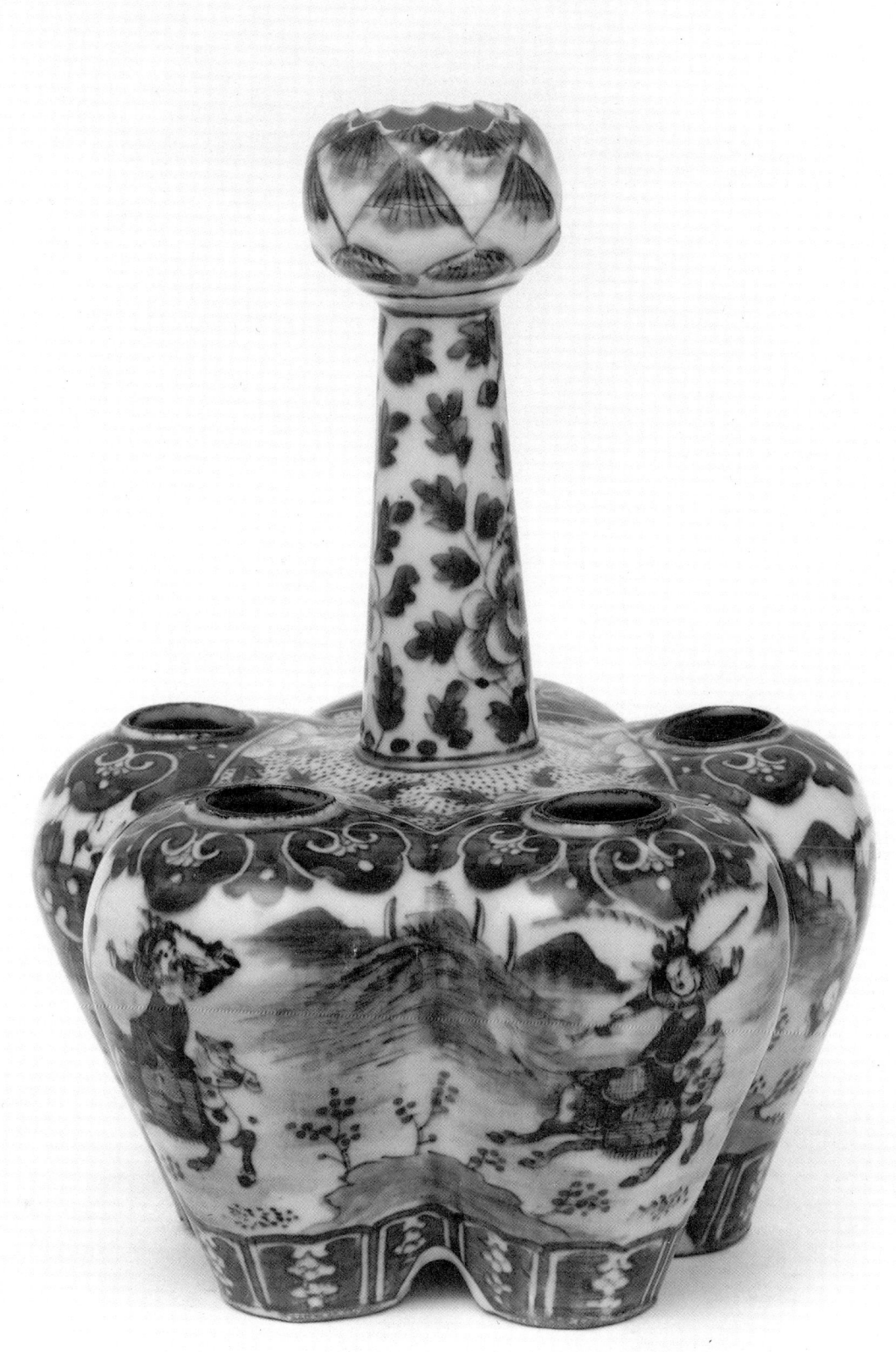

2.20. Bulb Pot, 1735–95. Chinese porcelain, 9¼ × 7 inches. The Brooklyn Museum 24.286, Gift of Mr. and Mrs. William Sterling Peters.

in the seventeenth century, however, their glass would have looked more like the Dutch or German rummer, or goblet, illustrated here (*fig. 2.21*). Fragments of rummers in green glass have been found in several seventeenth-century archaeological sites in New York.[28]

Silver objects, both foreign- and American-made, were also in use in colonial New York, and the estate inventories of the wealthiest citizens list silver in considerable quantity. At their deaths, for instance,

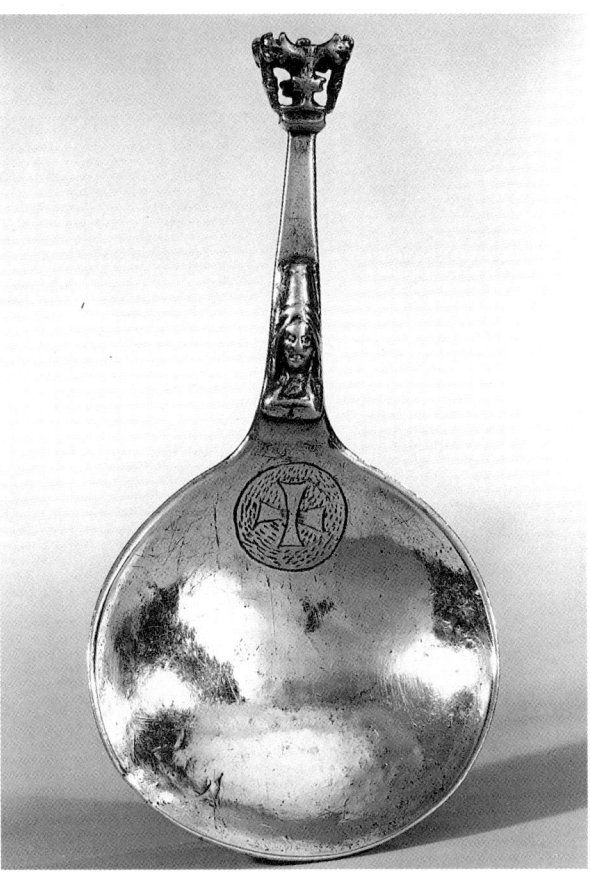

2.22. Spoon, *seventeenth century. Dutch. Silver, 4½ × 2½ inches. The Brooklyn Museum 79.29.2, Gift of Mr. Bruce F. Woodbury.*

Cornelis Steenwyck had 723 ounces of silver valued at £216. 18s., while François Rombout owned a more modest £20. 17s. worth.[29] Silver tankards, salt cellars, and beakers were valued not just for their usefulness and beauty; since they were made of the same material as money, they also provided a means of storing and displaying wealth. The importance people attached to even a single silver object is indicated by the fact that among the hundreds of items van Rensselaer imported on board the ship *den Otter* in 1659 was, for a man named Jan Thomass, "1 silver spoon which I owed him."[30] Such an item would have been much more highly cherished than a similar object today, and though the Schencks were not nearly as wealthy as Steenwyck and Rombout, they might at least have owned a silver spoon like the seventeenth-century Dutch example now seen in the north room (*fig. 2.22*). Indeed, according to legend, this spoon descended in the Schenck family.

Among the other furnishings in the room is a high chest of drawers (*fig. 2.23*) along the west wall, where, as mentioned earlier, there was a window in the installation of 1964. This chest, which appears to retain its original brasses, was probably made in New York between 1720 and 1740. Although its broad proportions and drawer arrangement have been compared to

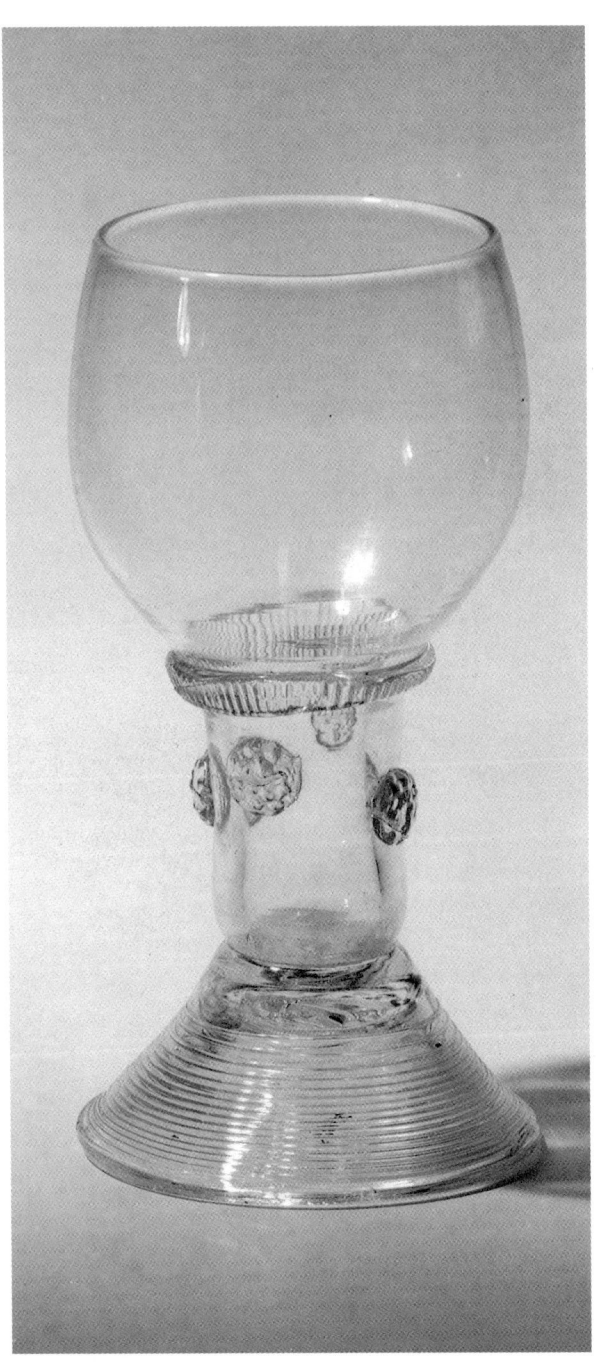

2.21. Goblet, *mid-seventeenth century. Dutch or German. Glass, 4¾ inches high. The Brooklyn Museum 13.530, Museum Purchase.*

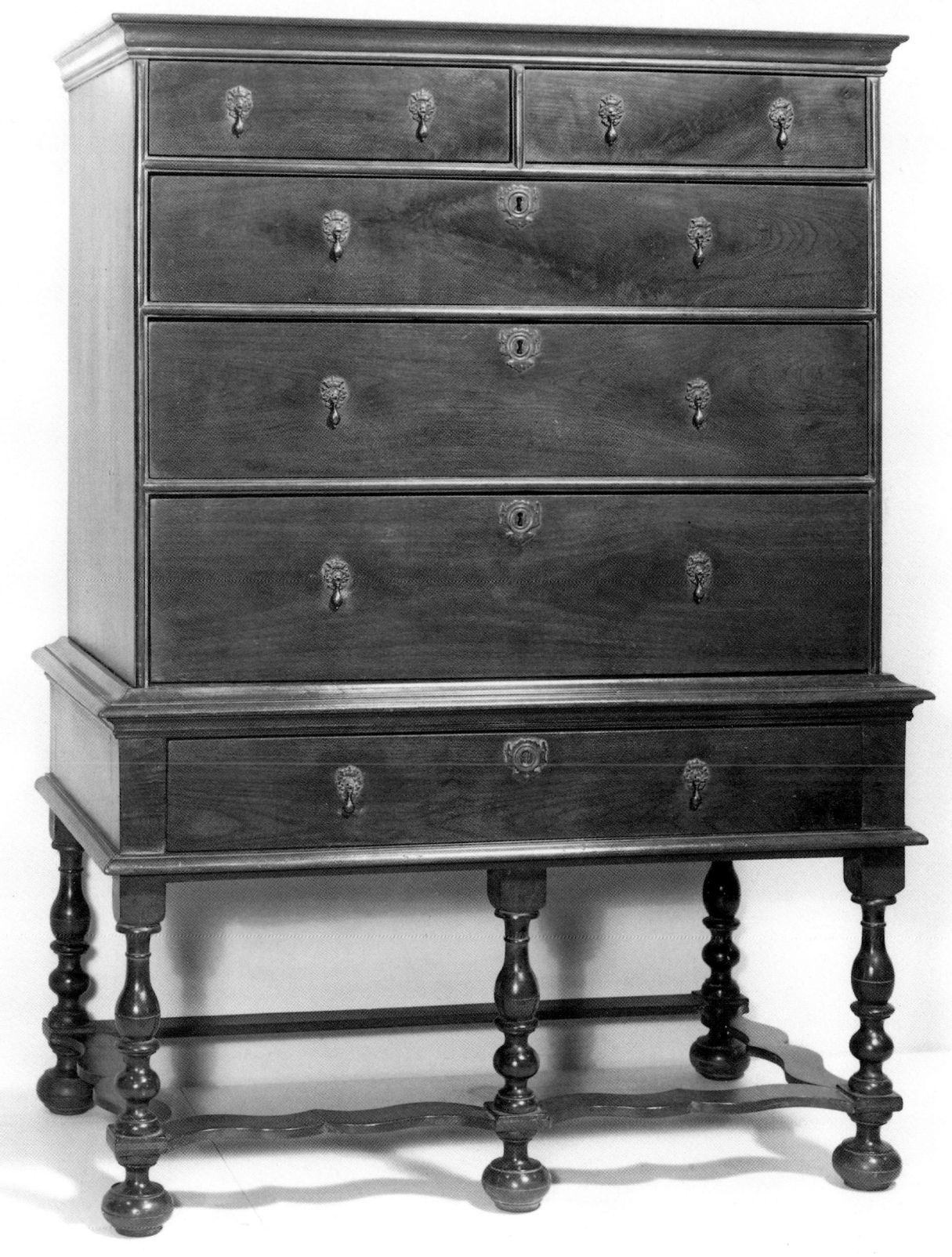

2.23. High Chest, *circa 1720–40. New York. Walnut and gumwood, 57½ × 40 × 22½ inches. The Brooklyn Museum 61.55.2, The Gamble Fund.*

New York *kassen* like the one in the Nicholas Schenck House (*see again fig.* 5.58), it has more in common with furniture of the English William and Mary style.[31] The box on top (*see again fig.* 2.7) was also made in New York, but earlier, in the last quarter of the seventeenth century. Its form relates to Dutch boxes called *kapdozen,* or dressing cases, which were used for the safekeeping of the caps and lace so valued as a part of the period costume.[32] Although its carving has often been associated with carving of the Dutch province of Friesland, the late decorative arts historian Benno Forman believed that it was made by the same craftsman who made a similar box of 1676 now in the Henry Francis du Pont Winterthur Museum in Winterthur, Delaware. Because the Winterthur box is inscribed in German, that craftsman was undoubtedly German rather than Dutch.[33]

Also displayed in this room, although not visible in recent photographs, is a walnut dressing table probably made in New York about 1700 (*see fig.* 2.24). The scrolled, S-curved legs of much more elaborate European Baroque examples have been reduced to their most basic form in this table in a manner typical of the American interpretation of sophisticated foreign styles.

Above the table in the installation of 1964 (*see again fig.* 2.5) was a mirror with a heavy, veneer frame and an elaborate crest. Such "looking glasses" are listed in many inventories of the period. The inventory taken of the estate of a New Yorker named Abraham de Lanoy in 1702, for example, lists a "great looking glass" worth £5.[34]

The walls of colonial New York houses were also often ornamented with prints and paintings. By the time of his death in 1685, for instance, Dr. de Lange had assembled sixty-one pictures in his home, nine in the *voorhuis,* or entrance hall, alone, and when a man by the name of Thomas Crundall died in 1652, five landscapes—two large and three small—were found in his house.[35] The Dutch in particular were apparently avid collectors of art, for as one English visitor to the Netherlands of the time observed:

> Their interior decorations are far more costly than our own not only in hangings and ornaments, but in pictures which are found even in the poorer houses. No farmer or even common laborer is found, that has not some kind of interior ornaments of all kinds, so that if all

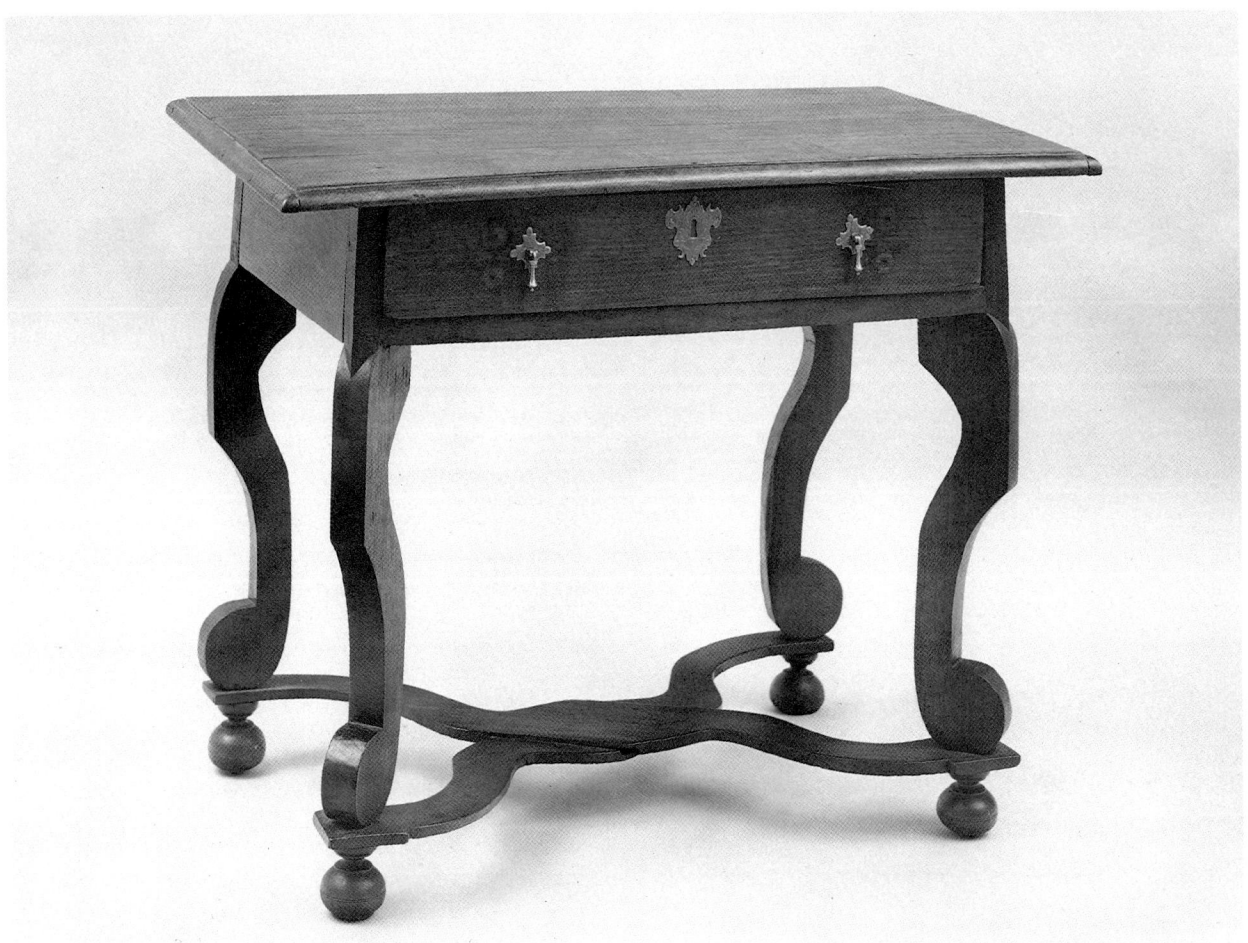

2.24. Dressing Table, *circa 1700. New York. Walnut and American white pine, 21 × 36½ × 28⅜ inches. The Brooklyn Museum   60.78, The Gamble Fund.*

were put together it often would fill a booth at the fair.[36]

The Schenck family likely continued this tradition of decoration here, perhaps displaying something like the two paintings on panels now seen in the north room (figs. 2.25 and 2.26), which were probably painted around 1730 by an artist of the Hudson River valley. These paintings, which descended in the Hewlett family of Merrick, Long Island, depict female figures, one holding an arrow and the other a small mirror or a miniature. Probably inspired by engravings, they may represent allegorical figures of Love and Vanity.

As a whole, the furnishings in the north room represent the kind of goods that might have been accumulated between 1675 and 1730 by a prosperous Long Island family like the Schencks. The room exhibits an interest in comfort and an inclination to follow the changing styles of the time, combining furnishings of the William and Mary style with earlier seventeenth-century Baroque pieces. Although much of the furniture was made in America, many other objects—such as the ceramics, glassware, and carpet—would have been acquired through a thriving network of trade with Europe and the East.

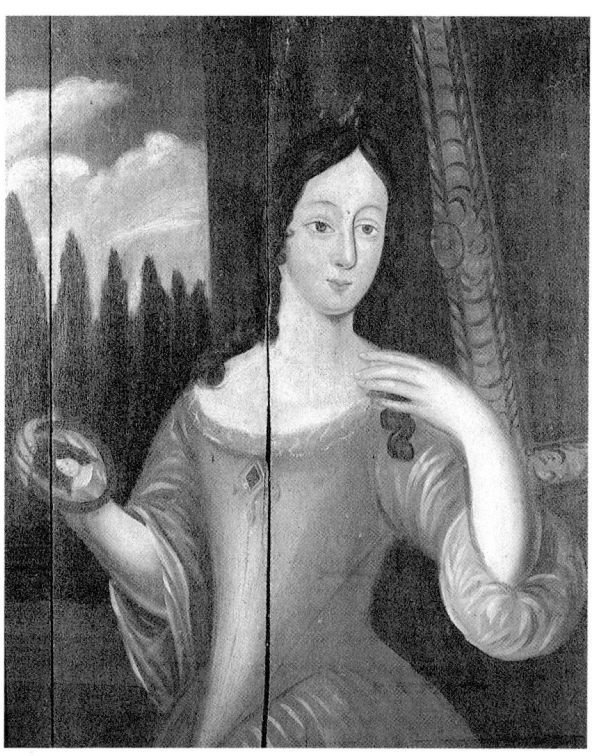

2.26. Artist unknown, American. Lady Holding a Miniature or a Looking Glass, circa 1730. Oil on panel, 29¼ × 24 inches. The Brooklyn Museum 64.89.2, The Gamble and Dick S. Ramsay Funds.

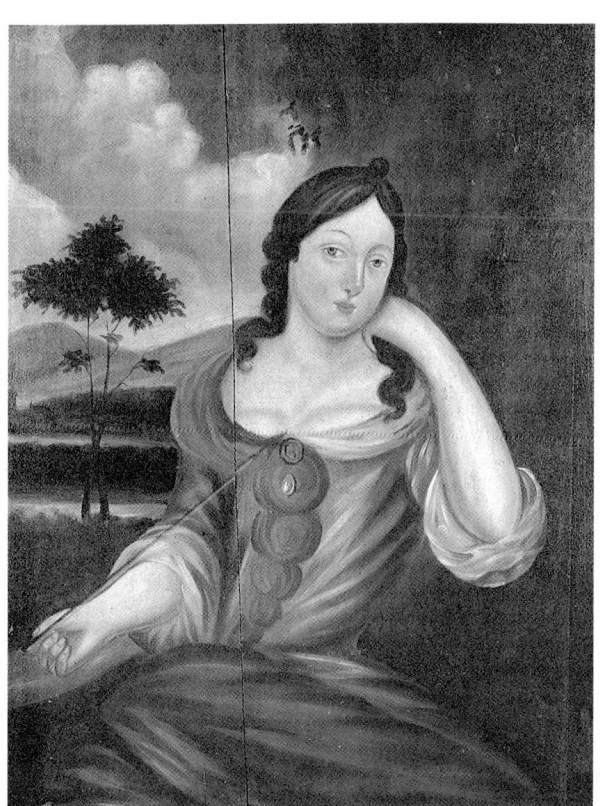

2.25. Artist unknown, American. Lady Holding an Arrow, circa 1730. Oil on panel, 27 × 21¼ inches. The Brooklyn Museum 64.89.1, The Gamble and Dick S. Ramsay Funds.

THE SOUTH ROOM

The best early photograph of the south room of the Jan Martense Schenck House, taken in 1905, is a view of the south wall showing the fireplace that was built there around 1800 to replace the central chimney (see fig. 2.27). Together with a later photograph of about 1934 (fig. 2.28), it demonstrates that the room's basic structural elements—its posts and beams—survived relatively unscathed. This was true up until the time the house was dismantled in 1952, though a photograph of that time (fig. 2.29) reveals that at some point the brace to the right of the southwest window (a window that was itself an alteration of the original structure) had been cut away, no doubt to accommodate a large piece of furniture. By this time, too, the fireplace had been walled up and a shelf added to the mantel.

As in the north room, those original elements that had disappeared, such as the central fireplace, were re-created (see figs. 2.30 and 2.31). The profile for the manteltree, simpler than the one in the north room, is based on a seventeenth-century example that still survives in the Jean Hasbrouck House in New Paltz, New York (see fig. 2.32).

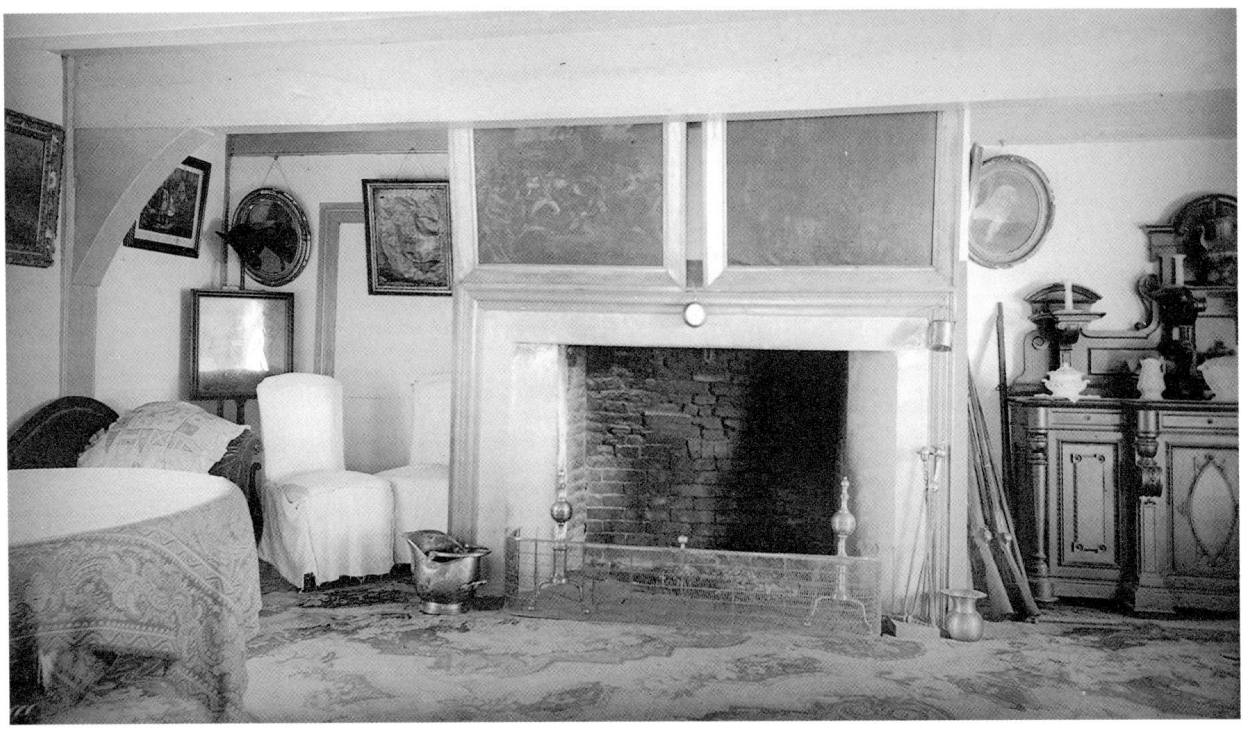

2.27. *South Room, Jan Martense Schenck House, in situ, 1905. Photograph courtesy of The New-York Historical Society.*

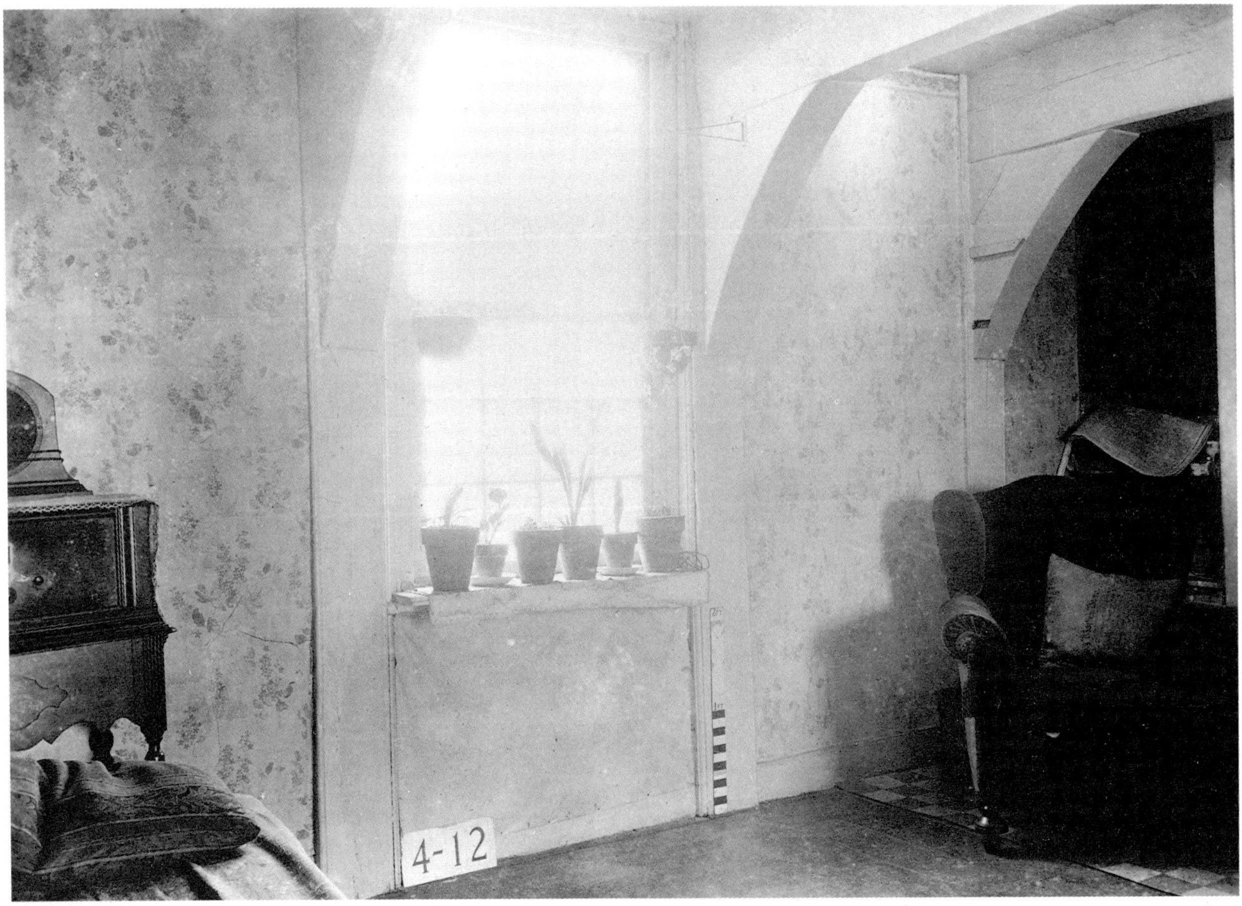

2.28. *South Room, Jan Martense Schenck House, in situ, circa 1934.*

OF CUPBOARD BEDS AND HEARTHS WITHOUT JAMBS

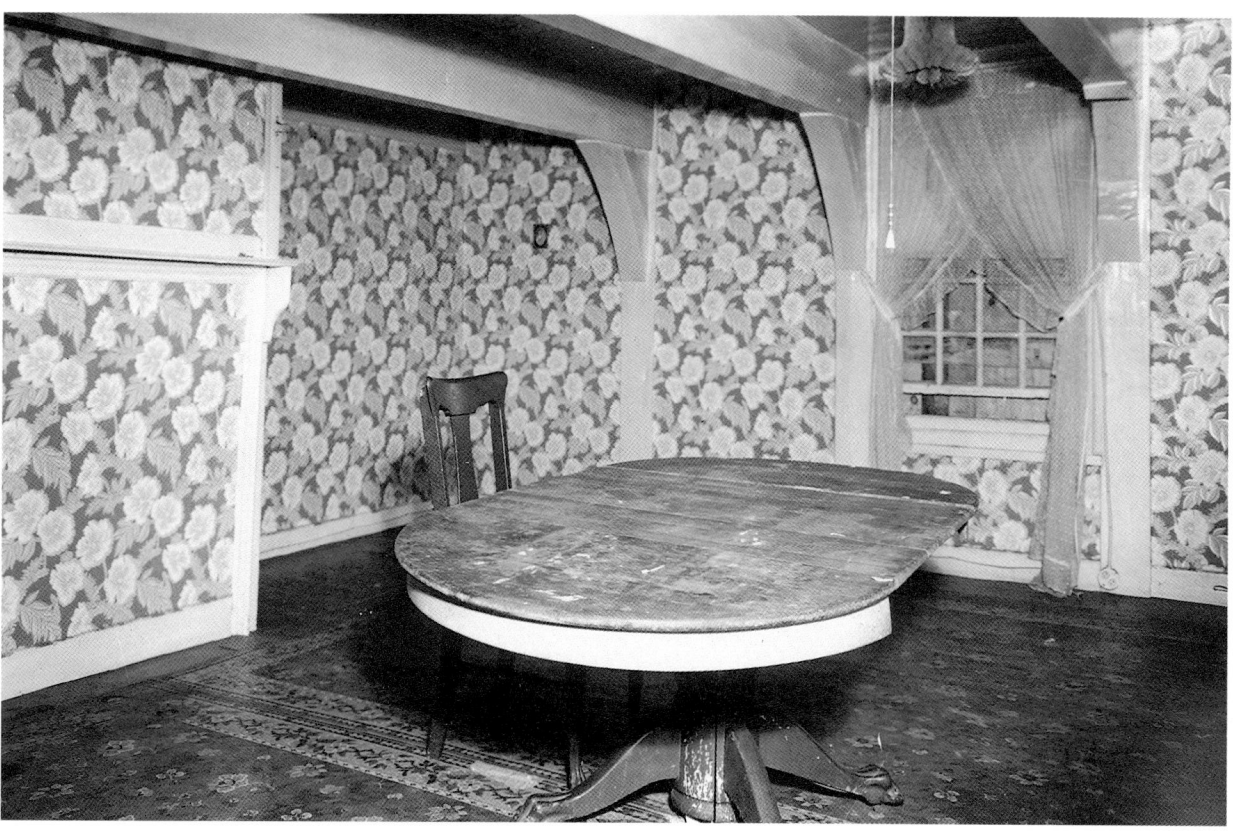

2.29. South Room, Jan Martense Schenck House, in situ, circa 1952.

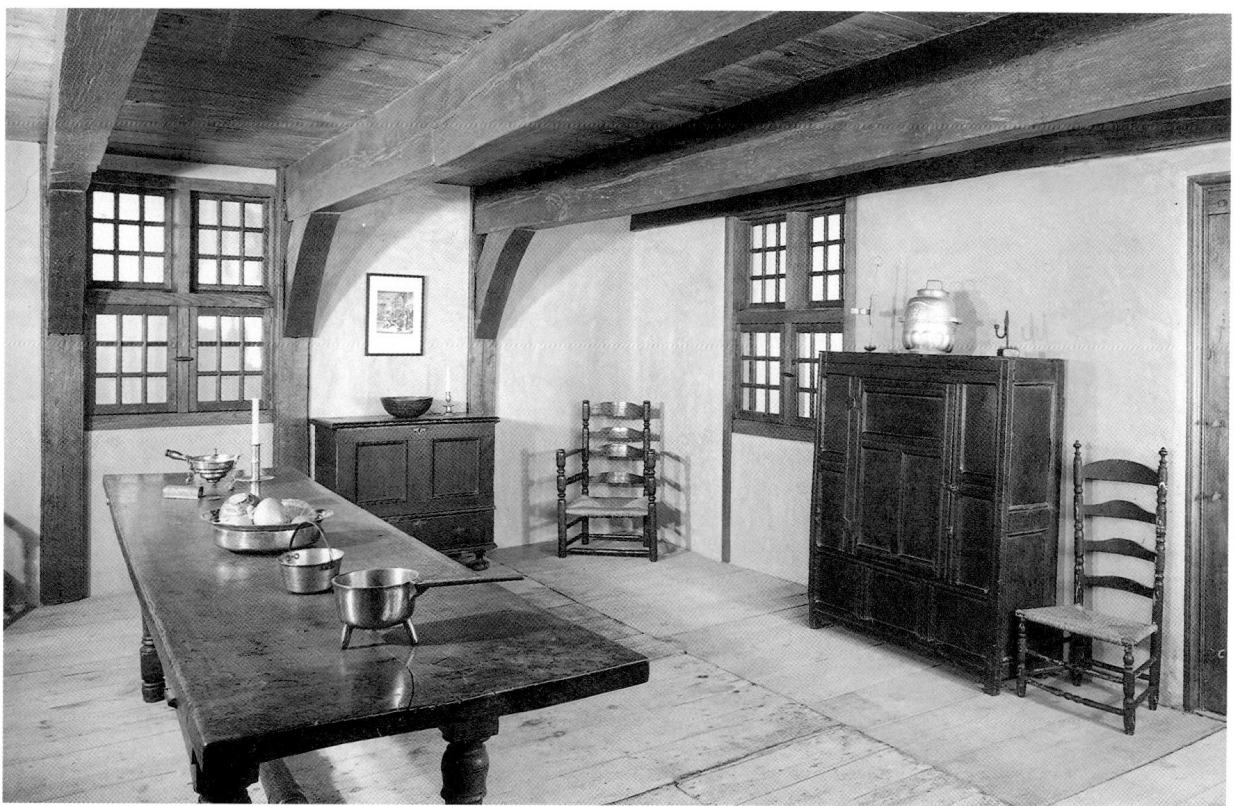

2.30. South Room, Jan Martense Schenck House, as installed in The Brooklyn Museum, circa 1964.

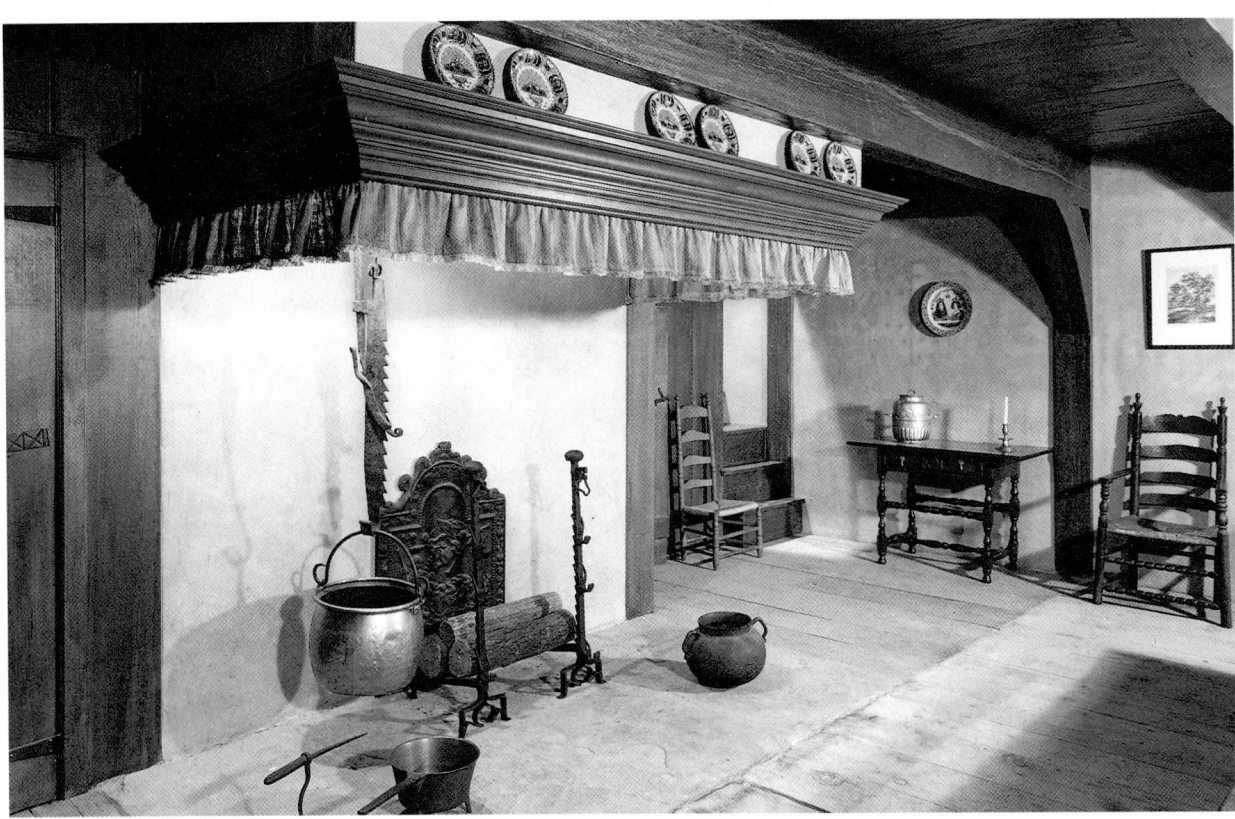

2.31. South Room, Jan Martense Schenck House, as installed in The Brooklyn Museum, circa 1964.

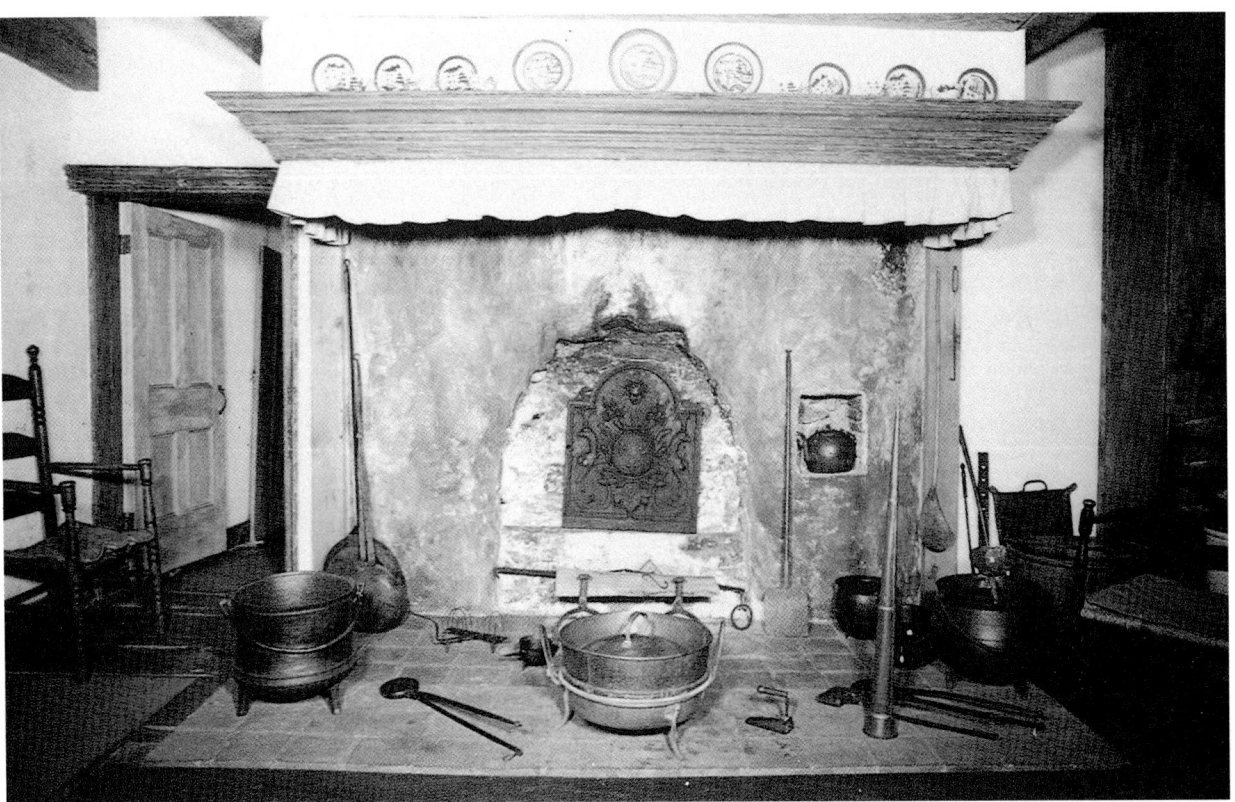

2.32. Seventeenth-century manteltree, Jean Hasbrouck House, New Paltz, New York. Photograph courtesy of the Huguenot Historical Society, New Paltz.

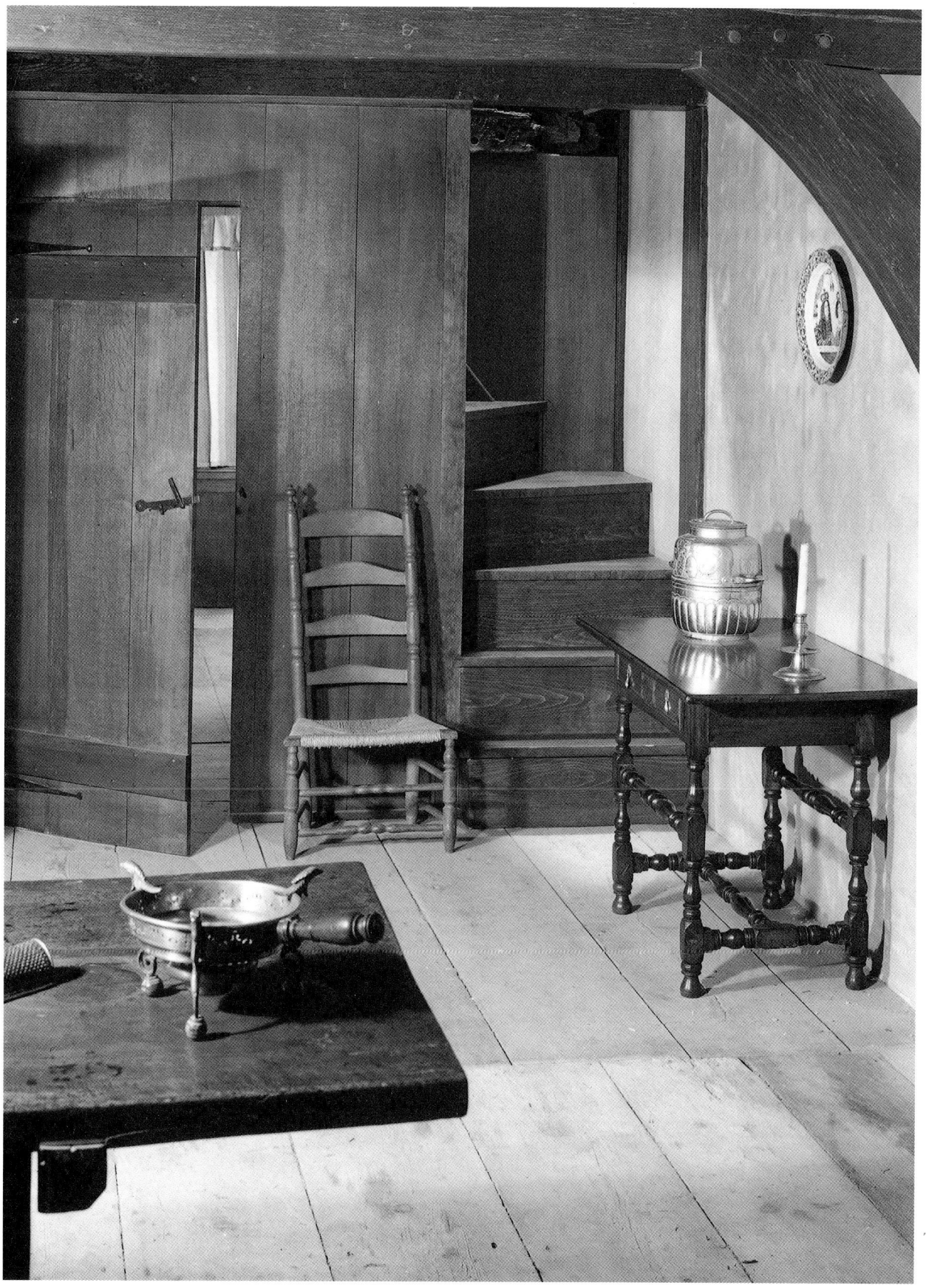

2.33. Staircase, South Room, Jan Martense Schenck House, as reconstructed in The Brooklyn Museum, 1964.

Just beyond the fireplace, on the east wall, is the entrance to an enclosed winding staircase (*fig. 2.33*) that may be similar to a "winding staircase in the foreroom" that Egbert van Borsum had the carpenters referred to earlier include in his Brooklyn ferry-house in 1655.[37] This, too, is a speculative reconstruction, for the original stairs did not survive and it is not known whether the entrance to them was in the south room or the north. Though it is here in the wall at the foot of the stairs that Henk J. Zantkuyl has suggested there would have been a window to provide light for work at the fireplace,[38] the only window in the east wall of the south room as the room was installed is located further to the right.

On the south wall, the early nineteenth-century fireplace has been removed and a window and a door placed where such openings were indicated by an examination of the wall. As Marvin Schwartz wrote in 1964:

> Neither door nor window in the south wall had survived in 1952. There were, however, two horizontal members found in the wall, that could be interpreted as the upper parts of doors or windows, and one door sill. This resulted in making one opening a door and the other a window. The door used had come from another Brooklyn house and dates about 1750.[39]

The south room is furnished more simply than the north room to indicate its function as the primary work and cooking space of the house (*see figs. 2.34 and 2.35*). In the middle of the room is a long seventeenth-century table with turned legs and a slab top. Of Continental origin, this table is an example of the simple, sturdy, functional furniture indispensable to the operation of the household. In front of it is a long bench, or form, a less expensive and therefore more common kind of seating than chairs in the seventeenth century. Jeremias van Rensselaer used pine benches in the council room of his estate until 1660, when he wrote to his mother in the Netherlands and asked her to send him eight Spanish chairs as a replacement.[40] The

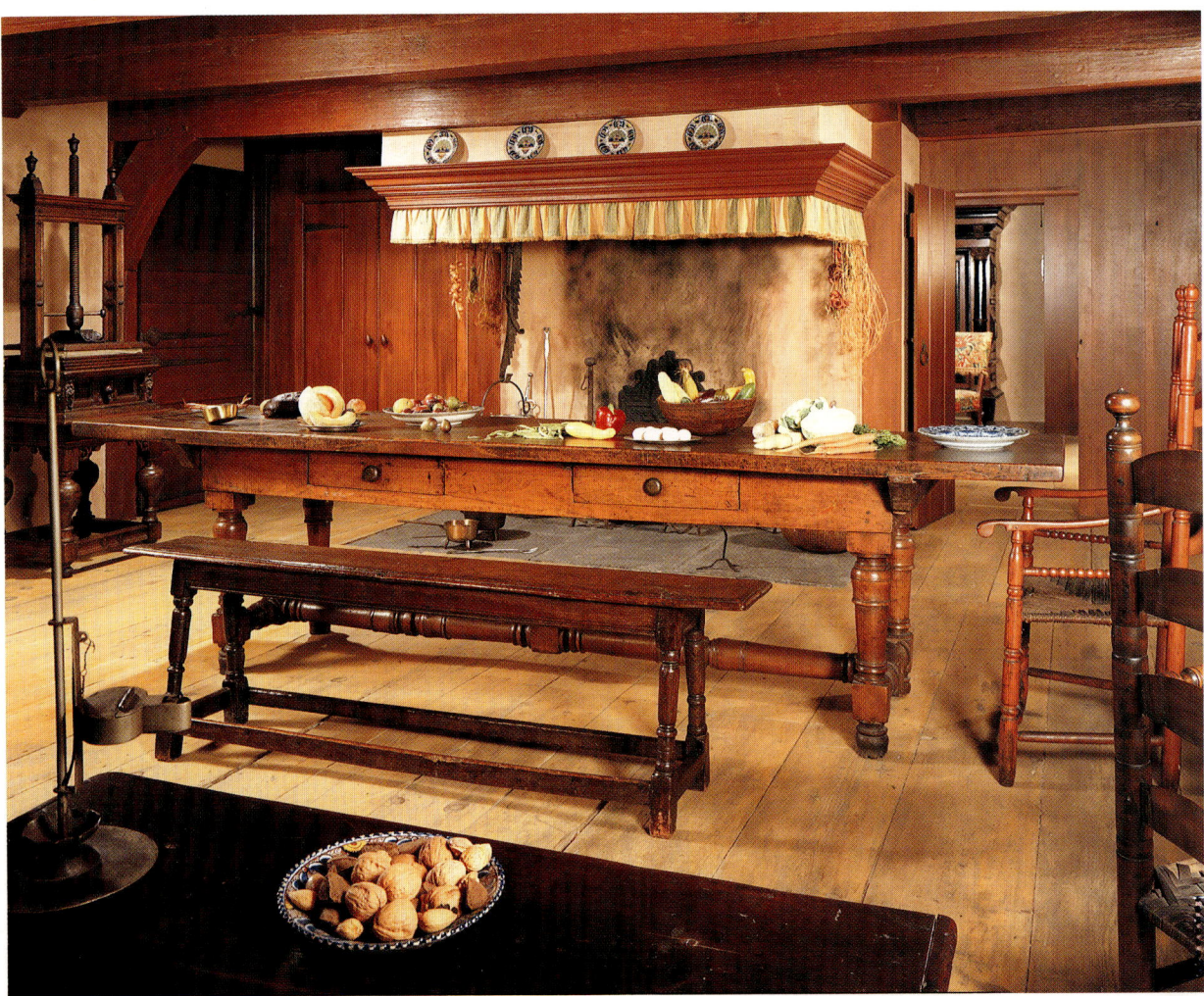

2.34. South Room, Jan Martense Schenck House, as installed in The Brooklyn Museum, 1987. Photograph by Paul Warchol.

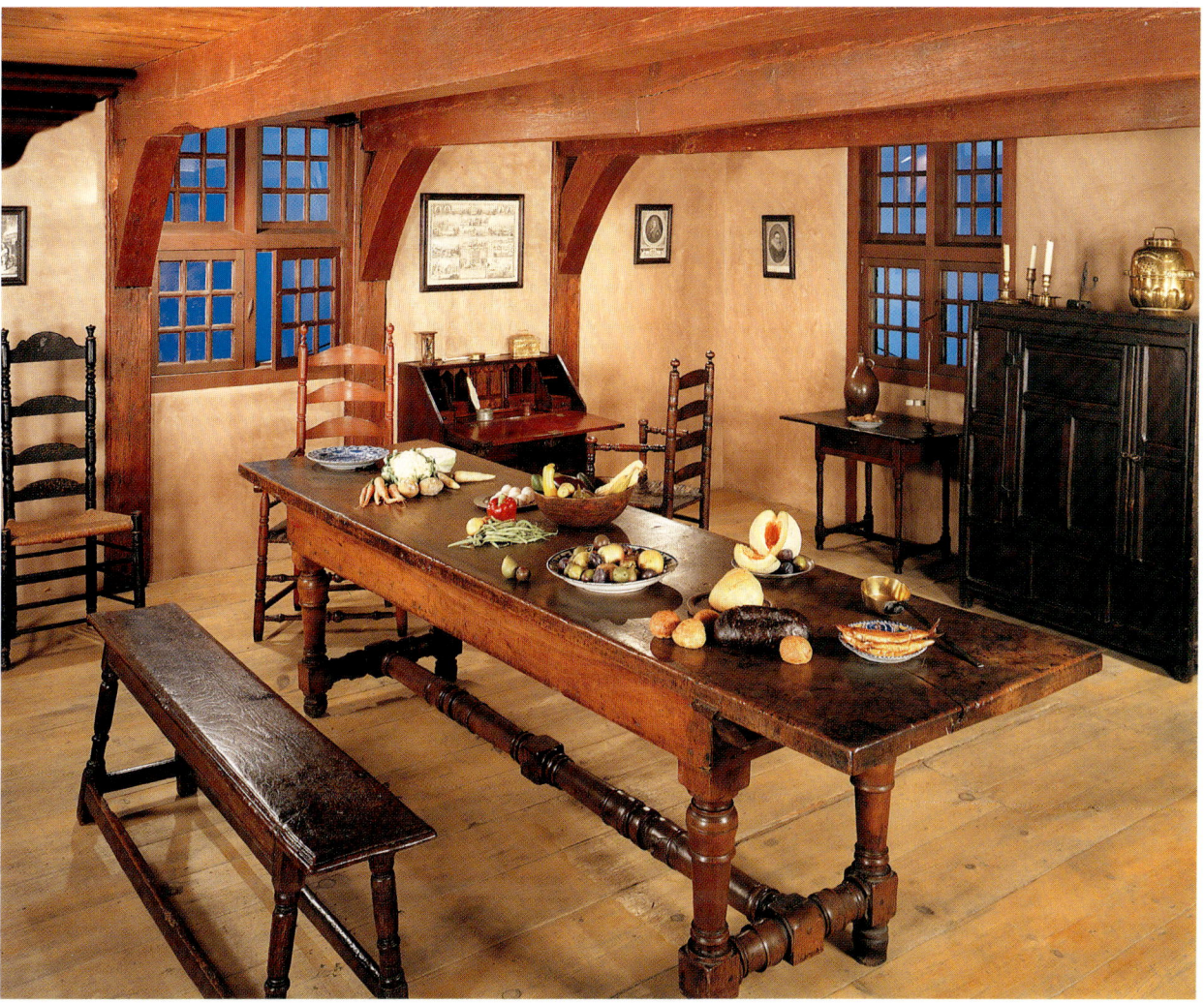

2.35. South Room, Jan Martense Schenck House, as installed in The Brooklyn Museum, 1987. Photograph by Paul Warchol.

Schencks, who were much less wealthy, would have used such benches far longer.

Nonetheless, by the early eighteenth century, they might well have owned turned wooden chairs as well. "Matted" or "matt" chairs with rush seats, slat backs, and turned rails and stiles are listed in many of the era's estate inventories along with "great" chairs, or armchairs (*see fig. 2.36*), and cushions to buffer the seats. Cornelis Steenwyck, for instance, had three "old matt chairs" in his kitchen and ten chairs with six chair cushions in the chamber above,[41] while a man named Anthony de Milt who died in 1693 owned ten "matt" chairs and two "great" chairs.[42]

On October 2, 1679, during their visit to New Amersfoort, Jasper Danckaerts and Peter Sluyter met a local man who made such chairs, called a turner because he turned the parts of the chair on a lathe. "In the evening," Danckaerts wrote, "we made the acquaintance of one Jean Poppe, formerly a skipper in the West Indies, whom I had known when I lived there. . . . He was tired of the sea, and not having accumulated much, he had come to settle down there, making his living out of the business of a turner, by which he could live bountifully."[43] Since Poppe is credited with delivering chairs on November 6, 1676, to Elbert Elbertsen, the merchant who sold the Mill Island property to Jan Martense Schenck, it is possible he also made chairs for the Schencks themselves, though the chairs now seen in the south room are of a somewhat later date.[44]

Also on display in this room is a large oak linen press (*fig. 2.37*). The elaborate nature of this piece, which like the *kas* in the north room was made in the seventeenth-century Netherlands, is appropriate to its role in the care of one of the household's most expensive items—the table linen, which would have been folded and placed between the object's boards to be pressed and neatly creased when the central screw was tightened.

The seventeenth-century oak cupboard on the south wall is a much simpler piece of furniture used to store household goods, including pressed linen. Though probably English, it relates in general form to seven-

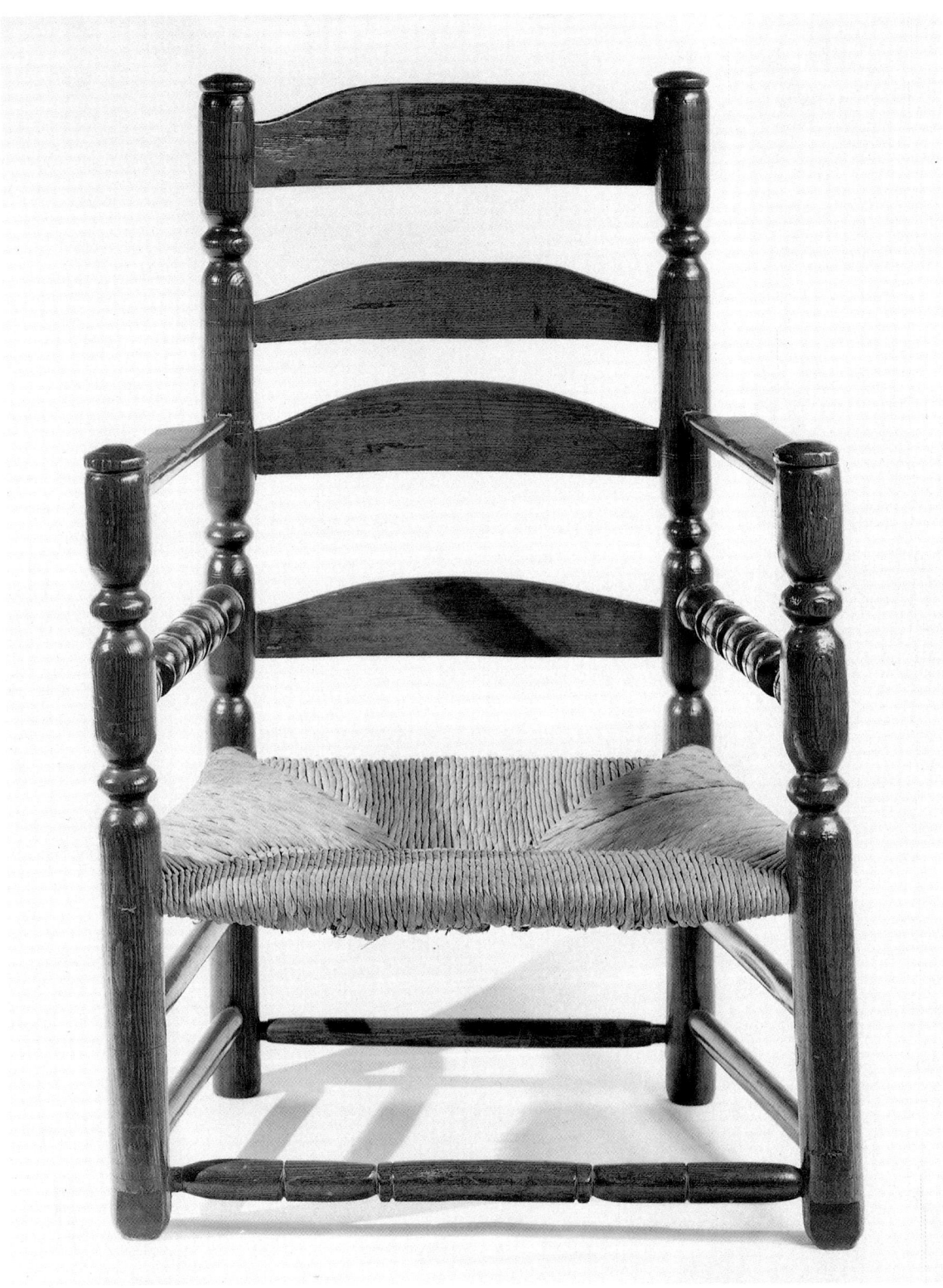

2.36. Armchair, circa 1700–25. American. Oak, 39 × 26 × 18 inches. The Brooklyn Museum 30.885, Henry L. Batterman Fund.

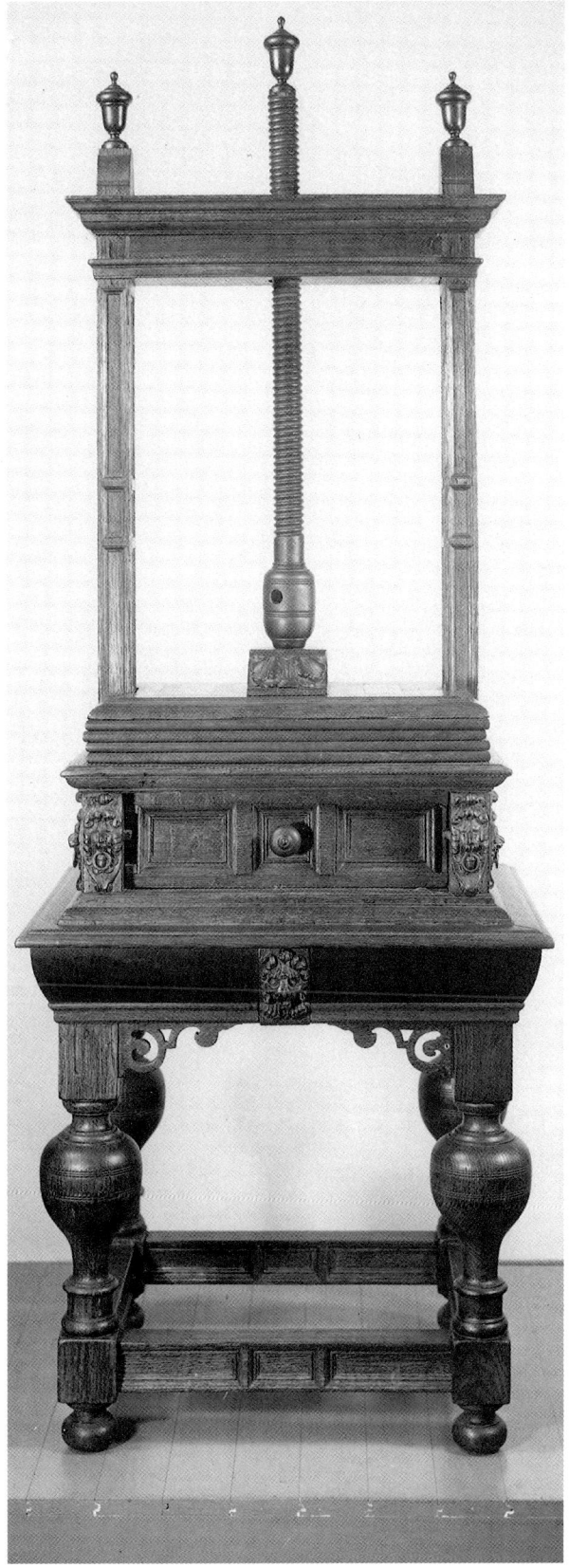

2.37. Linen Press, *seventeenth century. Dutch. Oak, 76¾ × 27¾ × 23½ inches. The Brooklyn Museum 12.877, A. Augustus Healy Fund and others.*

teenth-century oak cupboards made in New York.[45]

Facing it, along the east wall, is a desk (*fig. 2.38*) with a long history of ownership in Kings County, having descended in the Luquer family of Bushwick.[46] Made in New York between 1720 and 1740, this piece represents a possible acquisition by the Schencks about the time the house was first altered.

In addition to the furniture, the south room is equipped with a large assortment of implements and dishes used in the preparation and consumption of food. On the hearth are kettles and saucepans and other utensils of copper and brass, while on the mantel —where such things are still proudly displayed—are four delftware plates. Some additional kitchen items the Schencks might have used (though not, of course, in such numbers) are suggested by the inventory taken in 1702 of the estate of the wealthy New Yorker Pieter Jacob Marius, who, as we have seen, owned three-quarters of a ton of pewter. Besides nineteen earthenware dishes he kept on "ye mantle tree," Marius had in his kitchen at the time of his death:

> ...five brass kettles (44¾ pounds), three copper kettles (31½ pounds), three brass new pans and covers (31 pounds), two tart pans, two brass scales, one small metal pot and cover, five iron pots with covers (54 pounds), two iron chains, two spits, a brass mortar and pestle, a rolling-pin, two ladles, a kneading-trough, a tin apple roaster, a tin grater...two porringers, two chafing-dishes, a copper pail, a skillet, a saucepan, two brass skimmers, three brass frying-pans, two "old tin pye pans," a cullender, an iron dripping-pan, a flesh fork and ladle..."one gridding iron," [and] a brass bowl and ladle...[47]

During her visit to New York in 1704, Madame Knight found that Dutch New Yorkers kept their tables "as free to their Naybours as to themselves." On one occasion, she wrote, a certain Mr. Bourroughs "cary'd his spouse and Daughter and myself out to one Madame Dowes, a Gentlewoman that lived at a farm House, who gave us a handsome entertainment of five or six Dishes and choice Beer and metheglin [mead], Cyder, &c all which she said was the produce of her farm."[48]

Like her counterpart in the Netherlands, the Dutch New York housewife probably kept her kitchen space scrupulously scrubbed and orderly, polishing her copper and brass till it sparkled and sometimes wrapping it in gauze when not in use. As one English visitor to the Netherlands wrote:

> Now, if you have entered into their houses, the first that will strike your eyes is a large mirror, the other the pewter and brasswork, standing on a ledge along the walls like soldiers in their files—and everything is so neat and snug and clean, that it appears unto you like a golden and silver mountain, for nothing of all Gods

good things loses anything of its original beauty.... In the one house you will see the fire irons standing in the corner of the chimney, covered with fine netting, in another house, the warming pans covered with Italian open work designs and the handles carved, in the third the brass strainer, wrapped in cambric.[49]

Although conditions in rural western Long Island were surely difficult, the Schencks no doubt attempted to outfit their house in the Dutch manner and did their best to provide themselves with a reasonable degree of comfort and occasionally even a little luxury. As the historian Alice P. Kenney has written of the Dutch inhabitants of Fort Orange in the 1650s:

> [T]he same traders who complained bitterly of economic hardship were eating from elaborately decorated dishes and drinking from fine glassware, apparently attempting to maintain their accustomed European standard of living in the colonial wilderness.[50]

In this way Dutch customs and traditions were transplanted in the New World, where they would eventually play an important role in the development of American culture.

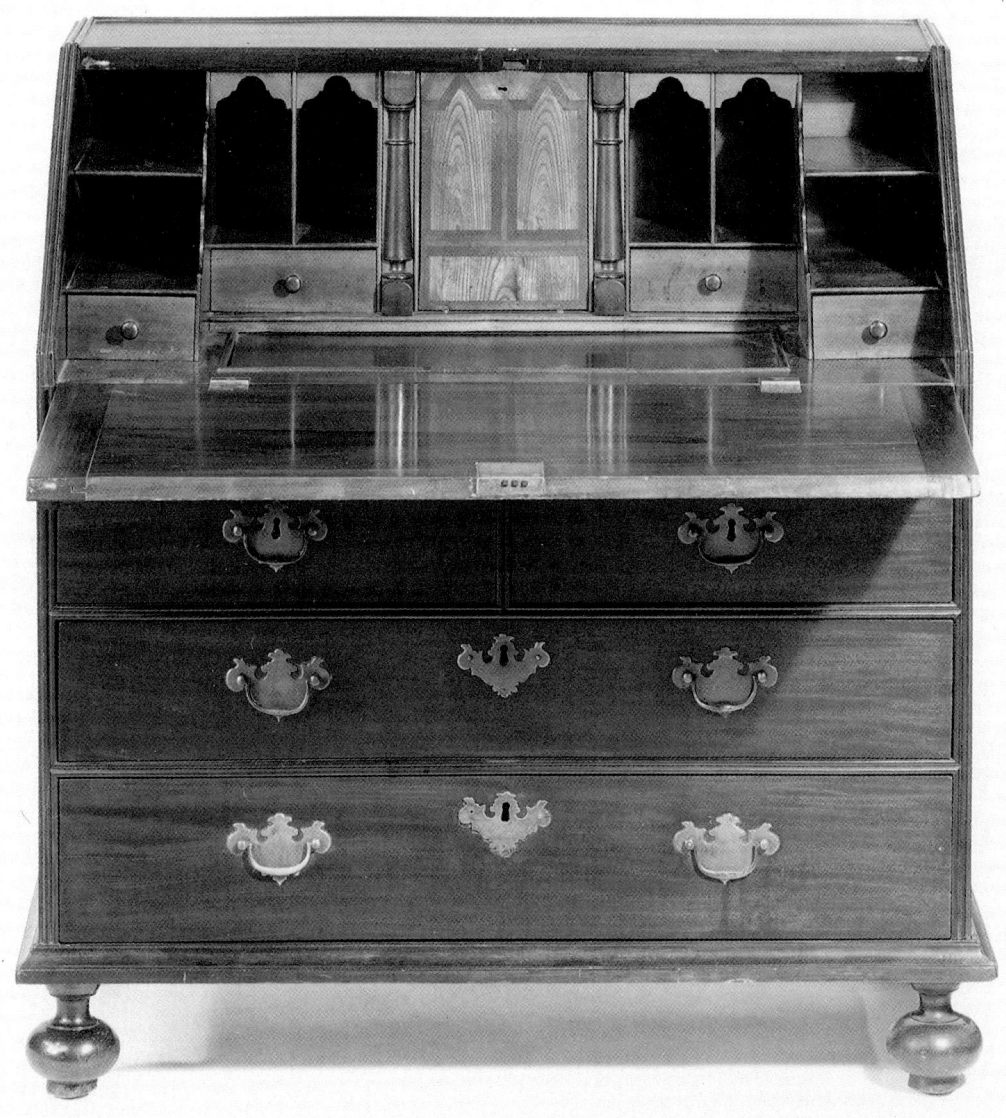

2.38. Desk, *circa 1720–40. New York. Mahogany, red gumwood, and poplar, 38⅛ × 37½ inches. The Brooklyn Museum 63.42, The Gamble Fund.*

CHAPTER
THREE

FROM DUTCH TO DUTCH AMERICAN

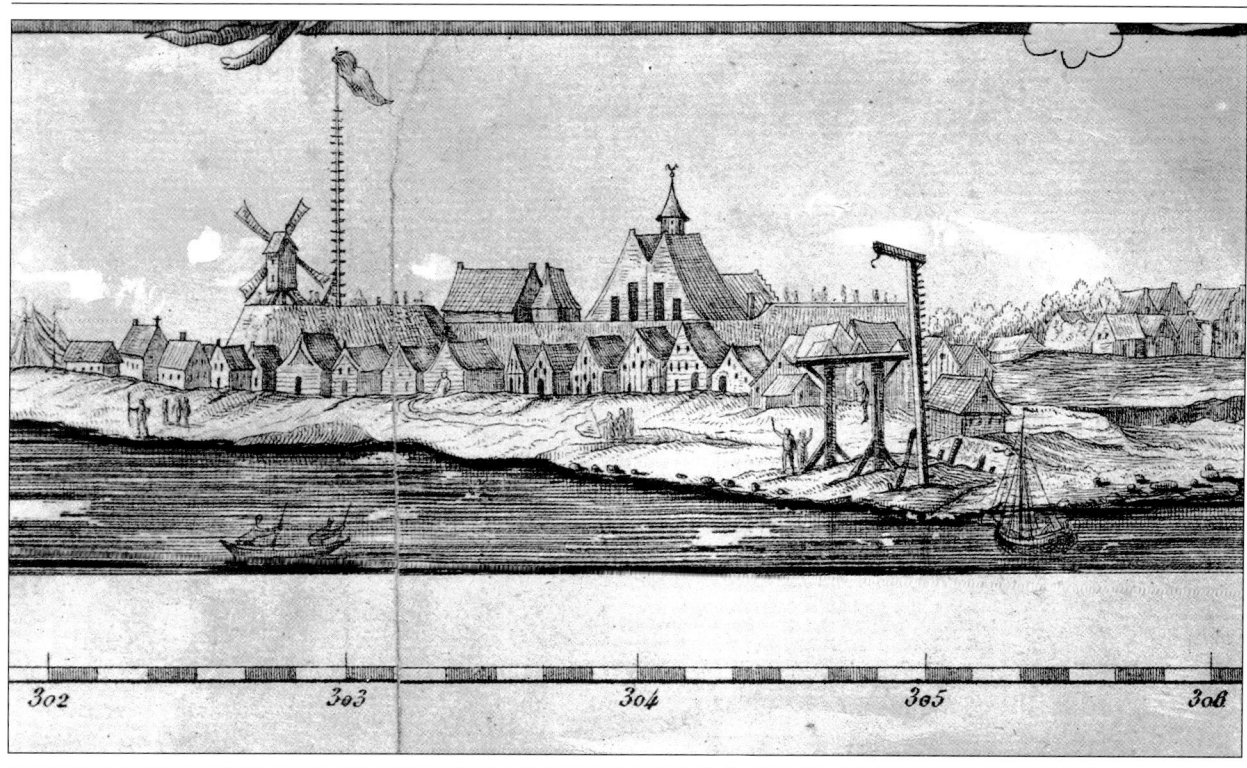

3.1. *View of New Amsterdam. Detail of a map by N. J. Visscher, Amsterdam, 1651. Photograph courtesy of The New-York Historical Society.*

In the century between the building of Jan Martense Schenck's house and the construction of the house of his grandson Nicholas, the American colonies developed the characteristics that would define a new and independent nation. Over the course of these years New York came to share more with New England and the Southern colonies than it shared with the Netherlands, while New England and the South developed stronger ties to New York than they had to Great Britain. The Dutch of New York became less and less Dutch and more and more American. But it was a slow process of evolution, and the Dutch heritage was absorbed by the developing culture rather than overwhelmed by it.

This process actually began even earlier, for long before the English conquest of New Netherland in 1664 the Dutch had inadvertently fashioned the cultural melting pot of their own assimilation. Mixed in New Netherland were both Northern and Southern Europeans, Africans both slave and free, and, of course, a number of different Indian nations. Of the more than nine hundred immigrants to the colony studied by historian David Steven Cohen, only a little more than half came from the Netherlands, while about eighteen percent came from such German states as East Friesland, Oldenburg, and Westphalia, and seven percent from the Spanish Netherlands' Walloon and Flemish provinces. There were also—in addition to the French and Scandinavians found by Cohen—Italians, Spanish, Portuguese, Poles, Scots, and Irish. Moreover, the Dutch themselves were a varied lot, exhibiting all the regional differences they did at home. Although most of the Dutch immigrants in Cohen's sample came from North Holland, substantial numbers also emigrated from Gelderland, Utrecht, South Holland, and Friesland.[1] By and large they were members of the Calvinist Dutch Reformed Church, but New Netherland was also home to a variety of religious groups, including North America's first major group of Jews, who arrived in 1654.[2] According to an account of 1646 by the French Jesuit missionary Isaac Jogues, himself an example of the population's diversity, the colonial capital (*fig. 3.1*) was a veritable Babel:

> On the island of Manhatte, and in its environs, there may well be four or five hundred men of different sects and nations: the Director General told me that there were men of eighteen different languages.... No religion is publicly exercised but the Calvinist, and orders are to admit none but Calvinists, but this is not observed; for there are in the Colony besides the Calvinists, Catholics, English Puritans, Lutherans, Anabaptists, here called Mnistes [Mennonites], &c. &c.[3]

That Dutch culture should have combined with the cultures of these and a host of other peoples to form a new, hybrid, American culture is ironic indeed, for getting involved in America is something that the Dutch at one time wanted greatly to avoid. They had no desire to settle here in the first place, and when they did they showed little interest in putting down roots.

The Dutch had first thought of America as a giant obstacle between themselves and the Spice Islands of Indonesia. In 1609 the Englishman Henry Hudson, sailing for the Dutch East India Company, tried to find a shortcut around or through it. But what he discovered instead soon changed Dutch minds, for America offered a land and a people ripe for exploitation. On Hudson's third day in Manhattan harbor one of his officers recorded, "[O]ur boats went on Land with our Net to Fish, and caught ten great Mullets, of a foot and a halfe long a peece, and a Ray as great as foure men could hale into the ship.... This day the people of the Countrey came aboord of us, seeming very glad of our comming, and brought green Tabacco, and gave us of it for Knives and Beads."[4] Although the signing that year of a truce in the Netherlands' long war for independence from Spain, which still claimed all of America, kept them from creating a colony here immediately, as soon as the truce expired in 1621 they established the Dutch *West* India Company for the purpose of challenging Iberian imperialism in not only the Old World (along the west coast of Africa) but also the New.

In founding New Netherland, which stretched in theory from the Delaware River in the southwest to the Connecticut River in the northeast, the company laid claim to some of the richest, best-situated land on North America's eastern seaboard. The seventeenth-century Dutch lawyer Adriaen van der Donck, among others, described it as a regular Eden. "New Netherlands," he wrote, "is a fine, acceptable, healthy, extensive and agreeable country, wherein all people can more easily gain a competent support, than in the Netherlands, or in any quarter of the globe, which is known to me or which I have visited."[5] A poem that prefaced the second, 1656 edition of his book *Description of the New Netherlands* echoed these sentiments, extolling the colony above even the lush South American land the Dutch had lost to Portugal two years earlier:

> Why mourn about Brazil, full of base Portuguese?
> When van der Donck shows us far much better fare;
> Where wheat fills golden ears, and grapes abound in trees;
> Where fruit and kine are good with little care;
> Men may mourn a loss, when vain would be their voice;
> But when their loss bring gain, they also may rejoice.[6]

The colony had one thing in particular in which the Dutch were keenly interested: an abundance of fur-bearing mammals. Barred by the French from trading for fur in Canada, they could now do business with New Netherland's natives, exchanging such things as kettles, cloth, guns, alcohol, and wampum (the strung seashells that served as the native currency) for pelts of beaver, mink, muskrat, and otter. Back in Europe a handsome profit could be had for such furs, especially beaver, which was in demand in Germany and Russia.

As the colony's proprietor, the West India Company recognized early the need for permanent settlements, if only to keep its traders supplied. Thus in 1624 it founded Fort Orange on the site of modern-day Albany as a center for trade with the Indians and in 1626 established New Amsterdam on Manhattan island as a port of entry for its ships.[7]

After that, however, because trade and not colonization was its primary concern, the company paid little attention to settlement, never really solving the problem of how to coax native-born Dutch to the wilds of America at the height of the Netherlands' Golden Age. In 1629 it did devise a scheme to award "patroonships," or large, feudal American estates, to any company member who could settle fifty adults in New Netherland for a year. But the patroons themselves were not required to emigrate, and the Dutch people found the thought of tenant farming for a feudal lord none too appealing.[8]

A prime example of the company's failure in this regard is what became of the stretch of New Netherland south of Staten Island between the Raritan and Delaware bays—the area now known as the Jersey shore. Here, it would seem, lay some of the most enticing land in the colony. As van der Donck wrote:

> Between those two bays, the coast, almost the whole distance, has double forelands, with many islands, which in some places lie two or three deep. Those forelands as well as the islands, are well situated for seaboard towns, and all kind of fisheries, and also for the cultivation of grain, vineyards, and gardening, and the keeping of stock, for which purposes the land is tolerably good. Those lands are now mostly overgrown with different kinds of trees and grape vines; having many plums, hazelnuts and strawberries, and much grass. The waters abound with oysters, having many convenient banks and beds where they may be taken.[9]

In the entire forty-year history of New Netherland, however, the Dutch established not a single settlement along this coast. In fact, the only New Netherland settlement to survive in what is now New Jersey was the town of Bergen (now Jersey City), which developed out of a failed patroonship called Pavonia founded in 1630 across the Hudson River from New Amsterdam. The Dutch did win a protracted struggle with Sweden over the Delaware River, but in the end their presence there was confined to the western, Delaware side around present-day New Castle and Wilmington.[10]

The population of the colony, then, was spread over a much less extensive area than the popular image of "Dutch New York and New Jersey" might suggest. Aside from New Amsterdam and the towns on the western end of Long Island, the principal settlements were strung out along or near the Hudson, from Yonkers (site of a patroonship founded by the *jonker*, or young nobleman, Adriaen van der Donck) in the south to Esopus (now Kingston) at the foot of the Catskills to Schenectady and Rensselaerswyck (the only patroonship that ever really succeeded) around Fort Orange.

According to the French-born Dutchman David Pietersz de Vries, who lived along the upper Hudson in 1638, the land there resembled parts of both France and the Netherlands.

> The ground on the mountains is bedecked with shrubs of bilberries or blueberries, such as in Holland come from Veeluwes [Veluwe, a range of hills in the province of Gelderland]. The level land . . . is covered with strawberries, which grow here so plentifully that they answer for food. There are also in the woods, as well as along the river, vines very abundant of two kinds, one bearing good blue grapes . . . of which good wine could be made. The other kind is like the grapes which grow in France on trellises—the large white ones which they make verjuice of in France—they are as large as the joints of the fingers.[11]

After it became clear that the West India Company's patroonship scheme was failing—that little of this bountiful land was being sown—the Dutch government stepped in, in September 1639, and passed a resolution that, in addition to lifting the company's monopoly of the fur trade, promised free passage to America for any farmer and his family. Once here, each family was to receive, for a yearly rent of 100 guilders and 80 pounds of butter, all the land it could plant.[12] Although many people posed as farmers for the chance to make a quick fortune in furs, the government's action did result in more farms, and by 1655 van der Donck could report that "the settlers who now come to the country raise their own provisions in the second year, and in the third year they have a surplus which they exchange for wares and tobacco."[13]

A Dutch farm family settling in New Netherland had first to clear the land—no easy task considering, as van der Donck put it, "the whole country is covered with wood, and in our manner of speaking there is all too much of it, and in our way."[14] Hindrance that it was at first, however, this wood ultimately redounded to the family's benefit. Once it was felled, van der Donck claimed, "The pursuit of agriculture is not heavy and expensive. . .as it is in the Netherlands. First because the. . .enclosing of the land does not cost much; for instead of the Netherlands dykes and ditches they set up post and rail, or palisado fences, and when new clearings are made, they commonly have fencing timber enough on the land to remove, which costs nothing but the labour."[15] Moreover, the colony's forests contained such a variety of trees that settlers could pick and choose among them the wood best suited for the purpose at hand. "We all agree," van der Donck wrote, for instance, "that no turf, or other common fuel is equal to nut-wood. When it is dry, it keeps fire and sparkles like matches. Our women prefer nut-coals to turf for their stoves."[16]

To supplement the grains and vegetables they grew and the livestock they raised for slaughter, New Netherland's farmers also fished and hunted, taking such game as birds, bears, rabbits, squirrels, and deer. "Buffaloes are also tolerably plenty," van der Donck wrote. "These animals mostly keep towards the southwest, where few people go. Their meat is excellent, and more desirable than the flesh of the deer, although it is much coarser."[17] As David de Vries's account of the hunting season around Fort Orange in 1638 demonstrates, surplus game—like surplus produce—served as barter in trade:

> There was this year, as they told me, a large quantity of deer at harvest and through the winter, very fat, having upon their ribs upwards of two fingers of tallow, so that they were nothing else than clear fat. They also had this

year, great numbers of turkeys. They could buy a deer for a loaf of bread, or for a knife, or even for a tobacco-pipe; at other times they give cloth, worth six or seven guilders. There are many partridges, heath-hens, and pigeons which fly together in thousands, and our people sometimes shoot thirty, forty, and fifty of them at a shot.[18]

Some of the colony's more prosperous farmers owned black slaves, though apparently rarely more than a single slave family. Through a series of raids on Portuguese trading posts in Angola, the Dutch for a time gained a monopoly of the African slave trade, but in sparsely populated New Netherland, which lacked the massive, single-crop plantations of, say, Virginia and South Carolina, large-scale slavery never developed.

Probably because of their limited numbers, slaves in New Netherland endured what some historians have labeled a "milder form" of slavery than evolved in the other American colonies, including New York under the English.[19] Slavery per se was never even legally sanctioned in New Netherland. Instead, the Dutch adopted an ad hoc approach, creating a de facto institution based on custom and usage. Though some slaves managed to obtain full freedom, it was apparently more common for a slave to be granted a sort of "half-free" status. In 1644, for example, the colony's first eleven slaves, who had been imported as bond servants of the West India Company in 1626, were set at liberty and given land on the condition that they continue to perform for the company a certain amount of *paid* labor while returning to the company each year a tax of 22½ bushels of corn, wheat, peas, or beans and one fat hog. If they failed to perform the required work or pay the annual tax, they were doomed to return to slavery. Moreover, their children "born or yet to be born" were to continue with the company as slaves.[20] A group of white citizens, including van der Donck, objected in part to these limitations, writing to the Dutch government, "There are...various...negroes in this country, some of whom have been made free for their long service, but their children have remained slaves, though it is contrary to the laws of every people that any one born of a free Christian mother should be a slave and be compelled to remain in servitude."[21] Nonetheless, the half-freedom system was clearly an improvement over total slavery. In fact, by blurring the distinction between slavery and freedom, it blurred the most racist distinction between blacks and whites and thus helped to assure that New Netherland would never have laws discriminating against blacks who were totally free.

The same factors that discouraged the importation of African slaves in the first place seem to have restrained the Dutch in their initial relations with Native Americans as well. Because of their limited interest in settlement, the Dutch occupied less Indian land than their English counterparts, and because of their overriding concern with trade, they tended to be better about paying for the land they did take.[22] In order to maintain the lively commerce in furs that was the colony's *raison d'être,* the Dutch needed to project an image of fairness—even friendship—and to some extent, in the colony's early years, they succeeded. "Though they are so revengeful towards their enemies, they are very friendly to us," David de Vries wrote of the Indians around Fort Orange in 1638. "We have no fear of them; we go with them into the woods; we meet each other sometimes at an hour or two's distance from any house, and we think nothing more of it than if a Christian met us. They also sleep in the chambers before our beds; but lying down upon the bare ground, with a stone or piece of wood under the head."[23]

The Dutch, whom the Indians called *Swannekens,* or people from the salt sea, had good reason to call the Indians friends, for in addition to furs and a taste for tobacco, they acquired from them a knowledge of how to eke a living from the American wilderness. That Native Americans introduced Europeans to maize— what the Europeans called corn—is a cliché of history. But that they also taught the colonists certain methods of land management is less well known. Even the Dutch, renowned for claiming land from the sea, learned a thing or two. As van der Donck wrote of one such native method:

> The Indians have a yearly custom which some of our Christians have also adopted of burning the woods, plains and meadows in the fall of the year, when leaves have fallen, and when the grass and vegetable substances are dry....This practice is called by us and the Indians, "bush-burning," which is done for several reasons: First to render hunting easier, as the bush and vegetable growth renders the walking difficult for the hunter, and the crackling of the dry substances betrays him and frightens way the game. Secondly, to thin out and clear the woods of all dead substances and grass, which grow better the ensuing spring. Thirdly, to circumscribe and enclose the game within the lines of the fire, when it is more easily taken, and also because the game is more easily traced over the burned parts of the woods.[24]

Despite everything they learned from the Indians, however, the Dutch still called them *wilden,* or savages, betraying an attitude that eventually led, in 1640, to a disastrous five-year war in which 1,600 Indians were killed and the colonists themselves were nearly wiped out.[25] As the Dutch attempted to rebuild the colony and to encourage greater settlement, three additional wars would follow, making the long-term implications of the Dutch presence all the more obvious. In time, van der Donck would preface an account of the Indians with the prescient and touching words: "[W]e deem it worth our attention to treat concerning the nature of the original native inhabitants of the land; that after the Christians have multiplied and the natives have disappeared and melted away, a memorial of them may be preserved."[26] As he saw it, the Indians were undermined by their very contact with the Dutch. "They are naturally civil and well disposed," he wrote, "and quick enough to distinguish between good and evil, but after they have associated amongst us, they become cunning and deceitful."[27]

For all their differences, the Dutch and Indians shared a common enemy in the English settlers of New England, who were constantly encroaching on both Indian- and Dutch-claimed land along the Connecticut River and on eastern Long Island. Even in this, however, their interests were not truly allied, for other New Englanders—such as the Anabaptists who settled Gravesend—fled to New Netherland as they would never have fled to the natives. Seeking religious refuge, these English subjects swore allegiance to the Dutch authorities, became citizens of the colony, and ultimately aided in the peaceful transition from Dutch to English rule.[28]

Indeed the cultural affinity between Dutch and English was such that the change in government probably scarcely affected the life of ordinary Dutch New Yorkers like Jan Martense Schenck. Besides, the English who finally succeeded in subduing New Netherland were not the Puritans of New England but the minions of James, Duke of York, who was invited to seize the colony by his brother Charles II after Charles regained the English throne following the death of the Puritan leader Oliver Cromwell. The Duke's people were too outnumbered and too concerned with the colony's economic development to tamper much with things as they found them. They promised to molest no private Dutch interest, either personal or proprietary, and to allow the Dutch six months' continued free trade with the Netherlands. In the area of religious tolerance they went the Dutch one better, guaranteeing not only the right to private liberty of conscience but also the right to worship publicly—an important step in the history of the developing American nation, for it served to isolate intolerant New England. Given such liberal terms, most of the Dutch chose to stay on, including the religious leaders, who were to prove important in the preservation of Dutch culture. "The Articles of Surrender stipulate that our religious services and doctrines, together with the preachers, shall remain and continue unchanged," the Dutch Reformed dominie Samuel Drisius wrote to the church in the Netherlands on September 15, 1664. "Therefore we could not separate ourselves from our congregation and hearers, but consider it our duty to remain with them for some time yet, that they may not scatter and run wild."[29]

Ironically, the Dutch failure at colonization now turned to Dutch advantage. As long as the colony remained underdeveloped, it was likely to stay predominantly Dutch, and, initially at least, the English proved nearly as inept at developing the territory as the Dutch themselves had been. At the end of July 1673, during the third Anglo-Dutch war, they were even forced to give it back to the Netherlands, which held it for fifteen months before finally deciding that peace was more important than a remote, unprofitable province surrounded by English possessions. After that, the English would resume their struggle with the colonial economy. Consequently, the widespread establishment of English ideas and institutions would not really begin until the early 1690s and then would happen only gradually.

Of all the conclusions historians have drawn about the effect of the English conquest perhaps none is more dramatic than that of the African-American jurist A. Leon Higginbotham, Jr. When the English assumed control of New York, Higginbotham writes, that takeover "marked the end of the period of nonhostile relations between blacks and whites in the colony." The English, he notes, eliminated the half-freedom system, substituted a harsh, legalized form of slavery for a mild, improvised one, and for the first time in the history of the territory placed repressive restrictions on free blacks as well as slaves.[30]

As with nearly everything related to anglicization, however, this escalation of racial tensions took place in gradual, well-spaced stages and depended to a major extent on the achievement of English commercial success. The Duke of York, who had a huge stake in the Royal African Company, the firm that controlled the English trade in slaves in the last quarter of the seventeenth century, encouraged the importation of slaves to the colony far more than the Dutch ever had. And yet during a visit to New York City in 1679 the Labadist missionary Jasper Danckaerts was impressed not so much by the number of slaves he found as by the large number of free blacks, who, he discovered, were living not in a ghetto but in an integrated community along Broadway. "Upon both sides of this way," he wrote, "were many habitations of negroes, mulattoes and whites. These negroes were formerly the proper slaves of the [West India] company, but, in consequence of the frequent changes and conquests of the country, they have obtained their freedom and settled themselves down where they have thought proper, and thus on this road, where they have ground enough to live on with their families."[31] Not till the early eighteenth century, when the colony finally developed to the point it could support increased slavery, would such legacies of the New Netherland experience really be threatened. Only then would the English enact their harshest slave codes and their most repressive racial laws; only then would they prohibit free blacks from owning any real estate.[32]

Like the Dutch, the English learned that one of the greatest impediments to the development of the territory was too little immigration, especially of their own people. From an estimated 8,000 inhabitants in 1664, the population of the colony actually declined to about 6,000 in 1673 before rising slowly to approximately 10,000 in 1680 and 18,067 in 1698.[33] Moreover, much of that growth was apparently the result of natural increase rather than new settlement. "I believe for these 7 years last past, there has not come over into this province twenty English, Scotch or Irish families," Governor Thomas Dongan wrote in 1687. "But on the contrary on Long Island the people encrease soe fast that they complain for want of land & many remove from thence into the neighboring province [East New Jersey, which was then a colony separate from West New Jersey]."[34]

As Dongan noted, New York at that time was actually becoming less English. "[O]f French," he wrote, "there have since my coming here several familys come both from St. Christopers & England & a great many more are expected as also from Holland are come several Dutch familys." Accordingly, he urged the Duke of York, now King James II, to add "to this Govermt the neighbouring English Colonys, that a more equal ballance may bee kept here between his Matys naturall born subjects and foreigners which latter are the most prevailing part."[35]

In 1688 James did indeed take this step, uniting New York and the Jerseys with the "megacolony" called the Dominion of New England that he had created two years before. Consolidation, however, only added to his problems, engendering enormous resentment abroad at a time when he was already despised at home for showing special favor to Catholics. Within a year the king had been overthrown by his daughter Mary and her Dutch Protestant husband, William of Orange, and when news of his demise reached America a group of Bostonians arrested the royal governor and declared the Dominion defunct.

In New York a number of prominent older Dutch families led by a German Calvinist merchant named Jacob Leisler used this occasion to seize the government, attempting to regain some of the political and commercial power they had lost to the newly emerged Anglo-Dutch elite. Although the colony was eventually restored to the crown and Leisler hanged for treason in 1691, instability born of pluralism would linger for years. As New York Mayor Charles Lodwick wrote, with a hint of xenophobia, in 1692, "Our chiefest unhappiness here is too great a mixture of nations, and English the least part.... The Dutch are generally the most frugal and laborious, and consequently the richest, whereas the English are the contrary."[36]

The population of colonial New York was diverse not only ethnically but geographically as well. Regional differences that had arisen under the Dutch were perpetuated by the English and in fact can still be seen today in the three-way rivalry between New York City, Upstate New York, and Long Island that continues to pervade New York politics.

Then, as now, Manhattan dominated the other two regions. It was the richest, most populous, most cosmopolitan place in the province, and consequently the Dutch there seem to have been more materialist and less resistant to change than their counterparts elsewhere in the colony. During her visit to the city in 1704, the Bostonian Sarah Kemble Knight found them downright frivolous:

[T]he Dutch, especially the middling sort, differ from our women, in their habbit go loose, wear French muches [called *mutjen* in Dutch] wch are like a Capp and a head band in one, leaving their ears bare, which are sett out wth Jewells of a large size and many in number. And their fingers hoop't with Rings, some with large stones in them of many Coullers as were their pendants in their ears, which You should see very old women wear as well as Young.

They have Vendues [auctions] very frequently and make their Earnings very well by them, for they treat with good Liquor Liberally and Generally pay for't as well, by paying for that which they Bidd up Briskly for, after the sack has gone plentifully about, tho' sometimes good penny worths are got there. Their Diversions in the Winter is Riding Sleys about three or four Miles out of Town, where they have Houses of entertainment at a place called the Bowery, and some go to friends Houses who handsomely treat them.... I believe we mett 50 or 60 slays [one] day—they fly with

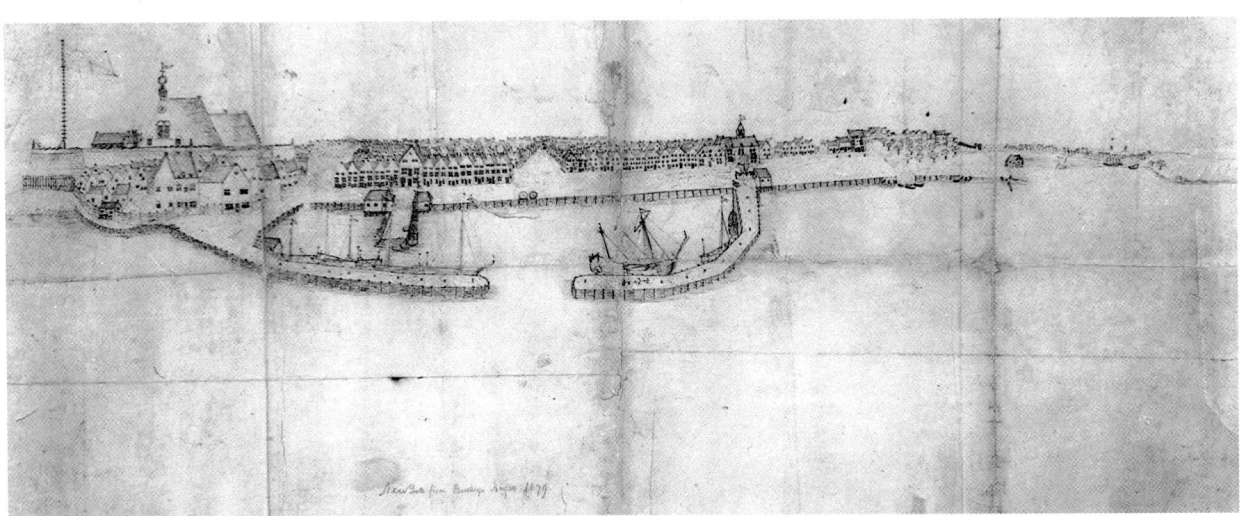

3.2. Jasper Danckaerts (Dutch, 1639–1702/4). *New York from Brooklyn Heights,* 1679–80. Pen and ink, 12⅝ × 31½ inches. The Brooklyn Historical Society.

FROM DUTCH TO DUTCH AMERICAN

great swiftness and some are so furious that they'le turn out of the path for none except a Loaden Cart.[37]

Compared to the bustling port of New York, the farming and fur-trading communities of the Hudson Valley were poor, isolated, and provincial. Hence, in many places in the valley the Dutch were a decided majority until the mid-1760s. Indeed, a Swedish botanist named Peter Kalm who visited the area in 1749 during a survey of North American natural history remarked that "the inhabitants of Albany and its environs are almost all Dutchmen."[38]

According to Kalm, Albany Dutch were a breed apart. "I cannot...," he wrote, "account for the difference between the inhabitants of Albany and the other descendants of so respectable a nation as the Dutch, who are settled in the lower part of New York province. The latter are civil, obliging, just in prices, and sincere; and though they are not ceremonious, yet they are well meaning and honest and their promises may be relied on."[39] In contrast, he added, "The avarice,

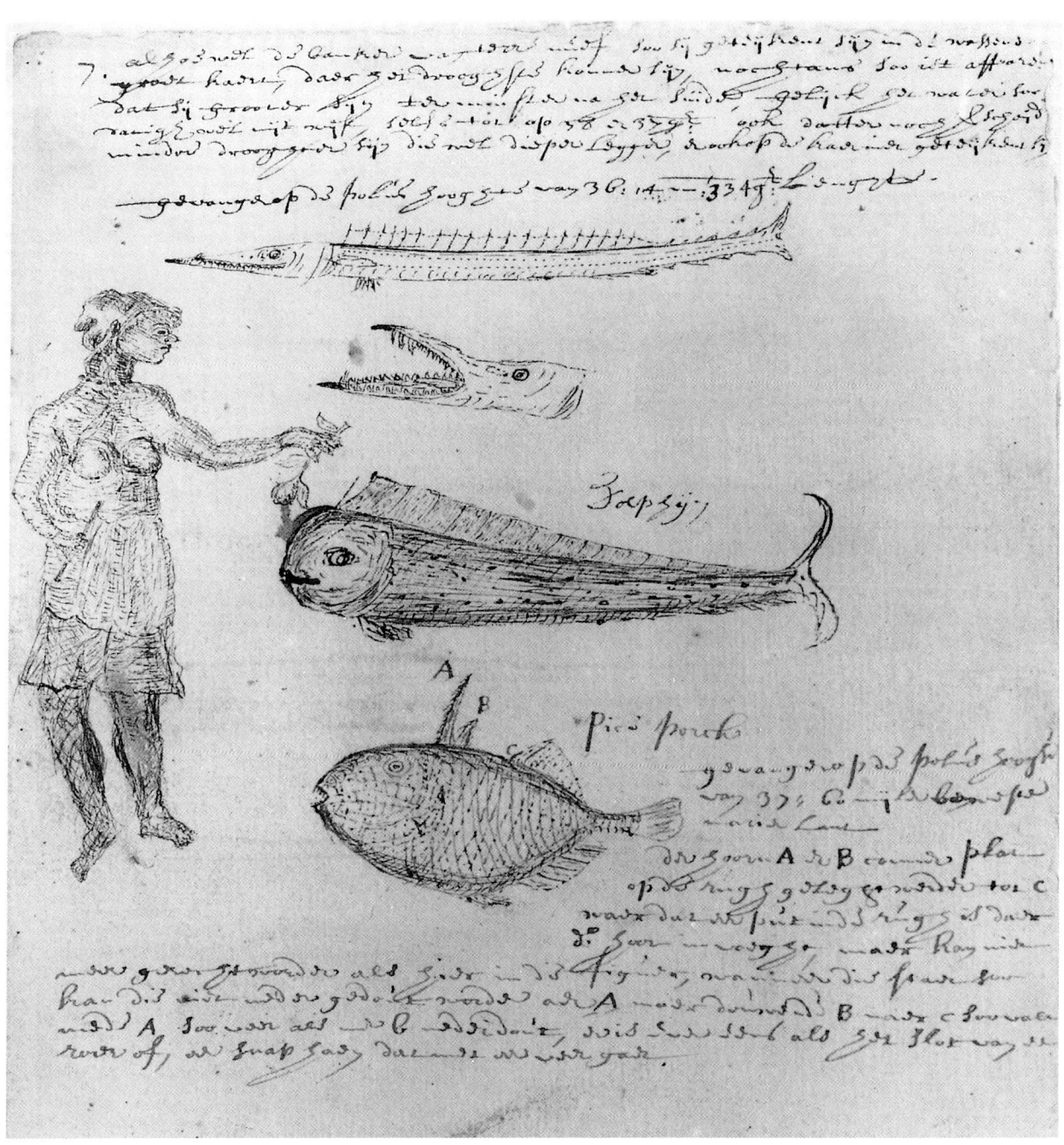

3.3. Page from a *"Journal of a Voyage to New York"* by Jasper Danckaerts and Peter Sluyter, 1679–80. The Brooklyn Historical Society.

selfishness and immeasurable love of money of the inhabitants of Albany are very well known throughout all North America... even by the Dutch.... In their homes [they] are much more sparing than the English and are stingier with their food. Generally what they serve is just enough for the meal and sometimes hardly that."[40] While Madame Knight had described Dutch Manhattanites as heavy drinkers, Kalm observed that among the Dutch at Albany "the punch bowl is much more rarely seen than among the English." And while she had found the Dutch women of New York City to be devil-may-care in their manner and ostentatious, or even gaudy, in their appearance, he discovered their sisters upriver to be "perfectly well acquainted with economy; they rise early, go to sleep very late, and are almost superstitiously clean in regard to the floor, which is frequently scoured several times in the week. Inside [their] homes [they] are neatly but not lavishly dressed."[41]

Dutch life in the Hudson Valley was shaped to a large extent by the semifeudal state of affairs that persisted there even into the 1800s. The English in New York had followed the patroonship precedent of awarding huge blocks of land, or what they called manors, to potential political allies, and the four largest such estates were located along the Hudson. One, in what is now Columbia County, was granted to Robert Livingston, a Scot raised in the Netherlands, while the other three—the Philipsburg and van Cortlandt manors in Westchester County and the former Fort Orange patroonship of Rensselaerswyck, which had its patent renewed by the English in 1685—were all Dutch-owned.[42] As Kalm wrote of this Dutch landed gentry, "Most of them being very rich, their envy of the English led them not to sell them any land, but at an excessive rate, a practice which is still punctually observed among their descendants. The English therefore, as well as people of other nations, have but little encouragement to settle here."[43] In a spiral of animosity, this greed born of envy led inevitably to English resentment of the Dutch, who in turn repaid that resentment in spades. "The hatred which the English bear against the people at Albany is very great," Kalm wrote, "but that of the Albanians is carried to a ten times higher degree. This hatred has subsisted ever since the time when the English conquered this section, and is not yet extinguished, though they could never have gotten larger advantages under the Dutch government than they have obtained under that of the English."[44]

If the Hudson Valley was a clannish Dutch backwater and New York City a tolerant cosmopolis, then Long Island, where the economy revolved around farming and whaling, was a restive English stronghold—the staging ground from which they would go forth to try to anglicize the entire province. Heavily outnumbered by English immigrants from New England, the Dutch concentrated themselves in the island's southwest corner in the five rural towns they had established before the English takeover. Yet, because of their proximity to Manhattan, they were probably never as insular as the Dutch around Albany. Early on, the Dutch town of Brooklyn became something of a port in its own right, funneling most of the traffic between New York and western Long Island. In 1679 Jasper Danckaerts, who has left us some invaluable sketches from his travels in the area (see figs. 3.2 and 3.3), wrote that the Brooklyn ferry to New York "is a considerable thoroughfare, this island [Long Island] being one of the most populous places in the vicinity. A considerable number of Indians live upon [the island]... and they, as well as others, just carry their articles to market over this ferry."[45] A steady stream of English Long Islanders would thus have passed through the Dutch communities of Kings County on their way to and from the city, and though this traffic probably sometimes led to tensions, it no doubt fostered acculturation and intermarriage as well.

As the two primary European cultures in New York grew together, the reality of English conquest began to sink in: in the end, no matter how the Dutch fought it, English culture would predominate in the hybrid taking shape. The only question was which aspects of Dutch culture would prove the most resilient.

In the area of decorative arts, some Dutch forms survived long enough to spread—occasionally by way of a third ethnic group—to the English. Thus, as noted earlier, the seventeenth-century Dutch *kas,* or cupboard, displayed in the Jan Martense Schenck House

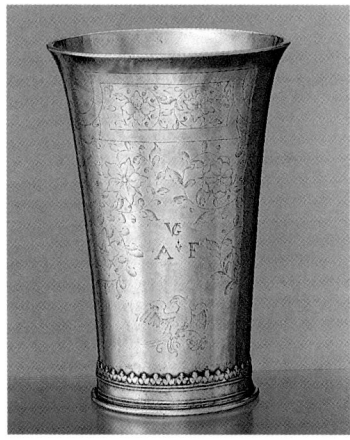

3.4. Attributed to Jurian Blanck, Jr. (Dutch American, 1645–1714). Beaker, 1680–90. New York. Silver, 6⅝ × 4 9/16 inches. Yale University Art Gallery, New Haven, Mabel Brady Garvan Collection.

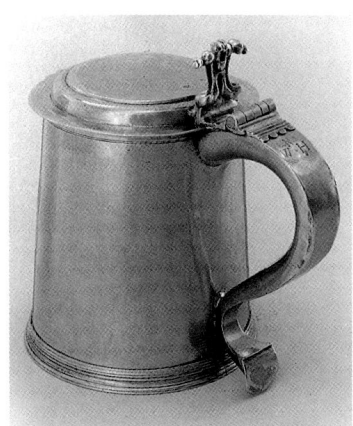

3.5. Tankard, 1680–81. Dublin. Silver, 7¼ × 5½ inches. The Colonial Williamsburg Foundation.

FROM DUTCH TO DUTCH AMERICAN

(*see again fig. 2.15*) was probably originally owned by the Walloon immigrant François Rombout and later passed, through his daughter's marriage, into an English family. Such *kassen*, as also noted, in turn served as prototypes for American-made ones like the mid-eighteenth-century example installed in the Nicholas Schenck House (*fig. 5.58*).

In other cases, the Dutch adopted English forms but attempted to put their own peculiar stamp on them. In the late seventeenth and the early eighteenth century, for instance, Dutch New Yorkers supplemented their traditional drinking vessel, the beaker (*see fig. 3.4*), with the English tankard (*fig. 3.5*). New York's Dutch silversmiths, however, took the tankard form, which was replicated in New England with little variation (*see fig. 3.6*), and applied to it the cut-card bands and meander wire decoration they had formerly used on their beakers, creating a new style of tankard (*fig. 3.7*) that reflected the colony's unique cultural mix. Still, by the second quarter of the eighteenth century all trace of Dutch ornament had disappeared from New York tankards.

When it came to architecture, the Dutch were particularly stubborn about retaining the old ways, especially in isolated areas like the upper Hudson Valley. Although the English versions offered clear advantages, Dutch architectural forms such as the jambless fireplace and the Continental framing of the Jan Martense Schenck House continued in use into the mid-1700s. Peter Kalm, during a visit to the area around Saratoga (now Schuylerville) in 1749, observed the construction of houses that evidently resembled in many ways the one built by Schenck seventy-five years earlier:

> They first put up the framework upon which the rafters and both roofs rested and then filled in the framework with unfired bricks. The inner side was brushed over with lime and whitewashed so that from the inside it looked like a stone house except where the perpendicular timbers which supported the rafters were visible. On the outside the houses were generally covered with clapboards so that the unfired brick might not be damaged by moisture, weather and wind. As a rule they did not have more perpendicular supports than they had cross beams, from three to five on each side or long wall.... The ceiling was horizontal and beamed [and the] roof was either of boards or shingles.... The fireplace for about six feet or more from the ground consisted of nothing more than the wall of the house.... There were no projections on the sides..., so it was possible to sit on all three sides of the fire and enjoy the warmth equally.... As the chimney was some distance above the floor they had put boards about these rafters, or as was more common, they had hung short curtains extending downward (and outward) to prevent the smoke from coming in. But in spite of this and because the fireplace had no sides, it frequently happened when the door was opened that the smoke was driven into the room. The hearth itself was always even with the floor [and the] fireplace was ordinarily six to eight feet in width. Occasionally a shelf had been made above it upon which teacups, etc. were placed.... In many houses in the town they had partitioned off the part of the room where the beds stood by placing large doors before them, (like cupboards), and thus completely concealing the beds from view.[46]

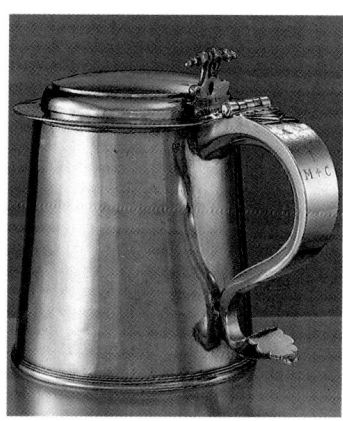

3.6. *John Coney (Anglo-American, 1656–1722). Tankard, 1685–95. Boston. Silver, 7⅛ × 5⁹⁄₁₆ inches. Yale University Art Gallery, New Haven, Mabel Brady Garvan Collection.*

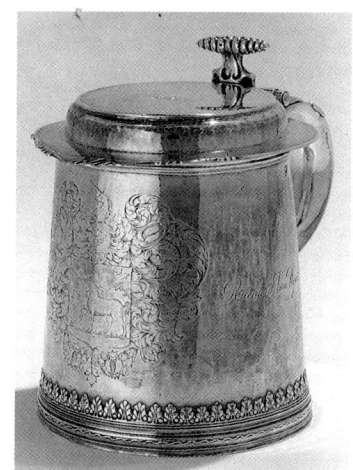

3.7. *Jacob Boelen (Dutch American, 1657–1729). Tankard, circa 1685. New York. Silver, 7⅛ × 5⅜ inches. The Brooklyn Museum 26.20, Presented in memory of Richard van Wyck by Mrs. Richard van Wyck and Mrs. Henry de Bevoise Schenck.*

Although Dutch New Yorkers gradually began to borrow certain English architectural forms, such as the gambrel (or dual-pitched) roof, sometime in the first half of the eighteenth century, they continued into the nineteenth to build their own distinctive type of house, which was eventually absorbed into the American architectural mainstream as the so-called Dutch Colonial style. As we shall see in our discussion of the Nicholas Schenck House, a prime early example of the type, this style was not really Dutch, but neither was it fully English. Even more than the Dutch-influenced New York tankard, it represented a peculiar Dutch-American form. (See figs. 3.8–3.11 for four examples

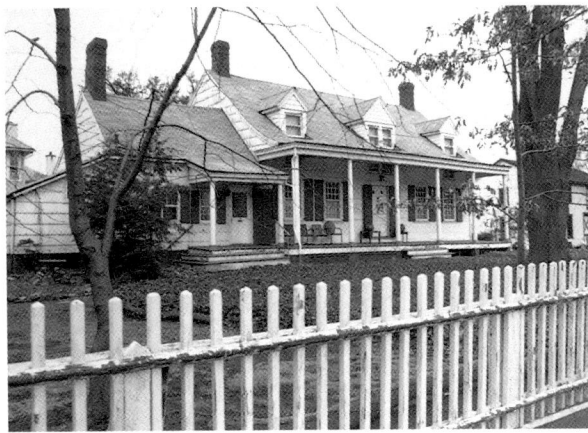

3.8. The Wyckoff-Bennett House, 1669 East 22nd Street, Gravesend, Brooklyn. Built circa 1766. Designated a New York City landmark 1968. Photograph by Michael Ferri.

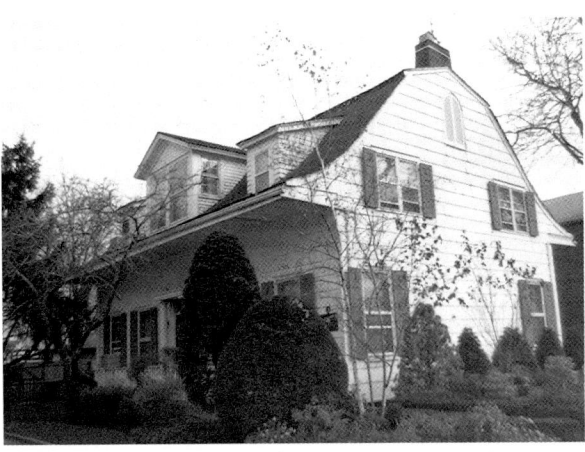

3.9. The Van Nuyse-Magaw House, 1041 East 22nd Street, Flatlands, Brooklyn. Built circa 1800–3. Designated a New York City landmark 1969. Photograph by Michael Ferri.

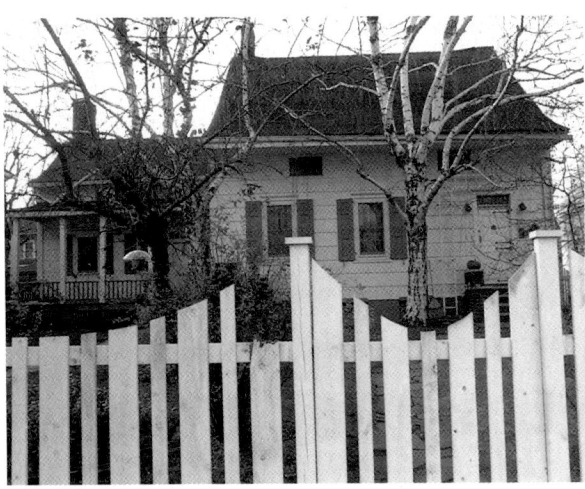

3.10. The Coe House, 1128–30 East 34th Street, Flatlands, Brooklyn. Left wing (1130 East 34th) built circa late 1730s–mid-1740s; right wing (1128) built circa 1793–1806. Designated a New York City landmark 1969. Photograph by Michael Ferri.

that were still standing in Kings County in 1990 when this book went to press.)

That Dutch Americans best preserved some sense of their separate identity in their domestic architecture should come as no surprise, for it was in the special occasions and daily routine of life in the home that they were most free to maintain their treasured customs, tastes, and traditions. The celebration of *Sinterklaas*, or St. Nicholas, Day; the making of *kool sla*, *koekjes*, and *wafels*—these and other Dutch household rituals were observed religiously until they found their way, albeit sometimes greatly altered, into the general American culture. Thus, in the old-fashioned Dutch houses of the upper Hudson Valley, Peter Kalm found an old-fashioned Dutch diet (though with a couple of new twists—one borrowed from the British and the other acquired from the Indians) as well:

> Their food and its preparation [in Albany] is very different from that of the English. Their breakfast is tea, commonly without milk. About thirty or forty years ago, tea was unknown to them, and they breakfasted either upon bread and butter, or bread and milk. They never put sugar into the cup, but take a small bit of it into their mouths while they drink [*see fig. 3.12*]. Along with the tea they eat bread and butter, with slices of dried beef. . . . Their dinner [the noon meal] is buttermilk and bread, to which they add sugar on special occasions, when it is a delicious dish for them, or fresh milk and bread, with boiled or roasted meat.[47]
>
> . . . In the evening [in Saratoga] they made a porridge of corn, poured it as customary into a dish, [and] made a large hole in the center into which they poured fresh milk, but more often buttermilk. They ate it taking half a spoonful of porridge and half of milk. As they ordinarily took more milk than porridge, the milk in the dish was soon consumed. Then more milk was poured. . . . After that they would eat some meat left over from the noonday meal, or bread and butter with cheese. If any of the porridge remained from the evening, it was boiled with buttermilk in the morning so that it became almost like a gruel. In order to make the buttermilk more tasty, they added either syrup or sugar, after it had been poured into the dish. Then they stirred it so that all of it should be equally sweet. Pudding or pie, the Englishman's perpetual dish, one seldom saw among the Dutch, neither here [Saratoga] nor in Albany. But they were indeed fond of meat.[48]

Outside the home, the last bastion of Dutch culture in America was the Dutch Reformed Church. Ironically, however, although the church played an important role in safeguarding Dutch ethnic identity, it also led the way to Americanization. Following the English takeover, the church had remained subservient to the Classis of Amsterdam, the ecclesiastical authority that had governed its affairs since the 1630s. At first, it looked to the classis for help in opposing the introduction of English ways. But as time went on and it grew more secure in its position, some in the church began to call for a measure of autonomy, particularly the right to ordain ministers in America rather than call them from the Netherlands. For much of the eighteenth century, a dispute raged between those who wanted an American ruling body and those who preferred to remain subordinate to Amsterdam. Finally, in 1771, a compromise was reached that gave the church virtual independence: American ordination was approved, though Dutch doctrine was fully accepted.[49]

This process of Americanization was mirrored in church architecture. During the first half century of English rule, when few in the church questioned the need for obedience to the classis, Dutch New Yorkers continued to build churches based on Dutch prototypes. One of the most popular styles was the octagonal church, patterned after the first Protestant church built in the Netherlands. Three such churches were constructed in Kings County: at Flatlands in 1663, at New Utrecht in 1700 (*see fig. 3.13*), and at Bushwick in 1705. Though all three eventually gave way to other, larger churches, their congregations treasured their memory for generations. So it was that during the

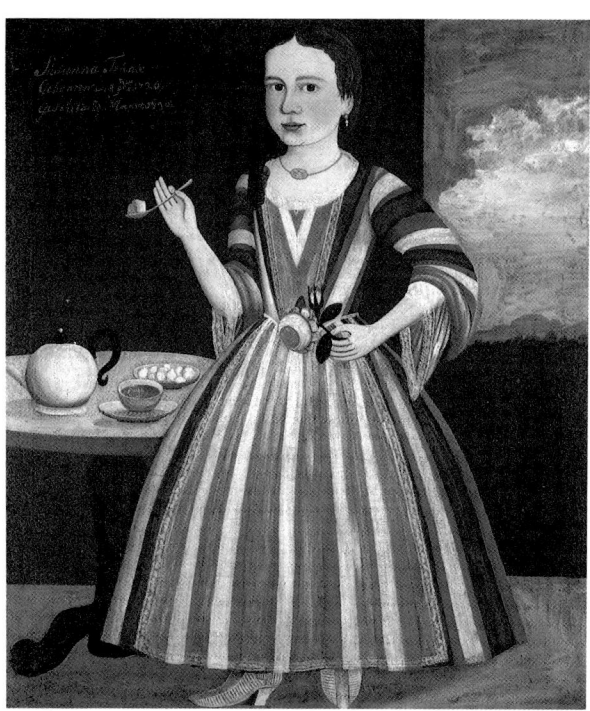

3.12. *Attributed to Pieter Vanderlyn (Dutch American, 1687–1778).* Susanna Truax (1726–1805), *Schenectady, New York, 1730. Oil on canvas, 37¾ × 32⅞ inches. National Gallery of Art, Washington, D.C.*

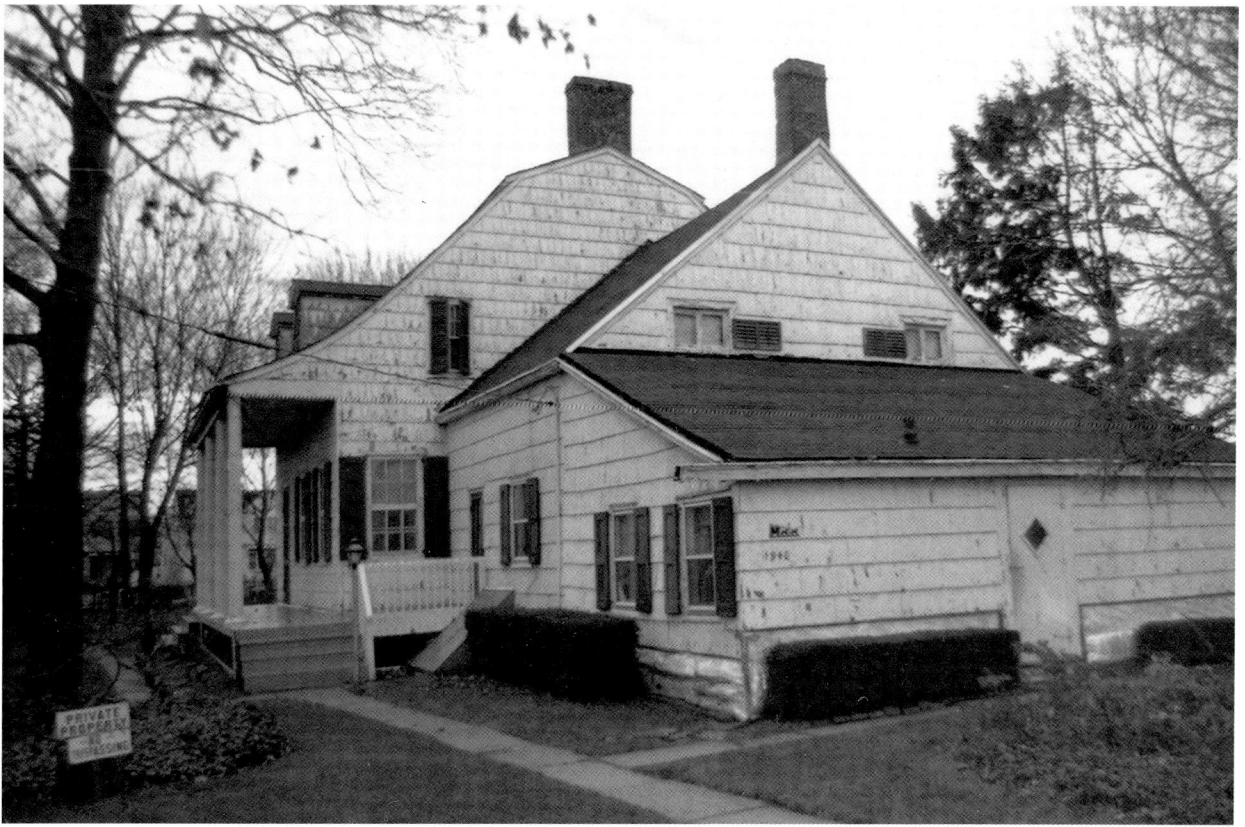

3.11. *The Lott House, 1940 East 36th Street, Flatlands, Brooklyn. Wing in foreground built circa 1720; middle section built circa 1800 with second flanking wing not visible in photograph. Designated a New York City landmark 1990. Photograph by Michael Ferri.*

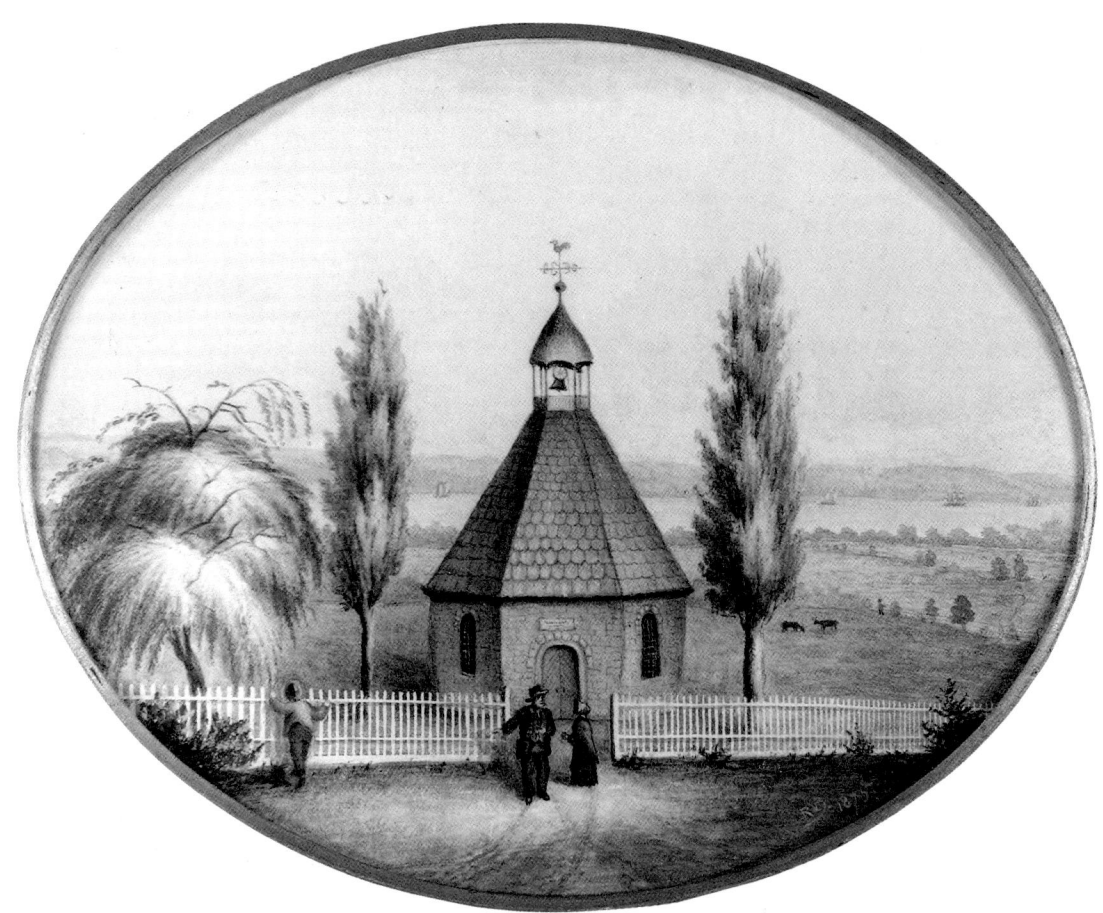

3.13. *James Ryder van Brunt (American, 1820–1916). New Utrecht Church, 1875. Watercolor on paper, 8½ × 10 inches. The Brooklyn Historical Society.*

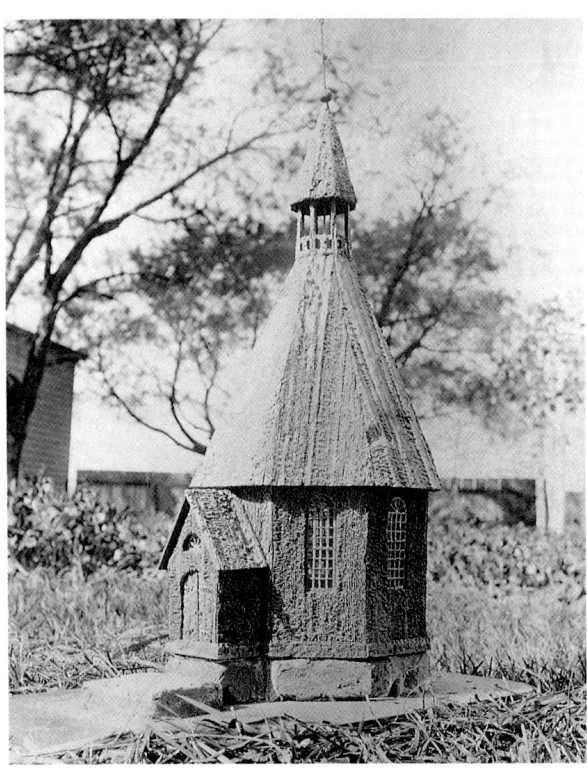

Reverend Schenck's visit to Flatlands in 1891 the local Dutch Reformed pastor showed him a replica of the town's original, eight-sided church (*see fig. 3.14*). "We examined in the hall of [the] parsonage," he wrote, "a very curious *model* of the very first and oldest Dutch church of the place. It is constructed of the identical brick and shingles of which the old church was composed."[50]

In the mid-1700s, as the church was torn between traditionalists and progressives, such old Dutch forms began to be replaced, at least in some places, by a church building whose profile, with its gambrel roof, was related to the Dutch-American house form then taking shape. The First Reformed Dutch Church of Brooklyn built a church of this type, on what is now Fulton Street between Duffield and Lawrence Streets, in 1766 (*see fig. 3.15*).

This form, too, eventually passed from use as the Dutch Reformed Church in America became independent of the mother church in the Netherlands. By the end of the eighteenth century, Dutch Reformed

3.14. *Model of first Dutch Reformed church of Flatlands. Photograph by the Reverend William Edward Schenck, 1891.*

congregations in New York were building Classical Revival churches typical of the American ecclesiastical architecture of the time. The Dutch Reformed Church of Flatbush, completed after three years of construction in December 1796 and still standing at the corner of Flatbush and Church Avenues, is a product of this period. It bears no clear trace of Dutch influence but is one of Brooklyn's finest surviving examples of the Federal style (*see fig. 3.16*).

Even after the Dutch Reformed Church acquired an American government and an ecumenical architecture, however, many of its members continued to worship in Dutch.[51] Not until 1763 was a sermon preached in English in the Reformed church in New York City, and Dutch preaching there was apparently not phased out entirely until 1803.[52] Rural congregations held out against the change in language for at least a generation longer, and in some churches when English was finally spoken a few people left the church altogether.[53] Likewise, in Dutch Reformed churchyards, Dutch inscriptions on tombstones were the norm until about 1770 and continued intermittently for some time thereafter.[54] (See figs. 3.17 and 3.18 for two still extant Schenck family gravestones illustrating the change.)

Language, perhaps more than any other aspect of Dutch culture, marked the assimilation of the Dutch people in America. Soon after the English takeover, many Dutch New Yorkers, especially those in high positions of government or trade, became bilingual out of necessity. Before the turn of the seventeenth century most official documents were written in English, and when Dutch *was* written the English style of script replaced the old Dutch handwriting style.[55] Still, throughout the colonial period Dutch remained the primary language of not only the Dutch but several other ethnic groups as well. It was not unusual in the 1770s, for instance, for an advertisement in the *New York Gazette* to say of a runaway slave, as was said of one in 1773, that he "can speak both English and Dutch but sounds mostly on the latter."[56]

American Dutch was, though, an increasingly corrupted form of Dutch, for its speakers began to borrow words from English, especially words of a legal nature after English common law supplanted Roman-Dutch civil law in 1691. Thus we find English terms, in one case misspelled, in the following Dutch phrases:

From 1690: "...& mitts gaeders een *warrant* getenkent door d' voorsz Leysler authorisierende Jochim Staets..."

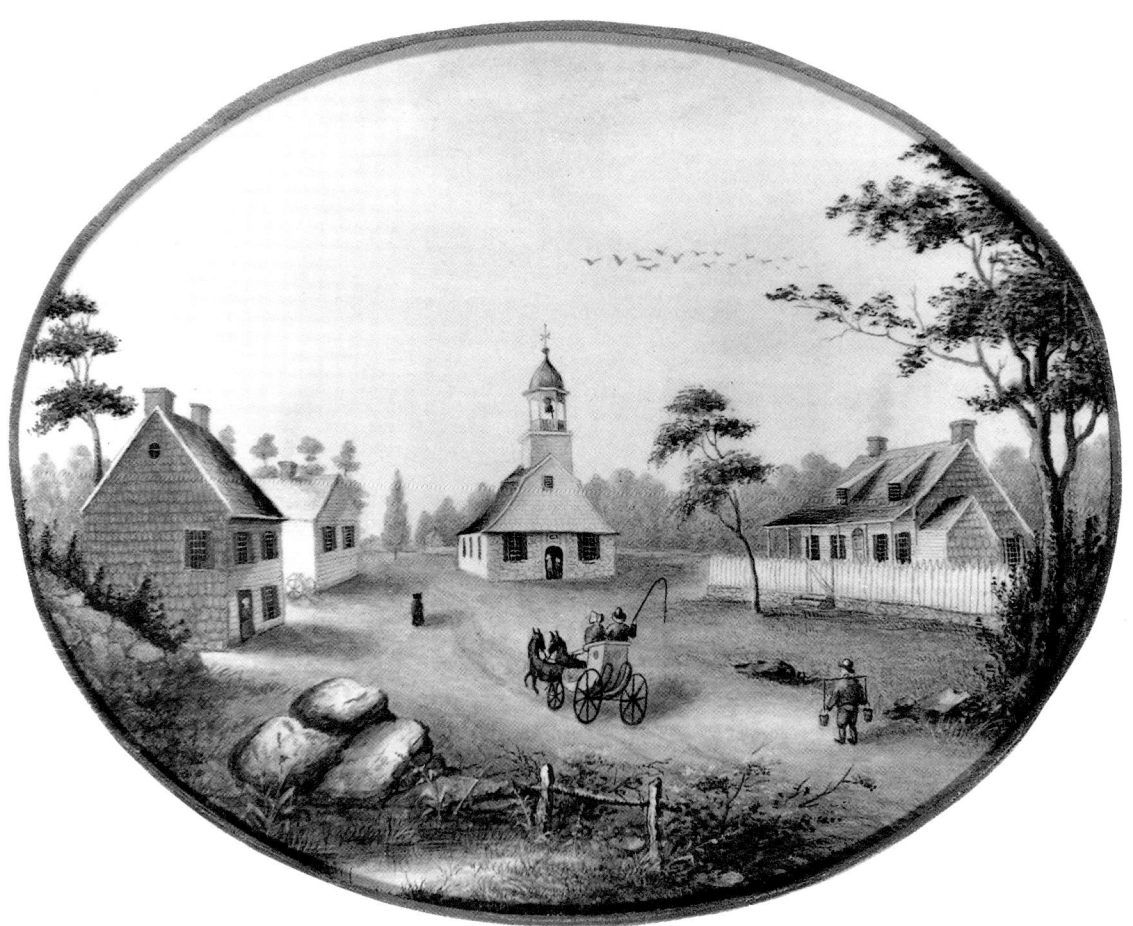

3.15. *James Ryder van Brunt (American, 1820–1916).* First Reformed Dutch Church, *1875. Watercolor on paper, 7½ × 9½ inches. The Brooklyn Historical Society.*

From 1772: "part in vershote gelt vor onkoste van een *law sute*."

And from 1791: "...vijftig pond *in cash*."[57]

In other cases, related words from the two languages were combined, so that in a document of 1773 the number 5 is spelled "vive" rather than the Dutch "vijf" or the English "five."[58] Moreover, Dutch morphology, or its system of word-forming elements, began to change. Dutch New Yorkers, for example, took to adding the English "s" instead of the Dutch "en" in order to make Dutch words plural.[59] A certain Dr. Alexander Hamilton of Maryland (not *the* Alexander Hamilton), after hearing this debased sort of Dutch being spoken among his fellow passengers on a boat trip between New York and Albany in 1744, described it as a "medley of Dutch and English as would have tired a horse."[60]

Of course, just as Dutch New Yorkers learned some English, English New Yorkers acquired some Dutch. The American English words sloop and stoop and yacht and boss, to name a few, all came directly from Dutch, only slightly altered in spelling.

As the eighteenth century progressed, however, the exchange of words grew more one-sided. Because the children of Dutch families needed to know English in order to function in the surrounding world, their parents began enrolling them in English schools. By 1757 so few families in New York City were still interested in a Dutch education that one of the city's two Dutch schools had to close; only ten students remained. Out of a total school-age population of more than three thousand, moreover, only forty-five or so attended the other Dutch school.[61] Just how much this English education of Dutch children hastened the decline of Dutch usage in particular and the assimilation of the Dutch people in general can be seen in Peter Kalm's account of the colony at mid-century, when the city was the only place such education was common:

> Dutch was generally the language which was spoken in Albany...and also in the places between Albany and New York.... In New York were also many homes in which Dutch was commonly spoken, especially by elderly people. The majority, however who were of Dutch descent [there], were succumbing to the English language. The younger generation scarcely ever spoke anything but English, and there were many who became offended if they were taken for Dutch because they preferred to pass for English. Therefore, it also happened that the majority of the young people attended the English church, although their parents remained loyal to the Dutch.[62]

Though the hold of the Dutch language was strong, Dutch was relegated more and more to the confines of the family, until ultimately Dutch parents even began to give their children English names.[63] Nicholas Schenck, Sr., born in 1732, had sisters named Jannetie, Antie, Willemtie, and Neeltie, but he named three of his own four daughters Anna, Adriana, and Nelly.[64]

For all that the English language did to subvert Dutch identity, however, it was undoubtedly the American Revolution that truly made the Dutch Americans. Though the Dutch had been developing common interests and a common culture with their fellow Americans for about a century and a half, before the unrest that led up to the Revolution few Americans—Dutch or otherwise—had developed an American national feeling. Americans joined forces to fight the British not because of any desire for common government but because, as the Dutch national motto put it, "Unity makes strength."

During the turmoil preceding the Revolution, the loyalties of Dutch Americans—like the loyalties of all Americans—were divided. Although many Dutch people had personal reasons for supporting one side or the other, neither side appeared clearly beneficial to the Dutch as a whole. Some joined the Patriot cause, some became Loyalists, and a good number remained uncommitted.[65] As the nineteenth-century Brooklyn historian Henry R. Stiles wrote of the Dutch inhabitants of Kings County, "[Their] sympathies were but slightly enlisted in behalf of the Revolutionary cause and [their]

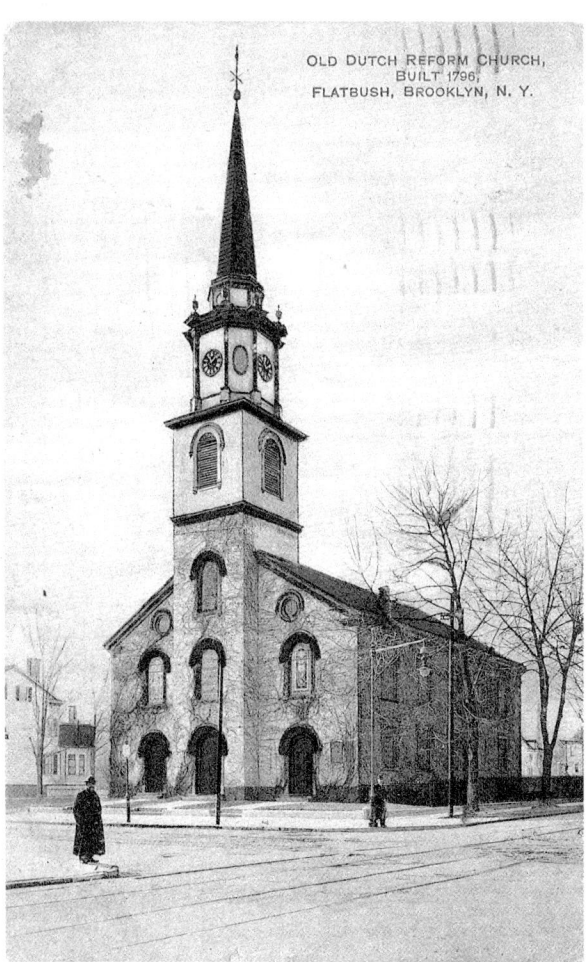

3.16. Postcard of the Dutch Reformed Church of Flatbush, circa 1910. Collection of John Antonides, Brooklyn.

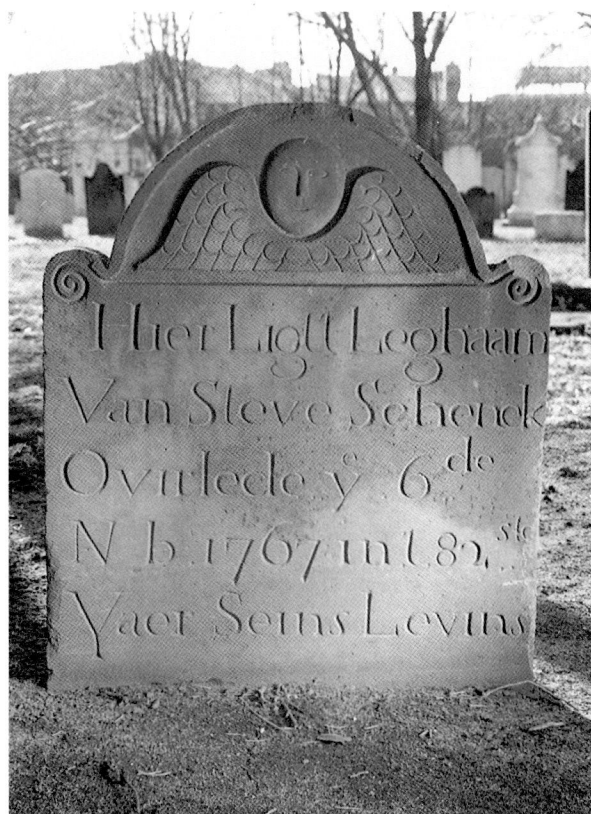

3.17. Tombstone of Stephen Janse Schenck (son of Jan Martense Schenck and father of Nicholas Schenck, Sr.), graveyard of the Flatlands Dutch Reformed Church, Kings Highway and East 40th Street, Brooklyn. Translation of epitaph: "Here Lies the Body of Steve Schenek [sic] Deceased the 6th of November 1767 in the 82nd Year of His Life." Photograph by Jim Hayes.

fear of pecuniary loss and personal inconvenience quite outweighed the more generous impulses of patriotism.... [They] seem to have viewed the approaching storm with perfect indifference, and to have acted tardily in defence of their rights."[66] In April 1775, when the New York Committee of Correspondence called for all the counties of the colony to appoint delegates to a general provincial convention for the purpose of electing representatives to the Second Continental Congress, the town of Flatlands even declined to participate in the Kings County appointment. Though it "would not put a negative on the proceedings," the county's delegates reported, the town "chose to remain neutral."[67]

It is not known whether Nicholas Schenck, a captain in the provincial militia, approved of his town's neutrality, but in any event he and his fellow Flatlanders soon found themselves under British occupation along with the rest of Kings County. On August 22, 1776, the British general William Howe began landing 15,000 men at Gravesend, and four days later, having occupied a wedge of the county from Flatlands to Flatbush to New Utrecht, they began marching north out of Flatlands along what is still called Kings Highway. By noon on the 27th, one witness later recalled, "the Red Coats were so thick in Flatlands you could walk on their heads."[68] Passing through the unguarded Jamaica Pass in what is now East New York, the British turned west, attacked the American troops from the rear, and, in what soon came to be known as The Battle of Long Island (*see fig. 3.19*), dealt them a drubbing. Only George Washington's brilliant evacuation of the American army to Manhattan under cover of darkness and dense fog prevented a total fiasco.

The British occupation of Long Island lasted till the end of the Revolution in 1783, giving the Dutch people of Kings County a more intimate knowledge of English ways than most of them probably ever cared to acquire.[69] The British army quartered its soldiers in Dutch homes, pillaged Dutch farms, plundered and torched Dutch houses, and eventually cut down almost all the wood in the entire county. Nicholas Schenck, because of his position in the militia, had a guard posted at his house,[70] and in 1781 he was ordered to

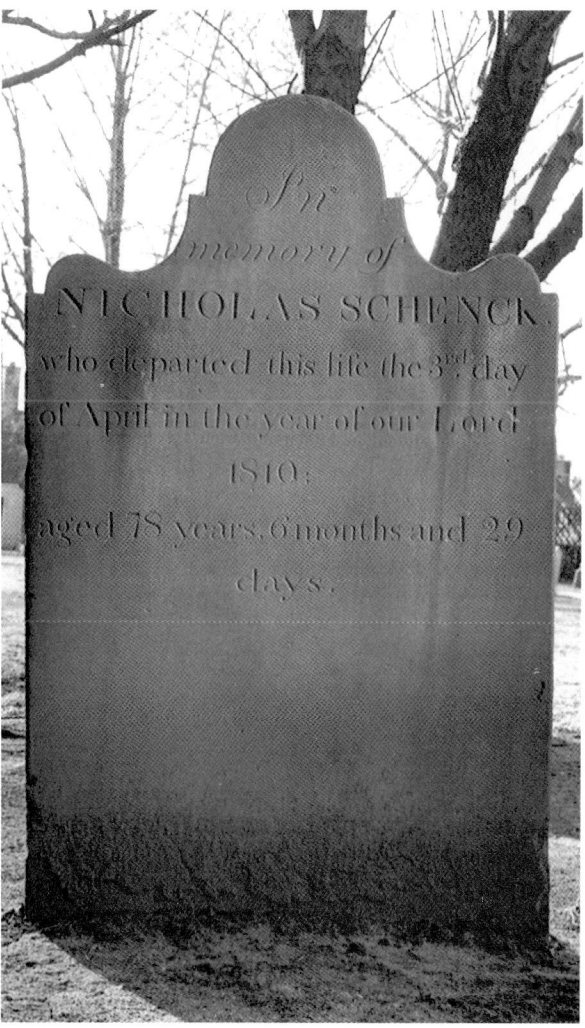

3.18. Tombstone of Nicholas Schenck, Sr., graveyard of the Flatlands Dutch Reformed Church. Photograph by Jim Hayes.

parade his troops meekly before the Loyalist colonel William Axtell, whose estates would be confiscated after the war.⁷¹ In 1777, when the British billeted paroled American prisoners among the families of Long Island, Schenck's family received two, one of whom, a soldier from Pennsylvania named Hezekiah Davis, married his daughter Anna in 1780.⁷² Supporting these prisoners, of course, strained the citizens' already strapped resources. Thus, in the recollections of a prisoner named Colonel Graydon who was billeted with the Suydam family of Flatbush, we see a Dutch diet that was considerably meaner than, though remarkably similar to, the one observed by Peter Kalm along the upper Hudson nearly thirty years earlier:

Though we were, in general, civilly enough received, it cannot be supposed we were very welcome to our Low Dutch hosts, whose habits were extremely parsimonious, and whose winter provision was barely sufficient for themselves. Had they been sure of receiving two dollars per week, Congress or ourselves being looked on as paymasters, it might have reconciled them. They were, however, a people who seemed thoroughly disposed to submit to any power that might be imposed on them, and whatever might have been their propensities or demonstrations at an earlier stage of the contest, they were now the dutiful

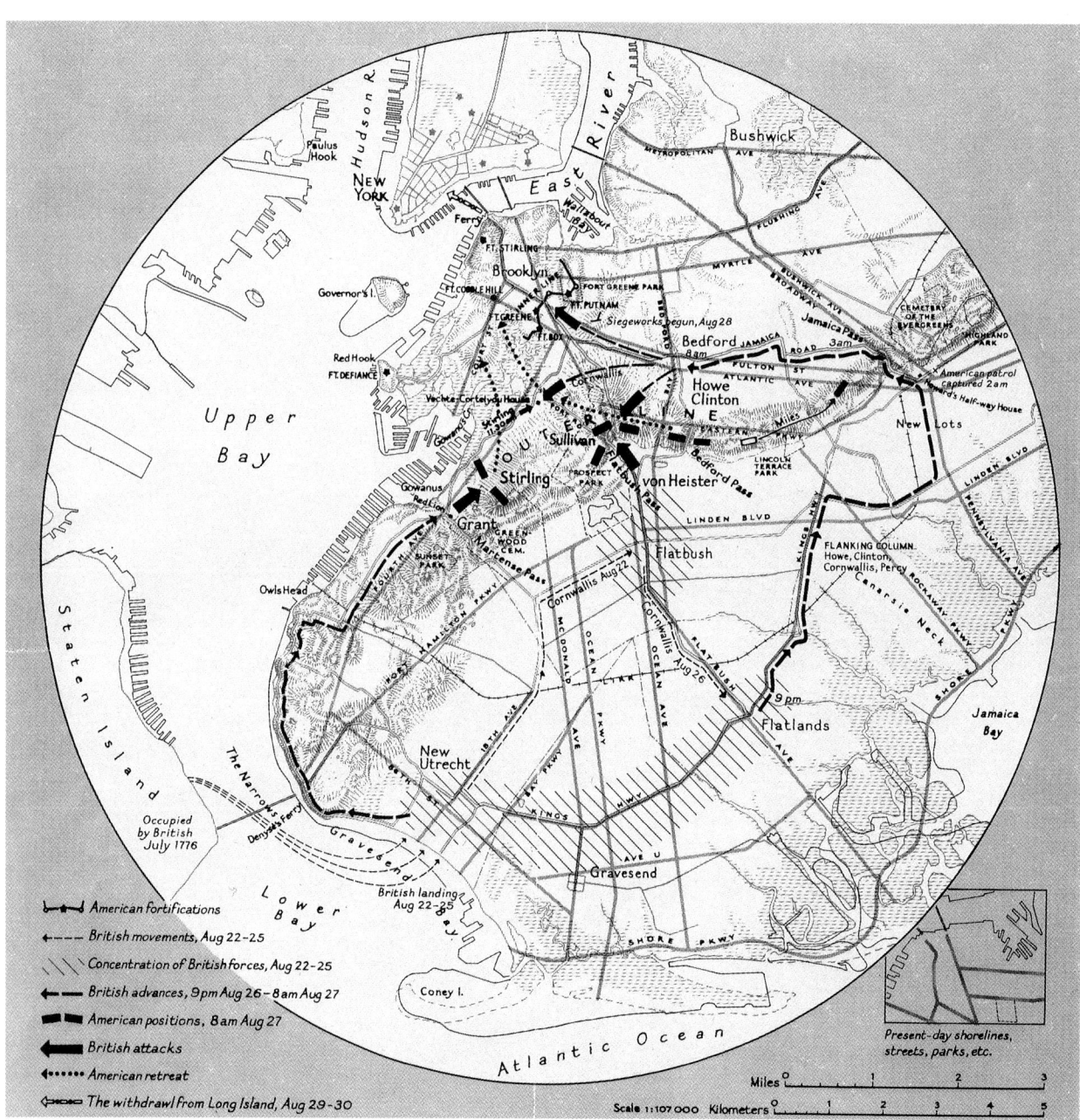

3.19. The Battle of Long Island, August 22–30, 1776. Map by George M. Colbert. Collection of The Brooklyn Historical Society.

and loyal subjects of His Majesty King George III., and entirely obedient to the behests of their military masters in New York. Their houses and beds we found clean, but their living extremely poor. A sorry wash, made up of a sprinkling of bohea [black tea] and the darkest sugar, on the verge of fluidity, with half baked bread (fuel being among the scarcest articles at Flatbush) and a little stale butter, constituted our breakfast. At our first coming, a small piece of pickled beef was occasionally boiled for dinner; but to the beef, which was soon consumed, there succeeded *clippers,* or clams; and our unvaried supper was *supon,* or mush, sometimes with skimmed milk, but more generally with buttermilk, blended with molasses, which was kept for weeks in a churn, as swill is saved for hogs. I found it, however, after a little use, very eatable, and supper soon became my best meal.... Their religious, like their other habits, were unostentatious and plain; and a simple, silent grace before meat, prevailed at the table of Jacob Suydam. When we were all seated he suddenly clapped his hands together, threw his head on one side, closed his eyes, and remained mute for about a minute. His niece and nephew followed his example; but with such an eager solicitude that the copied attitude should be prompt and simultaneous, as to give an air of absurdity to what might otherwise have been very decent. Although little of the vernacular accent remained on the tongues of these people, they had some peculiarities in their phraseology. Instead of asking you to sit down to table, they invited you to *sit by*.[73]

As if the hardships visited upon them by the British were not enough, the people of Kings County also occasionally fell prey to American privateers who had commissions to cruise the waters off Long Island in their whaleboats and plunder British vessels. Under pretense of seizing British goods, these privateers began landing on the island itself and robbing British and American alike. One night in June 1781, while the family of Nicholas Schenck was eating supper, the crews of two whaleboats under the command of a certain Captain Huyler raided their house and confiscated their silver.[74] Two months later, some of their neighbors suffered a similar indignity. "On the night of the 4th inst.," the *New York Gazette* reported August 12, "the crew of a rebel whale-boat from New Jersey landed near Flatlands on Long Island, and robbed the house of Col. Lott of about six hundred pounds, and carried off with them two of his slaves. [It is not clear whether the slaves were liberated or merely pilfered as property to be sold again.] They also robbed the house of Captain Lott of a considerable amount of specie."[75]

In the aftermath of the Revolution, of course, the excesses of the Patriot side would sooner be forgotten than the depredations of the British army. For the first time, out of an awareness of common sacrifice, Americans had developed a sense of nationalism that cut across regional and ethnic lines. If the Dutch had gone into the war a conquered people unsure of where their loyalties lay, they emerged part of a new nation—one whose motto, "Out of many, one," promised to include them as full partners. Now that they realized they had an American culture they could call their own, the preservation of Dutch culture would seem less important somehow.

Yet given the opportunity to help create a society in which the differences among Americans would truly matter less than their basic similarity, the Dutch—like America itself—fell short. The first New York State constitution, written at the height of the war in 1777, guaranteed the right to vote to all free propertied men, without reference to race, creed, or previous condition of servitude. Generous as that might sound, however, it excluded, at the most fundamental level of common interest, all women, slaves, and poor people. Apparently, though probably inadvertently, it did include propertied male Indians. But even if that were the case, it was practically meaningless, for the Revolution would facilitate, rather than end, the displacement of the Indians from the only property most of them knew—their communal hunting and fishing grounds. Presumably, Nicholas Schenck, Sr., dealt with a property-owning native in 1792 when he "got from David Cooper, a free Indian, one pockit Book," for which he paid 1s. 6d.[76] But by the early 1800s, according to local legend, there were only two Indians left—free, propertied, or otherwise—in all of Kings County: an old Canarsie man named Jim de Wilt, or "Jim the Wild Man," who died about 1830, and an old Canarsie woman called "Old Bess," who made a basket for a white woman named Margaret van Siclen Ditmas around 1804 (*see fig. 3.20*).[77]

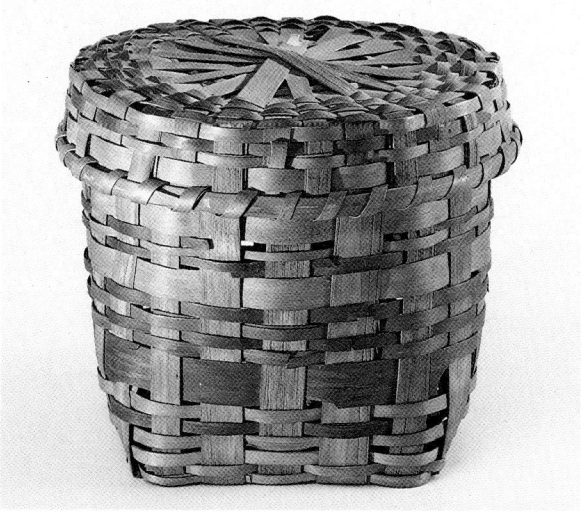

3.20. Basket, *circa 1804. Made by "Old Bess" of the Canarsie Indians, Flatlands, New York. Plaited splint, 7½ × 9⅛ inches. The Brooklyn Museum 48.150, Gift of Mrs. Charles A. Ditmas.*

Many Americans, to be sure, were troubled by their nation's failure to live up to its lofty ideals and moved to do something about it. During the Revolution, for example, a group of New Yorkers led by John Jay, America's first Chief Justice, sought to put an immediate end to their state's sanction of slavery.

Despite their efforts, however, slavery in New York continued at virtually the same level long after the Revolution. The black population of Kings County (almost all slaves), which had been about fifteen percent of the total in 1698 and had risen to about thirty-two percent in 1771, was still about thirty-two percent in 1790 – the highest proportion of any county north of the Mason-Dixon Line.[78] It was not until 1799 that the New York legislature was finally able to agree on a bill providing for the total elimination of slavery, and even then the process of emancipation was to drag on for decades. "The slaveholders at that time were chiefly Dutch," a representative named Erastus Root recalled years later. "They raved and swore by *dunder* and *blitzen* that we were robbing them of their property. We told them that they had none, and could hold none in human flesh while yet alive, and we passed the law."[79] But the law specified only that all children born to slave mothers after July 4 of that year were to be considered indentured servants, with all such male children freed of indenture at age twenty-eight and all females at age twenty-five. At that rate, slavery in New York State could have lasted till the end of the Civil War.[80]

As far as Nicholas Schenck was concerned, the passage of this so-called emancipation statute did nothing to deter him from actually increasing his ownership of slaves from two in 1790 to four at his death in 1810.[81] In fact, it may have helped him. Although the number of available slaves began to dwindle, the prices of the remaining slaves plummeted. A captive black child, though technically not a slave, could now be had for no money down. Under the law, a slaveholder who had no care to own children born of slave mothers after July 4, 1799, was to turn them over to the overseers of the poor to be bound out as indentured servants on the same terms as the children of paupers.[82] In 1811 Nicholas Schenck, Jr., evidently acquired such a child when the overseers of the poor of the town of Flatlands placed "a poor Black male Child named Peter," ten years old, under his supervision to "be instructed in the duties of a servant" until he was twenty-one. The child was thus bound to servitude only seven years less than he would have been had he remained with his original master, while Schenck had merely to provide "competent and sufficient meat drink and apparel lodging and washing...that [the child] may not be a charge to the Town."[83]

In 1817 the New York legislature did at last set a definite date for the complete eradication of any trace of slavery. Although it was not explicitly stated, it worked out to July 3, 1855. All slaves born before July 4, 1799, were to be freed July 4, 1827, while all children born of slave mothers in the interim twenty-eight-year period were to continue as indentured servants until they reached the ages specified in the statute of 1799.[84]

Two years after the passage of this law, Nicholas Schenck, Jr., apparently still had, in addition to the child just mentioned, at least one other indentured servant and at least one slave. The former, a "black slave child" of ten named Albert, he placed that year as a "slave servant" with Benjamin Bennet of Flatlands, while the latter, a "negro man slave" named Henry Ferguson, he manumitted the same year.[85] It is impossible to determine, of course, whether this manumission represented a heartfelt humanitarian gesture on Schenck's part or merely a financial decision.

There is no avoiding the sad conclusion, however, that such slaves had added to the prosperity that the Schencks – like most Dutch Americans – had come to enjoy in the new United States. Their ownership is an indication of an affluent family as surely as the bills of purchases that Nicholas Schenck, Sr., made from a merchant named David Masterton in the 1780s.

Still, Kings County was hardly plantation society. The Schencks were small farmers with no need of large numbers of slaves. They had a comfortable way of life, but they were by no means extravagant. They bought from Masterton a few luxuries like a pair of silk mitts and a red "pettecoat," and they ordered some fancy fabrics like a ½ yard of fine lawn, 2¼ yards of black lace, and 5¼ yards of "rich lace," but most of what they purchased was plain, such as 28½ yards of "Curtain Callico," 1 yard of muslin, and 2 yards of gauze.[86] In 1785 another merchant, named Henry Stanton, billed "Capt. Scank" for a saddle, a bridle, a length of carpet, 250 brass nails, and some repairs, probably of a carriage, which included "lining [the] chair body," "mending [the] braces," and "varnishing [the] body." Although Stanton received part of his payment in cash, he also gave Schenck £4 credit for 20 bushels of corn – a transaction typical of the barter economy of the day.[87] In short, the Nicholas Schenck family in the late eighteenth and the early nineteenth century probably resembled the Long Island farm families encountered somewhat later by a traveler named James Stewart. "[S]ome of the farmers of Long Island are wealthy," Stewart wrote, "but [they] are, in general, contented to live comfortably and hospitably, with all the ordinary necessities and conveniences of life, without ostentation or parade, and without seeming to care much, as other classes of people in this country do, about money."[88]

By all indications, there developed among the farmers of post-Revolutionary Kings County a strong sense of community. Even the Dutch, who had no tradition comparable to the New England town meeting, joined a movement toward greater popular participation in government. Nicholas Schenck, Sr., for instance, held numerous public offices, including commissioner of roads, commissioner of schools, election inspector, and tax assessor. His granddaughter Jane, who kept a journal (in English, notably) of her life between 1812 and 1816 (*see fig. 3.21*), came of age in a world in which people commonly pooled their labor in house

FROM DUTCH TO DUTCH AMERICAN

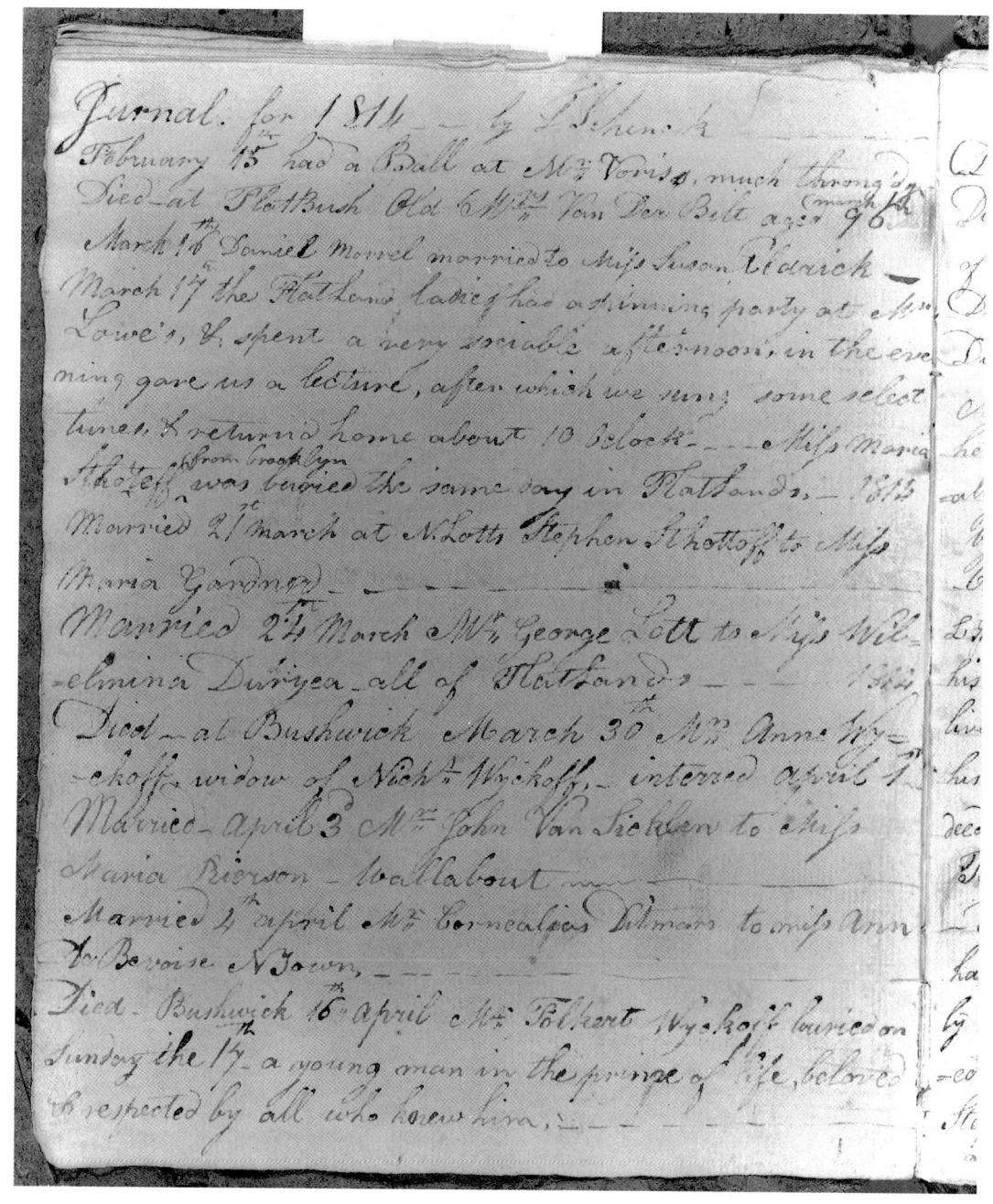

3.21. Page from a journal by Jane Schenck (Malbone). The Brooklyn Museum Library Collection.

raisings, spinning frolics, and quilting bees and often spent their free time visiting in one another's homes. Much of her journal is taken up with records of the births, deaths, and marriages of not only her relatives but also friends and acquaintances throughout the county and beyond. Elsewhere it tells of the Dutch and English youth socializing together freely, often till the wee hours of the morning and occasionally in ways that had once been peculiar to the Dutch but that now appear to have become part of the American cultural fabric.

For example, in the winter of 1813, when she was twenty-one, Jane Schenck sometimes joined her friends in sleighing parties much like the ones Madame Knight had observed the Dutch people of New York City enjoying more than a century earlier. Interestingly, although the English word for the vehicle in which they rode derived from the Dutch word *slee*, she attempted in writing about these parties to spell it phonetically, as Madame Knight had, in an English manner:

> Feby 1st went a slaying, join'd the Flatlands company at Mr C. Eldert's, where we sup'd, about 12 return'd to Mr Betts's, staid a short time & then return'd home.

Feby 2^d went out again, as far as Wiggins's with Mr Lambert Suydam and Mr John Lott, return'd to Mr Elderts about 10 OClock, sup'd and return'd home 3 OClock in the morning.[89]

Another Dutch custom that Jane Schenck's journal documents as surviving into the early nineteenth century, at least in part, is the practice of holding weddings not in church but in the house of the bride's parents, with the festivities continuing the following day at the house of the parents of the groom.[90] Although she made no note of where the wedding took place when her cousin Hetty Schenck married a man named Henry Suydam on March 4, 1813, she did write, "[N]ext day went all of us to his house in Bushwick with 3 waggons, & 1 chaise, spent the day in singing and other amusements, danced at night & return'd home 4 Oclock."[91]

Jane Schenck herself was married August 17, 1815, to a man from Killingly, Connecticut, named Ralph Malbone. Yet curiously there is no mention of Malbone in her journal up until the day of their wedding. Perhaps she considered their relationship too personal to write about, or perhaps their courtship took place, like so much else at the time, within the context of large social gatherings. For all we know, she and Malbone may well have met on an occasion such as the following:

Augt 4 [1814]. We had a large *Beach party* of about 30 ladies and 20 gentlemen.... Our party met at John Duryea's (Flatlands). We halted at Gravesend (Wyckoff's Hotel) and proceeded to the *Beach* with 7 waggons well loaded, we spent about one hour there, & return'd to Duryea's Tavern, where we had a delightful walk in the garden each one full of good humour & merriment, left Duryea's about 6, & proceeded to Begelow's Flatbush, where we were recei'd with the greatest attention, tea being ready we took a hearty repast of all the nice dainties before us, & withdrew to the Ballroom, where we commenced dancing (hot as it was) with all the avidity of youth, & display'd "animated nature" in its full extent. Our party seperated about 1 O'clock.[92]

In a way, the citizens of Kings County even made a party of the War of 1812, seeing to the common defense with the same good-natured spirit of cooperation they would have brought to a community corn husking. Though this war was highly unpopular in New England and other parts of New York, here, where the memory of British occupation was still fresh, there seems to have been little dissent. In 1813, as the British began extending their naval blockade up the East Coast, people who lived along the shore started keeping a careful watch on the enemy's movements, ready to sound the alarm of the feared invasion. On June 2, for instance, Jane Schenck wrote in her journal:

We seen two British Vessels of war coasting all day about our shores, a Schooner freighted with pine wood chanced to fall in their way, at 6 Oclock P.M. one of them fired three guns upon her, & the Schooner not heaving to, put in our inlet for safety & being unacquainted with the channel run aground, the English put out their barge in pursuit of her, & in a short time put her in flames, the men made for shore & made their escape.[93]

In August 1814, when word spread that the British were about to attack somewhere along the coast, Kings County became the scene of the kind of frenzied collective effort usually witnessed only in the face of a natural disaster. The goal was to build a line of fortifications encircling Brooklyn Heights in order to stop the British from marching through the county and seizing control of New York harbor as they had in 1776. A delegation of tanners and plumbers, a society of medical students, several church congregations, twelve hundred Irishmen, more than a thousand free blacks, a company of firemen, a lodge of Masons, a team of five hundred carpenters, a group of three hundred women, contingents from all six towns in the county — all these and more took turns digging trenches, building redoubts, and rehabilitating the three forts left over from the Revolution (including one, rechristened Fort Greene, that was to leave its name on a Brooklyn park and neighborhood). As they worked, these volunteers often sang a tune called "The Patriotic Diggers," written in their honor by Samuel Woodworth, better known as the author of "The Old Oaken Bucket." By the end of the month the fortifications were ready to be manned.[94] "Septr 2^d," Jane Schenck wrote in her journal, "our militia are called out under arms & have encamped at Brooklyn for 3 mos...."

But it was all, happily, for naught, for as she then added, evidently having just heard the news, "The British in Washington Augt 24th and destroyed the public buildings." The invasion had come farther south than expected, and after the successful defense of Fort McHenry near Baltimore on September 13 and 14 Kings County would have no more to worry about than an occasional incident like the following:

Octr 25th on Tuesday, a Brig, prize to an American Privateer, was chased ashore by a British Ship, near the Blockhouse on rockaway beach the crew after setting her on fire had time enough to make their escape. She was freighted mostly with dried *Cod fish*, which was mostly saved.[95]

Meanwhile, peace talks were under way in Europe, and by Christmas Eve a treaty that simply ended the state of hostilities, without any concessions by either side, was in hand. "Peace...," Jane Schenck wrote when the word at last reached America. "Feby 11, 1815 the news of *Peace*, signed at Ghent Decr 24th, 1814 between the American and British plenipotentiaries, arrived in New York, & the 17 Feby it was ratified by the President of the United States—an event that has produced universal joy throughout the Country."[96]

Both during and after the war, when it came to keeping the peace among themselves, the inhabitants of Kings County probably rarely resorted to force of arms, relying instead on enormous social pressure to conform. If this was a society in which neighbors readily came to one another's aid, it was no doubt also one in which everyone watched over everyone else's business, seldom hesitating to intervene if someone stepped out of line. The spirit of community would have given people a sense of identity associated with pride of place, but it would also have tended to stamp out individuality and to deaden the spirit of independent souls. Paradoxically, in this society built on mutual caring, a deeply troubled person might sometimes feel as if there were no place left to turn for help. Thus we find mentioned in Jane Schenck's journal a considerable number of suicides—reminders that the society was not as harmonious as it might at first appear. Take, for instance, the following example from 1814:

> On Saturday morning May 28th Jacobus Rider resident of Gravesend, L.I. cut the throat of his little son aged about 2 years & after that his own, the child died immediately of the wound, the father lived 11 days untill the 8 of june, he was about 35 years of age, his wife was in the field milking the cows when the dreadful deed was committed, he had previously written a letter to his Father, the contents of which are said to be very effecting. What has got into the people, a similar crime of the above has been comitted at Jamaica Little Plains [in neighboring Queens County] by Wm Doughty, an elderly man, who after cutting his throat expired instantly & was buried the same day that Jacobus Rider was.[97]

For answers to such questions, Jane Schenck undoubtedly turned to the Dutch Reformed Church. Relying on the church for spiritual guidance was, after all, a family tradition. Her grandfather Nicholas had been such a regular churchgoer that when the Flatlands congregation decided to build a new church in 1791 he subscribed to not one but two pews at ten shillings each per year.[98]

If she found solace in the church ministry just as he had, however, it is doubtful that she and her generation still looked to the church for the safeguarding of Dutch ways. The Reformed Church of Flatlands at this time was served by two ministers, one of whom, a revered old dominie by the name of Martinus Schoonmaker, spoke only in Dutch. But since her own primary language seems to have been English, she probably preferred to hear his English-speaking colleague, in all likelihood regarding Schoonmaker himself as something of a quaint curiosity. Just how old-fashioned he appeared to younger eyes can be seen in the following recollection penned by a pastor named Peter van Pelt in 1858:

> It was in 1819 that I last heard, or recollect to have seen, the venerable old dominie. It was at the funeral of one of his old friends and associates. A custom had very generally prevailed, which, though then very rarely observed, yet in this instance was literally

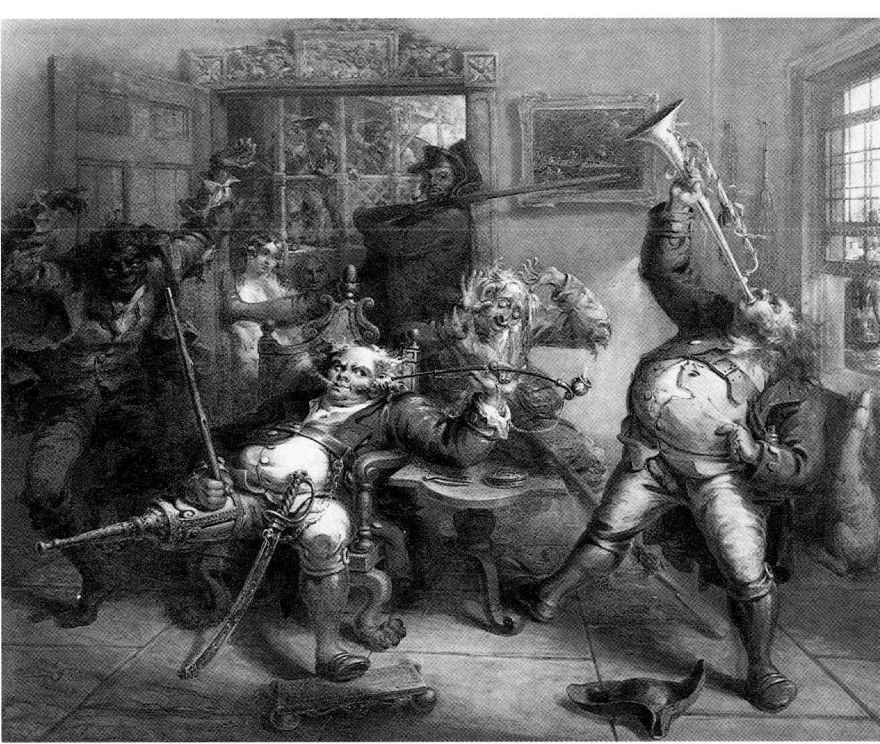

3.22. John Quidor (American, 1801–1881). Antony van Corlear Brought into the Presence of Peter Stuyvesant, *1839.* Oil on canvas, 27¾ × 34½ inches. Munson-Williams-Proctor Institute Museum of Art, Utica, New York.

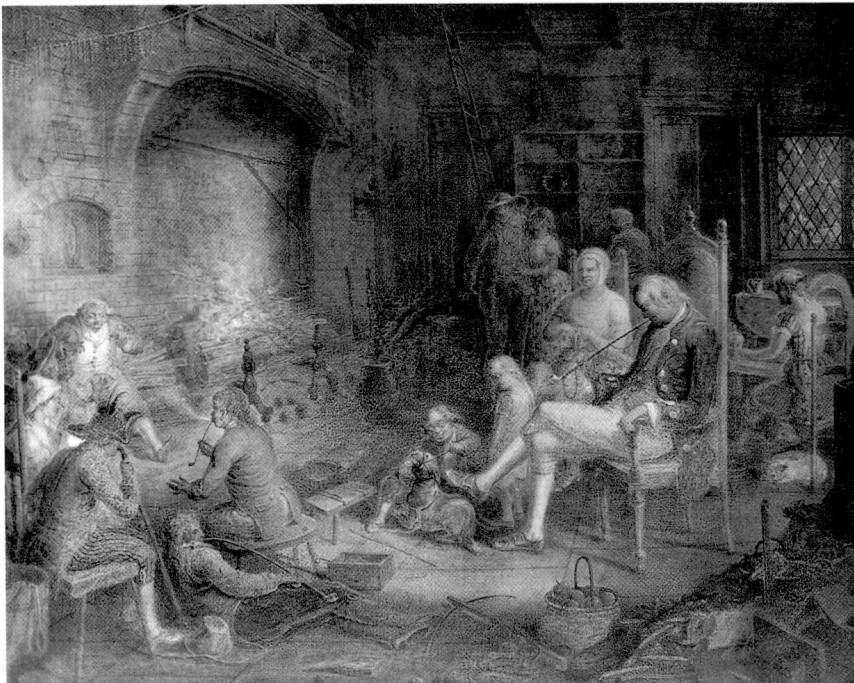

3.23. John Quidor
(American, 1801–1881).
The Knickerbocker Kitchen, *1865.*
*Oil on canvas, 27 × 33½ inches.
Addison Gallery of American
Art, Phillips Academy, Andover,
Massachusetts.*

adhered to. The deceased had, many years before, provided and laid away the materials for his own coffin. This one was of the best seasoned and smoothest boards, and beautifully grained. Other customs and ceremonies then existed, now almost forgotten. As I entered the room I observed the coffin elevated on a table in one corner. The dominie, abstracted and grave, was seated at the upper end; and around, in solemn silence, the venerable and hoary-headed friends of the deceased. All was still and serious. A simple recognition or a half-audible inquiry, as one after another arrived, was all that passed. Directly, the sexton, followed by a servant, made his appearance, with glasses and decanters. *Wine* was handed to each. Some declined; others drank a solitary glass. This ended, and again the sexton presented himself, with *pipes* and *tobacco.* The dominie smoked his pipe, and a few followed his example. The custom has become obsolete, and it is well that it has. When the whiffs of smoke had ceased to curl around the head of the dominie, he arose with evident feeling, and in a quiet, subdued tone, made a short but apparently impressive address. I judged solely by his appearance and manner; for, although boasting a Holland descent, it was to me speaking in an unknown tongue. A short prayer concluded the service; and then the sexton, taking the lead, was followed by the dominie, the doctor, and the pallbearers, with white scarfs and black gloves. The corpse, and a long procession of friends and neighbors, proceeded to the churchyard, where all that was mortal was committed to the earth, till the last trump shall sound and the grave shall give up the dead. No bustle, no confusion, no noise nor indecent haste, attended that funeral.[99]

When Dominie Schoonmaker himself died at the age of eighty-seven on May 20, 1824, it marked not only the end of Dutch preaching in the Reformed churches of Kings County but also, in many ways, the end of an era. By this time much of what had made up the structure and substance of daily life for Jan Martense Schenck and his contemporaries had passed away, or, more accurately, been transformed into something new and different.

Yet just as the Dutch roots of Dutch Americans began to fade beyond recall into the dim recesses of distant memory and vague legend, they were grasped back in a conscious effort to preserve them. Foremost among those who took an interest in Dutch-American history was the writer Washington Irving, who published *Knickerbocker's History of New York* in 1809 and *Rip van Winkle* and *The Legend of Sleepy Hollow* in 1820. Even if Irving's point of view was not altogether sympathetic or scholarly, at least he piqued the curiosity of not just those of Dutch descent but also the nation at large. In turn, the artist John Quidor, who came of age in the 1820s, would paint scenes from Irving's tales (*see, for example, figs. 3.22 and 3.23*) and thus further perpetuate the memory of the country's Dutch heritage and the Dutch contribution to American culture.[100]

It is to this point in time, in the 1820s, that the Nicholas Schenck House is now restored in The Brooklyn Museum.

CHAPTER
FOUR

A NEW IDENTITY, A NEW STYLE

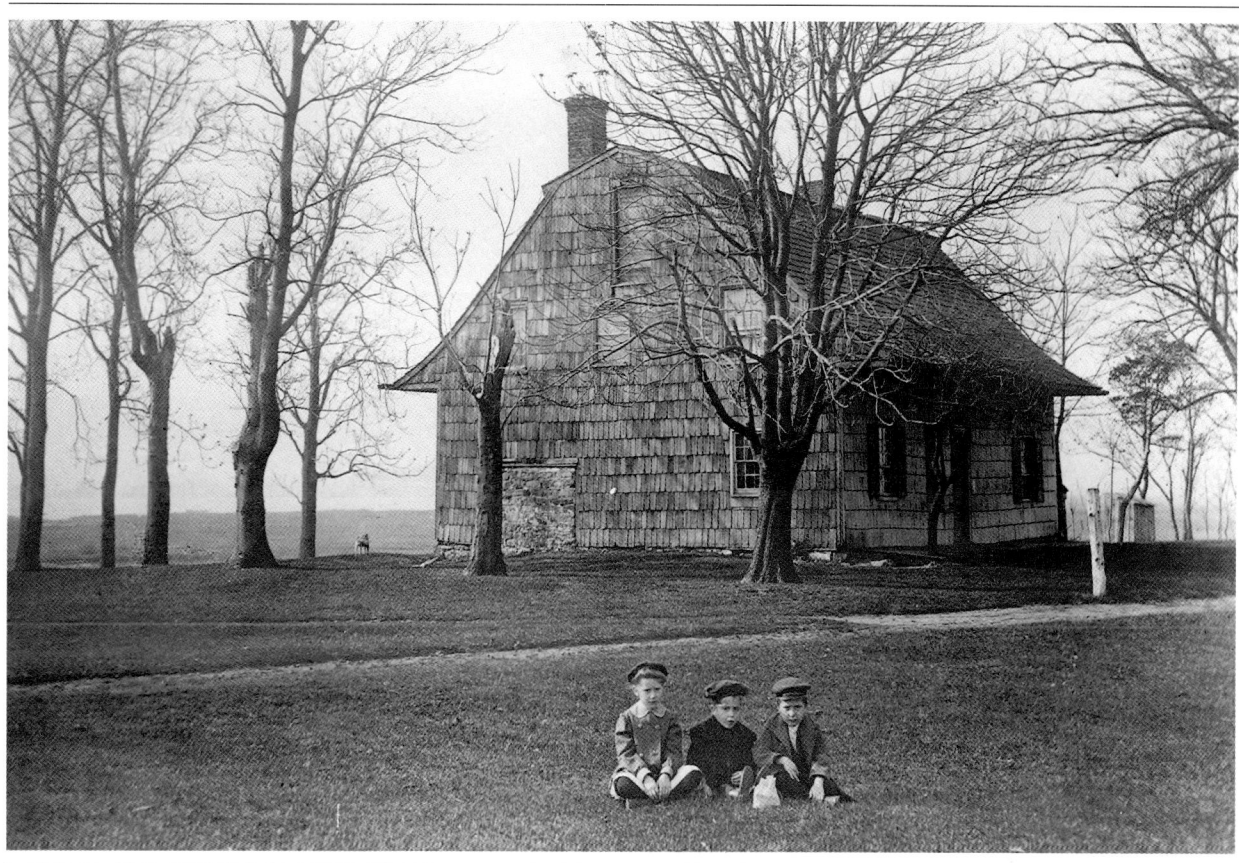

The Nicholas Schenck House *(fig. 4.1)* originally stood about a mile and a half northeast of the Mill Island house of Jan Martense Schenck on a neck of land jutting into Jamaica Bay *(see map, fig. 4.2).*[1] Here, in this remote location once known as Vischer's Hoek and now known as Canarsie, the descendants of Jan Schenck gradually lost touch with much of their Dutch heritage, clinging to what they could from their past as they took on a new identity as Americans. As they changed, their house changed with them, losing most, though not all, of its Dutch character and coming to represent a new style of architecture that in its hybrid nature was quintessentially American.

While the Jan Schenck House has been reconstructed in order to approximate, as nearly as possible, the way it first appeared, the Nicholas Schenck House has, in this regard, been left alone. In spite of a general refurbishing and a few quirks of its installation, it still reflects the radical transformation it underwent during the Schenck family's occupancy. Visitors are encouraged to "reconstruct" for themselves its original appearance—to discover, one might say, its Dutch foundations—and then to try to understand how it came to look the way it does today.

4.1. The Nicholas Schenck House, 1903.

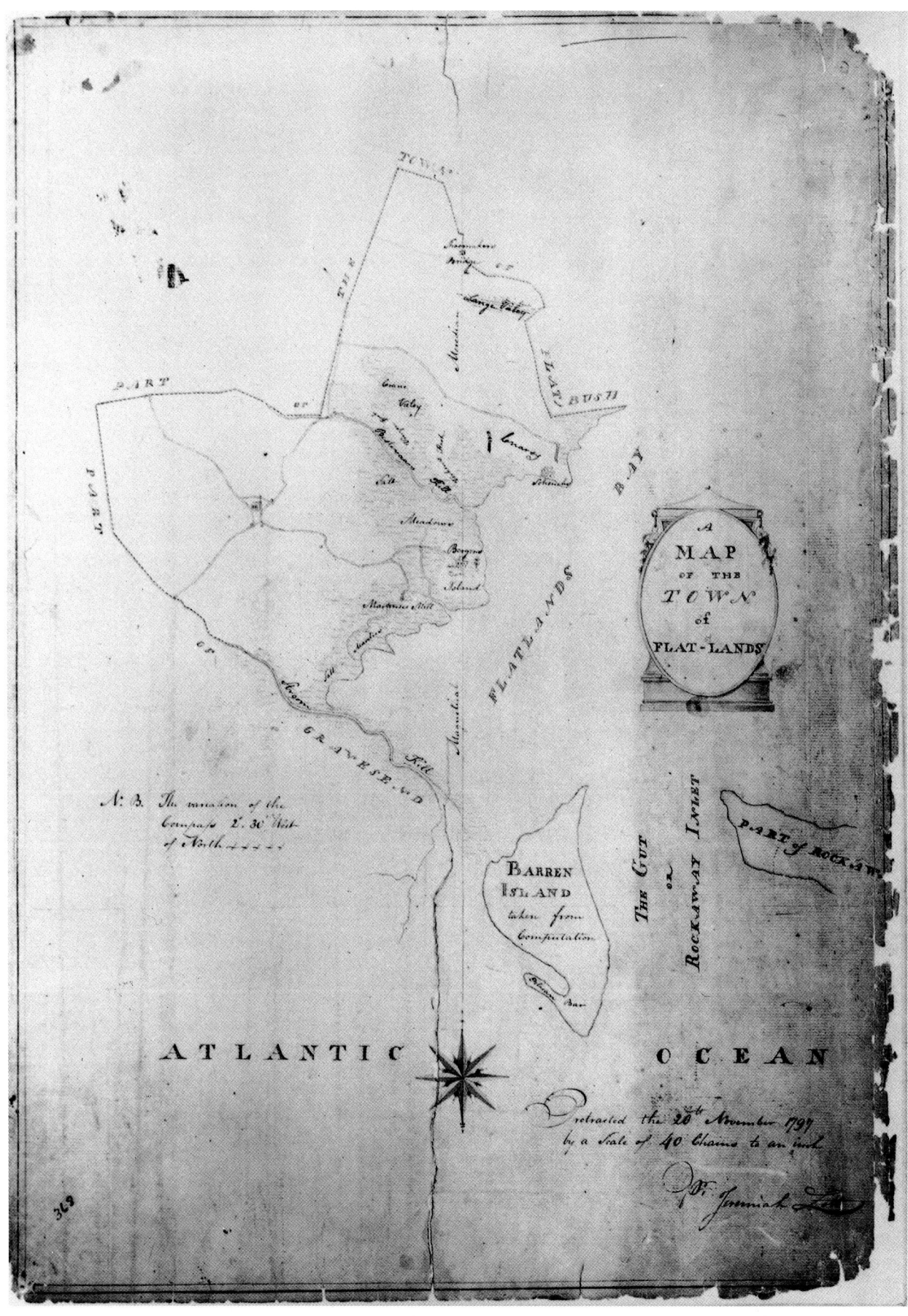

4.2. Map of Flatlands by Jeremiah Lott, dated November 20, 1797. Courtesy of the New York State Archives, Office of Cultural Education, State Education Department, Albany. Surveyor General roll map #368.

These are, admittedly, not easy tasks, and anyone who undertakes them is likely to end up with as many questions as answers. The pursuit, however, is worth the effort, for it sheds new light on one of America's most popular—but least understood—architectural forms.

For reasons that will soon become evident, our study begins not with the house itself but with the Canarsie property on which it was built. Canarsie, the last tract of land on western Long Island relinquished by the Canarsie Indians, was deeded to the town of Flatlands on April 23, 1665, for 150 fathoms of wampum, one coat, one pair of stockings, one pair of shoes, four adzes, two cans of brandy, and one-half barrel of beer.[2] Even before that, however, in 1661, a petition for the opening of farms there had been presented to the government of New Netherland, leading to the creation of six farms in the area by 1663.[3] Although five of these were eventually abandoned, returned to undeveloped woodland, and divided by lot among the citizens of Flatlands in 1719, one twenty-three acre parcel was apparently purchased in the interim by Jan Martense Schenck. It was this property, evidently, that he left to his four-year-old son, Stephen Janse Schenck, in 1689 when he bequeathed him "the lott land in the neck with the middow, to hoggs neck with all ye dependencies."[4]

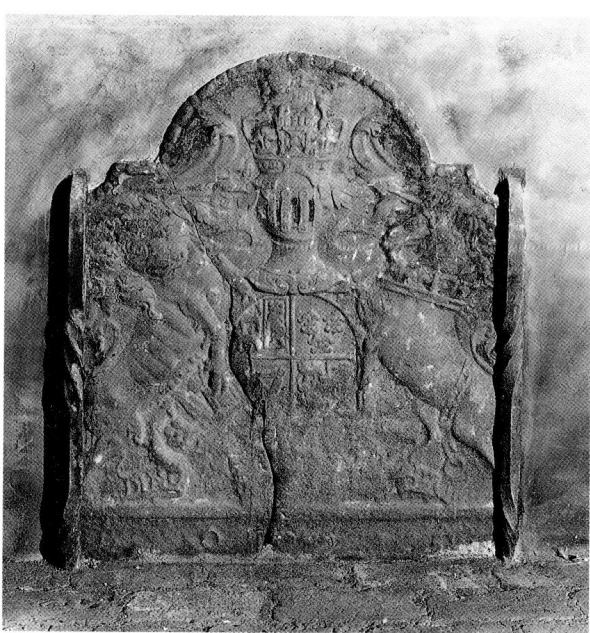

4.3. Fireback, 1745–58. Made by the Oxford Furnace, Warren County, New Jersey. Cast iron, 31⅞ × 29⅛ inches. The Brooklyn Museum   29.1592.1, Gift of the New York City Parks Department.

In any case, Stephen Schenck was the first of his family to occupy the land in Canarsie on which the Nicholas Schenck House once stood. Though he also owned property on the north shore of Long Island in the town of Oyster Bay (property that he left to his eldest son, John), it was here that he made his home. He farmed this land, raised nine children on it, and at his death in 1767 left it to his younger son, Nicholas, along with the buildings he had built upon it.

These buildings no doubt included a house. In fact, one source says Stephen Schenck built the *first* house in Canarsie.[5] And yet, curiously, no previous study of the Nicholas Schenck House has bothered to ask what became of it.

That oversight seems especially strange considering the Nicholas Schenck House has frequently been dated to around 1757—the year Nicholas Schenck married a woman by the name of Willemtje Wyckoff and the year before his father made out the will by which he would inherit the property a decade later. When the house was installed in the Museum in 1929, seeming evidence for such a date was discovered in the form of a cast-iron fireback found in the bricked-up fireplace in the dining room *(see fig. 4.3)*. This fireback, bearing the arms of England, was made at the Oxford Furnace in Warren County, New Jersey, a furnace that produced this particular model only between about 1745 and 1758.[6] Lacking further information, one might speculate that if the house were really built then, it might have been built not by Nicholas Schenck at all but by his father, Stephen. However, the scholars who used the fireback to date the house to the 1750s entertained no such notion. Either they were unaware of Stephen Schenck's tenure, missed its implications, or had access to some document that has since been lost to us.

Another possibility previously overlooked is that Stephen Schenck might at least have built the kitchen wing of the house seen in nineteenth-century photographs of the building *(see fig. 4.4)*. This wing, which had given way to a fairly substantial tree before the Museum acquired the house *(see fig. 4.5)*, featured a side-gabled roof that could indicate a somewhat earlier date than the gambrel roof of the main section because side-gabled roofs (tending toward a lower pitch in later examples) were used on Dutch houses in America long before the gambrel variety. One observer did write of the house in 1924, "Its oldest part, the kitchen, was removed a number of years ago. It dated before 1670."[7] And draftsmen for the Depression-era Historic American Buildings Survey apparently had the wing in mind when they dated the entire house to about that time. But in all likelihood the wing was not nearly so old (a roof of that period would probably have been much steeper), and at any rate such a date was far too early ever to raise the question of whether Stephen Schenck might have been the builder.

As it turns out, the idea that Stephen Schenck had anything to do with building either the main part of the house or its wing is most seriously challenged by the primary piece of evidence now used to date the house: a tax assessment of the Schencks' Canarsie farm con-

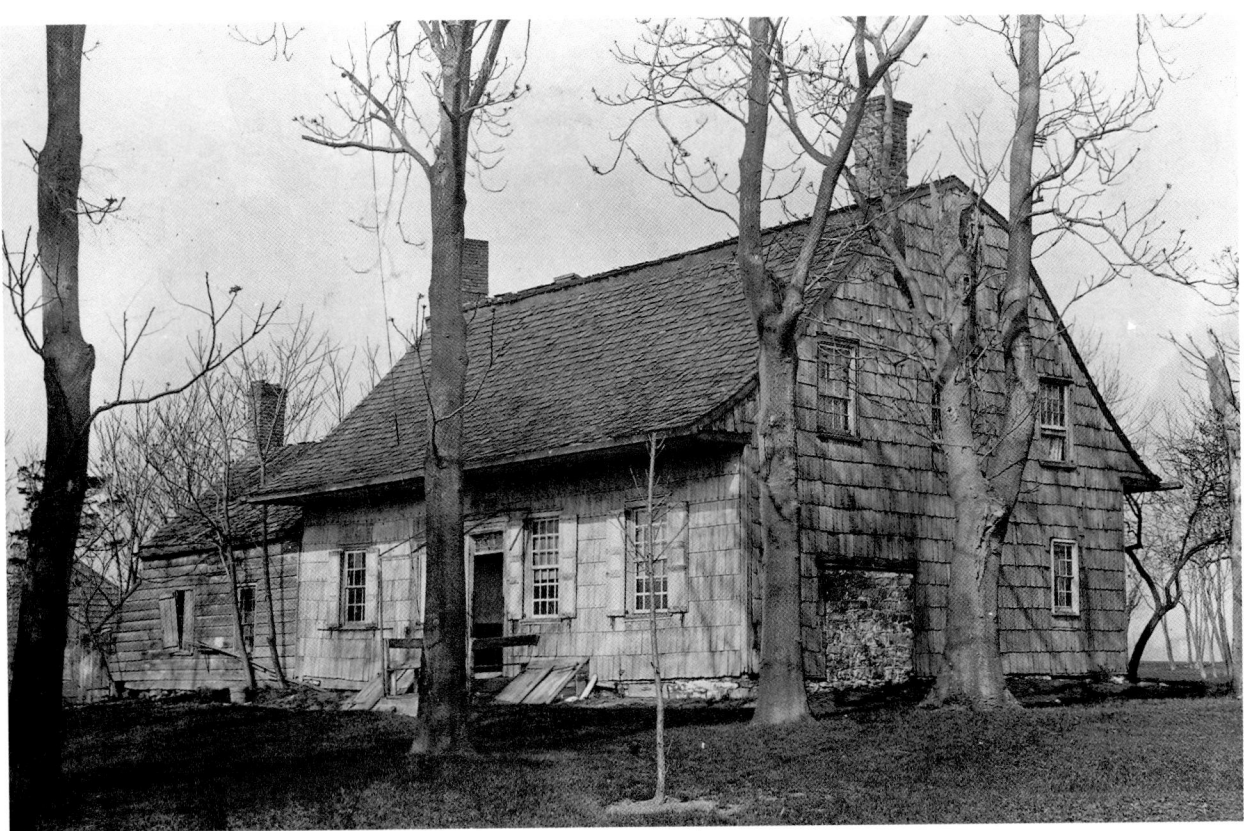

4.4. *The Nicholas Schenck House, circa 1885.*

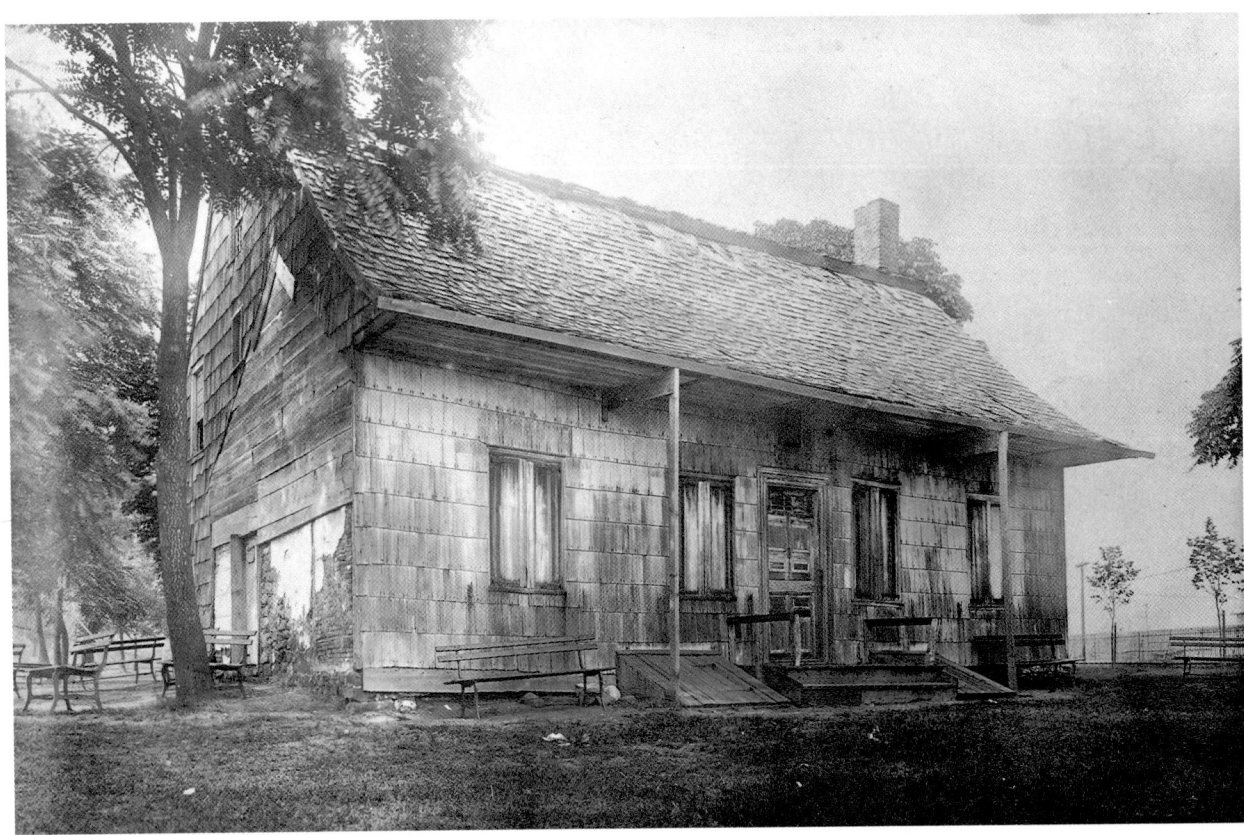

4.5. *The Nicholas Schenck House, circa 1925.*

ducted in 1796. In that assessment, the farm, with two barns—one 40 x 56 feet and the other 36 x 46—is valued at $3,390, while the house—42 x 33—is given the value of $850 and described as being in good condition.[8] The listed length of the house, practically the same as today, gives no indication of an extension, suggesting that the kitchen wing might in fact have been added later, while the stated age of the house, though probably an approximation, yields a date of around 1771, four years after Stephen Schenck's death. This dating, moreover, is supported by one of the earliest mentions of the house in print—a biographical sketch on Nicholas Schenck's grandson James, published while he was still alive, by the Brooklyn historian Henry Stiles. There the house is dated to 1772, very possibly based on information provided by James Schenck himself.[9]

Yet even though such a date assures us that Nicholas Schenck did indeed build the house now installed under his name in The Brooklyn Museum, it still does not answer that nagging question all other studies of the house have appeared to avoid: Whatever happened to the house Stephen Schenck must have built?

A possible explanation is suggested by the recently restored Pieter Claesen Wyckoff House, which still stands in Flatlands at the corner of Ralph Avenue and Clarendon Road. This old Dutch house *(fig. 4.6)* also comprises a main building with a kitchen wing, in much the same configuration as the Nicholas Schenck House once did, and it, too, raises questions. Scholars have differed greatly as to both its date and its manner of construction. Most have pointed to the steep roof of its wing (considerably steeper than the roof of the Schenck House extension) as evidence that the wing represents the earliest house on site, which they have dated variously to the late 1630s, the early 1650s, or the late seventeenth century.[10] Others, though, have argued that the wing is instead a later addition (built as late as 1784) and that the original house was three-fifths the depth of the main section, in which, they have

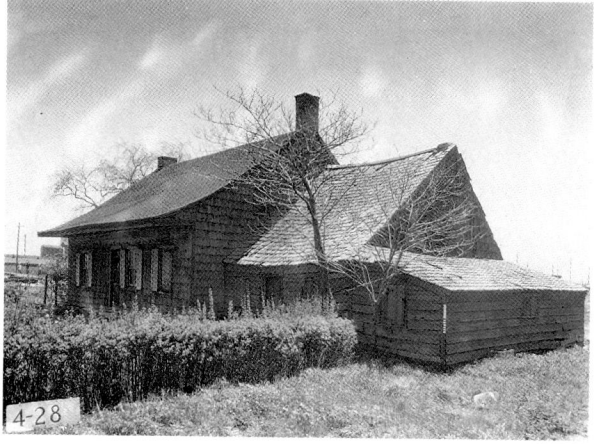

4.6. The Pieter Claesen Wyckoff House, Flatlands, circa 1934.

claimed, it is still contained.[11] Whatever their opinion, however, all these scholars have agreed on one thing: the Wyckoff House that stands today incorporates an earlier building in some way.

In her 1945 study of the old Dutch houses of Kings County, Maud Esther Dilliard implied that Nicholas Schenck's house replaced a seventeenth-century "hut" built by the fisherman Hoorn whose occupation provided the area with its old name Vischer's Hoek.[12] But if the Nicholas Schenck House replaced anything, it more likely replaced the house of Stephen Schenck, if not incorporating it as a kitchen wing as most scholars say the Wyckoff House incorporated its predecessor (a possibility questioned though, odd as it may seem, not necessarily excluded by the tax assessment of 1796), then perhaps at least cannibalizing it to some degree. Seen in this light, the cast-iron fireback discovered in the dining room represents not a piece of evidence dating the house to the 1750s but rather a possible indication that Nicholas Schenck used parts of his father's house (and maybe even parts of some of the other buildings constructed by his father) in building his own. Another such indication is found in the front part of the stair hall, where the central ceiling beam has a number of patches and filled mortise holes whose configuration—probably the result of the mortising in of a collar—suggests that it was originally a rafter anchor beam in another structure, perhaps even a building as large as a barn.[13] Of course the fireback might have been purchased unused years after its manufacture, or both it and the ceiling beam might have come from a building not even on site. But all we have learned thus far argues for the suspicion that if Stephen Schenck's house did not become a kitchen, the most likely place to look for a trace of it would be somewhere else within the house of his son. The Dutch farmers of Kings County might have modified and enlarged certain houses beyond recognition, might even have torn houses down and begun again, but they were usually in the habit of utilizing all they could of whatever came before.

However it came to be built, the Nicholas Schenck House is a typical example of the vernacular domestic architecture of late eighteenth-, early nineteenth-century rural Kings County, a house type probably forever branded in the American popular mind as the Dutch Colonial, even though most of the details associated with it are not actually Dutch and even though it reached its height in the first half century after the Revolution. The Schenck House incorporated many of the features that are commonly thought to define this style of house as it was built in New York and New Jersey, and it was particularly characteristic of the Kings County subtype of the style. When it stood on site it presented a classic Dutch Colonial profile, with a gently sloping gambrel roof and flaring, overhanging eaves. There was a large opening high in one gable end so that material could be hoisted into the loft for storage, and in front were a stoop, or porch, and a Dutch door that had its original upper panel replaced by a stationary transom sometime around 1880 *(see* fig. 4.7). The house was covered with shingles, which along with clapboards were used on Long Island and in parts of New Jersey where the soil was sandy and houses were usually built of wood because stone was scarce. Unlike the protruding chimneys built by the English, the two chimney stacks were kept within their respective walls, but, typically, the shingles were interrupted on the exterior where the fireplaces were located within. Inside the house as it is now installed in the Museum, the customary low ceilings with exposed beams supporting wide plank boards are still visible. The stair hall is wainscoted with a simple sheathing of flat boards (see fig. 5.33), and the fireplace ends of both the parlor and the dining room are paneled (see figs. 5.7 and 5.24) — a stylistic feature borrowed from the English. The paneling is characteristic of most Kings County farmhouses built during this period though not nearly as sophisticated as that found in some.

The origin of this so-called Dutch Colonial style that the Schenck House represents is as clouded as the origin of the house itself. During the twentieth century, scholars have, in due course, suggested that the style was indigenous to America with no precedent in Europe,[14] that the prototype for the flaring eaves could be found in the "flying gutters" of cottages in coastal Flanders,[15] that these eaves represented instead vestigial remains of the overhanging thatch roof common to the vernacular architecture of many nations,[16] that the gambrel roof was an English architectural trait borrowed by the Dutch,[17] and that, even if the Dutch did borrow the gambrel roof, the Dutch gambrel was distinct from the English.[18] Recently, the building type has been described as a hybrid born of the marriage of tradition and innovation in a land where the architectural customs of many national cultures were suddenly thrown together and the borrowing and recombination of countless forms and details resulted.[19]

Although at first glance the gambrel roof and the flaring eaves are the style's most distinguishing characteristics, the historian David Steven Cohen has lately argued that these are in fact secondary and that the primary characteristics that define the type are its framing and its floor plan. Cohen prefers to call the Dutch Colonial style of house the Dutch-American farmhouse, in order to distinguish it from what he calls the Dutch farmhouse in America. The latter, he maintains, is a house "whose framing and/or floor plan can be traced back to [Continental] Europe" like those of the Jan Martense Schenck House, while the former has both an English floor plan and a boxlike English frame.[20]

Cohen's elucidation of two crucial differences between the style of house the Dutch built in their early years in America and the type they were building in the late eighteenth and the early nineteenth century is helpful in understanding the evolution of both Dutch-American architecture in general and the Nicholas Schenck House in particular. In fact, applying Cohen's terms to the Schenck House yields a fascinating case study of how, as seen in a single dwelling, a new, American style of Dutch architecture developed out of the old.

According to Cohen's definition, the Schenck House as it stood when the Museum acquired it was beyond doubt a Dutch-American farmhouse, for it had both an English frame and an English floor plan — the so-called full Georgian plan, which consists of a central hall with two rooms on each side (see fig. 4.8). Contained within this plan, however, were ghosts of a different floor plan of the house's original construction, one related to a Continental plan Cohen has identified in such houses as the Peter A. Hopper House of Fair Lawn, New Jersey (see fig. 4.9): two rooms in front and three across the back. Thus, despite its flaring eaves and gambrel roof — two features Dutch Americans did not begin incorporating in their houses until the first half of the eighteenth century — the Schenck House originally represented, in Cohen's parlance, a Dutch farmhouse in America.

To explain how Dutch Americans made the switch from Continental forms like this to forms of English origin, Cohen has extended an analogy drawn by the folklorist Henry Glassie between the structure of buildings and the structure of language:

> When the English conquered New Netherland in 1664 and renamed it New York and New Jersey, important changes occurred both in the language and in the architecture.... [T]he Dutch people in this conquered land became bilingual, speaking English in public and

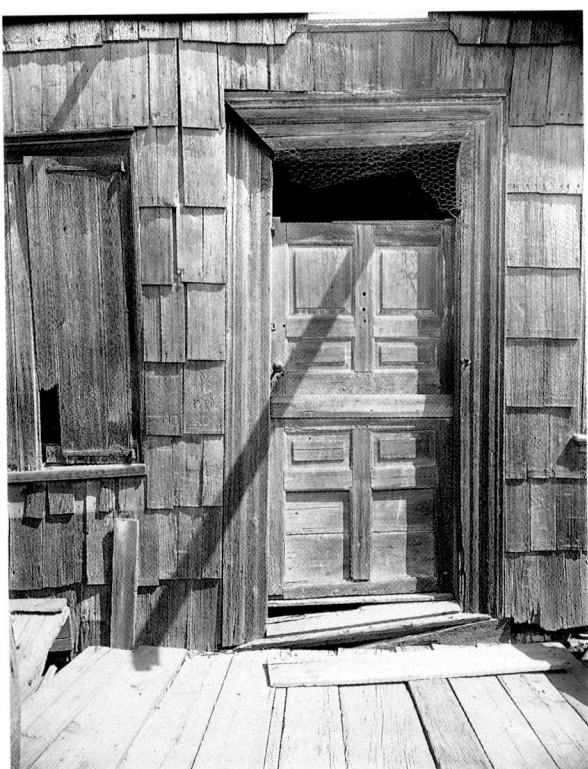

4.7. *Front door, the Nicholas Schenck House,* in situ, *circa 1925.*

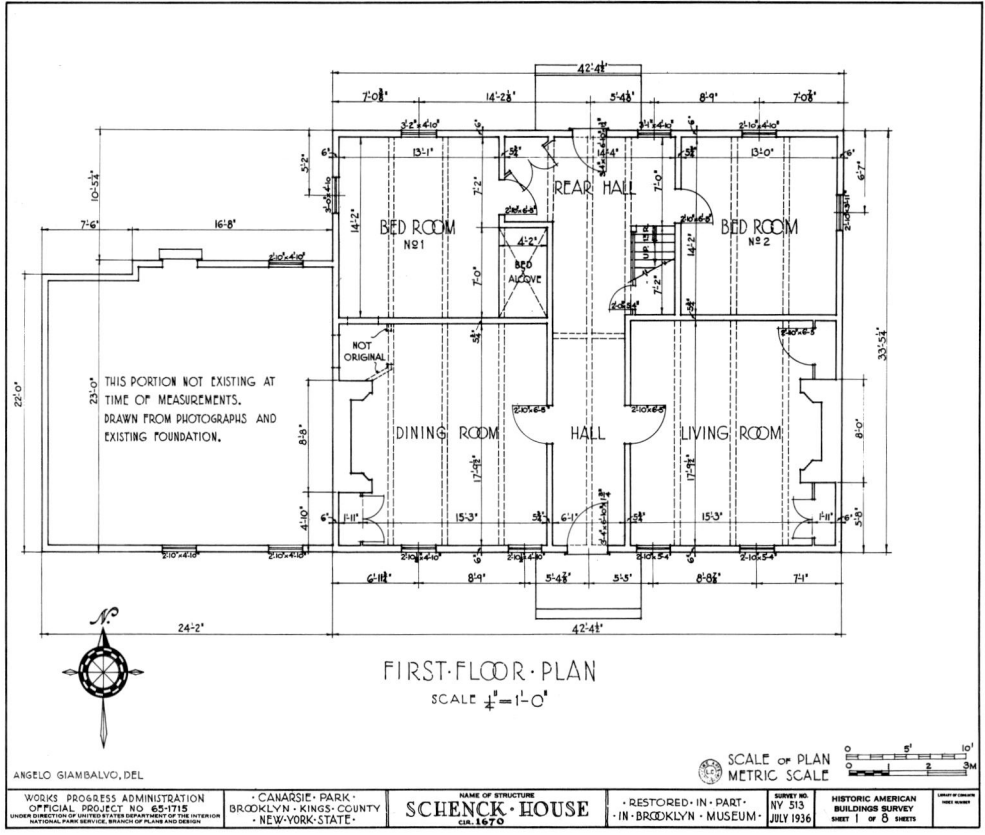

4.8. First-floor plan, the Nicholas Schenck House as it stood on site in the nineteenth century.

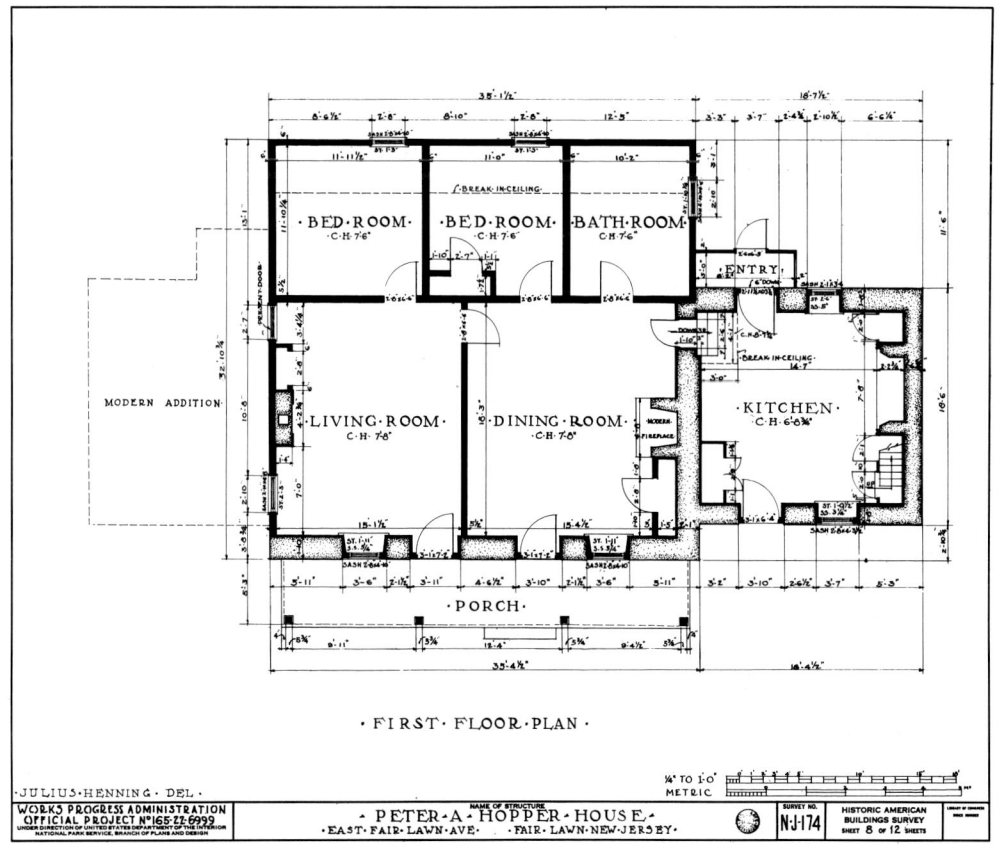

4.9. First-floor plan, the Peter A. Hopper House, Fair Lawn, New Jersey.

Dutch in the home. Finally they spoke English as their main language, and only a few Dutch words and expressions survived.... The same process can be seen in architecture.... After a while the basic structure of Dutch architecture was affected by [the] English influence. In both framing and floor plans the Dutch began to build in an English architectural idiom.... In other words, instead of building Dutch farmhouses in America they began building Dutch-American farmhouses.[21]

The Schencks, it seems, made this transition simply by remodeling. At some point, as Kings County grew more and more anglicized and the English Georgian floor plan became the norm, they remade their farmhouse to reflect the new taste. What had originally been the middle rear room was broken through and transformed into the rear portion of a central stair hall. A staircase was tucked into the southeast corner of the old middle room, and the southwest corner was eliminated by moving the southern portion of the inner wall of the west rear room from the third ceiling beam to the fourth, leaving evidence of the earlier arrangement in the third beam in the form of filled mortise holes with Roman numerals in sequence. In addition to narrowing the middle room and giving it the appearance of a central hall, the movement of the wall created an alcove in the west rear room. Moreover, the alteration also explains the mysterious appearance of a built-in cupboard by the rear door, a cupboard that was once part of a separate room, not misplaced in a stair hall.

At the time of this transformation, other elements of the Schenck House were also modernized: new door and window frames replaced old ones, fireplace mantels were added to earlier paneled walls, and an angled vestibule was built in the dining room at the entrance to the kitchen wing, suggesting that if the wing did not predate the main portion of the house it might have been added then. Some changes were possibly made in the second-story space as well. Although no physical evidence remains from the upper floor, a plan of that story drawn before the house was torn down (*fig. 4.10*) indicates that the original open loft was divided up rather haphazardly over time as the need arose. Rooms were tucked into both northern corners, a third room was built around the chimney over the dining room, and the rest of the floor was left an open storage area. Part of this arrangement may well have been created at the time the first floor was remodeled, for the top step of the new staircase was designed so that the upper floor could be entered from two directions — either straight ahead into the open storage space or to the side into the northeast room (*see fig. 5.35*). It is impossible to be certain, however, because

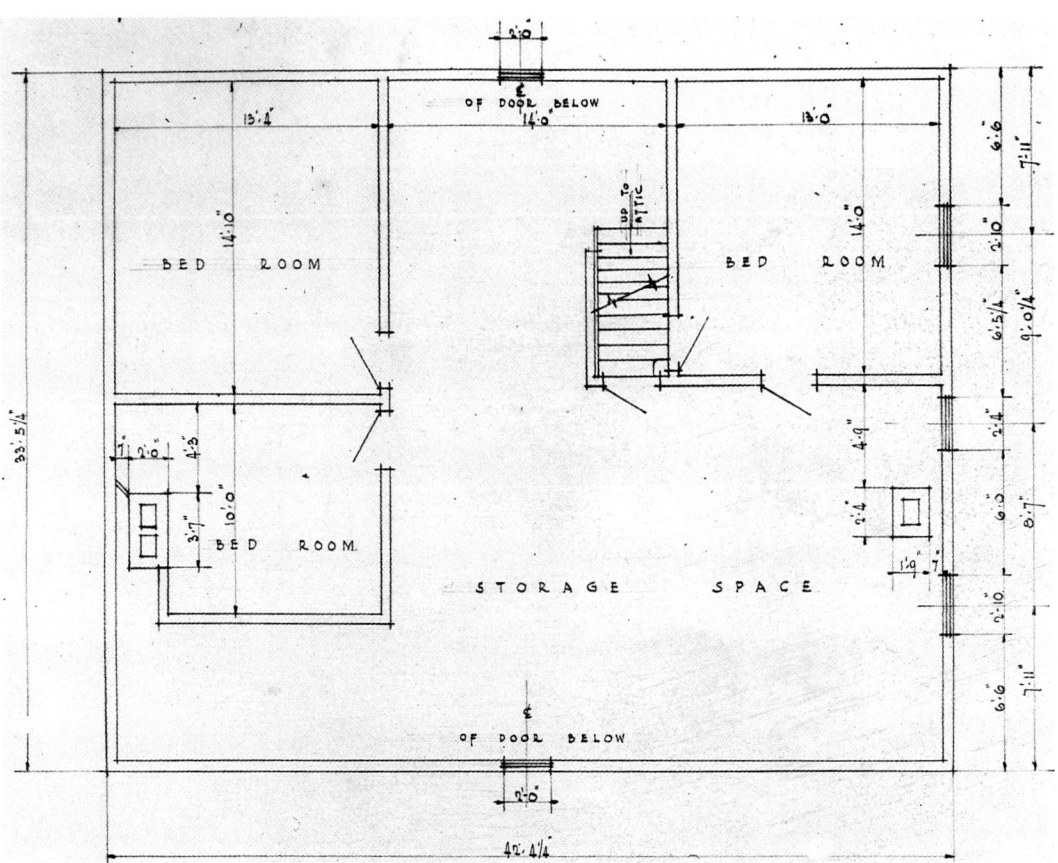

4.10. Second-floor plan, the Nicholas Schenck House as it stood on site in 1929.

both doors to the upper story predate the staircase itself; they may be original to their present location, they may have been moved during the remodeling from another part of the house, or they may have come from an earlier building on site.[22]

The exact date of the remodeling, like so much else about the house, is not known. Replaced molding details and the woodwork of the staircase appear to date from the first or second decade of the nineteenth century. A receipt now in the collection of The New-York Historical Society, however, might support a slightly earlier date, since it indicates that sometime in the 1790s (the last digit of the date is illegible) a certain Mr. Schenck (no first name is given) bought 5,000 shingles at a cost of £30. 5s.[23] Assuming this receipt represents a major renovation of the exterior of the house, one might surmise that the interior alterations also happened then. A more likely possibility, though, is that Nicholas Schenck's son Nicholas Schenck, Jr., remodeled the house when he inherited it from his father in 1810.

Such a remodeling, in any case, indicates that the family had considerable cash to spare and provides evidence of a prosperous homestead—something resembling the flourishing rural properties depicted by the nineteenth-century Brooklyn artist James Ryder van Brunt *(see figs. 4.11 and 4.12)*. Although van Brunt no doubt exaggerated his subjects' charms, a properly managed Kings County homestead was unquestionably capable of providing its owner with a bountiful income. Journals kept from the 1790s to the 1830s by the proprietors of one such farm—John Baxter and his son Gerret—tell of the harvesting of flax, turnips, corn, salt hay, potatoes, cucumbers, radishes, apples, pears, cherries, apricots, parsnips, melons, chestnuts, walnuts, oats, barley, rye, wheat, strawberries, blackberries, cranberries, currants, peppers, beets, and dandelions. Then, too, of course, there was livestock. In addition to turkeys and ducks, the Baxters kept hogs, which they butchered for sausage and smoked pork; chickens, which they raised for eggs and meat; and cattle, which they bred for milk and beef and which also yielded tallow for candles and soap. What they could not consume of this varied produce them-

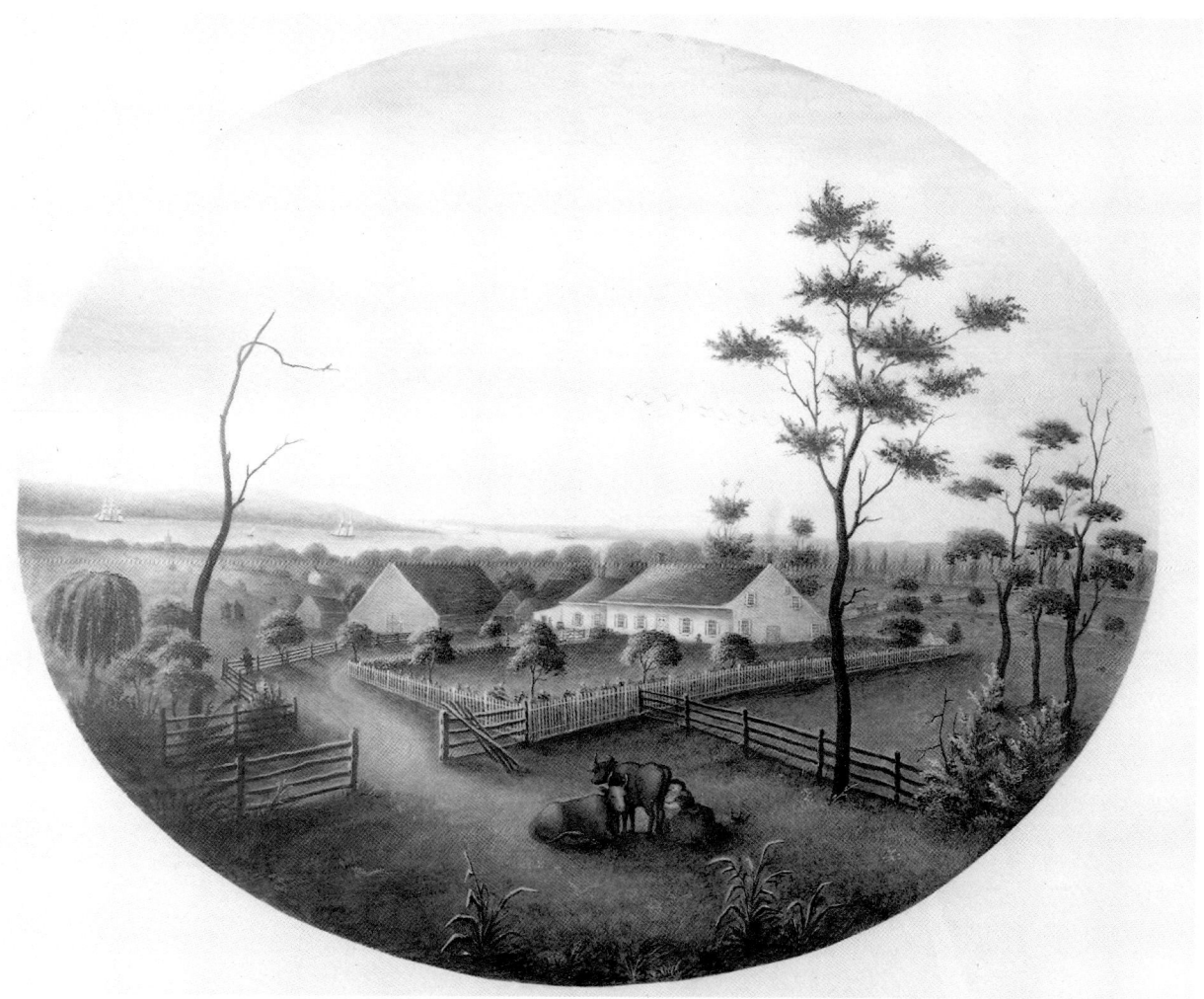

4.11. *James Ryder van Brunt (American, 1820–1916).* Dutch Homestead, *1864. Watercolor on paper, 13¾ x 16¾ inches. The Brooklyn Historical Society.*

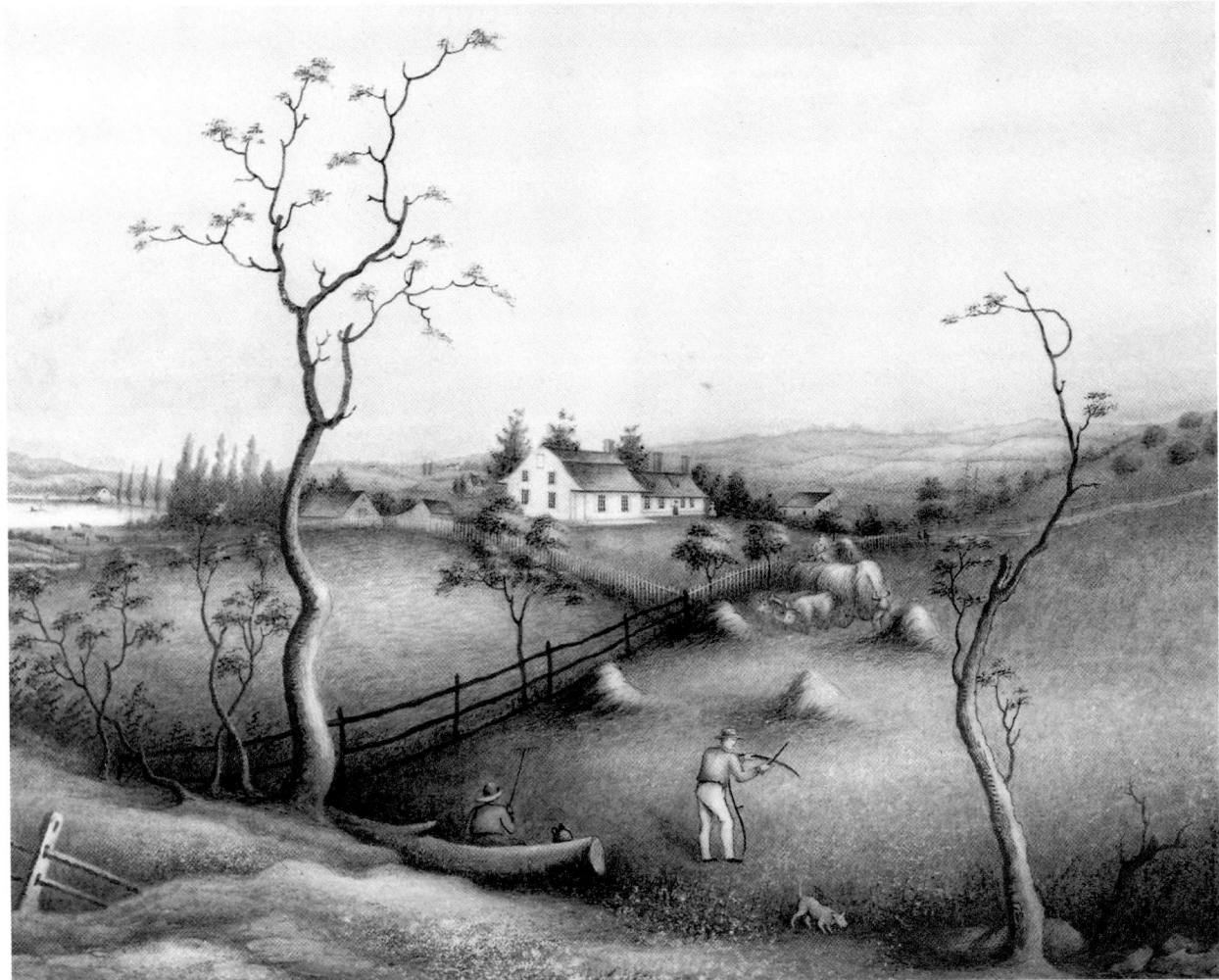

4.12. James Ryder van Brunt (American, 1820–1916). Homestead of Cornelius van Brunt, circa 1890. Watercolor on paper, 13 x 16¾ inches. The Brooklyn Historical Society.

selves they sent to market in Brooklyn or, in the case of barley, rye, and wheat, to local mills and then on to Brooklyn distillers.[24]

Obviously, life on such a homestead revolved as much around the barn as it did around the house. In fact, according to the Frenchman Michel-Guillaume-St. Jean de Crèvecoeur, who immigrated to New York in 1759, "The barn, with regard to its situation, size, convenience, and good finishing, is an object, in the mind of a farmer, superior even to that of his dwelling. Many don't care how they are lodged, provided that they have a good barn and barn-yard, and indeed it is the criterion by which I always judge of a farmer's prosperity. On this building he never begrudges his money."[25]

Since economic and sometimes literal survival depended on the safekeeping of livestock and crops during the harsh New York winters, the barn was almost always constructed before a permanent dwelling was built for the family. At least one of the two barns mentioned in the tax assessment of the Nicholas Schenck homestead in 1796, therefore, probably predated the first house on the property.

Although these barns are lost to us, it is possible to form a fairly clear picture of how they must have looked. Just as there existed a typical form of domestic architecture in areas of Dutch settlement in America so too there was a typical style of barn, seen here in a photograph of a barn built by the Vanderveer family of Flatbush around 1810 *(fig. 4.13)*. Unlike its Old World counterpart, the Dutch-American barn was constructed entirely of wood, with no stone or thatch. Although its spacious interior was the scene of such tasks as the cleaning of flax and the husking of corn, and although Crèvecoeur wrote that "in the summer the women resort to it, in order to spin their wool,"[26] it included no living quarters for people as European barns usually did.[27] Like the Schenck barns, which as mentioned earlier measured 40 x 56 and 36 x 46, most Dutch-American barns were rectangular in plan. "The middle-sized ones are commonly 50 x 30 feet," Crèvecoeur noted; "mine is 60 x 35 and cost $220.00."[28]

In his journeys in America from 1748 to 1751, the Swede Peter Kalm found such barns throughout New Jersey and New York from Trenton to north of Albany.

A NEW IDENTITY, A NEW STYLE

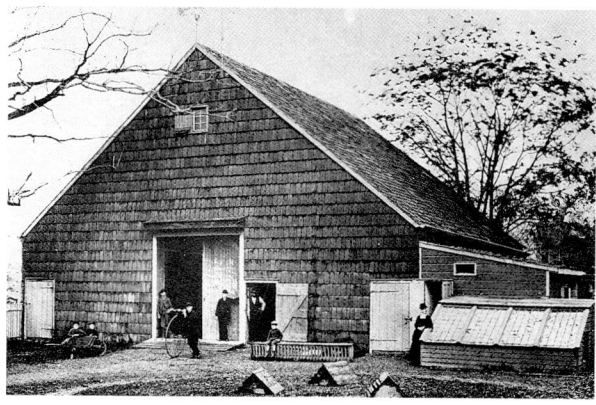

4.13. Vanderveer barn, Flatbush, circa 1875. Photograph courtesy of The Brooklyn Historical Society.

After visiting one near Princeton, he wrote:

> The barns had a peculiar kind of construction in this locality, of which I shall give a concise description. The main building was very large, almost the size of a small church; the roof was high, covered with wooden shingles, sloping on both sides, but not steep. The walls which supported it were not much higher than a full grown man; but on the other hand the breadth of the building was all the greater. In the middle was the threshing floor and above it, or in the loft or garret, they put the unthrashed grain, the straw, or anything else, according to the season. On one side were stables for the horses, and on the other for the cows. The young stock had also their particular stables or stalls, and in both ends of the building were large doors, so that one could drive in with a cart and horses through one of them, and go out the other. Here under one roof therefore were the thrashing floor, the barn, the stables, the hay loft, the coach house, etc.[29]

The Schenck barns probably stood as long as the homestead was used as a working farm, which as far as we can tell was until late in the nineteenth century. After inheriting the homestead in 1810 in return for a payment of $1,000 to his father's estate,[30] Nicholas Schenck, Jr., expanded the farm, buying an adjoining piece of property from a man by the name of Johannes Ditmars; this enlarged homestead he in turn bequeathed to his sons James and Stephen at his death in 1836.[31] Stephen died in 1842, but James, who was something of an eccentric, continued to occupy the place until almost the time of his death more than four decades later. Under his care the house began to fall into disrepair, and eventually, sometime after the Civil War, he leased both the house and the farm to a man named James Whittaker.

Much of what we know about Whittaker's tenancy derives from his granddaughter Lillian Tyler Pelham Bantz, who wrote to Museum curator Marvin Schwartz in 1964, sending along sketches of the house she herself had drawn from old family photographs *(see figs. 4.14 and 4.15)*. Mrs. Bantz had been told by her mother, Ida Whittaker Pelham, who claimed to have been born in the house, that Whittaker moved there with his wife and parents in 1867.[32] Never having married, James Schenck lived on in the house with his tenants and, according to another source, with a black man, called Uncle Sam, and the man's wife.[33] Recalling that her mother had told her that the Whittaker children referred to their family's landlord as Uncle Jimmie, Mrs. Bantz related a poignant account of James Schenck's last days:

> When my grandfather moved into the house, he rented it from James Schenck for $500.00. ... Uncle Jimmie got his rent but hoarded the money. He couldn't spend it on anything. My grandmother fed him, nursed him when he was ill and darned his socks. One day my Aunt Martha was sent in disgrace to an old dusty room full of newspapers. She started to read them and found dollar bills between the pages. It was Uncle Jimmie's hoard. My grandmother turned the money over to his relations. They came to claim it and take James Schenck away and he cried all the way down the lane.[34]

James Schenck died, in 1885, a wealthy man. His estate totaled $147,533.60, but of this only about $100 represented the value of his household goods—a reflection of his parsimony. Since he had no descendants, the homestead was divided into small lots and sold to the public, though according to Mrs. Bantz the Whittakers remained in the house until sometime between 1890 and 1894.[35] Thus the property passed out of the family that had owned it for two centuries. In 1896 the Brooklyn Parks Commission purchased the lot on which the house stood, near Seaview Avenue between Remsen Avenue and Canarsie Road, and incorporated it into Canarsie Beach Park.

Despite the efforts of a man named George Leinfelder, who became caretaker of the park in 1904 and took an active interest in the history of the house, the deterioration of the building was allowed to continue.[36] Although officials of the New York City Parks Department (which took over the Brooklyn parks when Brooklyn joined the city in 1898) made plans in 1922 to restore the house on site and requested $5,000 in their next year's budget for the purpose, these plans, despite rising public interest in the house, were never carried out.

In March 1923 the building was seriously damaged by a storm that blew off part of its roof. Though the planned restoration was perhaps no longer feasible after this pivotal calamity, the nascent historic-preservation movement remained hopeful, and an article in *The New York Times* in December 1924 took restoration of the house for granted. "It is interesting to note that there are three old Schenck family houses in Brooklyn [including the Jan Martense Schenck House],"

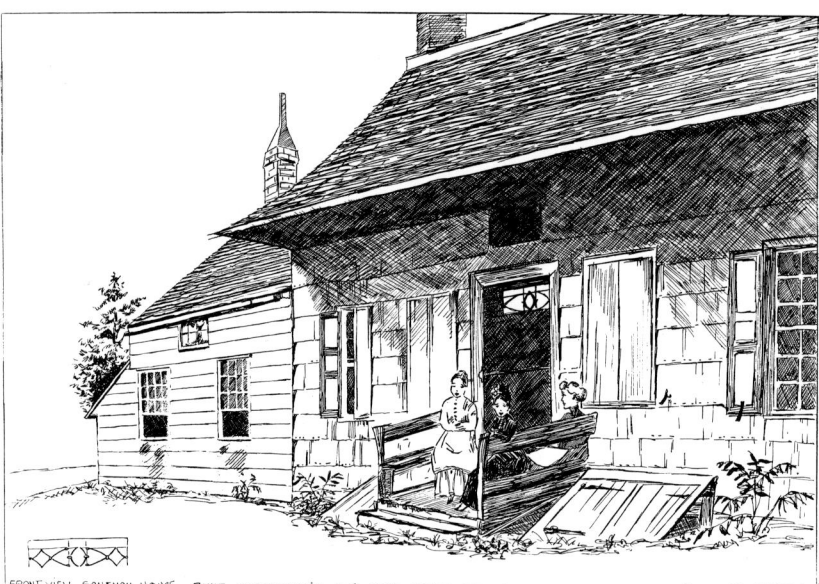

4.14. *Front view of the Nicholas Schenck House. Drawn by Lillian Tyler Pelham Bantz from a photograph of circa 1890.*

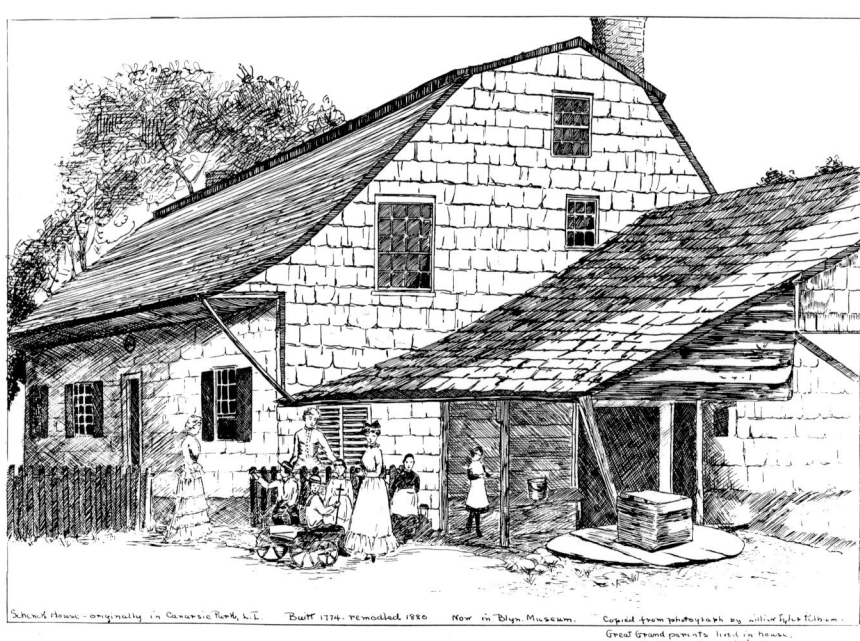

4.15. *Rear view of the Nicholas Schenck House. Drawn by Lillian Tyler Pelham Bantz from a photograph of circa 1890.*

the *Times* reported. "Two of them are already owned by the city, being assured of permanent preservation in two Brooklyn parks. One is in Highland Park [the Cornell-Schenck House, destroyed by fire in 1944] and the other is in Canarsie Park."[37] This article in turn prompted letters to the editor urging that the house be preserved because of its "immense value as a history lesson to the many children who go there"[38] and "to show our architects how much better are the lines of the Colonial houses ... than the wooden effigies of stone Greek temples, insinuated to our Northern climate, that they have given us for many years."[39]

The optimism expressed in the *Times* article proved unwarranted, however, for in spite of concern from many quarters nothing was done to stabilize the house, let alone restore it. By the late 1920s the building had been fenced off and turned into a storage shed for the park concession stand—a kiosk tacked ingloriously to its rear *(see fig. 4.16)*. By this time, too, the roof had collapsed almost entirely *(see figs. 4.17 and 4.18)*. In short, the house seemed doomed.

No doubt it would soon have disappeared altogether but for the interest that was then emerging in the concept of museum period rooms. In 1924 New York's Metropolitan Museum of Art had become the first American art museum to install a permanent collection of period rooms when it opened its renowned American Wing, and at The Brooklyn Museum the noted decorative arts historian Luke Vincent Lockwood had been making plans to install a similar collection since 1915.[40] Just as Lockwood was putting the finishing touches on the Museum's intallation in 1929,

A NEW IDENTITY, A NEW STYLE

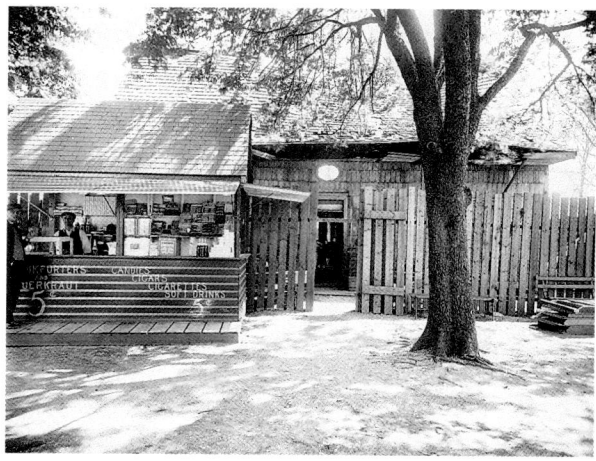

4.16. *The Nicholas Schenck House, circa 1929.*

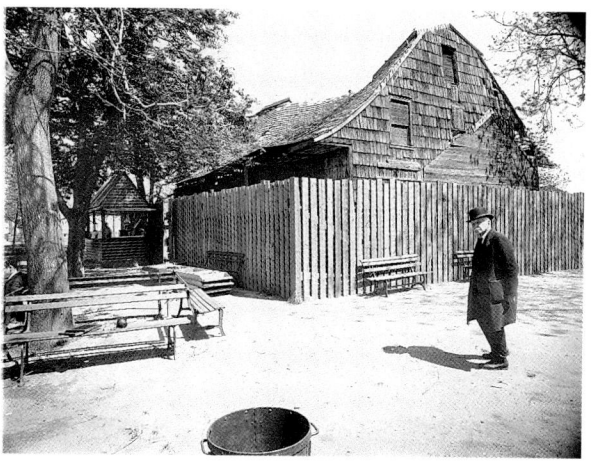

4.17. *The Nicholas Schenck House, circa 1929.*

a city budget crisis led to the last-minute acquisition of the Schenck rooms. As William Henry Fox, then the Museum's director, later recalled:

> It happened that in South Brooklyn [*sic*] there was a wooden house once in possession of the Schenck family, one of the original Dutch settlers. It was on a farm which was taken over by the City as a public park. In the course of time New York was attacked by one of its numerous spells of economic stringency produced by causes that required investigation, and on account of the expense of keeping the property in order, the authorities withdrew the caretakers. In consequence the neighbors of that immediate section began to help themselves to shutters, doors, shingles and various other parts of the old residence until it became evident that in a short time there would be nothing remaining of the Schenck House but the uprights and beams and being of combustible material, they were likely to disappear also. Aroused to this situation by the Brooklyn newspapers, the Commissioner of Parks begged the Museum to come to the rescue.[41]

Thus, in October 1929, all four ground floor rooms and the central stair hall of the Schenck House were transferred to the Museum's Department of Colonial and Early American Furniture, as the Department of Decorative Arts was then called. By December, they and the Museum's fourteen other period rooms had been installed and were ready to be opened to the public, marking the end of the effort to preserve the house on site.

Unfortunately, no records survive to document either the Schenck rooms' installation in the Museum or their removal from Canarsie. Evidence that would be routinely recorded today, such as indications of how the rooms were originally constructed, was apparently not gathered. In fact, the only information we have regarding the rooms *in situ* was assembled not by Museum

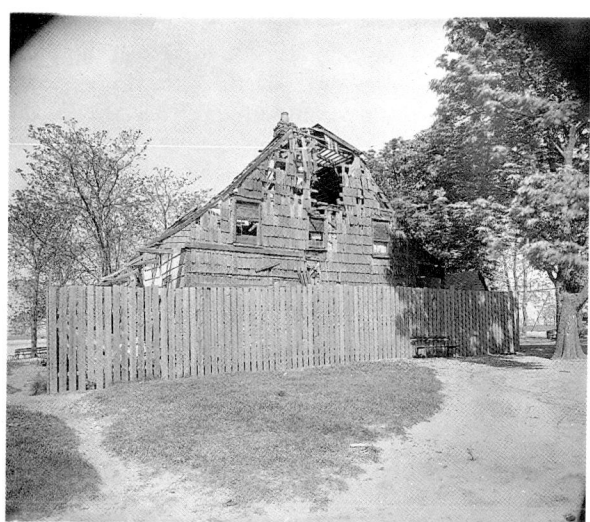

4.18. *The Nicholas Schenck House, circa 1929.*

curators but by the Canarsie Park caretaker George Leinfelder, who noted in 1922 that the insulation between the outer shingles and the interior walls was a "thick layer of clay and meadow grass hard as mortar after all these years."[42] Thanks to Leinfelder, we also know that the laths of the house were of oak, as were the structural horizontal and vertical members, and that the original floors (replaced when the rooms came to the Museum) were of white pine cut in wide, thick planks. Lacking a detailed description of the rooms before their removal, however, we cannot know with any certainty precisely how much of the material now seen in the house as it is installed in the Museum was originally part of the house as it stood on site. The best we can do is to compare photographs of the rooms *in situ* with the rooms in place, a process that seems to indicate that most of the elements now at the Museum are original rather than replacements.

This question of the extent of the rooms' originality becomes all the more puzzling when we consider that the shell of the Nicholas Schenck House remained standing in Canarsie Beach Park at least until July 1936, when draftsmen of the Historic American Buildings Survey documented the house with measured drawings and noted on these that the house had been "restored in part in [The] Brooklyn Museum." The chief draftsman of the survey, Robert G. Kron, recalled in 1976 that portions of the house were still standing in late 1936 or early 1937 and that some of the interior fittings, including part of a chair rail and certain elements of the wainscoting, had not yet been removed.[43] Whether these fittings and other material came to the Museum when the building was finally and entirely torn down is not known. But it seems unlikely that such essential structural members as the ceiling beams could have been removed while the house still stood in any form.

As if a lack of documentation were not enough to preclude positive identification of just what elements came to the Museum and when, the rooms were installed at the Museum as a mirror image of their original arrangement on site. To appreciate how difficult it can be to determine exactly what was originally where, one need only compare the floor plan of the house drawn by the Historic American Buildings Survey *(fig. 4.8)* with a plan of the house showing the rooms reversed as they are in the Museum *(fig. 4.19)*.

In the process of making this reversal, which was probably done in order to satisfy certain requirements of gallery organization, the installers made alterations in a number of the architectural elements, some of which were necessary in order to accommodate the switch and others of which are inexplicable. The rear entry door, for example, had its hinges and doorknob reversed, and in the parlor the cupboard that was originally next to the exterior wall exchanged places with the cupboard that abutted the opposite wall. In the dining room the antechamber to the kitchen wing remained along the interior wall, but it was made square rather than angled and its relationship to the central area of paneling around the fireplace was altered *(compare figs. 5.16 and 5.21)*.

Despite these alterations, however, the Nicholas

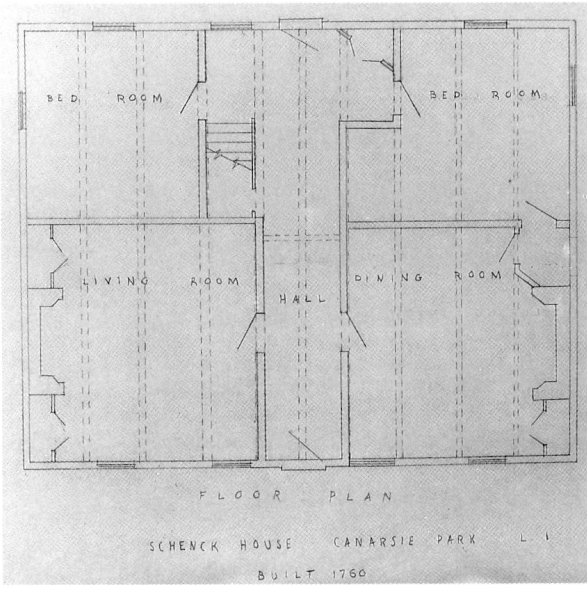

4.19. Floor plan, the Nicholas Schenck House as installed in The Brooklyn Museum.

Schenck House rooms at The Brooklyn Museum retain for all intents and purposes both their on-site character and their historical value. They not only exhibit the style of a particular period but also give us some idea of how that style came about by revealing the major remodeling of a building that was a living, evolving entity. In so doing, they illustrate the development of the distinctive architecture of rural Dutch Kings County from the late eighteenth to the early nineteenth century and reflect how the society that produced that architecture managed to preserve a sense of its separate culture even as it accepted more and more from the culture of the larger, more heterogeneous society into which it was being assimilated. If they also present a number of unsolved mysteries, therein lies both a challenge and a hope: that, with further research, some of these mysteries may yet be solved.

CHAPTER
FIVE

Consumer Goods and Family Heirlooms, or The Morn of Independence

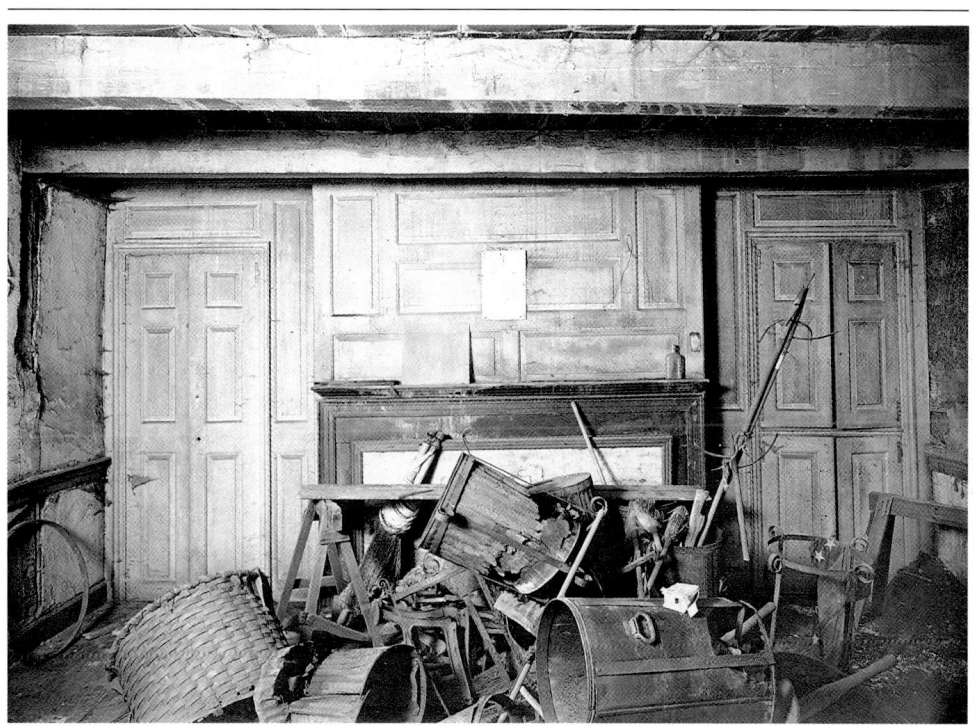

5.1. *Parlor, Nicholas Schenck House, in situ,* circa 1929.

Over the course of years between 1929, when they were first installed in The Brooklyn Museum, and the late 1960s, when they were closed to the public and turned into a storage space for part of the Museum's furniture collection, the four rooms and central stair hall of the Nicholas Schenck House changed repeatedly as each generation of curators gathered more knowledge about life in early New York, refined the interpretation of history offered by the Museum's period room galleries, and added more and better objects to the rooms from the Museum's ever-improving collection of decorative arts. Yet one thing remained constant: the rooms were, for the most part, presented to the public as interiors dating to the third quarter of the eighteenth century, even though they showed clear signs of the major alterations the house had undergone either in the late 1790s or, more likely, in the early nineteenth century.

In the early 1980s, when plans were made for the current reinstallation of the rooms, these alterations posed a difficult question. Should they be ignored as they had been in the past? Should the house be reconstructed, or "restored," to achieve a look in keeping with what we know about its original construction? Or should the rooms be exhibited for what they really are: examples of 1770s interior architecture remodeled in the late eighteenth or the early nineteenth century as the tastes and needs of their occupants changed?

To take the first option seemed dishonest, while the second option, in turn, appeared impractical, since the alterations were so extensive that reconstruction of an eighteenth-century ideal would be based at best on speculation. The final option, however, represented an opportunity to exhibit rooms that, together with the Jan Martense Schenck House, would demonstrate the changing lifestyles of one Dutch-American family over the course of several generations and more than a century of time. It allowed, indeed called for, the exhibition of a living architecture, one which, like that of most buildings, changed over time rather than remaining static.

The rooms were installed, accordingly, as they might have looked in the 1820s during the life of Nicholas Schenck, Jr., son of the original builder. Although each of the rooms has its own reasons for looking the way it does in the current installation, they all have certain features in common—features that reflect the economic, social, and cultural history of Dutch families in America in the early nineteenth century.

Like most Dutch-American farm families of the time, the Schencks were a family with a reasonable income but apparently few pretensions to style. As such, they would have lived out their active lives in these rooms among objects whose primary purpose was use and not decoration. In early nineteenth-century genre paintings and family portraits showing comparable rural interiors one thing becomes immediately evident: such rooms were seldom decorated consistently in the style of any one period. Rather, old things that were still useful took their place beside newer, more stylish furniture. The Schenck rooms, therefore, are furnished to suggest how they might have evolved as generations of household goods accumulated, as if they had grown as naturally as a country garden until there was a comfortable clutter of dissimilar objects that had all finally found their proper place and use.

The rooms also reflect how the Dutch, as have so many ethnic groups since, struggled to maintain some trace of their own cultural identity while blending into the mainstream American society they were helping to create. By this time, in the 1820s, the Dutch had spent two centuries in America. Their cultural memory had faded, their language had changed, and many of their customs had passed away. Not much more than their names remained Dutch, and their primary identity was now American. Dutch heritage had become a curious fact—perhaps a source of pride but hardly their principal allegiance. Still, old customs die hard, and their material remains are left behind. So the Schenck rooms include, among articles and architecture that reflect the pervasive Englishness of early nineteenth-century American culture, items such as a *kas* that attest to the Dutch roots of a people with a distinctive past. Stasis and change are seen side by side as the process of assimilation nears completion. Speeding this process along, moreover, is a new force—the Industrial Revolution—which now made available to a wide public, through mass production, goods previously enjoyed only by the rich.

In a more general sense, the Nicholas Schenck rooms illustrate as well a major, relatively recent development in Western domestic living: the assignment of particular functions to particular rooms. Thus, unlike the two multipurpose rooms of the Jan Schenck House, which as we have seen are called merely the north room and the south room, these rooms have names that give some indication of the use to which they would have been put.

THE PARLOR

This room, originally the front east room of the house, was probably always the "best" room. It was adorned along the fireplace wall with elaborate paneling and was located on the opposite side of the house from the kitchen wing, away from the odors and activities of cooking. Nicholas Schenck, Sr., considered it of such status that before he died in 1810 he stipulated in his will "that my dear wife—Jane—Schenck [apparently his second wife, though no such marriage is recorded] shall have to her own use the easternmost front room in my Dwelling house for and During the time she shall remain my Widow."[1] Following eighteenth-century custom, this room had probably originally been a room of mixed usage, and it likely served Jane Schenck as both a parlor and a bedroom. The possibility exists that she continued to use it as such through the 1820s, for though the date of her death cannot be established with any certainty, the *Long Island Star* of December 12, 1832, notes the death in Flatlands of a Jane Schenck described as the eighty-nine-year-old widow of Captain Nicholas Schenck. Today in the Museum, however, in order to demonstrate the trend toward specific room usage that developed in the early nineteenth century, the room is installed as if it had been converted to exclusive use as a parlor.

In the house's final days on site at Canarsie Beach Park, the room was used for the storage of equipment and trash and suffered much abuse. Still, except for a side wall of peeling wallpaper, a photograph taken shortly before the room's removal to the Museum in 1929 (*fig. 5.1*) reveals little actual decay, showing an intact fireplace wall and an apparently well-preserved ceiling of rough-hewn beams supporting exposed floorboards above.

For its first installation at the Museum, the room was scrubbed clean and equipped with a new floor that was stained and polished in a twentieth-century manner (*see figs. 5.2 and 5.3*). The walls and ceiling were painted white, as was all the woodwork except the

5.2. Parlor, Nicholas Schenck House, as installed in The Brooklyn Museum, circa 1929.

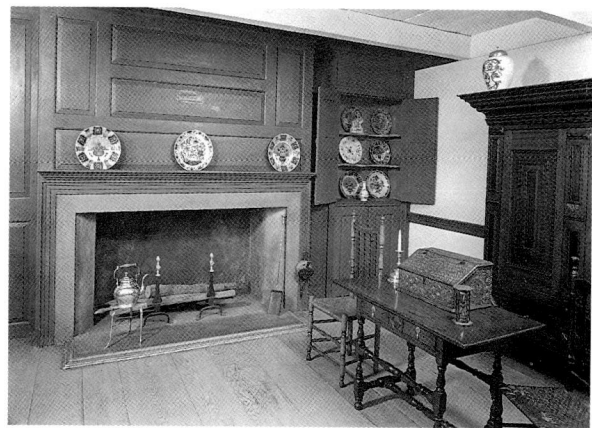

5.4. Parlor, Nicholas Schenck House, as installed in The Brooklyn Museum, late 1930s or early 1940s.

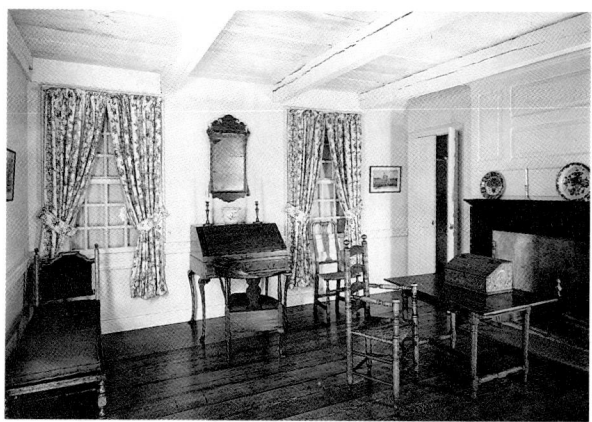

5.3. Parlor, Nicholas Schenck House, as installed in The Brooklyn Museum, circa 1929.

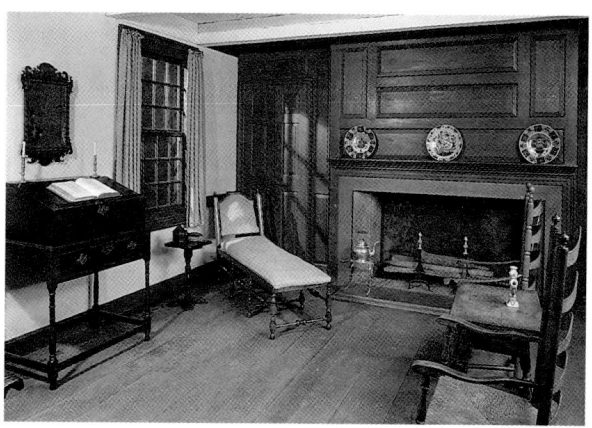

5.5. Parlor, Nicholas Schenck House, as installed in The Brooklyn Museum, late 1930s or early 1940s.

early nineteenth-century mantelpiece, which was painted black or possibly dark brown.[2] Modern chintz curtains were hung at the windows to cover the nineteenth-century window frames; assorted eighteenth-century furniture, including a New York *kas,* was distributed generously throughout the room; and Dutch delft ceramics were displayed in one of the cupboards and used to decorate the mantel.

Although the installation reflected an honest attempt to envision the eighteenth century, especially considering the limited knowledge of the time and the Museum's then-meager collection of objects, by today's standards it fell short. We now know, for example, that the woodwork was probably not originally white and that such stiffly tailored curtains were never used in the 1700s. Furthermore, in the eighteenth century, furniture would not have been so casually arranged but would have been placed against the walls when not in use and brought out when needed. Evidently the curators of the late 1920s, though they eschewed Victorian furniture and decoration in favor of the colonial, were unable to reject the comfortable Victorian arrangement of furniture in a room.

The installation apparently changed little during the next several years, for a guide to the Museum's period rooms published in 1936 shows it looking just as it did in 1929. However, sometime before the entire house was refurbished in 1967 (most likely in the late 1930s or the early 1940s), the woodwork was stripped of all its old paint and painted a dull blue-gray, possibly on the basis of visual evidence found at the time. In addition, the floor was stripped and lightened in color, the furniture was moved around, and the curtains were changed (*see figs. 5.4 and 5.5*). The effect, though, remained much the same: an eighteenth-century room with nineteenth-century alterations furnished with eighteenth-century furniture arranged in a nineteenth- or twentieth-century manner.

Nor was this effect significantly altered by the refurbishing of 1967. At that time tin-glazed earthenware tiles representing scenes from the Bible were installed around the fireplace opening and some of the delft plates were hung on the wall by means of wire strung through the pierced holes originally placed in their foot rims for that purpose. But the principal change of 1967 did not concern the look of the room or its furnishings at all, involving instead the installation of a system of taped commentary, available at the push of a button, and the addition of a mannequin representing Nicholas Schenck, Sr.'s first wife, Willemtje, placing linens in the family *kas* (*see fig. 5.6*).[3] This attempt to bring the room to life and to convey some sense of its social history was to prove short-lived, for the house was closed to the public a year or so after the renovation and was to remain closed until the completion of the current reinstallation in October 1984.

For this latest installation, the room has assumed a radically different look (*see figs. 5.7 and 5.8*), conveying the spirit of a parlor redecorated in the 1820s with a mix of slightly old-fashioned furniture and more up-to-date stylish pieces, including the sort of manufactured goods, both imported and American, then becoming more available to the rural middle class. A simple rural interior whose character was suggested by such period paintings as Deborah Goldsmith's portrait of the Talcott family (*fig. 5.9*), done in 1832, and Jacob Maentel's watercolor of John Hamm (*fig. 5.10*), painted about 1830, it combines wallpaper sprinkled with a small floral print with a vividly colored striped carpet called a Venetian, thus also reflecting — besides a natural combination of old and new furnishings — a visual sensibility that accepted large adjacent areas of unrelated patterns more easily than current taste is able to do.

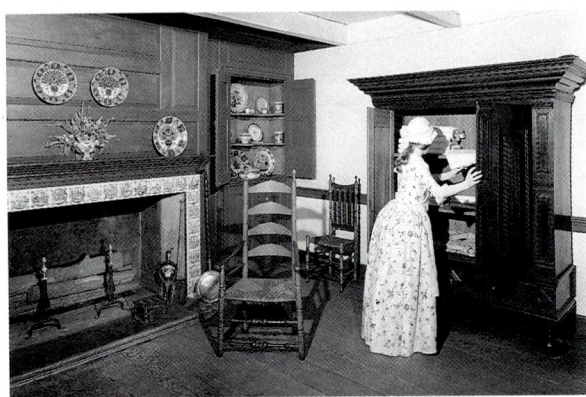

5.6. *Parlor, Nicholas Schenck House, as installed in The Brooklyn Museum, circa 1968.*

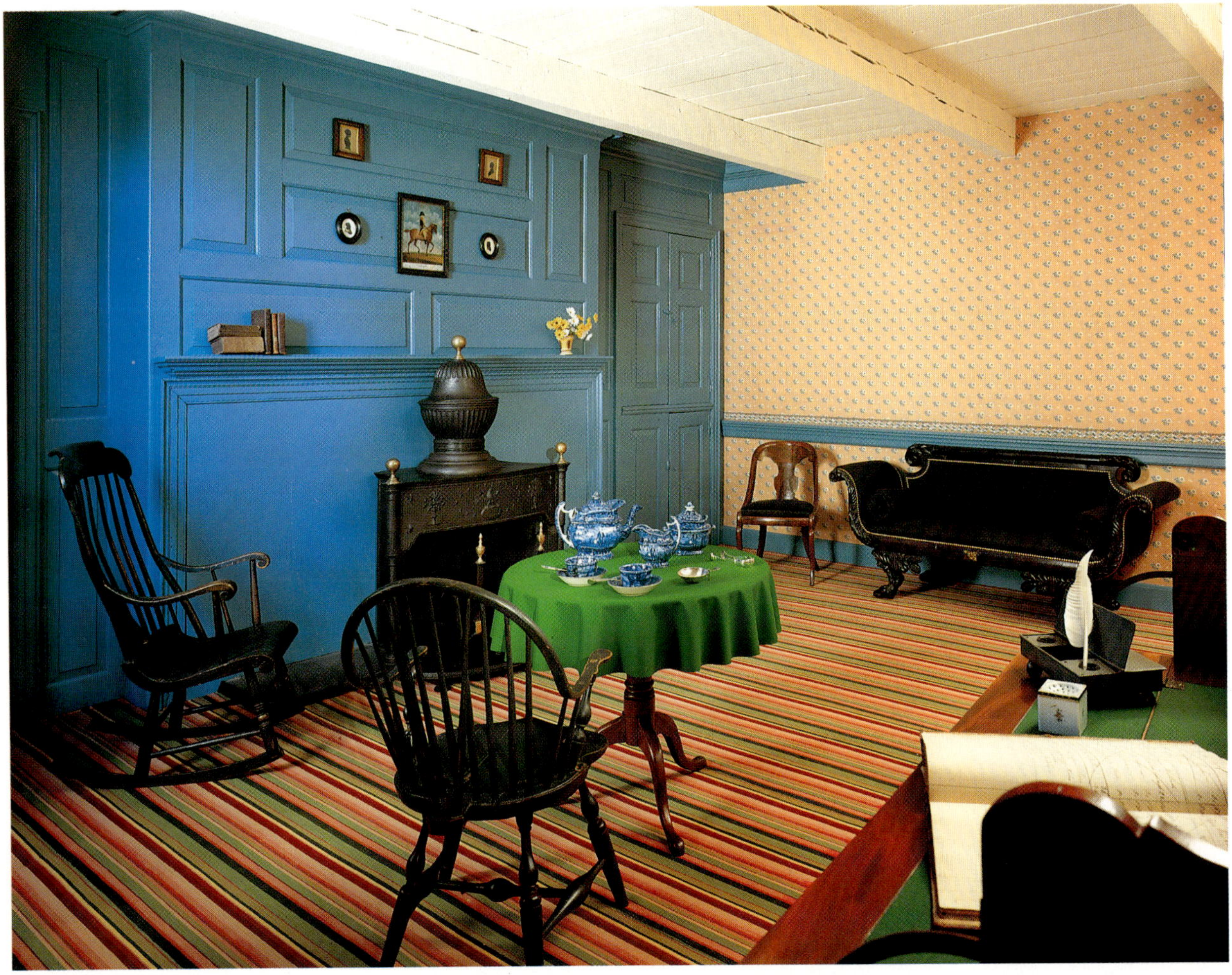

5.7. *Parlor, Nicholas Schenck House, as installed in The Brooklyn Museum, 1984. Photograph by Paul Warchol.*

5.8. *Parlor, Nicholas Schenck House, as installed in The Brooklyn Museum, 1984. Photograph by Paul Warchol.*

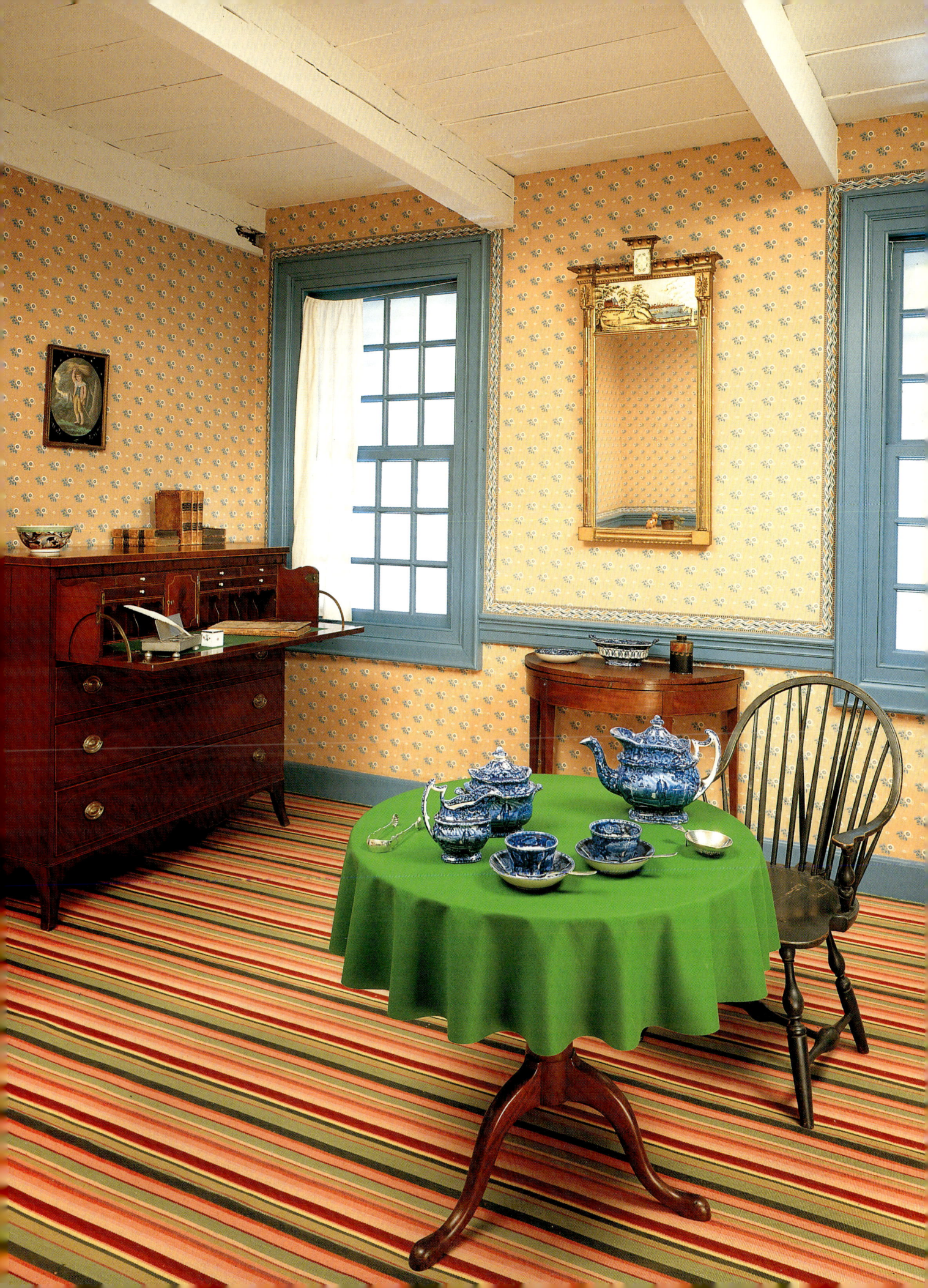

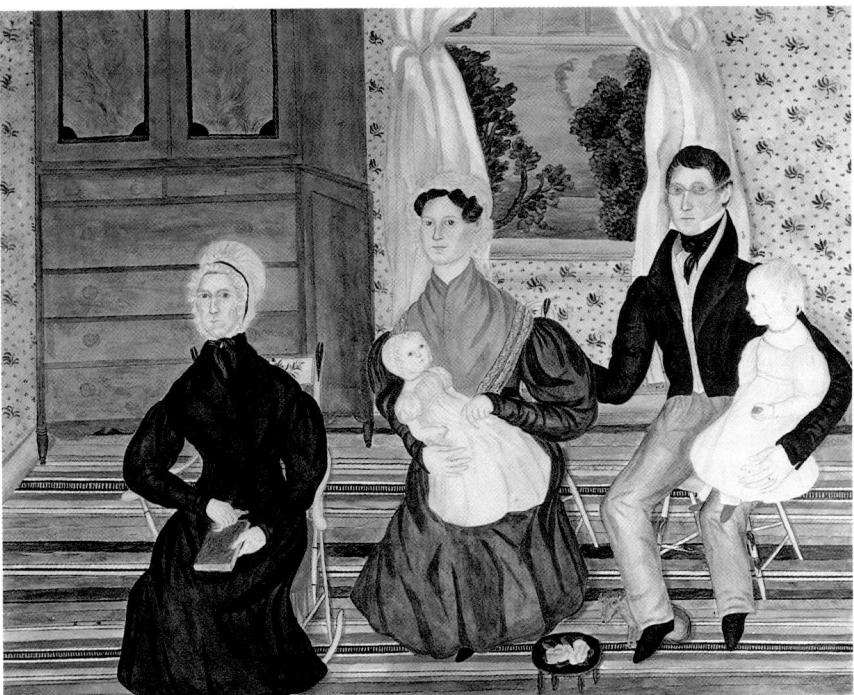

5.9. *Deborah Goldsmith (American, 1808–1836).* The Talcott Family, *1832. Watercolor on paper, 14 × 18 inches. Abby Aldrich Rockefeller Folk Art Center, Williamsburg, Virginia.*

5.10. *Jacob Maentel (American, 1763–1863).* John Hamm, *circa 1830. Watercolor on paper, 13¼ × 9¾ inches. Photograph courtesy of Sotheby's, New York.*

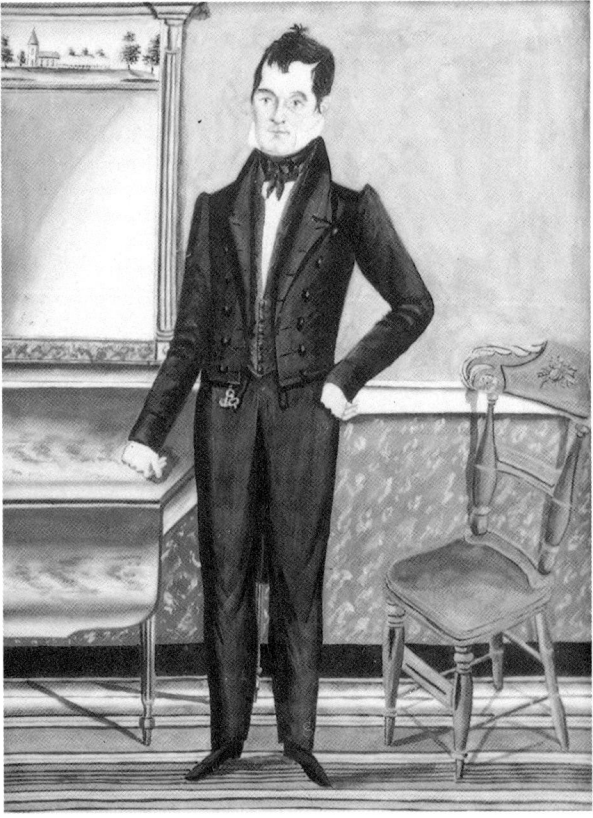

The room's wallpaper is a reproduction, by Brunschwig & Fils, of a French document paper dating from 1825–35 in the Musée des Arts Décoratifs, Paris. Although the original has a mauve ground, the reproduction is on pale orange, or terra-cotta, another popular color of the period and one that is also found — along with blue, black, and white — on the room's border paper.

This border paper, reproduced by Brunschwig from a period example in the Society for the Preservation of New England Antiquities, is used in the parlor to surround the door and window frames and to outline the chair rail. In the late eighteenth and the early nineteenth century, border papers were frequently installed in this way, serving not only to add finish and to provide decoration but also to conceal uneven edges on the wallpaper itself. Their use in this manner is well documented in interiors ranging from the Harrison Gray Otis House in Boston, in which wallpaper was installed in 1796, to the French-Robertson House on the St. Lawrence River in Canada, in which paper was hung in the early 1820s.[4]

Newspaper advertisements of the time indicate that the Schencks would have been able to choose wallpaper and border from a wide selection of imported and domestic papers available in New York. As early as November 12, 1800, the New York merchant Caleb Alder advertised "a large and elegant assortment of English glazed and plain Paper-Hangings, of the newest pattern with rich borders to suit."[5] In November 1803 his widow announced that "she has just received, and has now open for sale, an Elegant and Extensive Assortment of Paper Hangings, of English, French and American manufacture."[6] And in the same year the New York dealers Cornelius and John Crygier boasted that their stock included "about 10,000 pieces from their own manufacturing in this city, which are equal to any imported, superior to any manufactured in the United States and at least fifteen percent cheaper."[7]

Venetian carpeting (which despite its name apparently has nothing to do with Venice) was just as easy to obtain. In fact, the Schencks could have made it themselves; that at least one branch of the family might have made such carpeting is suggested by the 1833 inventory of the estate of Nicholas Schenck, Jr.'s brother John, which includes one loom and five spinning wheels.[8] A simply woven fabric whose pattern is derived from colored wool warp threads, Venetian carpeting was often made at home in rural settings, either by the women of the household or by itinerant weavers. By the 1820s, however, the Schencks could simply have bought such a carpet from one of the countless New York carpet dealers who advertised Venetians along with Brussels, ingrain, and Scotch carpeting.

The many New York inventories in which Venetian carpets are listed, sometimes by the yard, indicate that Venetians were relatively inexpensive. The inventory taken of the estate of a New Yorker named Garrit B. Akeel in December 1829, for instance, lists in an upper-story "middle" room of Akeel's house a Venetian carpet valued at $3, considerably less than the Brussels carpet listed in a parlor at the back of the house at a value of $75.[9]

Examples of Venetians preserved in textile collections throughout the country demonstrate that dozens of variations existed on the theme of the multicolored, striped carpet. Despite years of use and fading, many of these are still vividly colored.[10] Durable and decorative, then, in addition to affordable, Venetian carpeting would have been a likely addition to the parlor of a family like the Schencks.

Another manufactured item the Schencks might well have acquired for this room by the 1820s is a cast-iron stove like the one now installed in front of the closed-up fireplace. Although this fireplace, set in the wall and surrounded by paneling in the English fashion, represented an improvement over the large hooded fireplace without jambs used by the elder Nicholas Schenck's grandfather Jan Martense Schenck, it was still an inefficient means of heating and probably would have been sealed when iron stoves became readily available. That it was closed up at some point is confirmed by the photograph of the room *in situ* referred to earlier (*fig. 5.1*), and that its function was assumed by a stove is indicated by the 1885 inventory of the estate of James Schenck, the last family occupant, which lists two stoves in this house.

The stove chosen for the installation, actually more like an open fireplace of cast iron, is an outgrowth of Benjamin Franklin's invention of 1742. Although unmarked, it bears a clear resemblance to stoves patented by James Wilson of Poughkeepsie, New York, in 1816, exhibiting the pervasive neoclassical taste of the time in the eagle decoration on its front panel and the classical maidens on its interior jambs. The fluted urn on top is both a decorative feature and a device for trapping heat and radiating it throughout the room.[11]

Stoves similar to this were certainly used in Kings County. In fact, the aforementioned 1833 inventory of the estate of the younger Nicholas Schenck's brother John, who also lived in Flatlands, includes a Franklin stove valued at $12.[12]

During work on the reinstallation of the parlor in the early 1980s, the removal of the mantel above the stove revealed on the woodwork underneath an area of bright blue paint that professional analysis suggested was original. Although all the woodwork in the house had been stripped at least once since the rooms' removal to the Museum, this indication of the house's paint history had luckily been spared, no doubt because it was hidden. While it most likely represents the eighteenth-century color of the room's woodwork, it is quite possible that the woodwork was painted blue well into the nineteenth century. Blue, it should be noted, was a popular color for woodwork on Long Island in the early 1800s, although the blue most often used was not as bright as this. In any event, bright blue is the only color for which there is any evidence of use in this house on site, and so the woodwork throughout the house, including of course the mantel itself, has been painted an intense blue (Munsell #5B 5/6).

In addition to being convenient shelves for the storage of commonly used items, mantels, along with the chimney breasts above them, are a natural focus of decoration. In the early nineteenth century they were often adorned with ceramics while chimney breasts were frequently ornamented with silhouettes or patriotic prints in a symmetrical arrangement. Such customs can be seen in John Lewis Krimmel's *Quilting Frolic* of 1813 (*fig. 5.11*) and his *Country Wedding: Bishop White Officiating* of 1819 (*fig. 5.12*). In the Schenck parlor the spirit of this decoration has been re-created with silhouettes and an églomisé painting of George Washington on horseback. On the mantel, books are casually stored for ready use and flowers fill an English creamware vase.

This type of creamware, decorated with various colors to imitate mocha stone, or moss agate, was popular in America in the 1820s. Often called mocha ware, it features a glaze produced by spattering a mixture of tobacco juice, stale urine, and turpentine onto a wet, colored slip. The drops of the mixture form assorted branching shapes that resemble the markings on moss agate.

Unlike the ceramics in the Jan Martense Schenck House—objects of Chinese porcelain and Dutch tin-glazed delftware that would have represented large expenditures to their owners—early nineteenth-century ceramics like mocha ware were inexpensive, having been mass-produced for a broad market. They are liberally used, accordingly, throughout not only this room but the entire house as well in order to illustrate that the Industrial Revolution and advances in ceramic technology had by this time made ceramics highly affordable to the American middle class.

These ceramics, however, were still imported rather than made in America. Some, like the sander, or pounce pot, on the parlor desk, were made in China expressly for the Western market. But most were English, including many wares designed specifically for cheap sale to Americans.

One such ware, transfer-printed earthenware decorated with American views and patriotic subjects, is represented in the parlor by the tea service on the mahogany tilt-top tea table, which has been drawn out into the room and covered with a green baize cloth as if for an afternoon tea. Made in England by Enoch Wood and Sons (in business from 1819 to 1846), this service depicts George Washington standing in New York's Bowling Green. Displayed with it on the table are coin silver spoons by various New York silversmiths and a silver tea strainer by Elias Pelletreau (1726–1810) of Southampton, Long Island.

The table itself (*fig. 5.13*) is attributed to Nathaniel Dominy V, a member of the famous family of craftsmen who worked in East Hampton, Long Island, from the 1760s to about 1840. It may have been made in 1792, for besides two tea tables the Dominys kept for themselves in 1796, Dominy family business accounts list only three such tables made for sale, all of them produced in 1792 and sold for either £1. 4s. or £1. 14s.[13]

By the 1820s, this style of table would have seemed out-of-date. In fact, the cabriole legs, snake feet, and general form of the table would have made it conservative in design even at the time of its manufacture. It was a valuable and functional piece of furniture, however, and would have continued to find use for many generations.

The Windsor chair next to the table also represents an old-fashioned form. Such chairs were used in the eighteenth century in a wide variety of places, from rural and urban taverns to Independence Hall in Philadelphia. Sturdy and attractive, they became a standard form of seating in middle-class homes. The Schencks quite likely did keep one in this room in the 1820s, for the Windsor's popularity hardly waned in the nineteenth century. Related chairs are seen in the Krimmel paintings, and Windsors are listed in many Kings County inventories of the 1830s.

The parlor Windsor is branded "I. Always," which suggests that it was made by either James or John Always, two brothers who worked in New York between 1786 and 1815. (The initial *J.* was commonly written *I.* at the time.) In 1801, James Always advertised that he wished "to inform his customers, and the public in general, that he continues to carry on the Windsor Chair Business, at No. 40 James-street, where may be had, Windsor Chairs of every description, both plain and fancy colors." This chair's dark green finish, the most common color found on Windsors, was no doubt considered plain, as another part of the Always advertisement indicates. "He will paint them green or

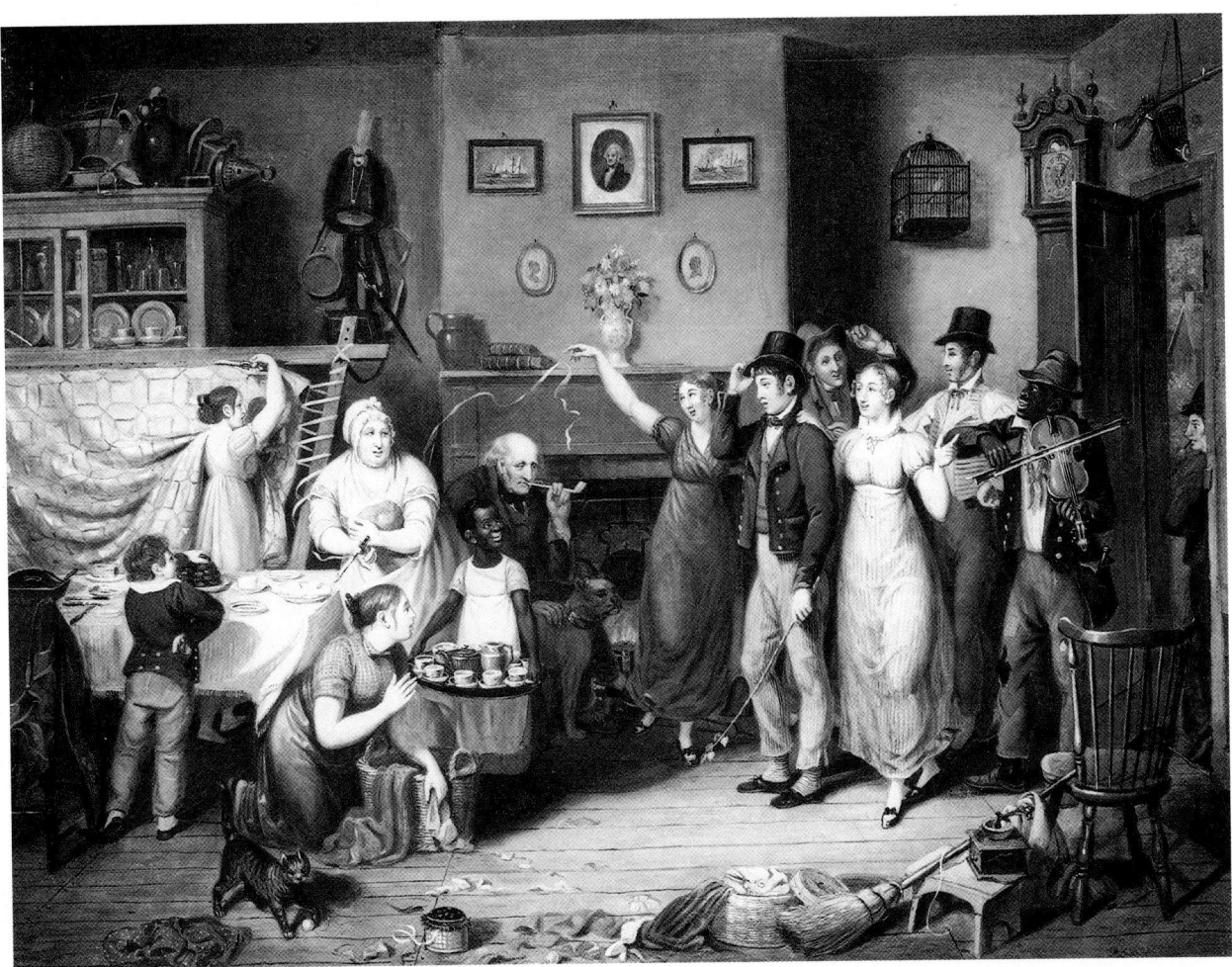

5.11. John Lewis Krimmel (American, born Germany, 1787–1821). Quilting Frolic, 1813. Oil on canvas, 16⅞ × 22⅜ inches. The Henry Francis du Pont Winterthur Museum, Winterthur, Delaware.

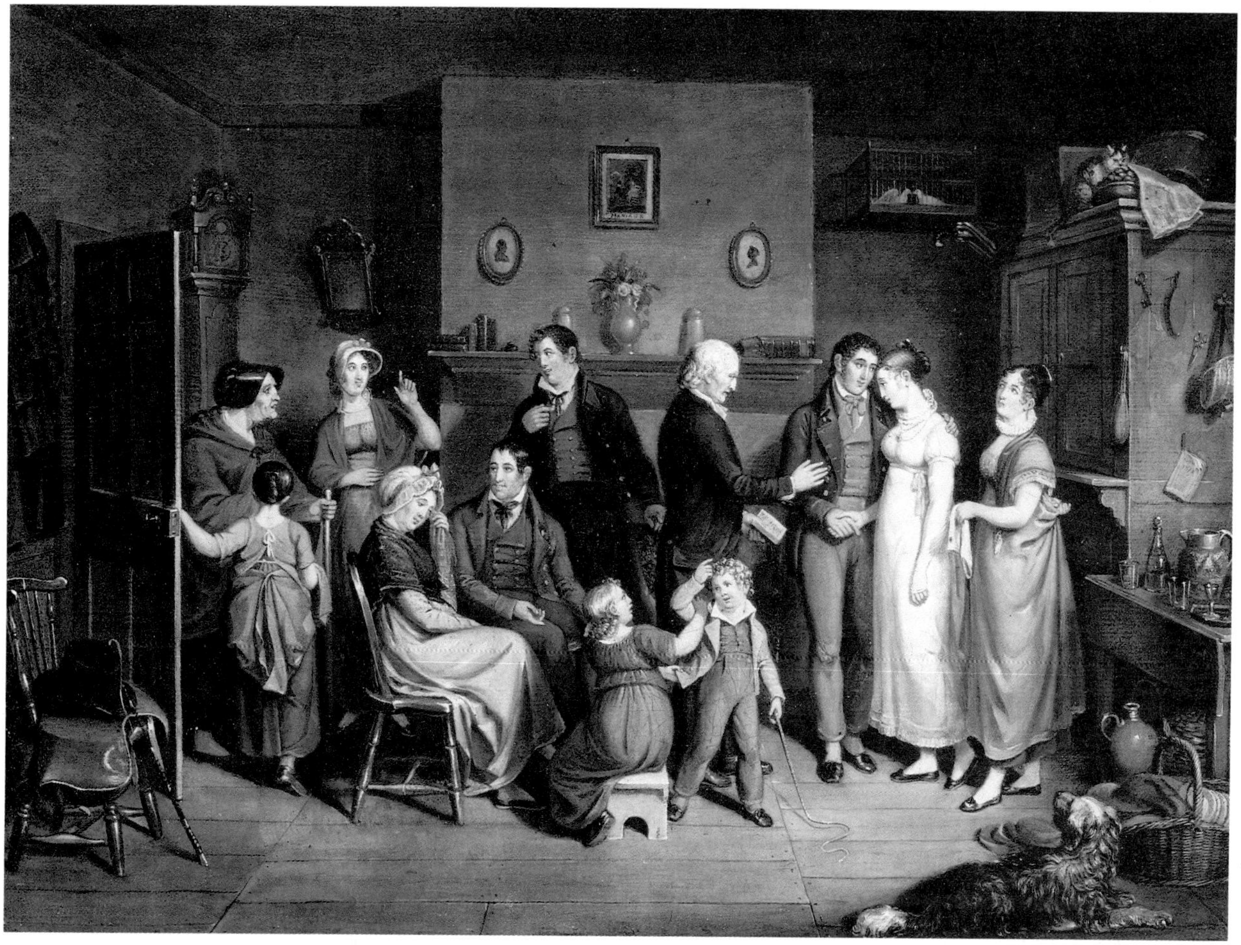

CONSUMER GOODS AND FAMILY HEIRLOOMS, OR THE MORN OF INDEPENDENCE

5.12. John Lewis Krimmel (American, born Germany, 1787–1821). *Country Wedding: Bishop White Officiating, 1819.* Oil on canvas, 16¾ × 22½ inches. The Pennsylvania Academy of the Fine Arts, Philadelphia.

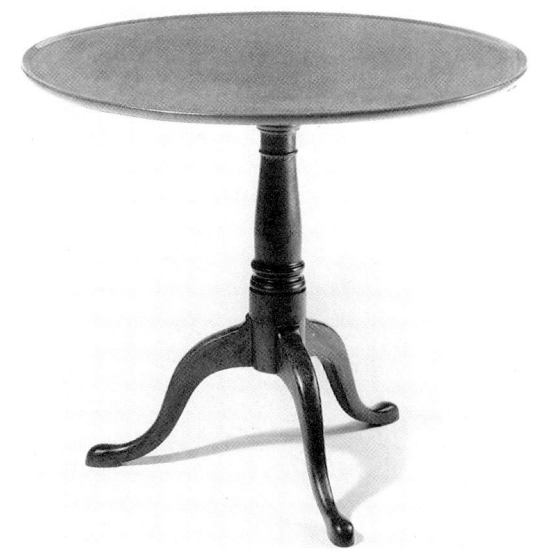

5.13. Attributed to Nathaniel Dominy V (American, 1770–1852). *Tea Table, 1790–1800.* East Hampton, New York. Mahogany, 27½ × 32 × 32 inches. The Brooklyn Museum 1989.67, *Gift of the Wunsch Americana Foundation, Inc.*

[alternatively] any fancy color," it reads, "in the best manner, at a very low price."[14]

Two pieces that would have been a bit more up-to-date than the tea table and the chair are the card table between the windows (*fig. 5.14*) and the secretary by the door (*fig. 5.15*), although they, too, would have been out of style by the 1820s. The work of anonymous New York craftsmen, both are in the pared-down Federal, or American neoclassical, style of the turn of the century. The card table, which according to family legend has a history of use in this house, may be one of three mahogany tables valued at $1.50 each in the 1885 inventory of James Schenck's estate. Its lack of inlaid decoration indicates that, although stylish when it was made, it was a relatively inexpensive model of its form. Folded and placed against the wall when not in use, it might well have been paired with a looking glass like the one now hung above it, which is a good example of a type of glass popular around 1810 and is on loan to the Museum from a descendant of the Schencks. The secretary, which has a history of ownership in yet another branch of the family and is inscribed "Nelly Allen's Secretary for Elisabeth S. Schenck," is of finer craftsmanship than the table and

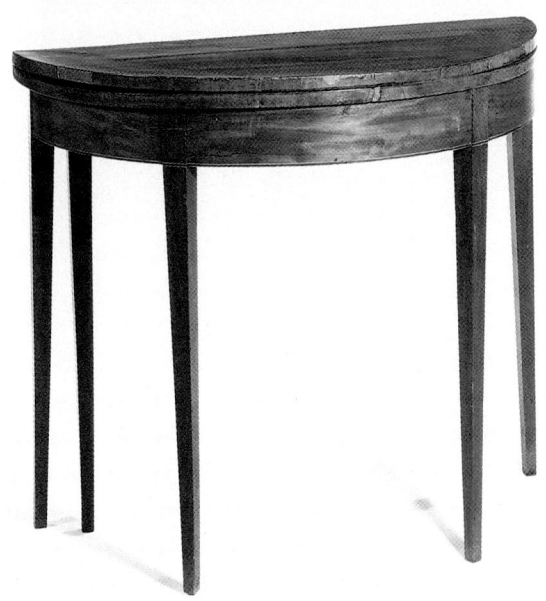

5.14. Card Table, *circa 1800. New York. Mahogany veneer, 28⅜ × 35 × 17½ inches. The Brooklyn Museum 49.176.1, Gift of Elsie O. Hincken.*

because of its careful inlay would have been expensive in its day. That Nicholas Schenck, Jr., and his wife might have owned a comparable piece and continued to use it even into the 1830s is supported by the presence of a secretary-bookcase in the same Talcott family portrait (*fig. 5.9*) that helped suggest the room's carpet and wallpaper.

Of course, not all old furniture is so well worth

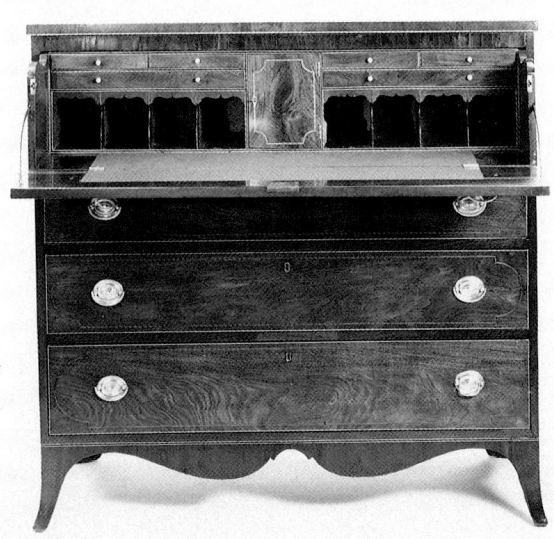

5.15. Secretary, *1790–1810. New York. Mahogany and other veneers, 45½ × 46¼ × 21½ inches. The Brooklyn Museum 69.5.1, Gift of Gunnar Maske.*

keeping, and the Schencks no doubt would have discarded some old pieces in favor of new items in the latest styles. One such piece they might have bought is a rocking chair like the one to the left of the fireplace. Commodious, solid, and decorated on its crest with a stenciled basket of flowers, this chair represents both a later outgrowth of the tradition of sturdy Windsors and another indication of the range of consumer goods then becoming more available as a result of new techniques in manufacturing and marketing. It could not, it should be noted, have been in this room in the 1820s, since it is labeled on the back of its crest "Hitchcock, Alford and Company," a firm that did not even exist until 1832. But rockers similar to this one, as well as related side and armchairs, *were* made in large quantity in the 1820s by Lambert Hitchcock—the Hitchcock of Hitchcock, Alford.

Hitchcock got his start in 1818 in Hitchcocks-ville (now Riverton), Connecticut, making chair parts that he shipped to other locations for later assembly. Eventually, using division of labor and interchangeable parts, he began the cheap mass production of the completed chairs that made him famous, aggressively developing new markets in what was then the West as well as along the East Coast. A disastrous fire in 1829 forced his company into a period of trusteeship, but he rebounded three years later by forming a partnership with Alfred Alford.[15]

In addition to a well-built but rather simple chair like the Hitchcock rocker, the Schencks in the 1820s might have acquired some finer, more expensive items like the scroll-armed sofa and the mahogany side chair arranged along the wall opposite the windows. The sofa, which was probably made in New York around 1825, is in the heavier, more ornately carved style of the late Federal period and is based on Greco-Roman prototypes, or, more directly, on French furniture of the Empire style. Its upholstery, reproduced by John Boyd & Co. of England, is a horsehair, or haircloth, fabric with a small damask pattern. Haircloth, popular for its glossy sheen and durability, was advertised by many New York upholsterers in the 1820s, and such sofas, common in New York homes at the time, were typically covered with haircloth upholstery outlined, as on this example, with shiny brass tacks. To further emphasize the fabric's popularity, horsehair has also been used on the mahogany side chair, a related piece of furniture that reflects the influence of the post-Empire French Restauration style.

These last two objects, together with all the other furniture and decoration of the Nicholas Schenck House parlor, speak of a family that had become, by the 1820s, more American than Dutch, a family whose belongings would have reflected America's strong social and commercial ties with England. Like most Americans of European extraction, the Schencks no doubt readily accepted the most recent styles and acquired all they could of the consumer goods available to them. At the same time, however, they undoubtedly continued to cling to, rather than reject, the familiar and useful from their own recent past.

THE DINING ROOM

Across the central stair hall from the parlor is the room now installed as a dining room and a general work and living area. If the main part of the house predated the kitchen wing, this room was probably originally also used for cooking. In any event, it was likely known in the 1700s as a hall, as such multipurpose dining and living spaces were then called. Only in the nineteenth century would it have come to be referred to as it is today, though even then it would not have been used solely for dining.

A photograph of the room on site (*fig. 5.16*) indicates that it has been altered more significantly than the parlor since its removal to the Museum. Although only the fireplace wall is paneled in the room as it is now installed, the photograph also shows paneling on the window wall. No photographs exist to indicate whether the other two walls were paneled as well, but in any case the additional paneling would have resulted in a room quite different in effect from the one we now see. Houses of this type usually had paneling only on their fireplace walls,[16] and one might expect an exception in this case to be in the "best" room, or parlor. But since this is the room in which the business of the farm would have been conducted with neighbors and other visitors, it is perhaps not so peculiar that it had such impressive paneling. What is more curious is that the paneling on the fireplace wall was not made to extend to the floorboards above, as in the parlor, but was fashioned to accommodate a dropped board ceiling that was installed only as far as the first beam.

Like the other rooms in the house, the dining room was moved from one side of the hall to the other when the house came to the Museum. In this instance, though, the move was complicated by the presence, at one end of the fireplace wall, of the built-out antechamber to the kitchen wing. Had the wall simply been installed as it was found on site, as was done in the parlor, this antechamber would have wound up next to the window wall, instead of abutting the interior wall as it had in the house *in situ*. Even though the wing had disappeared from the site years earlier and was not recreated in the installation, the Museum curators wanted to preserve a correct indication of where the connection to it had been. Therefore, they moved the cupboard seen at the left of the fireplace in the photograph of the room on site to the right of the fireplace in the room at the Museum (*see fig. 5.17*), thus altering the antechamber's relationship to the fireplace but maintaining its position vis-à-vis the interior wall.

For all the care they took in preserving the antechamber's situation, however, the curators did not preserve the antechamber itself. When the house was on site, this small, closetlike passage, clearly an early nineteenth-century addition, was irregularly shaped (*see again fig. 5.16 and floor plan, fig. 4.8*). But in the reconstruction at the Museum its shape was squared and its plastered walls were replaced by paneling related to that on the fireplace wall.

Besides illustrating these changes, photographs of the earliest installation (*figs. 5.17–5.19*) show a room painted entirely white except for the early nineteenth-

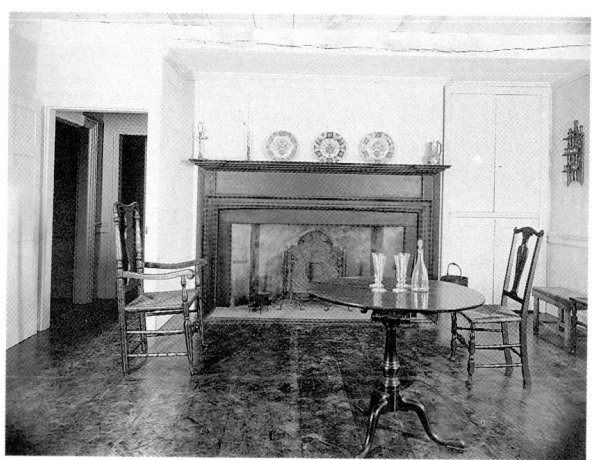

5.17. *Dining Room, Nicholas Schenck House, as installed in The Brooklyn Museum, circa 1929.*

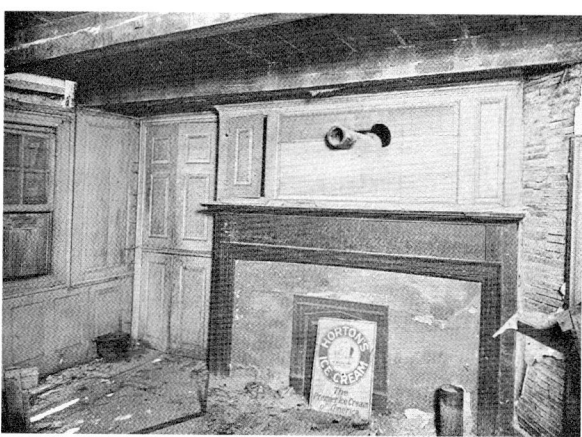

5.16. *Dining Room, Nicholas Schenck House, in situ, circa 1929.*

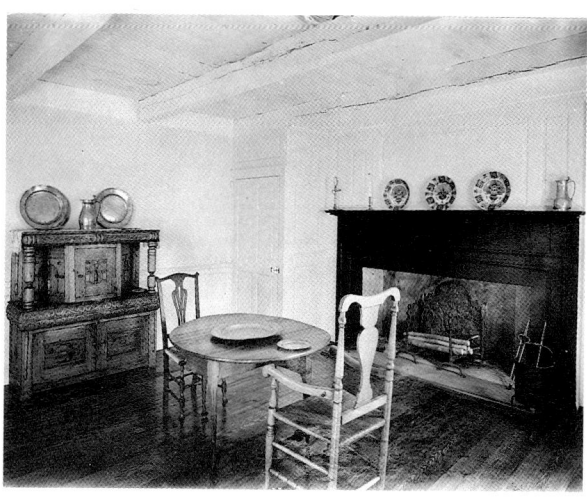

5.18. *Dining Room, Nicholas Schenck House, as installed in The Brooklyn Museum, circa 1929–36.*

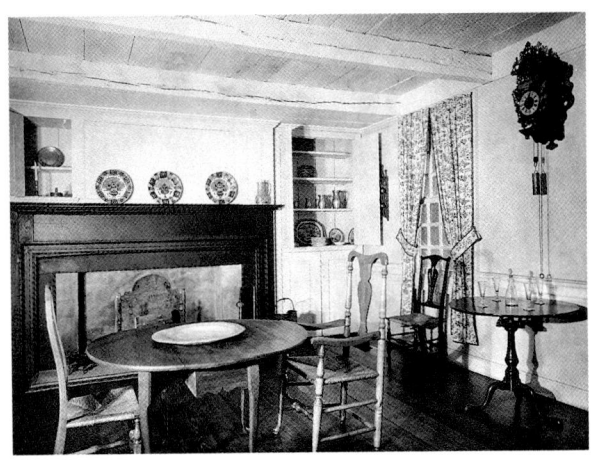

5.19. Dining Room, Nicholas Schenck House, as installed in The Brooklyn Museum, circa 1929–36.

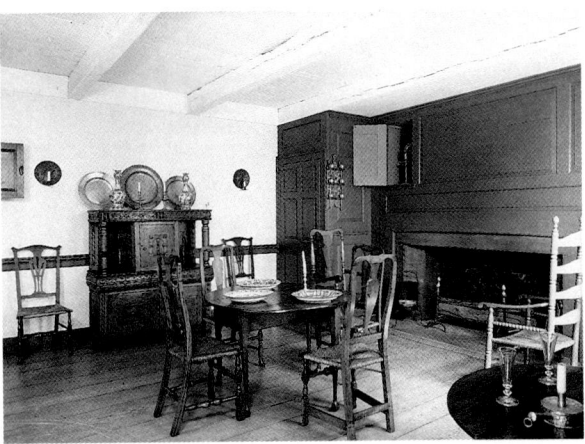

5.20. Dining Room, Nicholas Schenck House, as installed in The Brooklyn Museum, late 1930s or early 1940s.

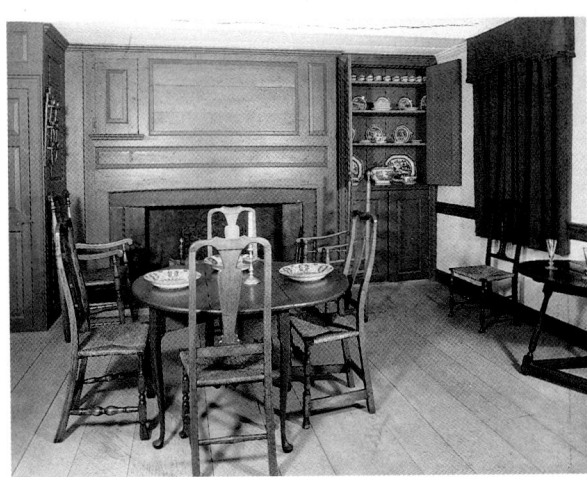

5.21. Dining Room, Nicholas Schenck House, as installed in The Brooklyn Museum, late 1930s or early 1940s.

5.22. Dining Room, Nicholas Schenck House, as installed in The Brooklyn Museum, circa 1965.

century mantelpiece, which was painted black or perhaps dark brown. As in the earliest installation of the parlor, the floors were stained a rich dark color and chintz curtains were hung at the windows. The room was austerely furnished with "country" furniture, including a late seventeenth-century oak press cupboard from Connecticut, an armchair of a Long Island type, and a simple Chippendale side chair. An elaborate Dutch clock was hung on the window wall, and ceramics ranging from seventeenth-century Dutch delftware to nineteenth-century Chinese export ware were set about along with American pewter and English glassware. The fireplace, which had been bricked up and fitted with a small cast-iron insert dating to the mid-1800s in the house *in situ* (*see again fig. 5.16*), was opened to reveal the mid-eighteenth-century cast-iron fireback that, as noted in Chapter 4, was found within (*see fig. 4.3*).

Later, probably in the late 1930s or the early 1940s, the room underwent a number of changes similar to those made in the parlor (*see figs. 5.20 and 5.21*). The paneled woodwork and the chair rail were painted dark (most likely the same dull blue-gray used in the parlor), the floor was stripped and allowed to acquire a patina of wear (these were the days when visitors walked right into the rooms at the Museum), and the chintz window hangings were replaced with curtains and valances that appear to have been fabricated of heavy wool. Clearly, an attempt had been made to provide the room with a more consistent eighteenth-century appearance, for the nineteenth-century mantel was removed from the fireplace as well. But other, less noticeable nineteenth-century woodwork was left in place around the windows and the door to the hall, and early nineteenth-century Chinese export ceramics were still quite visible in the cupboard.

Around 1965 a few pieces of furniture were changed (*see fig. 5.22*), and during the refurbishing of 1967 more objects were added and the window hangings were simplified (*see fig. 5.23*). Yet despite these and all the other alterations that had been made over the years, the basic character of the room changed only a little. In fact, some of the furniture seen in the installation of 1929 was still in the room in 1968 shortly before it was closed.

For its reopening in 1984, however, the room was

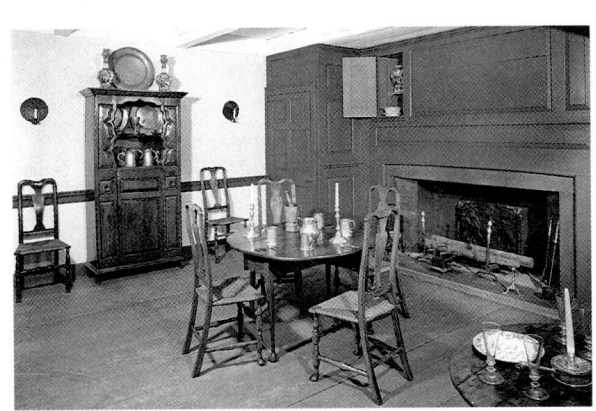

changed considerably (*see figs. 5.24 and 5.25*), not only to reflect a date in the 1820s but also to convey more emphatically that the room was used not merely for dining but for family gatherings, household work, and farm business as well. This effect was achieved in large measure through the consultation of nineteenth-century genre scenes depicting such activities in comparable interiors—scenes like the aforementioned Krimmel paintings of 1813 and 1819 (*figs. 5.11 and 5.12*), Asher B. Durand's *The Peddler Displaying His Wares* of 1836 (*fig. 5.26*), and Richard Caton Woodville's *Soldier's Experience* of 1844 (*fig. 5.27*). Although such paintings should be interpreted with care, since the representation of a room might be affected by an artist's desire to aggrandize a sitter or deliver a satire on rural life, they provide valuable clues to the ways in which people actually used their rooms and to how their daily lives and everyday objects were fitted together. Because the texture of material culture and the texture of human life are interwoven, the juxtapositions of objects these works suggest can serve to arouse ghosts.

In some cases certain details found in a painting have been quoted quite literally in this room. The drop-

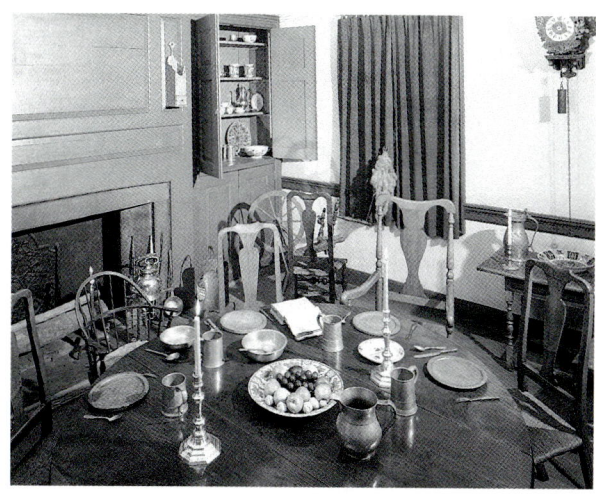

5.23. Dining Room, Nicholas Schenck House, as installed in The Brooklyn Museum, circa 1968.

5.24. Dining Room, Nicholas Schenck House, as installed in The Brooklyn Museum, 1984. Photograph by Paul Warchol.

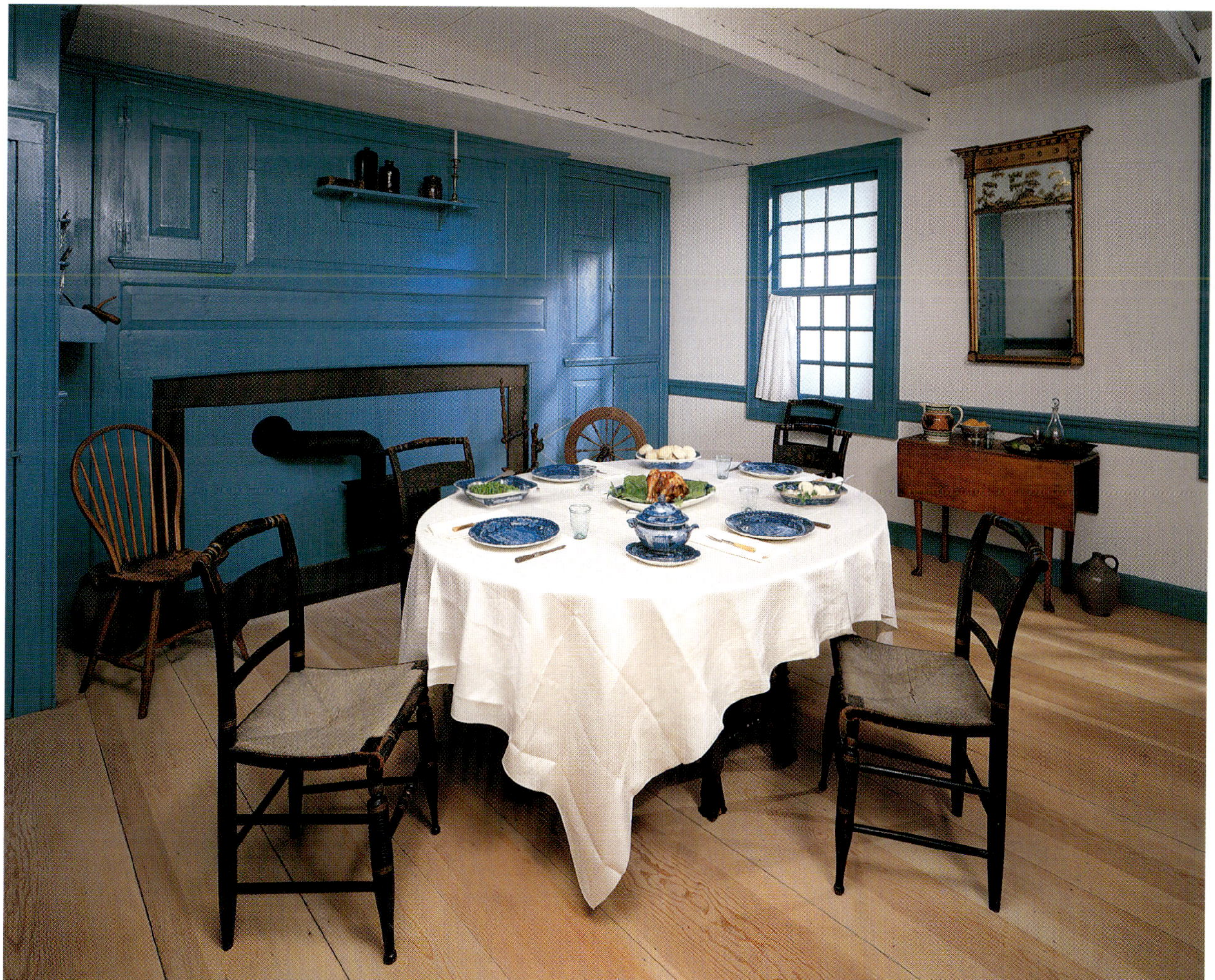

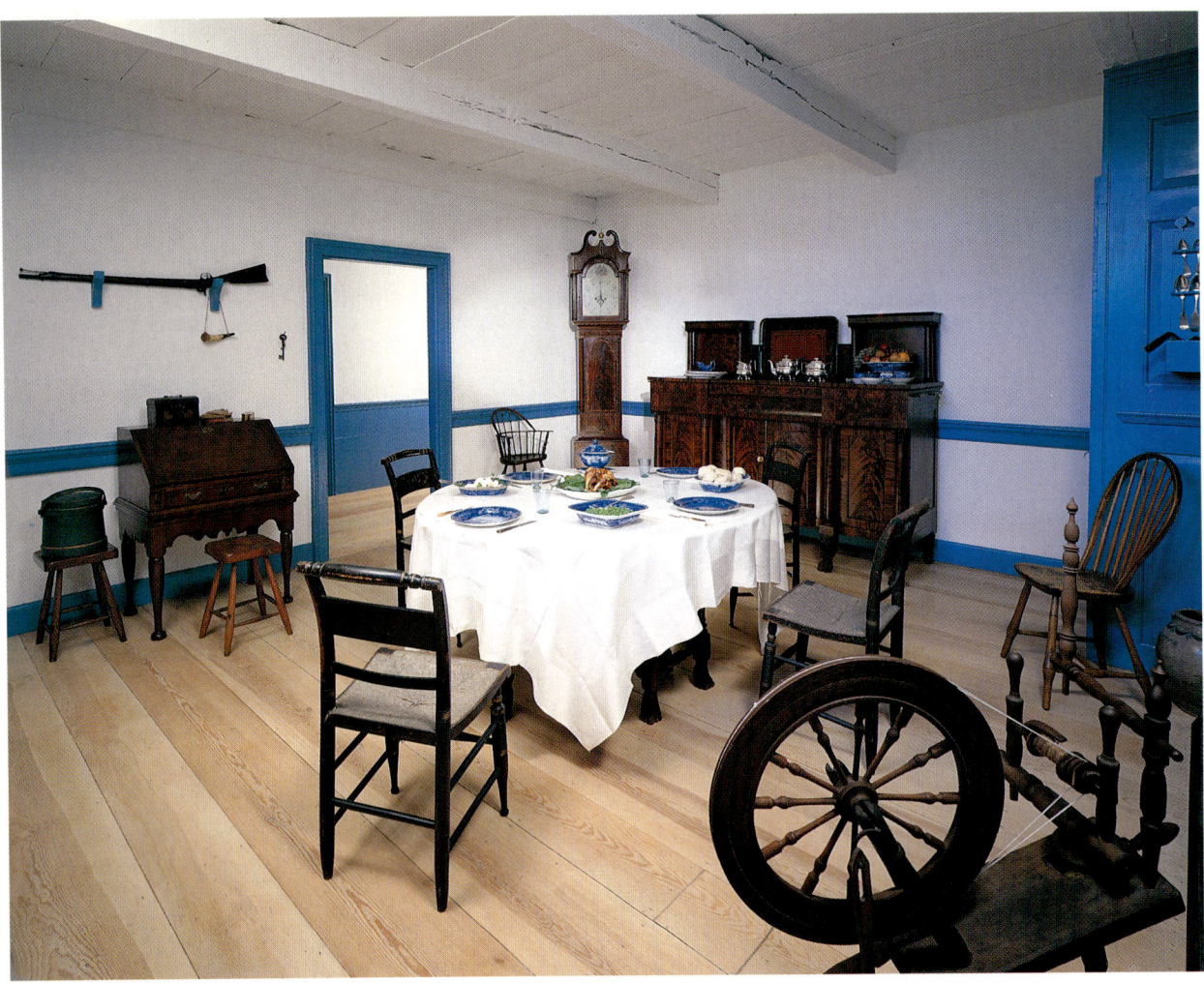

5.25. *Dining Room, Nicholas Schenck House, as installed in The Brooklyn Museum, 1984. Photograph by Paul Warchol.*

leaf maple table between the windows, for instance, is arranged to resemble the table on the right in Krimmel's *Country Wedding,* set for the service of drinks with a glass decanter, tumblers, stemware, a mocha-ware pitcher, and a tole, or painted tin, tray. Beneath it is a stoneware jug by J. Remmey of Manhattan Wells, New York, which no doubt held spirits, and above it a looking glass that is a simpler version of the glass in the parlor. Likewise, the small shelf on the chimney breast is hung close to the ceiling and casually cluttered—with bottles, a jar, a book, and a candlestick—as a similar shelf is shown by Durand.

In other cases, genre scenes supplied evidence of what would have been an object's standard placement. For example, Krimmel's painting *Quilting Frolic,* among others, suggested that the typical place to stand a tall clock was in a corner. The dining room's tall clock, therefore, has been placed in the corner to the right of the door and diagonally positioned so that it can be clearly seen from various points in the room. Although this clock belonged to the Haslett family of New York, it is possible the Schencks owned a similar piece, for the most valuable item listed in James Schenck's estate inventory of 1885 is a clock valued at $30.[17] In like manner, because Woodville's *Soldier's Experience* and other paintings suggested that guns were usually hung on the wall and often near a door for ready access, a rifle has been mounted on brackets to the left of the door in the area now installed as the householder's office space. The powder horn hung with it, said to have been found in the house shortly before the rooms' removal to the Museum, has crude scrimshaw decorations of flying birds and a sailing ship (*see fig. 5.28*). Dated 1821 and initialed A.S., it probably belonged to Abraham Schenck, a son of Nicholas, Jr., and a brother of James who would have been nineteen that year. Hung slightly to the right are the household keys, and placed immediately below is a desk with a history of ownership in Flatbush that was collected by Luke Vincent Lockwood in the early part of this century (*see fig. 5.29*).[18] On top of the desk are account books, a tole document box, a clay pipe, and a Dutch brass tobacco box.

The furniture in this room, as in the parlor, is a mixture of the old and the new. Thus we see two early Windsors, one a child's high chair, together with a set

CONSUMER GOODS AND FAMILY HEIRLOOMS, OR THE MORN OF INDEPENDENCE

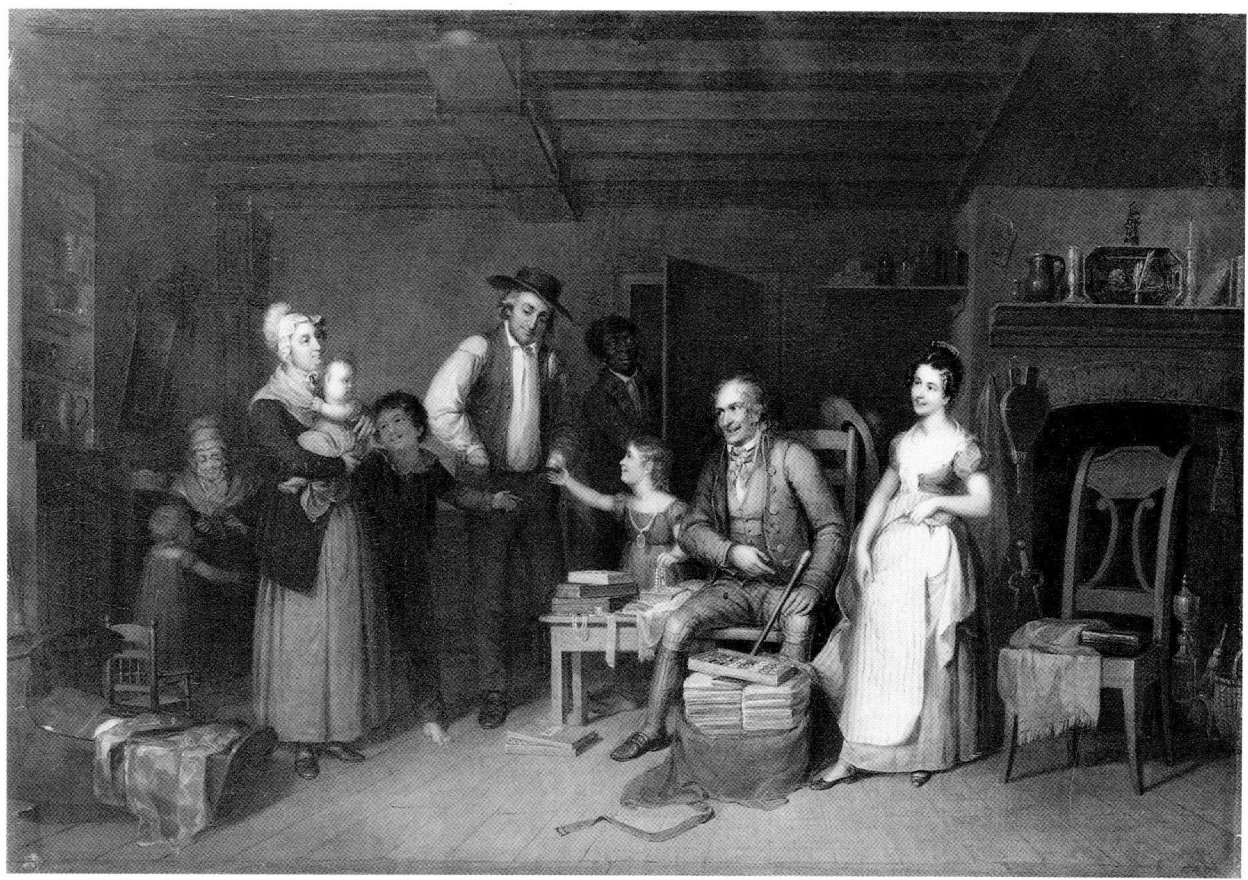

5.26. Asher B. Durand (American, 1796–1886). The Peddler Displaying His Wares, 1836. Oil on canvas, 24 × 34½ inches. The New-York Historical Society.

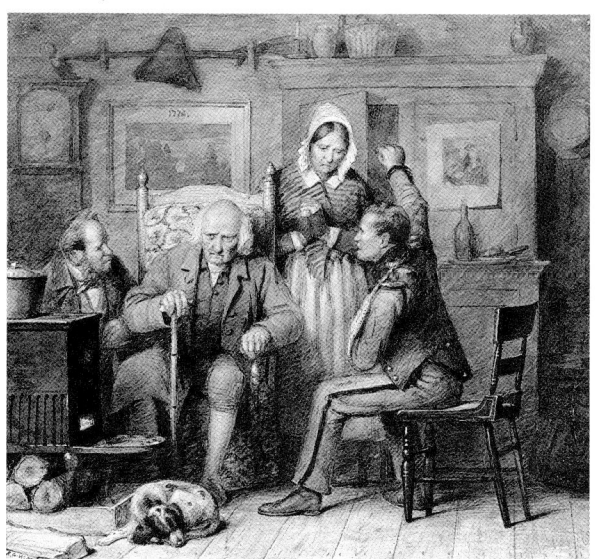

5.27. Richard Caton Woodville (American, 1825–1855). Soldier's Experience, 1844. Watercolor on paper, 11 × 10 inches. Walters Art Gallery, Baltimore.

5.28. Attributed to Abraham Schenck (American, b. 1802), Powder Horn, 1821. Flatlands, New York. Cow's horn, 6 × 2¼ inches. The Brooklyn Museum 41.1140, Gift of Louis E. Birdseye.

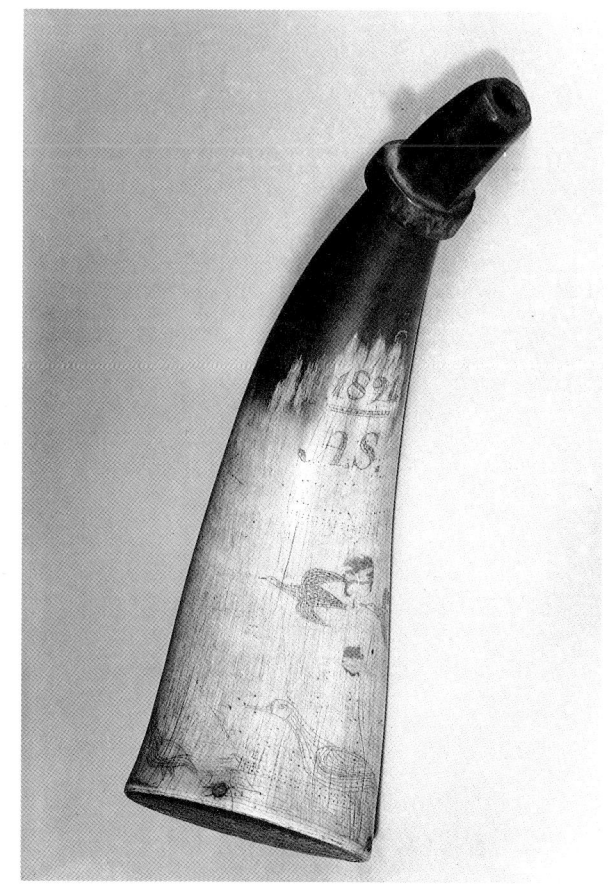

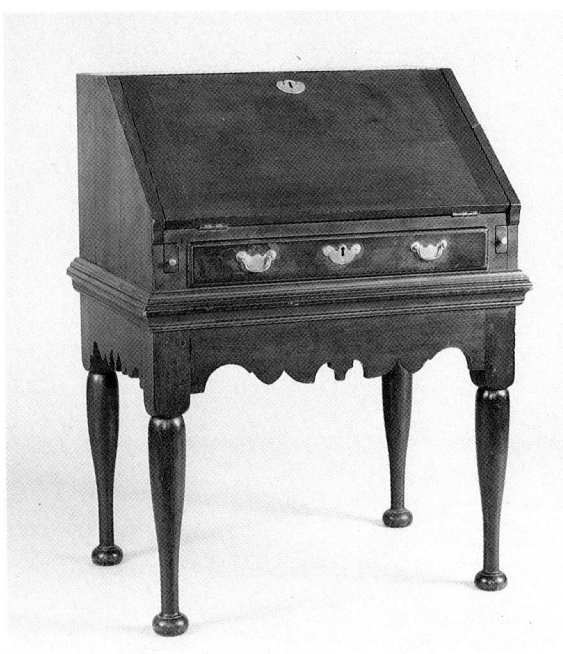

5.29. Desk, circa 1725–40. Long Island, New York. Walnut, 38 × 30 × 21 inches. The Brooklyn Museum 42.176, Gift of Mrs. Luke Vincent Lockwood.

of six fancy chairs made by Lambert Hitchcock between 1825 and 1832, before his partnership with Alford. The drop-leaf table and the desk are eighteenth-century pieces, while the tall clock, like the secretary in the parlor, dates from around 1800 and is in the early Federal style. The sideboard to the right of the clock, on the other hand, represents the sort of expensive, stylish object the Schencks might have purchased for this room in the 1820s (see fig. 5.30). It is in the heavier, late Federal style, embellished with freestanding classical columns and richly veneered with mahogany. Probably made around 1825, it bears the label of the New York cabinetmaker Michael Allison.[19]

Prominently displayed on the sideboard along with some of the English transfer-printed earthenware used on the dining table is a matched silver tea service that is also in the late Federal style and, though unmarked, was no doubt also made in New York (see fig. 5.31). Originally owned by Martin and Sarah Skillman Schenck, distant relatives of the Nicholas Schencks, it not only exhibits the period's fondness for large heavy forms but also shows the influence of industrialization on the decorative arts in its machine-made die-rolled ornament. Since the Schencks, as noted in Chapter 3, had their silver stolen during the Revolution,

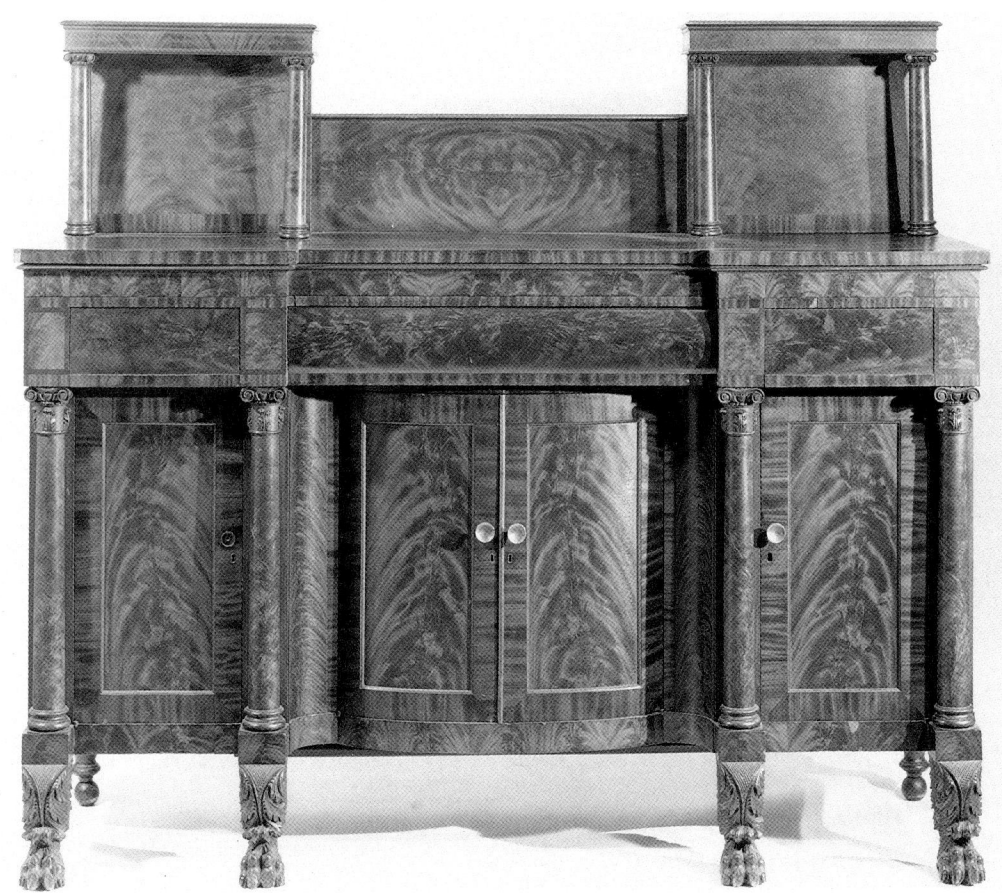

5.30. Michael Allison (American, active 1800–1845). Sideboard, circa 1825. New York. Mahogany, 61¾ (to top of shelf) × 73¼ × 24 inches. The Brooklyn Museum 65.140, Gift of Mr. and Mrs. H. Stewart Peyton.

CONSUMER GOODS AND FAMILY HEIRLOOMS, OR THE MORN OF INDEPENDENCE

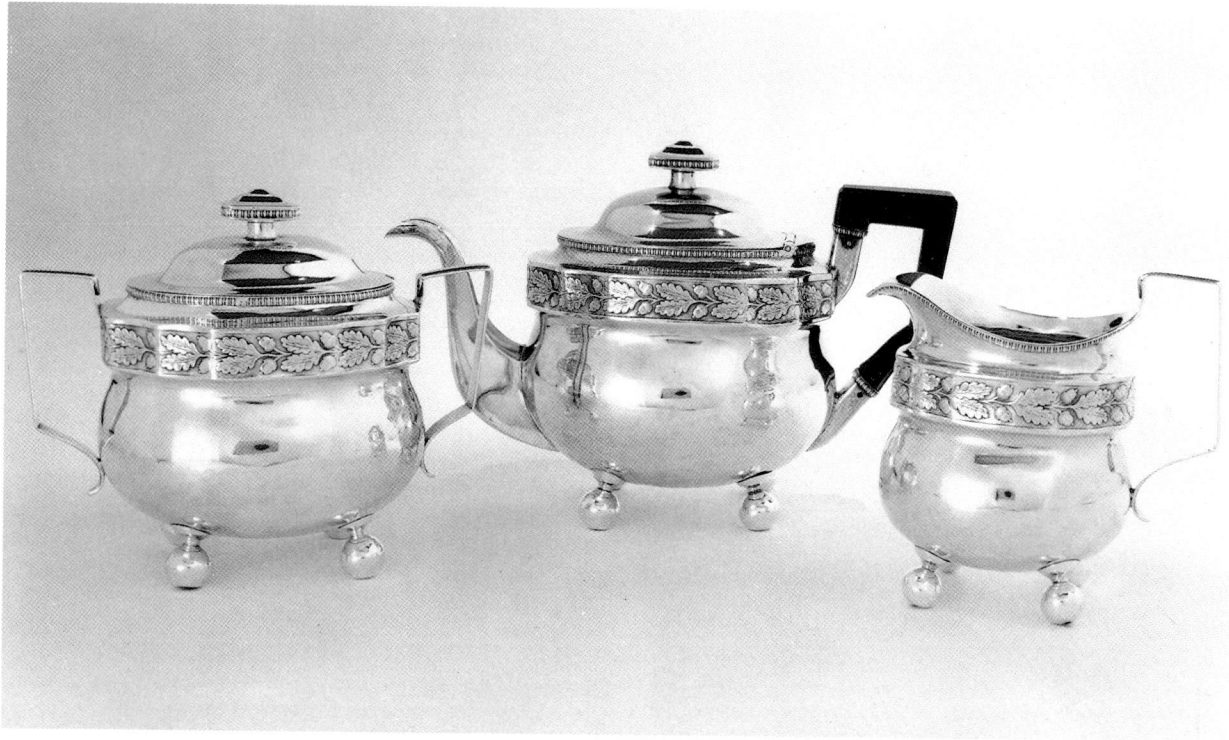

5.31. Tea Service, circa 1820. New York. Silver, 6 × 11 × 5¼ inches (dimensions of teapot). The Brooklyn Museum 83.152.1–3, Gift of Barbara Dickerson.

they might well have acquired such a service in the 1820s, by which time mechanization had made silver objects more affordable.

Additional silver is seen, in the form of coin silver spoons, in the spoon rack on the side of the antechamber. Such racks were popular among Dutch settlers in New York and New Jersey,[20] and a study of Kings County estate inventories of the 1830s (inventories that reflect households of the preceding decade) shows that silver spoons were commonly owned. "Large silver spoons" or "silver table spoons" were often found in sets of six, sometimes with teaspoons as well.[21]

All the paintings consulted in the decoration of this room suggested that the floor should be left bare and unfinished to approximate the look of a floor heavily used and frequently scrubbed with sand. The common wisdom of the time held that such floors should almost never be cleaned with soap. As the English housewife Susanna Whatman instructed in her manuscript *Housekeeping Book*, written between 1776 and 1800 to guide her servants, "Use as little soap as possible (if any) in scouring rooms. Fuller's earth and fine sand preserves the colour of the boards, and does not leave a white appearance as soap does. All the rooms [are] to be dry scrubbed with white sand."[22]

At least two of the paintings studied, Krimmel's *Quilting Frolic* and Durand's *Peddler Displaying His Wares*, depict an open fireplace, but since the on-site photograph referred to earlier (*fig. 5.16*) shows a sealed fireplace, a cast-iron insert, and a stovepipe in the paneling above, the fireplace was sealed once again and this time fitted with a small cast-iron stove similar to the one seen in Woodville's *Soldier's Experience*. Made by J. H. Shear in Albany, this stove, according to family legend, was used to heat the home of the van Wyck family of Brooklyn. Although it is later than the other objects in the room, box, or six-plate, stoves like it were in use well before the middle of the nineteenth century. Ideally, the early nineteenth-century mantelpiece that was removed from the wall behind it sometime in the late 1930s or the early 1940s would have been reinstalled, but it could not be found.

To the right of the fireplace is a spinning wheel, indicating another type of labor that would have been performed in this room. We know from the inventory of James Schenck's estate that three spinning wheels, valued at 10 cents each, were still in this house as late as 1885. Whether they were similar to this one is not known, but wheels of this kind, though based on a German prototype, were used by Americans of both English and Dutch descent.[23] Because they were easily disassembled and could be stored away when not in use in order to save space, the appearance of one in a room so obviously arranged for a formal meal may seem a bit incongruous. During the periods of time when spinning was done, however, the wheel would have remained standing even when a meal was in progress. Today its presence serves as a reminder that for all the consumer goods they would have enjoyed that their ancestors had not, the Schencks in the 1820s would still have made many things themselves.

The Stair Hall

As noted in Chapter 4, the central stair hall that leads to the bedrooms at the back of the house was not a part of the original structure. It was created, most likely in the early nineteenth century, by eliminating the third, middle room that originally existed in the rear, and it still holds a reminder of that room in the form of an eighteenth-century corner cupboard. Aside from this cupboard, its most distinguishing feature is the treatment of the walls below its chair rail, which are sheathed with flat boards beaded at the joints—a practice common in Dutch-American houses of this type.[24]

A comparison of a photograph of the hall *in situ* (*fig. 5.32*) with a view of the hall as it now appears (*fig. 5.33*) shows how it was altered to accommodate the reverse installation of the rooms around it. The staircase has been moved from one side of the hall to the other, and the window that was originally to the right of the rear door has been switched with the corner cupboard, which, as another on-site photograph indicates, was originally to the left of the door (*see fig. 5.34*).

The earliest photograph we have of the hall installed in the Museum is a view probably from the late 1930s or the early 1940s looking toward the front door (*fig. 5.35*). In addition to showing that the ceiling beams were then painted dark (most likely blue-gray) and that balusters had been added to the stair rail, it reveals that at least one piece of furniture had been placed there. Indeed, this space, especially the wide area near the staircase, would not have been wasted but would have been furnished to serve a useful purpose.

Unfortunately, the stair hall must now remain empty of furnishings in order to provide access to visitors. Unadorned as it is, however, it has gained greater authenticity simply by virtue of the reinterpretation of the rooms around it as interiors dating to the 1820s. In earlier installations, when the rooms were mainly presented as interiors dating to the third quarter of the 1700s, the hall was an anomaly that could not be explained.

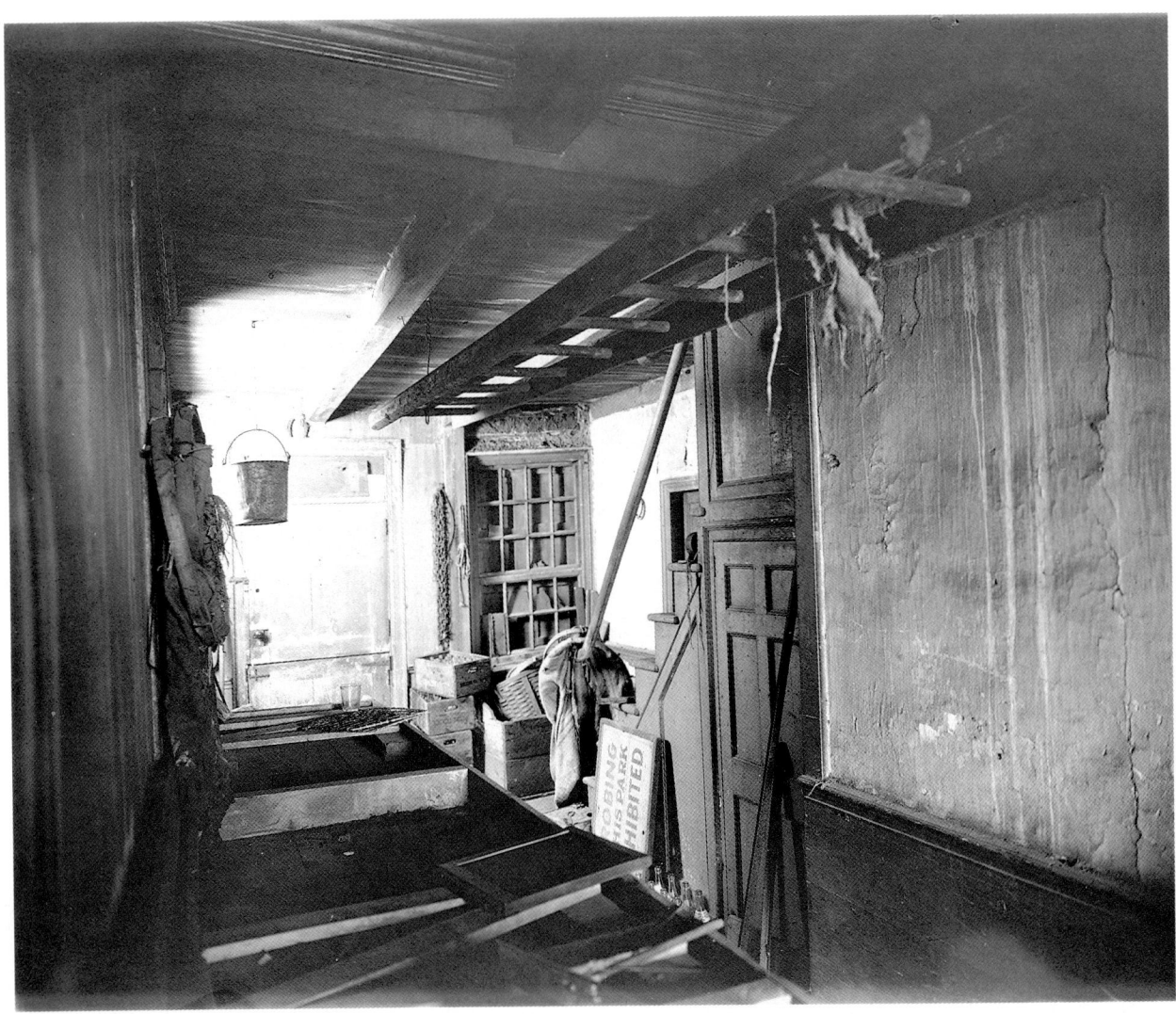

5.32. *Stair Hall, Nicholas Schenck House, in situ, circa 1929.*

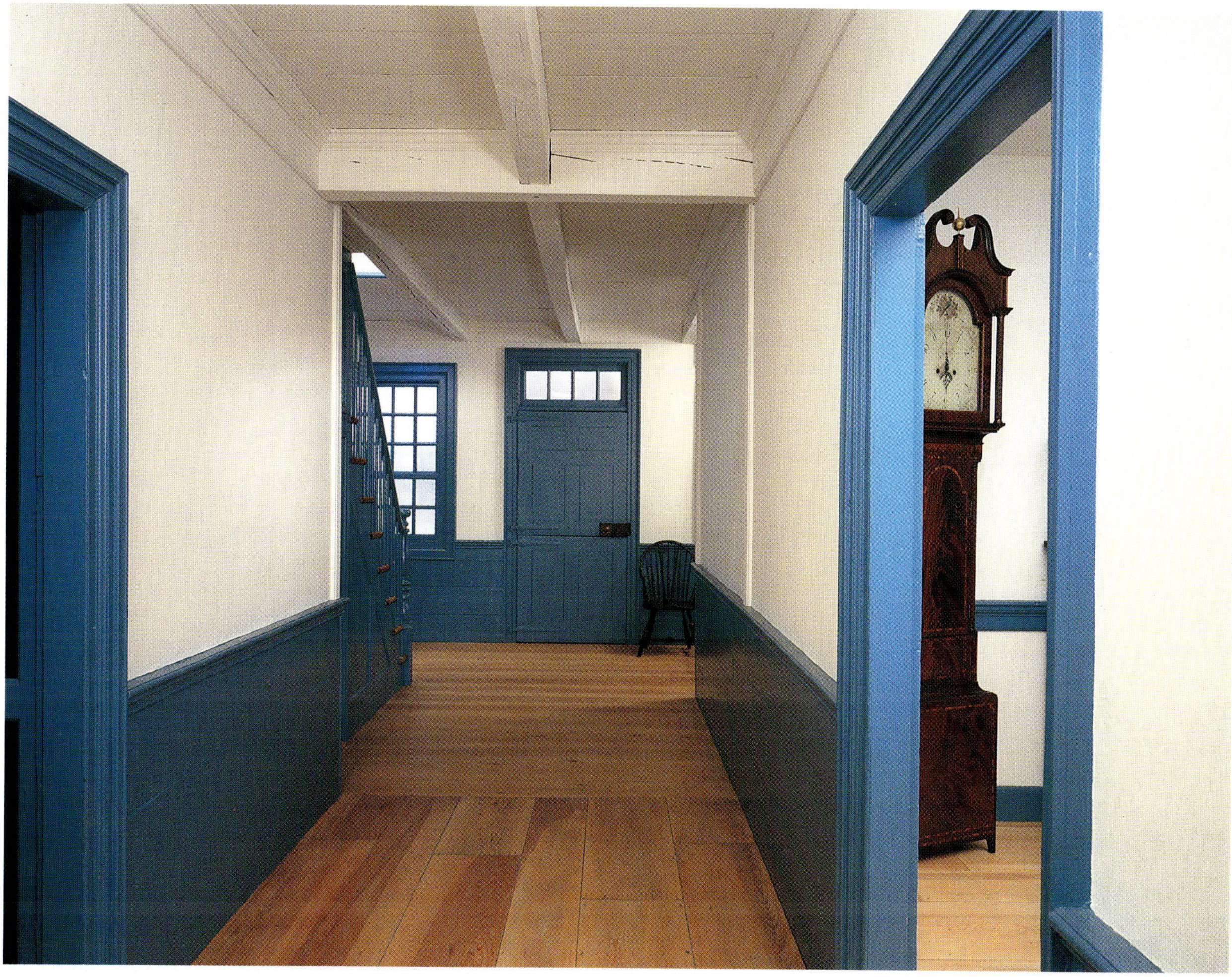

5.33. Stair Hall, Nicholas Schenck House, as installed in The Brooklyn Museum, 1985. Photograph by Paul Warchol.

5.34. Left: Stair Hall, Nicholas Schenck House, in situ, circa 1929.

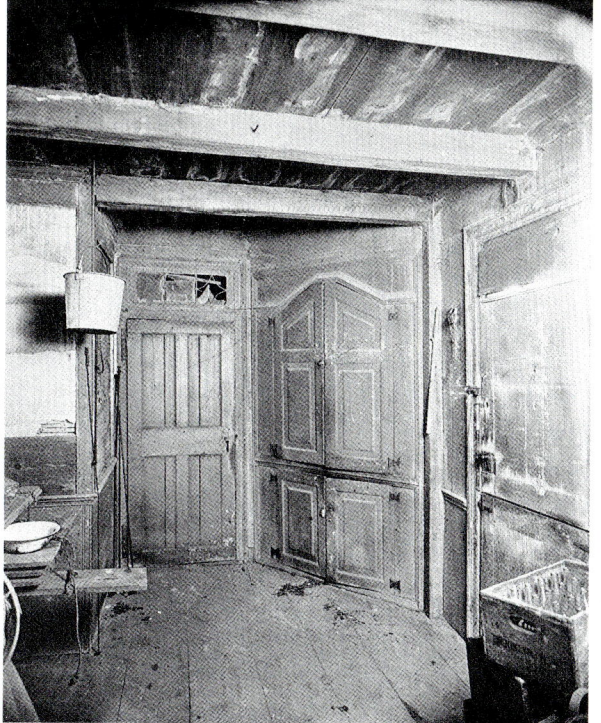

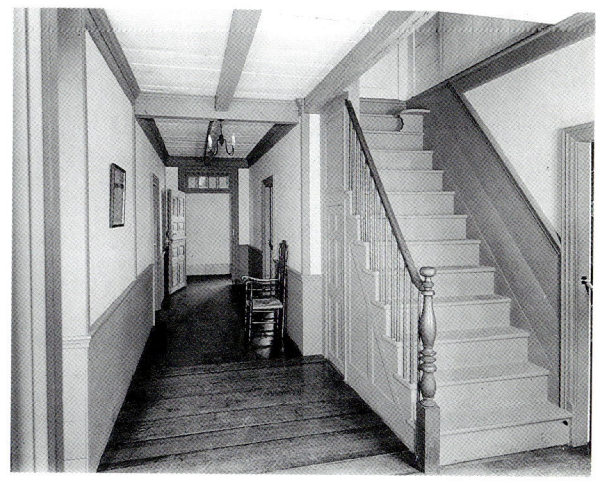

5.35. Stair Hall, Nicholas Schenck House, as installed in The Brooklyn Museum, late 1930s or early 1940s.

The Bedroom behind the Parlor

When the Schencks added the stair hall, the bedroom behind the parlor was the only one of the three rear rooms (now two bedrooms and the rear part of the hall itself) to retain its original form. It did not, however, remain unaltered. As in the other rooms, new door and window frames were installed and a chair rail was added. Moreover a photograph of the room on site (*fig. 5.36*) reveals that at some point in its history horizontal boards (now removed) were used to sheathe the walls above the chair rail and a molding was placed at the top of the walls just beneath the beams, perhaps in tandem with the introduction of a lowered plaster or board ceiling. Although the physical evidence still remaining is inconclusive, there is some indication on the beams of this room, and on the beams of the bedroom across the hall, of nail holes that could have been made by the addition of laths for just such a ceiling. Strangely enough, however, except for the small area of dropped ceiling between the paneled wall and the beam next to it in the dining room, such evidence is lacking in the front rooms, where one might more logically expect the old-fashioned beams to have been covered.

In an apparent attempt to demonstrate how the furnishing of the house might have changed in the first few decades after it was built, this bedroom, which would have been called a chamber in the eighteenth century (or a *kamer* by the Dutch), was decorated in the fashion of a slightly later date than the other rooms of the house—sometime in the 1790s—in its earliest installation at the Museum. The guide to the Museum's period rooms published in 1936 shows it furnished with a Federal chest of drawers, an elaborate neoclassical mirror, simple woolen curtains with valances, and an eighteenth-century field bed (*see fig. 5.37*). Later, presumably in the late 1930s or the early 1940s, the furniture was moved around a bit, the chair rail was painted dark, and the curtains and valances were

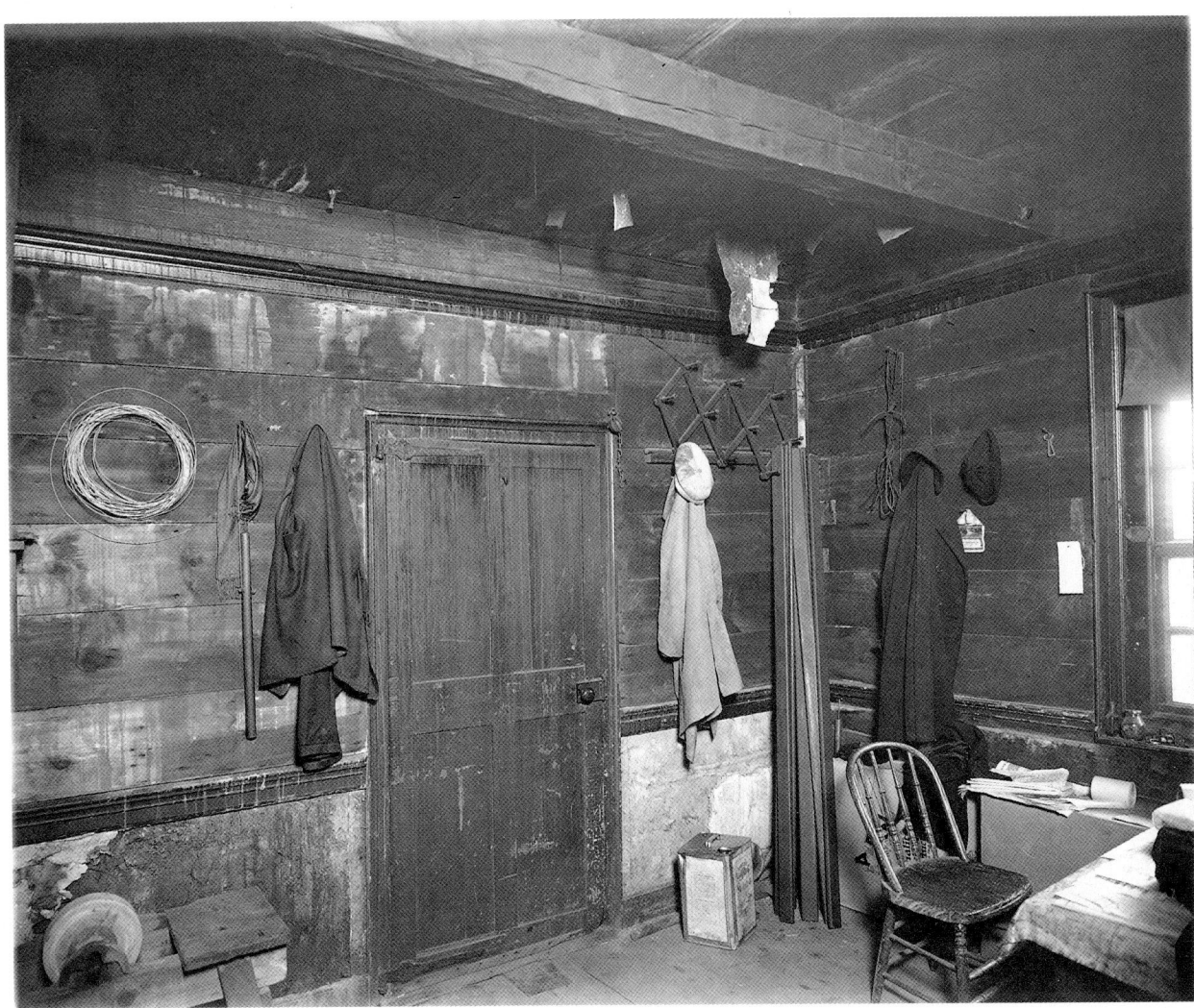

5.36. *Bedroom behind the Parlor, Nicholas Schenck House, in situ, circa 1929.*

CONSUMER GOODS AND FAMILY HEIRLOOMS, OR THE MORN OF INDEPENDENCE

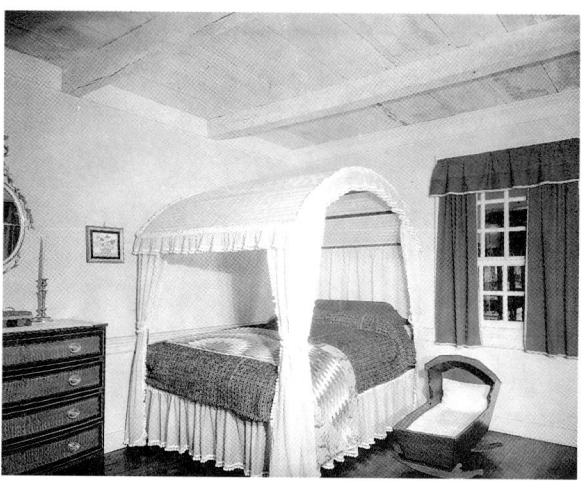

5.37. Bedroom behind the Parlor, Nicholas Schenck House, as installed in The Brooklyn Museum, 1936.

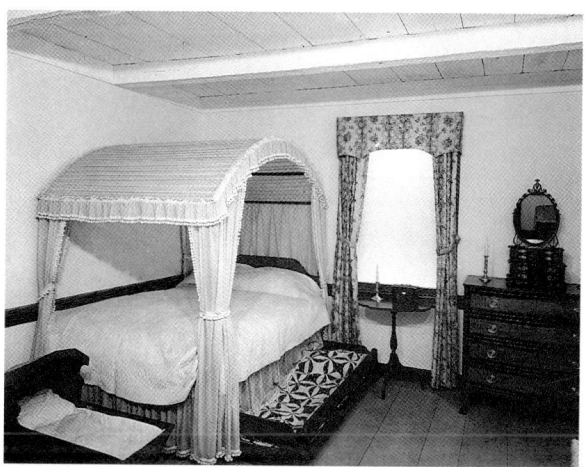

5.38. Bedroom behind the Parlor, Nicholas Schenck House, as installed in The Brooklyn Museum, late 1930s or early 1940s.

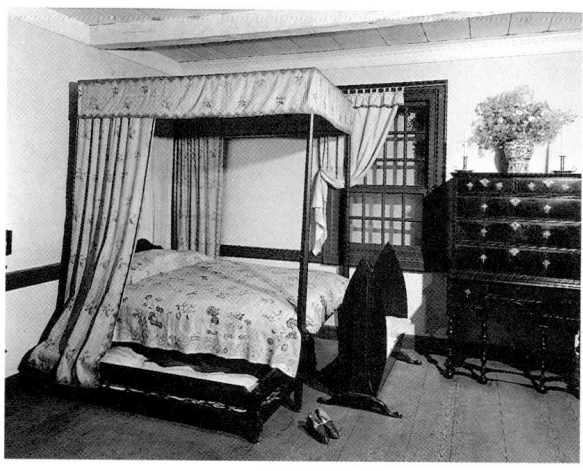

5.39. Bedroom behind the Parlor, Nicholas Schenck House, as installed in The Brooklyn Museum, circa 1968.

changed (see fig. 5.38). But nothing was done to alter the impression that this room was intended to represent an interior that, compared to the other rooms, had been redecorated.

With the refurbishing of 1967, however, this approach was finally abandoned and the room given the same misleading pre-Revolutionary appearance conferred on the rest of the house (see figs. 5.39 and 5.40). An earlier bed adorned with embroidered hangings and an eighteenth-century coverlet was installed, and the Federal chest of drawers gave way to a William and Mary high chest and a mid-eighteenth-century Long Island chest with drawers. At the windows, yet another set of curtains appeared, hung by tapes from a rod, but this time without valances.

The current installation, of course, takes this room once again forward in time (see figs. 5.41 and 5.42). This is accomplished largely through the decoration of the bed, which is dressed as it might have been had it been refurbished in the 1820s.

Indeed, Nicholas Schenck, Jr., and his wife might well have refurbished their bed at that time. We know that Nicholas Schenck, Sr., had probably had new bed curtains made in 1789 since the bill he received from the merchant David Masterton that year for 28½ yards of "Curtain Callico" (at the considerable price of £7.

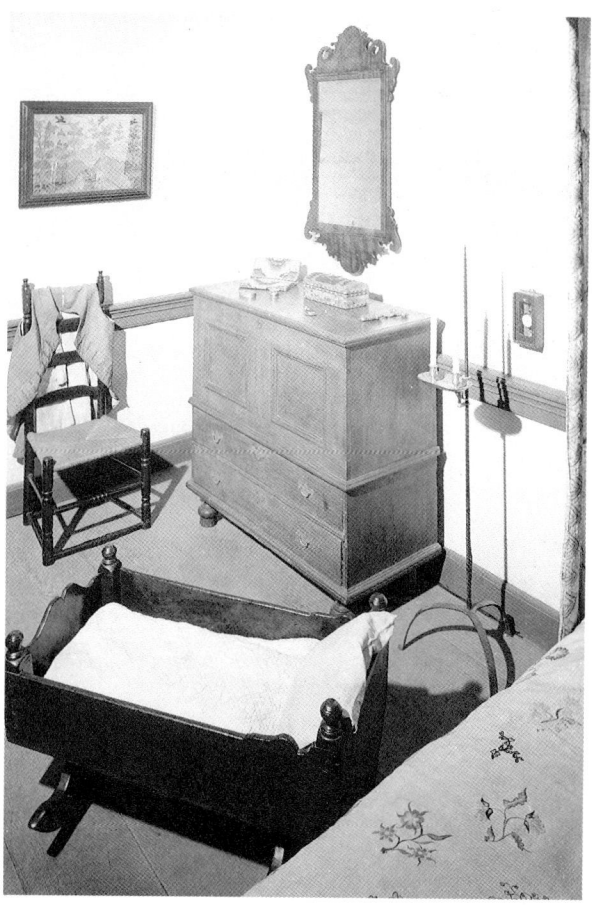

5.40. Bedroom behind the Parlor, Nicholas Schenck House, as installed in The Brooklyn Museum, circa 1968.

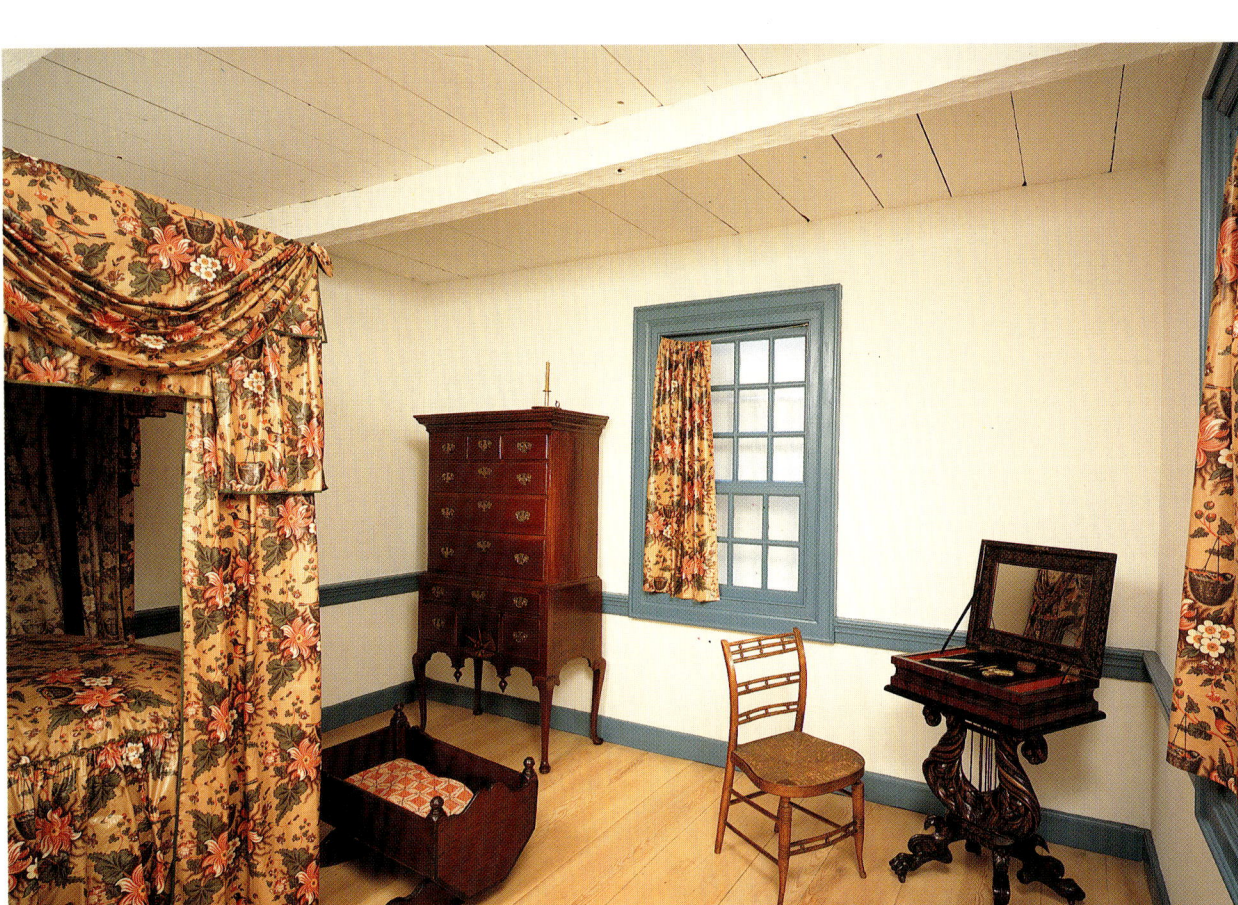

5.41. *Bedroom behind the Parlor, Nicholas Schenck House, as installed in The Brooklyn Museum, 1984. Photograph by Paul Warchol.*

16s. 9d.) also included one piece of bed ticking and three yards of bed binding.[25] By the 1820s, however, these hangings would have been unfashionable and shabby and ready to be replaced.

Although Sarah Josepha Hale, in her famous *Godey's Lady's Book,* would criticize bed hangings as unhealthful in 1839 because they "confine the air about us as we sleep,"[26] estate inventories indicate that they were still popular in Kings County as late as the early 1830s. Since they were often one of the most valuable items listed in such inventories, they undoubtedly represented not only comfort and privacy but a tangible status symbol as well.

Naturally, the richly draped bed had a certain prescribed look, and in this, as in so many matters of fashion, Americans of the time took their cue from the English. For the middle class, there were a number of British books to provide guidance. *The Workwoman's Guide* published in London in 1840, for instance, described not only the various elements that should be included in bed hangings, or what it called bed furniture, but also the proper way to arrange them:

Bed furniture is composed of a top, a back, two head curtains, two foot curtains, one top outer and one top inner valance, one bottom valance, and sometimes extra drapery laid on the back of the bed. When beds are lined, the lining is put inside the curtains, and within the top and back of the bed....The curtains should just touch the ground, as also should the foot valance....The valances accord with the rest, having often fringe added to give a greater finish.[27]

The hangings used in this room are based on a set of bed curtains bequeathed to the Essex Institute in Salem, Massachusetts, in 1897 by a Salem family that had owned them since the early nineteenth century (*see fig. 5.43*).[28] Unsurprisingly, these prototype curtains are not only arranged in an English fashion but also made of an English fabric. Just as English ceramics dominated the American market then, so did English textiles.

The fabric used in the Museum's reproduction

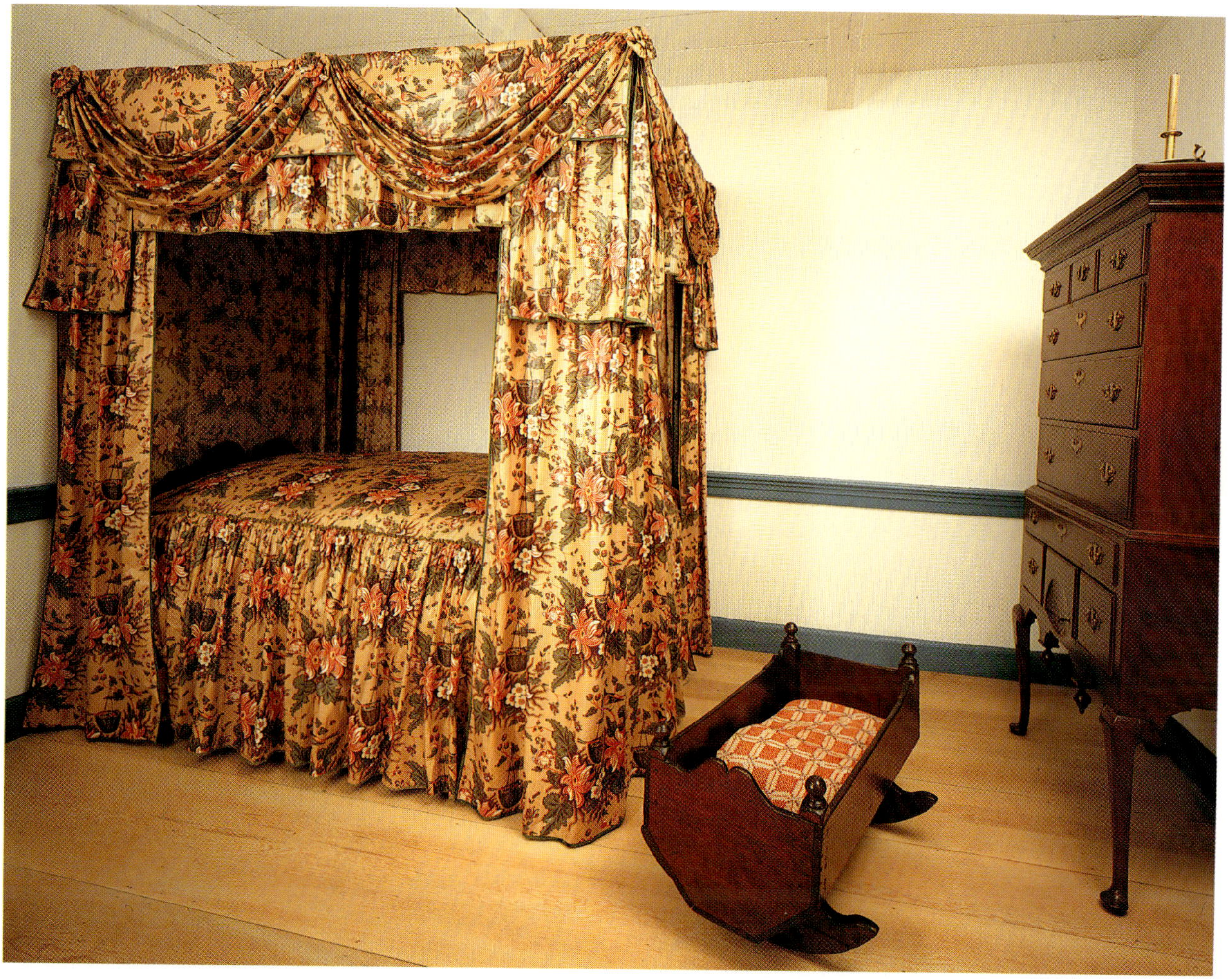

5.42. *Bedroom behind the Parlor, Nicholas Schenck House, as installed in The Brooklyn Museum, 1984. Photograph by Paul Warchol.*

5.43. Bed Hangings, *early nineteenth century. Made in Massachusetts of copper-plate English chintz. The Essex Institute, Salem, Massachusetts.*

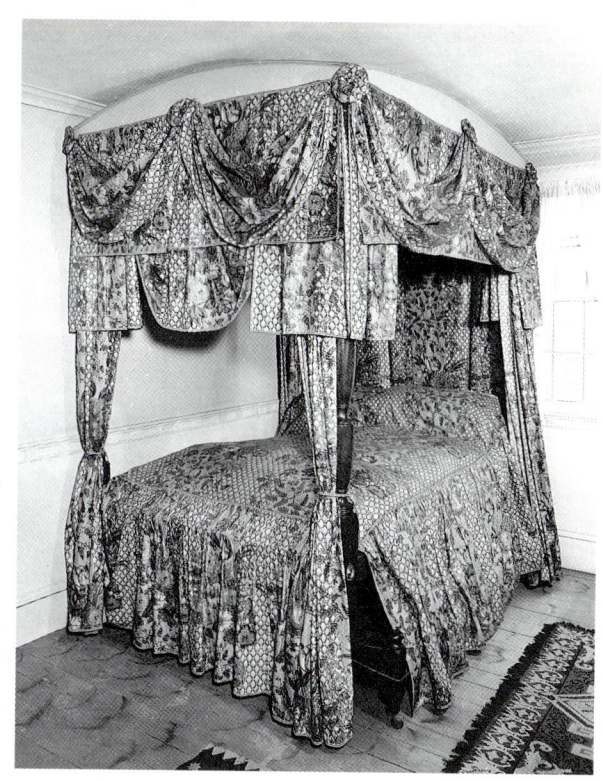

of the Essex hangings is itself a reproduction, by Brunschwig & Fils, of a document print of about 1830 in the Henry Francis du Pont Winterthur Museum. It is typical of the bold cotton chintzes printed in England in the early nineteenth century with the use of mechanized rollers rather than wood blocks or copper plates. Cheaply produced, such roller-printed textiles found a ready market in America. This particular print, originally part of a series of English fabrics depicting native American birds, shows Baltimore orioles nesting among flowering branches.[29] Because the use of fabrics in a room *en suite* was a common practice in the 1820s, it has also been used for the window curtains and for the slipcover placed on an easy chair beside the door (*see fig. 5.44*).

Then, as now, slipcovers were used both to provide protection for the permanent upholstery of new chairs and to update or refurbish old-fashioned or timeworn pieces inexpensively. Unlike the tailored slipcovers of the twentieth century, however, the slipcover used in this case is a loose-fitting sack slipped over the frame of the chair. Such covers can be seen in illustrations and paintings dating from the late eighteenth century (*fig. 5.45*) well into the nineteenth (*fig. 5.46*).

In addition to the bed and the easy chair, the room's furniture also includes a dressing table and chair, a cradle, and a high chest. Like the sofa in the parlor and the sideboard in the dining room, the dressing table represents the sort of piece that would have been new in the 1820s, purchased from a fashionable New York cabinetmaker and in the latest style (*see fig. 5.47*). On the other hand, the cradle, which descended in the Kouwenhoven family of Kings County, represents a relic brought out of storage for the child of a guest since the Schencks themselves had no children in need of a cradle then, while the Queen Anne–style high chest (*fig. 5.48*) is an example of a piece of older furniture that would have remained useful enough to earn a place in a refurbished room.

Although New Yorkers in general preferred the chest-on-chest, an upper case resting on a solid lower case rather than raised on legs, high chests *were* made and used in New York, especially in eastern Long Island, where tastes more closely resembled those of New England.[30] This particular chest has a history of ownership in the family of General Jeremiah Johnson (1766–1852), the third Mayor of Brooklyn, and may have belonged originally to his parents, Barent and Anne Remsen Johnson, who were married in 1764. Queen Anne–style chests like it were most popular around the middle of the eighteenth century but continued to be made until the end of the century by Long Island's conservative craftsmen.[31]

Though, as noted, the major reason for keeping

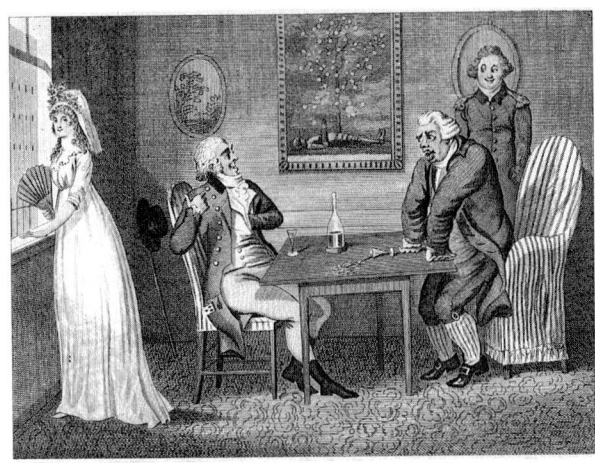

5.45. *Illustration from* Speculation: or, A New Way of Saving a Thousand Pounds *(London: Laurie & Whittle, 1798). Photograph courtesy of the Lewis Walpole Library, Yale University, New Haven.*

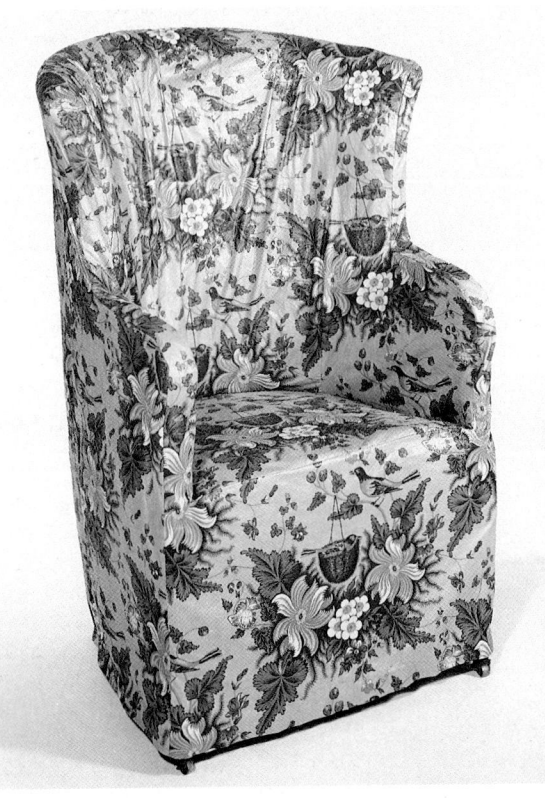

5.44. *Easy Chair with Reproduction Slipcover, circa 1815. American. Cherry wood, 44¾ × 22 × 26½ inches. The Brooklyn Museum L40.320, Lent by Louise Egbert Sailer.*

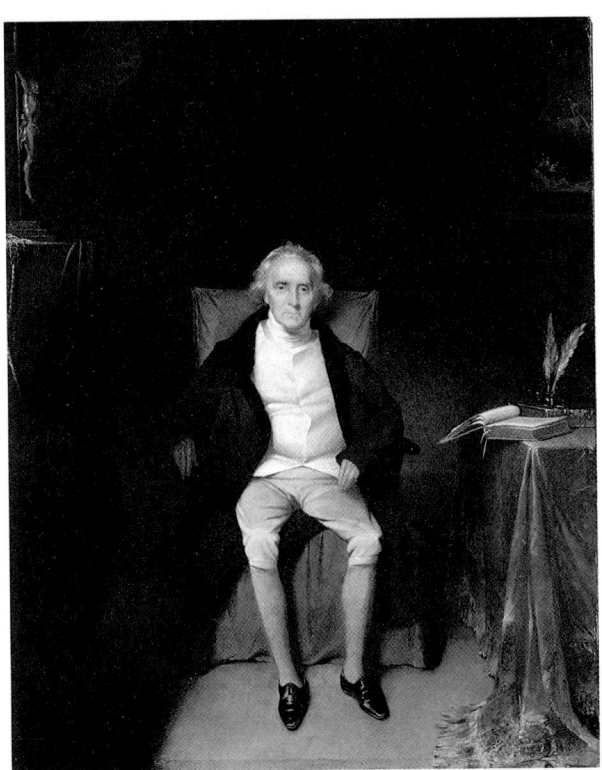

5.46. *William James Hubard (American, 1807–1862). Charles Carroll of Carrollton, circa 1830. Oil on panel, 18¾ × 14½ inches. The Metropolitan Museum of Art, New York, Rogers Fund.*

such an old-fashioned piece of furniture would have been its usefulness, the influence of sentiment and nostalgia may have played a role as well. As the New England social historian Joseph B. Felt wrote of such chests in 1853:

> Not a few of such tall venerable-looking pieces of furniture still survive. They were owned by some of our early settlers and made of cherry and black walnut woods. Supported on high legs, they had drawers of different lengths and depths, all forming an agreeable *tout ensemble*. Some of them have much ornamental work. They are still used by a few families, who carefully preserve them for the sake of their revered ancestors. They are keepsakes from those who were once familiar with them, but [who] have long since been conversant with the momentous realities of the spiritual world.[32]

Although Felt was speaking of the customs of mid-century New England, similar sentiments were no doubt also held in the New York of the 1820s, where, as suggested earlier, Washington Irving's works had begun to create an aura of romanticism around the past. Such an old-fashioned high chest, although it had no roots in Dutch design or culture but rather was an American creation based on English traditions, might well have been revered by a Dutch-American family of the time. (As a matter of fact, the family in which this particular high chest became an heirloom was, despite its anglicized name, itself Dutch.[33]) That such objects provided no link to the Netherlands is beside the point. They could have been treasured simply for their age and thus survive to provide a record of a family's early steps toward Americanization.

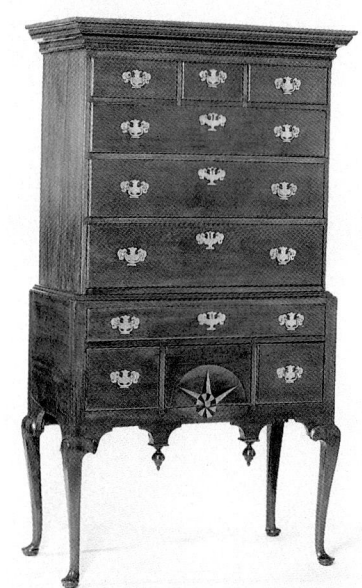

5.48. High Chest, 1760–1800. Probably New York. Walnut and cherry; poplar and chestnut, 71 × 40½ × 20 inches. The Brooklyn Museum 77.47, Gift of The Roebling Society and Mrs. Remsen Johnson, Jr.

THE BEDROOM BEHIND THE DINING ROOM

This room was originally nearly identical in size and shape to the bedroom behind the parlor. As a photograph of the room on site (*fig. 5.49*) shows, however, it came to the Museum a quite different interior, having gained a corner alcove when the original rear middle room was turned into a hallway. This alcove, as noted in Chapter 4, was created by moving a portion of the bedroom's inner wall, which had originally been totally flush with the door to the middle room. Now, at regular intervals along the lower edge of the beam beside the door (which is seen in the on-site photograph with a transom that was added in the late nineteenth century and hence not included in the installation) there are filled mortise holes from the studs that once defined the portion of the wall that was moved. Near each hole is a Roman numeral following in sequence the studs of the remaining original wall.

When the room was first installed at the Museum (*see figs. 5.50–5.52*), the alcove was interpreted as a built-in, or cupboard, bed and was thought to represent a rare instance of the survival into the eighteenth century of the Dutch custom of sleeping in cupboard beds. Years later, in 1964, Lillian Tyler Pelham Bantz would provide support for this theory when she wrote to the Museum with memories of the house passed on to her by her mother, Ida Whittaker Pelham, who, as noted in Chapter 4, had lived there with her parents during the occupancy of James Schenck, or, as she called him, Uncle Jimmie. "'Uncle Jimmie' went with the lease," Mrs. Bantz recalled her mother telling her, "and he slept in the cupboard bedstead built into a

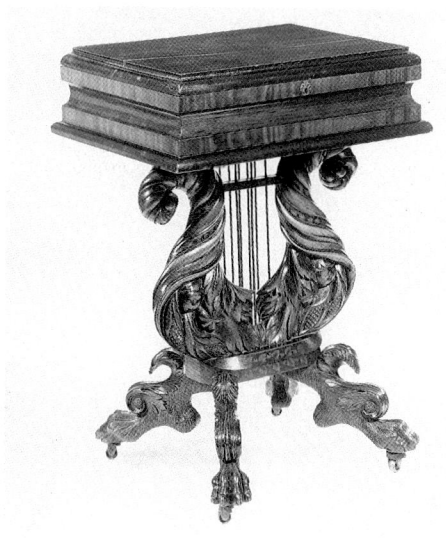

5.47. Dressing Table, circa 1825. New York. Cherry and poplar with mahogany veneer, 35 × 23¼ × 18½ inches. The Brooklyn Museum 81.32.1, Gift of Mrs. Donald Oenslager.

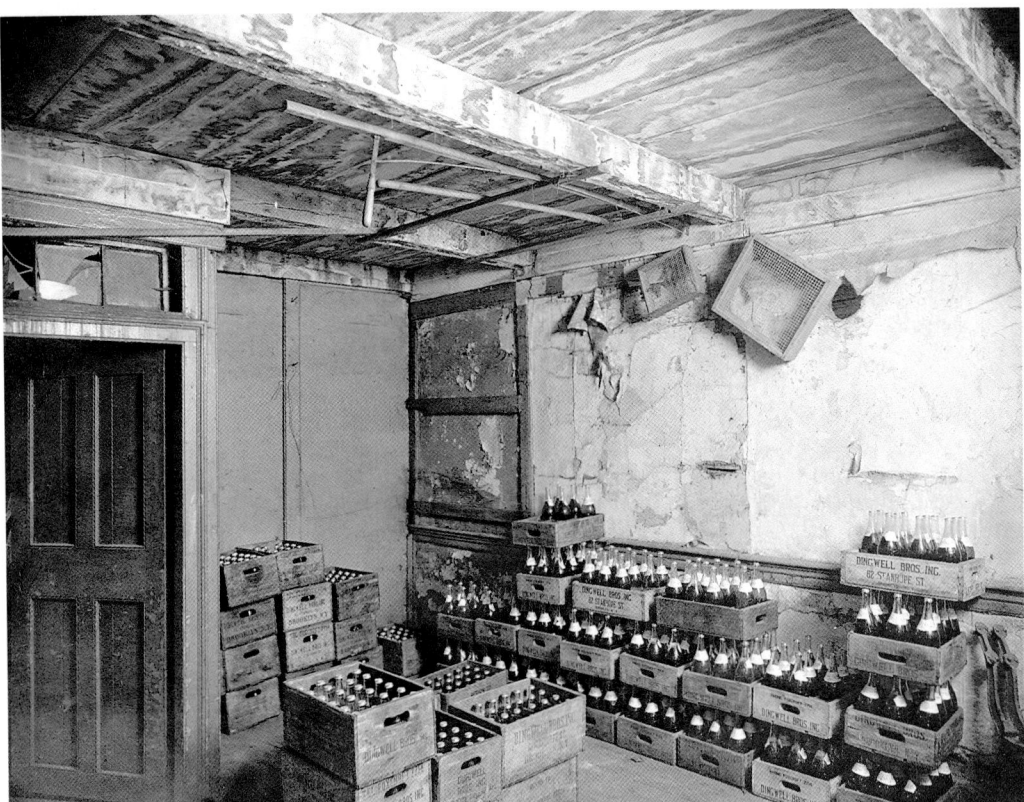

5.49. Bedroom behind the Dining Room, Nicholas Schenck House, in situ, *circa 1929.*

5.50–5.51. Bedroom behind the Dining Room, Nicholas Schenck House, as installed in The Brooklyn Museum, *circa 1929–36.*

small alcove, which was closed off from the bedroom with curtains."[34]

There is, however, no physical evidence that the alcove was intended to be used as a cupboard bed, and the presence of an early nineteenth-century chair rail along the short wall of the alcove in the on-site photograph indicates that when the room was first remodeled the alcove was treated simply as an extension of the room. In any case, since the alcove dates from around 1800, its use as a cupboard bedstead could represent at best a revival of an old tradition rather than a survival; more likely it was transformed into a cupboard bed much later in the century by the eccentric "Uncle Jimmie."

In addition to the speculative re-creation of the cupboard bedstead with eighteenth-century-style paneling, photographs of the earliest installation show a room painted entirely white and equipped with eighteenth-century furniture, including at various times to the right of the door to the dining room either a New England high chest (see figs. 5.50 and 5.51) or a related New England chest-on-chest (fig. 5.52). At the windows and the bed, curtains of checked fabric were hung.

Later, as in the rest of the house, the woodwork was painted dark, and during the refurbishing of 1967 the New England chests were replaced by a more appropriate New York *kas* (see fig. 5.53) and the desk now used in the dining room was installed in the corner by the window (see fig. 5.54). Over all this time, however, the corner alcove continued to be treated as a cupboard bed.

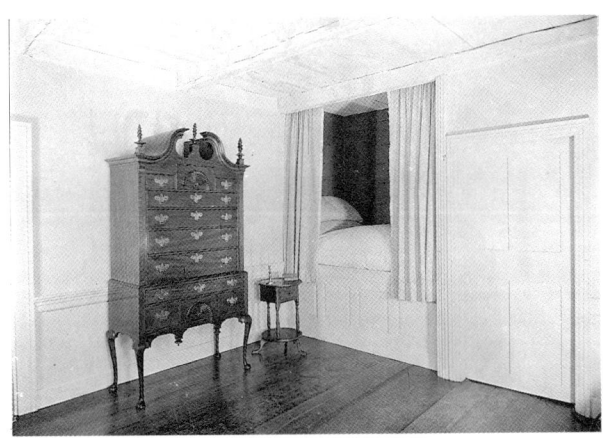

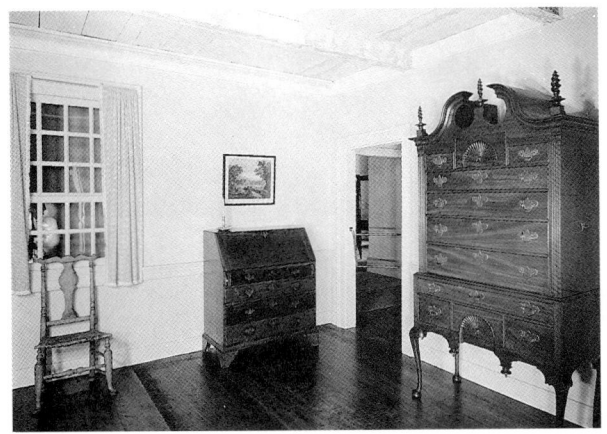

CONSUMER GOODS AND FAMILY HEIRLOOMS, OR THE MORN OF INDEPENDENCE

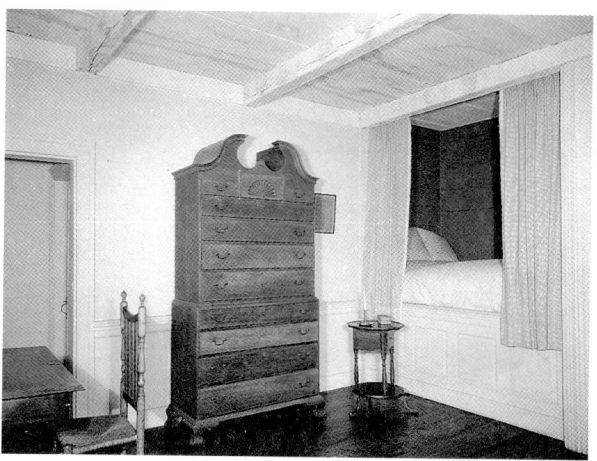

5.52. *Bedroom behind the Dining Room, Nicholas Schenck House, as installed in The Brooklyn Museum, circa 1929–36.*

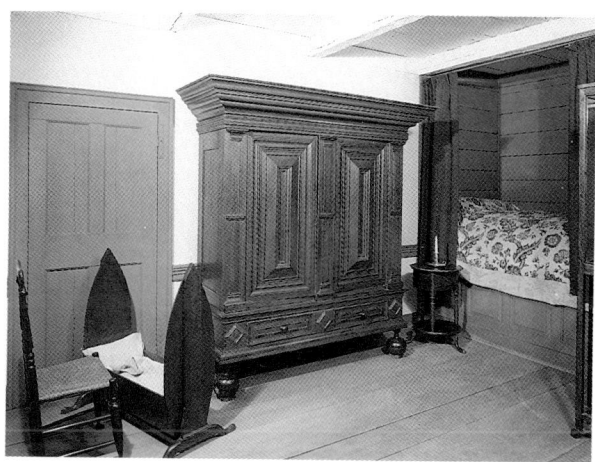

5.53. *Bedroom behind the Dining Room, Nicholas Schenck House, as installed in The Brooklyn Museum, circa 1968.*

During the reinstallation of the room in the early 1980s, the conviction that this space should be restored to a simple nook led to the addition of a freestanding bed that entirely altered the room's appearance. Now the installation is intended to give the impression of a simple, practical interior whose look just happened without specific planning, like the bedroom seen through the doorway in Charles Bird King's *The Itinerant Artist* of circa 1830 (fig. 5.55). It is casually arranged, therefore, for the sake of convenience, incorporating a number of literal quotes from the King painting (see figs. 5.56 and 5.57). A looking glass in an old-fashioned Chippendale-style frame, for instance, hangs near a window where there would have been plenty of light,[35] while on a rocking chair below are a pewter basin for morning washing and, draped over the crest of the chair, a linen towel. A simple linen panel is hung on a string at the window, and a trundle bed is pulled out a bit from beneath the low-post bedstead,

which is placed flush with the right half of the windowsill. Nearby, a coat hangs conveniently on a hook in the wall.

Some of the furniture in the room represents old Dutch or Long Island forms relegated to the back of the house like a memory at the back of the mind. Foremost among these is a mid-eighteenth-century New York *kas* (fig. 5.58), placed, as in the installation of 1967, to the right of the door to the dining room where the New England pieces formerly stood. This *kas* came to the Museum in 1921 from a Brooklyn family whose genealogy includes ties to the Cortelyous, the Bergens, the Leffertses, the van Brunts, and the Kouwenhovens, all early Kings County families, any one of which might have been the original owners.[36]

Such American *kassen* were simpler versions of elaborate seventeenth-century Dutch *kassen* like the one seen in the Jan Schenck House in the full-blown Baroque style (fig. 2.15). Made throughout the eighteenth century, they continued in service well into the nineteenth, their use spreading, probably through intermarriage, from the Dutch to the English. Thus it is not at all unusual to find among the estate inventories of the time a case like that of a resident of the old English settlement of Gravesend named Daniel Stillwell, whose possessions at his death in 1834 included "1 Dutch cupboard."[37]

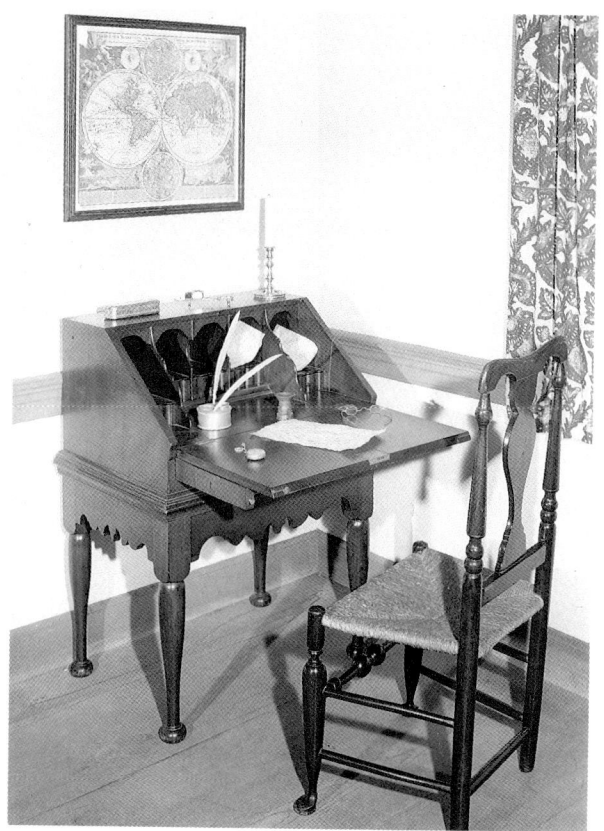

5.54. *Bedroom behind the Dining Room, Nicholas Schenck House, as installed in The Brooklyn Museum, circa 1968.*

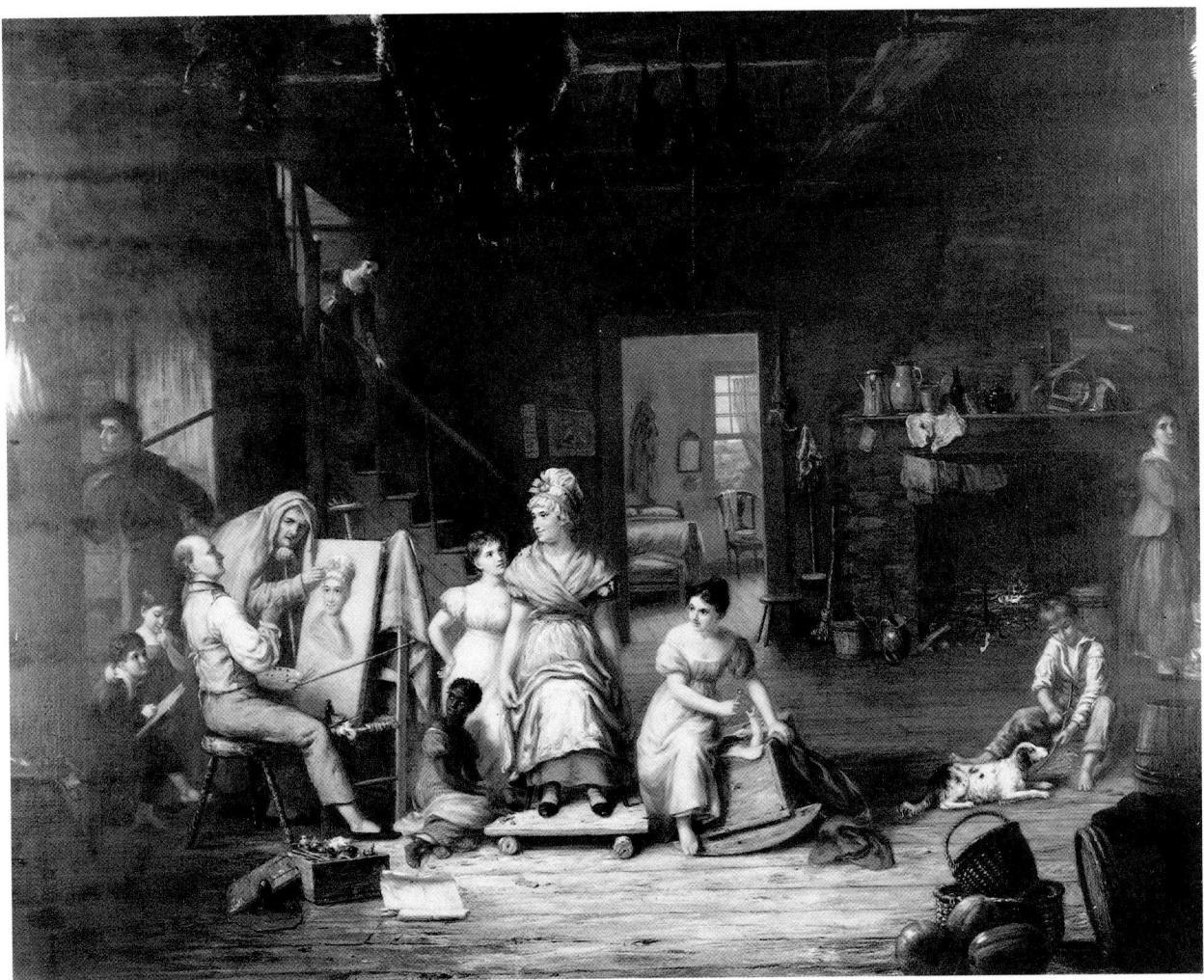

5.55. *Charles Bird King (American, 1785–1862).* The Itinerant Artist, *circa 1830. Oil on canvas 44¾ × 57 inches. New York State Historical Association, Cooperstown.*

If the Nicholas Schenck family owned such a piece —and a listing for a "wardrobe" valued at $5 in James Schenck's estate inventory of 1885 (the second most valuable item listed there) suggests they might have—it was undoubtedly first used in the "best" room of the house for the storage of linen. By the 1820s, however, the Schencks probably would have considered it too old-fashioned to fit in with their more up-to-date decor, though still functional enough to be put to use in a bedroom at the back. There it might have remained another fifty years or so, for the earliest indication we have of kassen falling totally from grace dates to 1881, when Gertrude Lefferts Vanderbilt wrote in *The Social History of Flatbush:*

> The old cupboards have been banished to the garret or consigned to the cellar; only a few of them still remain with paneled doors and dark cherry-wood shelves, seeming to bid defiance to the ravages of time and to mock by their endurance the veneering of model furniture.
>
> Those which have not been altered have very heavy overhanging moldings upon the top, and stand on huge ball feet. The inconvenience of moving such heavy furniture resulted in the cutting off of all unnecessary ornamentation, and thus many of these curious old articles of furniture have been remodeled into ordinary clothes-presses.[38]

The makers of American *kassen* relied on a number of design sources—from Dutch *kassen* in America to their own and their patrons' memories to printed material like plates from Crispen de Passe II's *Furnituremaker's Workshop*, published in Amsterdam in 1642.[39] They substituted local woods—walnut or cherry with secondary woods of pine and poplar—for rosewood and ebony, and they favored applied pilasters over carved ornament and freestanding columns, but they never abandoned the Baroque ideal of a strong architectural presence. With its vigorously articulated paneled doors and deep, heavy cornice molding, the *kas* shown here is a particularly fine and robust example of the best of their art, reflecting a continuing Baroque fascination with the three-dimensional effect of an architectural form in space.

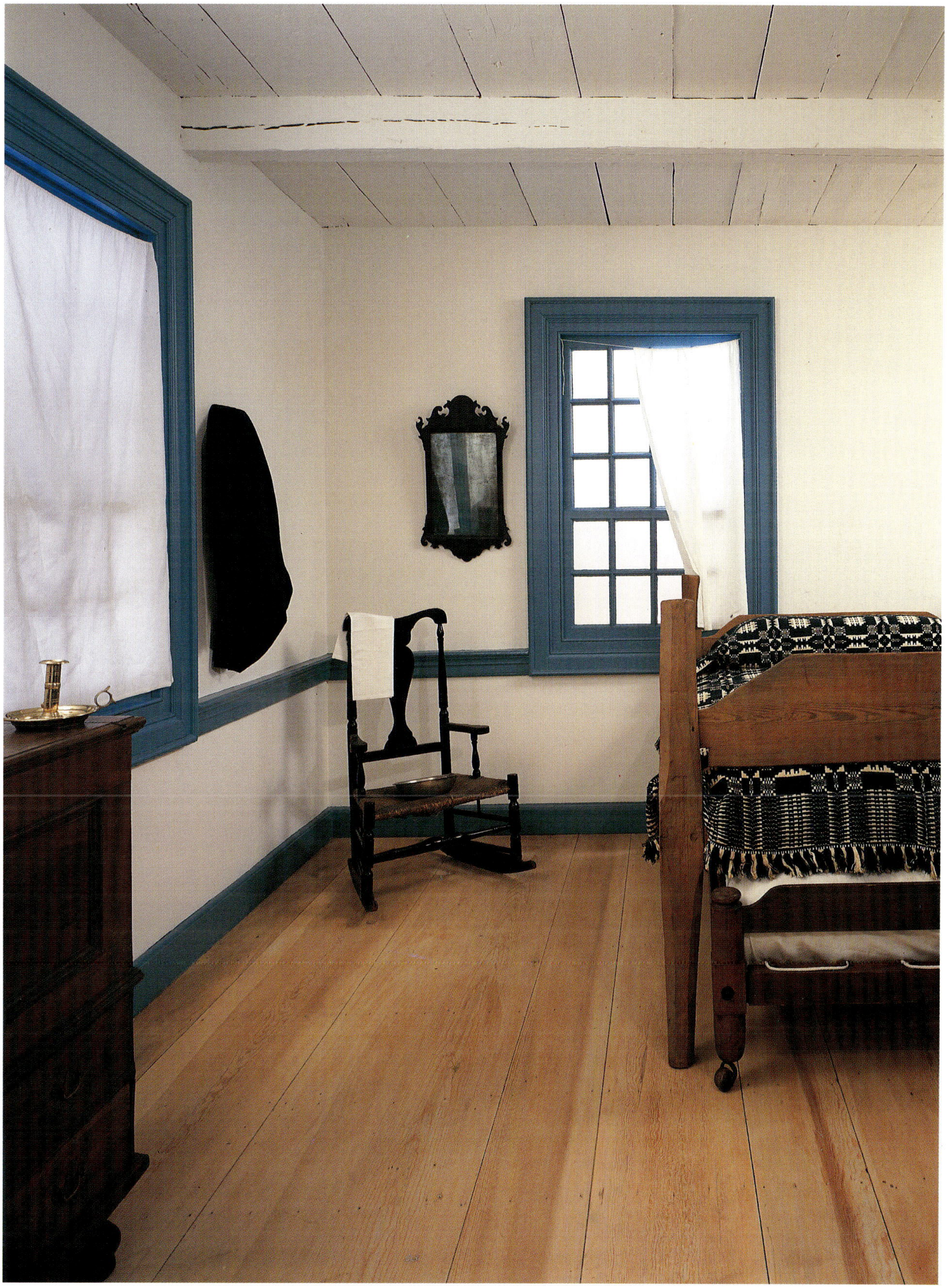

5.56. Bedroom behind the Dining Room, Nicholas Schenck House, as installed in The Brooklyn Museum, 1984. Photograph by Paul Warchol.

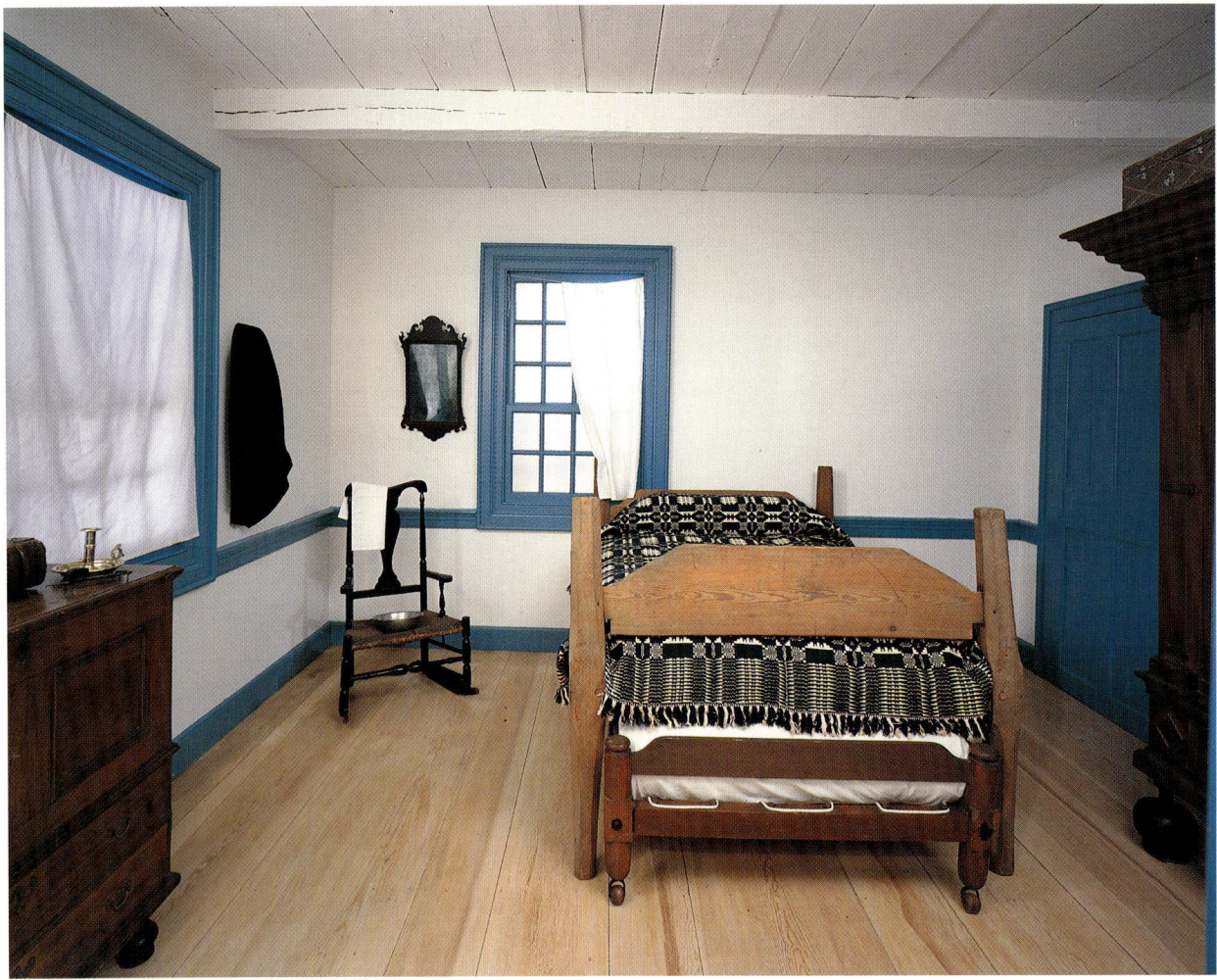

5.57. *Bedroom behind the Dining Room, Nicholas Schenck House, as installed in The Brooklyn Museum, 1984. Photograph by Paul Warchol.*

A similarly sturdy piece of old-fashioned furniture—a double-paneled Long Island chest with drawers that also dates from the mid-eighteenth century (*see fig. 5.59*)—is located against the wall opposite the *kas*, to the left of the window. Formerly used in the room across the hall in the installation of 1967, it too represents an outmoded style of storage that would have been exiled to a minor room. Unlike the *kas*, however, this piece is probably an Anglo-American furniture form. Made with either one or two drawers beneath a chest with a hinged top, such pieces seem to be unique to Long Island, and most have histories in the eastern part of Queens County. They were made from about 1710 to about 1810 with only minor concessions to changing styles.[40]

Yet another Long Island item in the room is the rocking chair in the corner (*see fig. 5.60*). Like the paneled chest, chairs of this sort—with fiddlebacks, yolk crests, and turned rails and stiles—were produced for a long period of time during the eighteenth and the early nineteenth century. Since they were popular in areas with strong Dutch communities, they were once called not only fiddlebacks but also Dutch splat backs. Recent research, however, indicates that, like Long Island paneled chests, they were more frequently associated with families of English origin.[41] Usually made as armchairs or side chairs, they were also produced by the early nineteenth century as rocking chairs.[42] This particular chair, though, probably started its life in the late eighteenth century as a side chair and, like the house itself, was remodeled as tastes and needs changed. Its arms and rockers were most likely added in the early nineteenth century, a common practice then.

Although the bedstead used in this room was made in Alabama, its form is typical of simple beds used in rural areas throughout the country at the time. Trundle beds like the one beneath it served as space savers in households where large families occupied a small number of rooms and are listed in many Kings County inventories of the 1830s. The 1832 inventory of the estate of one Peter Stryker of Flatlands, for example, lists together with a bed found in the sitting room of Stryker's house a "trundle bed for same," and the estate

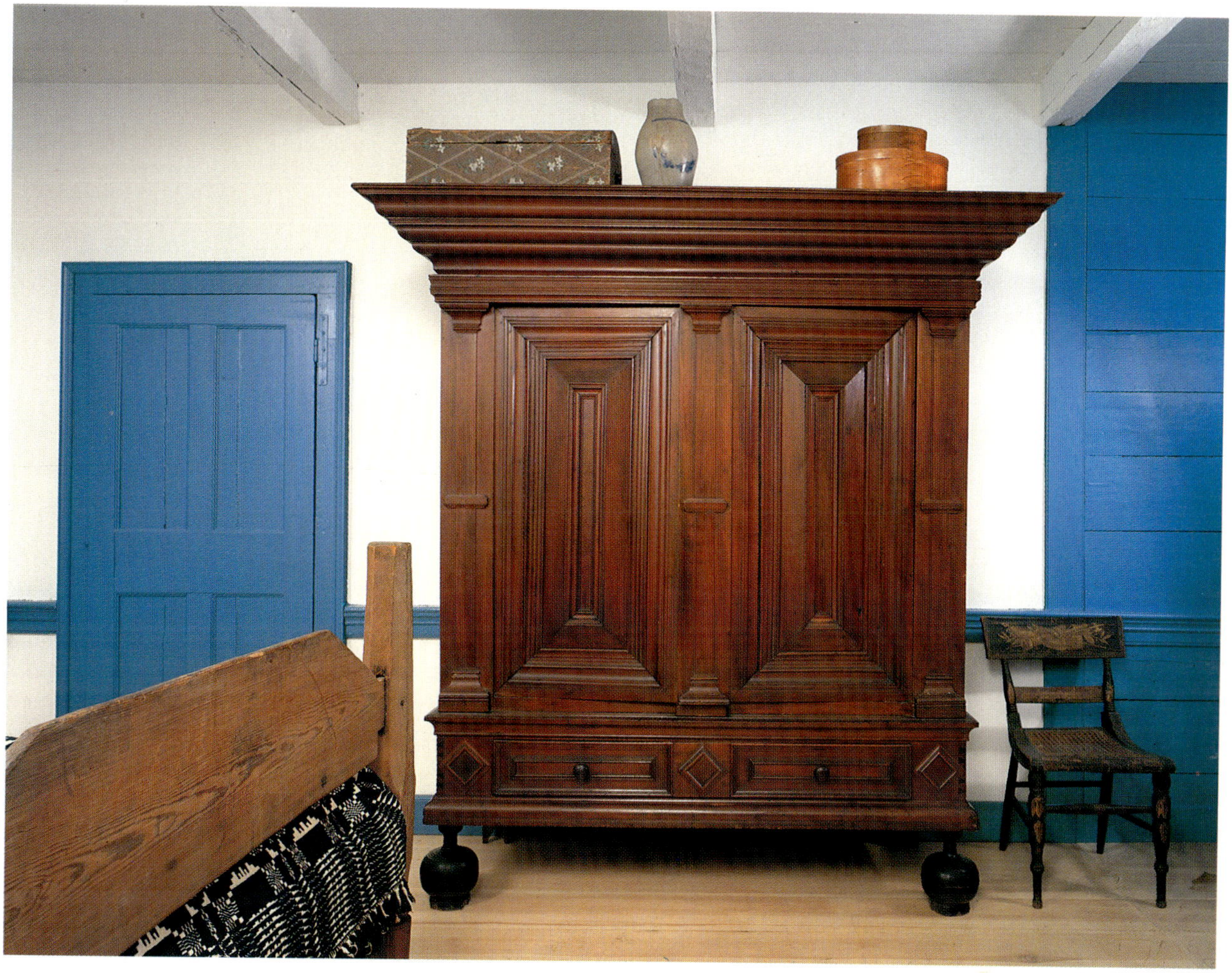

CONSUMER GOODS AND FAMILY HEIRLOOMS, OR THE MORN OF INDEPENDENCE

5.58. Kas, circa 1750. Long Island, New York. Cherry and walnut, 81 × 62 × 30 inches. The Brooklyn Museum 21.438, Gift of Mrs. Gertrude Cortelyou Bunn. Photograph by Paul Warchol.

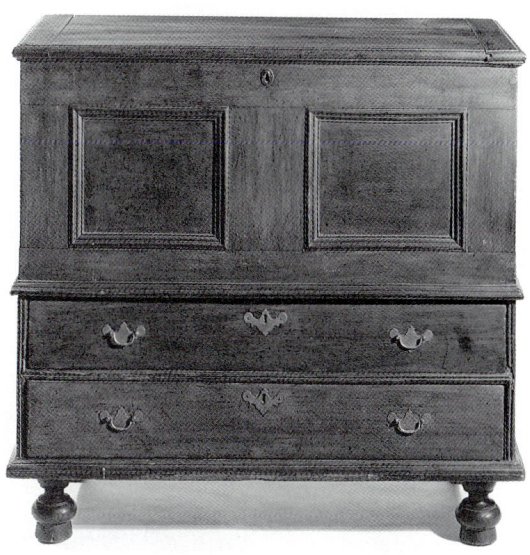

5.59. Chest with Drawers, circa 1750. Long Island, New York. Painted pine, 40 × 40 × 18¾ inches. The Brooklyn Museum 66.181, H. Randolph Lever Fund.

inventory of Stephen Voorhees, a carpenter from Gravesend who died in 1835, includes a "trunnel" bed.[43] In 1881 Gertrude Lefferts Vanderbilt remembered that such a bed was referred to in Dutch as "*een slaapbank op rollen.*"[44]

Among the accessories in the room are a few with special significance to the history of Dutch Americans. One, a large leather-bound Dutch Bible with brass fastening clasps on the Long Island paneled chest, is a reminder of the continued importance of the Dutch Reformed Church in their daily lives. Published in Dordrecht in 1741, it belonged originally not to the Schencks but to the Ditmars family of Kings County. Nonetheless, it bears a strong resemblance to the family Bible of Nicholas Schenck, Sr., which is still in private hands, in that its register of the births and deaths of the Ditmars family is in Dutch up until 1781 and in English after 1783. The Schenck family Bible records the births of all the children of Nicholas, Sr., and his first wife Willemtje in Dutch up until the birth of their last child, a daughter, in 1776 and also notes the death of Willemtje Schenck herself in Dutch in 1779.[45]

Although such Bibles were in a language fewer and fewer Dutch Americans understood, they continued to be cherished into the early nineteenth century, as evidenced by the fact that when a certain John Barrett of Bushwick died in 1820 a "large Dutch family Bible" was included in his will. Some idea of their monetary worth is provided by the inventory of the estate of a resident of Flatlands named Elias Hubbard who died in 1833. Though the language of the "large Bible" listed there is not mentioned, the Bible itself is valued at $4.[46] James Schenck's estate inventory of 1885, on the other hand, describes the "three family Bibles" found among his possessions as having "no value," perhaps because they too were in Dutch and by that time Dutch had fallen totally from use.

If the family Bible displayed in this room represents the Schencks' continued attachment to certain of their Dutch traditions, the linen sampler on the wall above it (*fig. 5.61*) signifies their pride at having assimilated into the larger American culture. Made by the younger Nicholas Schenck's daughter Jane in January 1805, when she was twelve years old, this sampler is one of the few objects now in the house that was probably also a part of the household in the early nineteenth century. Young girls frequently made such pieces to demonstrate their accomplishment at needlework, but this one reveals a good deal more—and merely by the spelling of the date, which is English, not Dutch. Clearly, Jane Schenck had been schooled to give up the ancestral tongue.

This is the same Jane Schenck who began, seven years later, to keep the journal discussed in Chapter 3. Hers, it seems, is one ghost the current installation

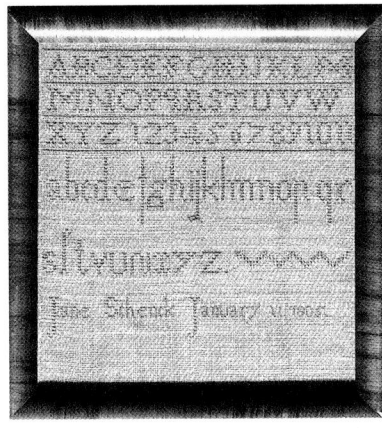

5.61. Jane Schenck (American, 1792–1843). Sampler, 1805. Flatlands, New York. Linen, 9⅛ × 8¾ inches. The Brooklyn Museum 49.176.2, Gift of Elsie O. Hincken.

of the house has managed to stir, for it was during the preparation of this book in 1987 that her journal resurfaced in a drawer in the Museum's Decorative Arts Department. Although it had been safely preserved, it had long been forgotten and had never before been closely examined. On inspection, it proved to be a fruitful document, for as one can see in the following passage of 1814, it brings these rooms to life and conveys a sense of their social history in a way no mannequin or system of taped commentary could ever hope to do:

> Remsen, Julia & myself took a trip to Jamaica [in Queens County], went to the Dutch church in the forenoon, in the afternoon to the Presbyterian meeting. R & J return'd home Sunday afternoon without me. . . .The night previous to my coming away I staid at Oldfield Bergens, where his Parents stopt for me at 1 Oclock in the night, to come down to Brooklyn in their waggon & a jolly ride we had, for whenever I felt sleepy, Mr. B. would rouse me up & call for a song. It was the morn of Independence, & we serenaded the neighbouring houses as we passed with several . . . songs, such as "the old maids last prayer," "Sailors advise," "Yorkshire Merchant," etc.[47]

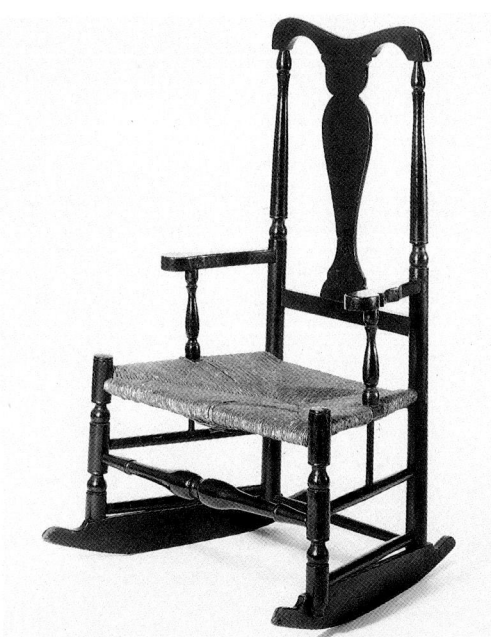

5.60. Side Chair, *late eighteenth century (converted to rocking chair early nineteenth century). Long Island, New York. Painted wood, 40 × 24⁷⁄₁₆ × 16 inches. The Brooklyn Museum   34.1152, Gift of Mrs. Clair McKelway.*

Just as the rooms of the house in which she lived combined the old with the new, the Dutch with the English, so did Jane Schenck herself. Tellingly, she could go to a Reformed church in the morning (where the service may have been in Dutch) and a Presbyterian in the afternoon (where the meeting was no doubt in English) and think nothing of it. In part that was because both churches were Calvinist in doctrine and presbyterian with a small *p* in government. But more to the point is that she had acquired a new identity whose noblest sentiments encouraged her to look beyond the old divisions among peoples and institutions and seek the common ground. In the end, it is the morning of July 4 that raises her spirits and moves her to song. If one could meet her, one would undoubtedly form the same impression one gets in walking through her house: the Schencks were, by this time, fully American.

NOTES

CHAPTER ONE: THE VENERABLE FOREFATHER

1. The Reverend William Edward Schenck, "Account of my trips to Holmdel, N.J. & to Flatlands, L.I.," unpublished journal, The Brooklyn Museum Library Collection, 1891, pp. 15–16. The Reverend Schenck mistakenly believed that the house had been built by Roeloff Schenck, Jan's brother. I would like to thank George T. Griswold for bringing this journal to my attention and depositing it at the Museum.
2. The deed reads as follows:

   Petrus Stuyvesant & the Council of New Netherland have granted to Jan Martensen land near the village of Amesfoort on the northwest side of Peter Claessen, and southwest side [of] a small meadow, south east a kil [creek], containing 12 morgens [1 morgen = 2.116 acres] 182 r[o]ds; also a parcel of flatland bounded on the southwest side by Peter Wophertsen van Couwenhoven, on the northwest by Govert Loockermans, in width 38 rods and in length 162 rods, containing 10 morgens. fort Amsterdam 20 August, 1660.

   From Berthold Fernow, ed., *Documents Relative to the Colonial History of the State of New York,* vol. 14 (Albany: Weed, Parsons & Co., 1883), p. 479.

3. Fernow, vol. 14, p. 479, says that "on August 28, 1660, the same 'Jan Martense' conveyed to Pieter Claesen (van Norden) the twelve morgens first named in the previous deed, on the north west side of the land of Pieter Claesz by virtue of a deed dated August 20, 1660, granted to the party appearing by Governor Stuyvesant." See also Charles Arthur Hoppin, *The Washington Ancestry and Records of the McClain, Johnson, and Forty Other Colonial American Families* (Greenfield, OH: privately printed, 1932), vol. 3, pp. 148–49; English Transcript of Flatlands Town Records, Deeds, Miscellaneous, 1661–1831, St. Francis College, Brooklyn, p. 54; Rosalie Fellows Bailey, *Pre-Revolutionary Dutch Houses and Families in Northern New Jersey and Southern New York* (1936; reprint ed., New York: Dover, 1968), p. 66.
4. Edmund Bailey O'Callaghan, ed., *The Documentary History of the State of New York,* vol. 1 (Albany: Weed, Parsons & Co., 1849–51), p. 429; Bailey 1968, p. 66; Hoppin, p. 148.
5. Hoppin, pp. 147–48.
6. Ibid., p. 111.
7. See Rosalie Fellows Bailey, unpublished research report, The Brooklyn Museum, January 1964; also William J. Hoffman, *New York Genealogical and Biographical Record,* vol. 68 (1937), pp. 114–18.
8. Bailey 1964; see also Fernow, vol. 14, p. 511.
9. Hoppin, p. 148; Flatlands Church Records, p. 19.
10. The deed reads as follows:

    On this 29th of December sixteen hundred and seventy five, appeared before me Michil Hainelle, licensed clerk of the 5 Dutch towns on Long Island, the worthy Capt. Elbert Elbertse, residing at Amsfort, who in the presence of the undersigned witnesses transports cedes and conveys with these presents for him and his heirs and descendants to and in behalf of Jan Martense a certain half mill situated under the jurisdiction of Amsfort on the place called Mill Islet (*molen Eilandje*) with the same small island with the kill included...which he the party appearing with these presents transports free and unincumbered, saving the Lord's right, desisting with these presents from all his ownership and equity, in order to invest therewith the above mentioned Jan Martense, whom the party appearing with these presents places in full possession to own forever and to dispose of according to his desire, in as much as he the party appearing by the above mentioned Jan Martense acknowledges honorably and clearly to be satisfied, and promises to free the same from all subsequent demands. Done at Amsfort day and date as above.
    Koert Stevensen
    Sijmon Jansen   Elbert Elbertsen

    As quoted in Frederick van Wyck, *Keskachauge or the First White Settlement on Long Island* (New York: Putnam, 1924), p. 724.

11. Van Wyck, p. 711; Bailey 1968, p. 66.
12. Bailey 1968, p. 66; see also Bailey 1964 and note 29 below.
13. Jasper Danckaerts and Peter Sluyter, "Journal of a Voyage to New York and a Tour in Several of the American Colonies in 1679–1680," *Memoirs of The Long Island Historical Society,* vol. 1 (Brooklyn, 1867), pp. 130–31. Danckaerts and Sluyter were traveling in America to examine sites of possible settlement for the Labadists. The sect established a colony a few years later at the head of the Chesapeake Bay, but the colony did not prosper.
14. Stoothoff Papers, The Brooklyn Historical Society; Marvin D. Schwartz, *The Jan Martense Schenck House* (Brooklyn: The Brooklyn Museum, 1964), p. 25. Schwartz's book, now out of print, has provided a substantial portion of the information used in the current volume.
15. Fernow, vol. 2, p. 495; Bailey 1964; Schwartz, in *The Jan Martense Schenck House,* points out that in 1676 Schenck's property included:

    1 poll 3 horses 1 do. of 2 yrs. 1 do. of 2 yrs. 2 do. of
    1 yr. 3 cows 2 do. of 1 yr. £83
    10 morg. land & valley 30

    In 1683 it had grown to:

    one man, one negro, 2 horses, 1 of 3 yrs. 5 cows 2 of 3 yrs. 2 of 2 yrs. 2 of 1 yr. & 28 morgens land. . . . . £11. 9s.
    [approximately £141 in the currency of 1676]

16. Bailey 1964.

17. Van Wyck, p. 725; see also note 29 below.
18. Col. A. D. Schenck, "American Ancestry," *The Blyenbeck and Afferden Branch of the Family Schenck van Nydeck* (Hampton, VA: Normal School Press, 1885), pp. 25–26.
19. Ibid.; Bailey 1964.
20. Bailey 1964 points out that Schenck had probably not taken possession of the Mill Island property before September 1676, since he is not taxed for the property on the tax assessment of that date. In that assessment and in the assessment of August 24, 1675, he is taxed only for the remaining 21-odd acres of the 46½ or so he acquired in 1660. See assessment lists in O'Callaghan, vol. 2, p. 495; vol. 4, p. 155.
21. David Steven Cohen, "Defining the Dutch-American Farmhouse," unpublished manuscript, New Jersey Historical Commission, Trenton, 1986, p. 8.
22. Schwartz, *The Jan Martense Schenck House*, pp. 12 and 13.
23. Cohen, p. 10. Cohen designates the wood-frame houses of Kings County, New York, and Monmouth County, New Jersey, as one of four regional subtypes built by Dutch Americans. The other subtypes he identifies as the red sandstone houses of Bergen, Morris, and Passaic Counties, New Jersey, and Rockland County, New York; the gray fieldstone houses of the middle Hudson Valley and the upper Delaware Valley; and the brick houses of the upper Hudson Valley.
24. Isaac Jogues, "Description of New Netherlands," August 3, 1646. In "The Jogues Papers," trans. by John Gilmay Shea in *Collections of The New-York Historical Society*, 2nd series, vol. 3, part 1 (New York: D. Appleton & Co., 1857), p. 217.
25. Stoothoff Papers, The Brooklyn Historical Society, translated typescript, p. 25; Schwartz, *The Jan Martense Schenck House*, p. 22.
26. Schwartz, *The Jan Martense Schenck House*, p. 17.
27. Ibid., p. 14.
28. Henk J. Zantkuyl, "Reconstructie van Enkele Nederlanse Huizen in Nieuw-Nederland uit de Zeventiende Eeuw," *Bulletin KNOB*, vol. 84, no. 2/3 (June 1985), pp. 166–79; supplemented by consultation with Zantkuyl July–October 1986. Zantkuyl's 1985–86 conception of the house modifies an earlier conception he proposed in 1964. See Henk J. Zantkuyl, "Het Jan Martense Schenckhuis Te Brooklyn," *Bulletin KNOB*, 6th series, vol. 17 (1964). Marvin Schwartz mentions the possibility of a partition in the north room in "The Jan Martense Schenck House in The Brooklyn Museum," *Antiques*, vol. 85, no. 4 (April 1964), p. 421.
29. The will reads as follows:

> In the name of Jesus Christ in the yeare when wee writt 1688/9 ye 28th January JOHN MARTENSE present sickly a bedd butt with perfect knowledge is willing ffirst and beffore all to dispose of his temporale estate. IMPIRIS his wife Jannetie Stephens shall remaine in ffull possession of ye estate moveable and immovable. Second she shall remaine till ye yongest child shall be at age, or come to marriage. Thirdly then shall Marten Johnson take in his possession viz the old land with ye small island and mill and dependencies thereoff with this condition that the sd Marten Johnson shall every yeare render to his mother the sume of Six hundred Guildens during her life. Fourthly the youngest sunn Viz Stephen Johnson shall have the lott land in the neck with the middow, to hoggs neck with all ye dependencies. Fiffthly the other children shall have ffor theire portion out ye estate Viz Stephen Johnson shall have One hundred pieces off eight Jannetje Johnson shall have ffor her portion One hundred pieces off eight with two cows, one bedd or a due outsetting and Willemtie Johnson ye like portion Viz One hundred pieces of eight two cows, one bedd or a due outsetting Neeltie Johnson shall have the saime portion, my wiffe present with child in case She shall have a sunn he shall have ffor his portion ye monny standing out att New Yorke the summ off Sixteen hundred gildens, butt in case itt shall be a daughter then she shall have no more than ye s^d other daughters viz One hundred pieces off eight two Cowes, one bedd or a due outsetting with ye others, when the said Martin Johnson shall take ye estate in possession and beeing settled, then ye other children shall have each ffor his part the sume off Ffive hundred guildens except Steven Johnson, in case itt shall be a sonn as afores he shall receive this Ffive hundred guildens like wise, in case ye underaged children shall come to dye ye survivants shall sheare that part or parts equally, day and date as above in Kings County in Amesffortt. 1688/9 ye 28th January
> Signed
> Jan Martense Schenck
>
> Testis
> Jan van Dyckhuyse
> William Gerritsen van Couwenhoven
>
> Recorded by ordre off the court of sessions held the 2nd day off April 1689 In Kings County being the original will in dayth. Proved and the above named witnesses sworne.

As quoted in van Wyck, pp. 725–26.
30. Bailey 1968, p. 67.
31. Schwartz, *The Jan Martense Schenck House*, pp. 15–17. Schwartz also proposes that another door was added then, opposite the other side of the south room's fireplace. But if anything was added there, it was more likely the window proposed by Zantkuyl.
32. Bailey 1968, p. 67.
33. Ibid.
34. See van Wyck, pp. 726–27.
35. Bailey 1968, pp. 67–68.
36. Henry R. Stiles, *The Civil, Political, Professional and Ecclesiastical History and Commercial and Industrial Record of the County of Kings and the City of Brooklyn, N.Y. from 1683 to 1884* (New York and Brooklyn: W. W. Munsell & Co., 1884), vol. 1, p. 69; Bailey 1968, p. 67.
37. Bailey 1968, p. 68, documents the descent as follows:

> Joris Martense, bap. May 29, 1724, d. May 23, 1791, married and had two sons who died in infancy, another son who was a bachelor, and a married daughter who inherited the mill property. The daughter Susan Martense, b. Jan. 15, 1777, married Feb. 11, 1802 John H. Cowenhoven of New Utrecht (1769–1806) and had two daughters who remained in New Utrecht; she married secondly Patrick Caton and had one daughter before he died April 13, 1818. This daughter, Margaret Caton, b. May 31, 1815, d. March 8, 1858, married Nov. 26, 1837 Gen. Philip S. Crooke; they lived in the old Martense home in Flatbush. Mrs. Caton devised the mill and other property in trust for her daughter Margaret, wife of Philip S. Crooke, and she in turn willed the property in trust for her children. After eleven conveyances between various members of the Crooke family, the first dated July 5, 1870 from Philip to Robert for 500 acres of meadows and 5 acres on Mill Island with grist mill and mill dam and 66

acres of upland, the title to the Mill Island part of the property became vested in Robert L. Crooke.
38. The Reverend Schenck, pp. 16–17.
39. Teunis G. Bergen, *Early Settlers of Kings County* (New York: S. W. Green's Son, 1881), p. 250.
40. The Reverend Schenck, pp. 17–18.
41. Ibid., pp. 18–19.
42. "Private Captain Schenck," *The Kings County Journal*, vol. 8, no. 16 (August 5, 1891). From an unpaged typescript in the files of The Brooklyn Museum Department of Decorative Arts.
43. The Reverend Schenck, p. 23.
44. Charles Andrew Ditmas, *Historic Homesteads of Kings County* (Brooklyn: Charles A. Ditmas, 1909), p. 21.
45. *The New York Times*, December 7, 1924.
46. Ibid., April 20, 1933.

CHAPTER TWO:
OF CUPBOARD BEDS AND HEARTHS WITHOUT JAMBS

1. Sarah Kemble Knight, *The Journal of Madame Knight*, introductory note by Malcolm Freiberg (Boston: David R. Godine, 1972), p. 29.
2. Ibid.
3. Esther Singleton, *Dutch New York* (New York: Dodd Mead & Co., 1909), p. 93.
4. A. J. F. van Laer, trans. and ed., *Correspondence of Jeremias van Rensselaer, 1651–1674* (Albany: University of the State of New York, 1932), p. 238.
5. Knight, p. 29.
6. Marvin D. Schwartz, *The Jan Martense Schenck House* (Brooklyn: The Brooklyn Museum), p. 17.
7. Ibid.
8. Adriaen van der Donck, *A Description of the New Netherlands*, Thomas F. O'Donnell, ed. (Syracuse, NY: Syracuse University Press, 1968), p. 23; originally published in Amsterdam, 1655.
9. Henk J. Zantkuyl, "Reconstructie van Enkele Nederlanse Huizen in Nieuw-Nederland uit de Zeventiende Eeuw," *Bulletin KNOB*, vol. 84, no. 2/3 (June 1985), pp. 166–79.
10. See Appendix.
11. Singleton, p. 44. For their labor, the carpenters were paid "five hundred and fifty guilders, one-third in beavers, one-third in good merchantable wampum, one-third in good silver coin, and free passage over the ferry so long as the work continues, and small beer to be drunk during work."
12. Schwartz, *The Jan Martense Schenck House*, p. 30.
13. Manuscript letters from Mary van Kleeck in the files of The Brooklyn Museum Department of Decorative Arts; Singleton, p. 99; D. T. Valentine, *Manual of the Corporation of the City of New York for 1858* (New York: Clerk of the Common Council, 1858), pp. 512–14; I. N. Phelps Stokes, *Iconography of Manhattan Island, 1498–1909* (New York: Robert H. Dodd, 1922), p. 318.
14. Singleton, p. 91.
15. Valentine, p. 514.
16. Singleton, p. 91.
17. Ibid., p. 98.
18. Ibid.
19. Ibid., p. 99.
20. These chairs were acquired in London in 1925 and are nearly identical to an example acquired by the Victoria and Albert Museum in 1926. Although it is likely the frames are early twentieth-century copies made in seventeenth-century style specifically to accommodate the Turkey work, the upholstery itself appears to date from around 1650.
21. Singleton, p. 97.
22. See Charlotte Wilcoxen, "Household Artifacts of New Netherland from its Archaeological and Documentary Records," *Bulletin KNOB*, vol. 84, no. 2/3 (June 1985), pp. 120–28; see also Alice P. Kenney, "Neglected Heritage: Hudson River Valley Dutch National Culture," *Winterthur Portfolio*, vol. 20, no. 1 (Spring 1985), p. 61.
23. Valentine, p. 513; Singleton, p. 99.
24. Singleton, pp. 93–94.
25. Van Laer, p. 291.
26. Singleton, p. 92.
27. Van Laer, p. 28. The invoice for the shipment reads as follows:

> [List] of the goods loaded in the ship den Otter, Pieter Janse Aemilius, master, which are entrusted to cousin Jeremias van Renselaer to be sold by him to our best advantage:
>
> 329 gill goblets @ fl. 7 per 100......fl. 23–
> 100 quarter-pint goblets @ fl. 10 per 100...10:–
> 62 half-pint goblets @ 3 st. apiece...9:6
> 25 pint goblets @ 4 st. apiece.....5:–
> 25 half-gill vials....–:15
> 25 fine beer glasses @ 3 st......3:15
> 125 half-gill goblets @ 4.50 per 100...5:12:8
> 24 pint measuring glasses @ 1½ st. apiece ..1:16
>
> 24 ditto half-pint glasses.....1:–
> For the case...3:15
>
> 739 pieces.....fl. 63:19:8
> (...) lbs of all kinds of silk, amounting to 27:–
> For duty, convoy and supervision.....3:–
> For insurance, valuation fl. 100....6:–:8
>   fl. 100:–:
>   Your willing servants
>   GERRET LAMBERTSZ COCK
>   and JAN VAN WELY

28. Wilcoxen, p. 125.
29. Singleton, pp. 94, 101.
30. Van Laer, p. 139.
31. Donald C. Peirce, "New York Furniture at The Brooklyn Museum," *Antiques*, vol. 115, no. 5 (May 1979), p. 995.
32. Files of The Brooklyn Museum Department of Decorative Arts.
33. Letter from Benno Forman to Wendy Cooper, February 8, 1973, in the files of The Brooklyn Museum Department of Decorative Arts.
34. Singleton, p. 89.
35. Ibid., pp. 90, 97.
36. Ibid., p. 104.
37. Ibid., p. 44. Van Borsum also paid the carpenters "to make a chimney mantel and to wainscot the foreroom below, and divide it in the centre across with a door in the partition; [and] to set a window frame with two glass lights therein."
38. Consultation with Henk J. Zantkuyl, July–October 1986.
39. See Appendix.
40. Wilcoxen, p. 126; van Laer, p. 238.
41. Singleton, p. 94.
42. Ibid., p. 101.
43. Jasper Danckaerts and Peter Sluyter, "Journal of a Voyage to New York and a Tour in Several of the American Colonies in 1679–1680," *Memoirs of The Long Island Historical Society*, vol. 1 (Brooklyn, 1867), pp. 131–32.

44. Marvin D. Schwartz, "The Jan Martense Schenck House in The Brooklyn Museum," *Antiques,* vol. 85, no. 4 (April 1964), p. 425; Stoothoff Papers, The Brooklyn Historical Society.
45. See Roderic H. Blackburn, "Dutch Arts and Culture in Colonial America," *Antiques,* vol. 130, no. 1 (July 1986), fig. 9.
46. Peirce, p. 996.
47. Singleton, pp. 96, 97.
48. Knight, p. 31.
49. Singleton, pp. 137, 138.
50. Kenney, p. 66.

Chapter Three:
From Dutch to Dutch American

1. Sixteen percent came from North Holland, ten percent from Gelderland, eight percent from Utrecht, three percent from South Holland, and three percent from Friesland. See David Steven Cohen, "How Dutch Were the Dutch of New Netherland?" *New York History* (January 1981), pp. 43–60.
2. Anita Libman Lebeson, "The American Jewish Chronicle," in Louis Finkelstein, ed., *The Jews: Their History, Culture, and Religion* (New York: Harper & Bros., 1949), vol. 1, p. 317; see also *The Jewish Community in Early New York, 1654–1800,* exhibition catalogue, Fraunces Tavern Museum (New York, 1979).
3. Isaac Jogues, "Description of New Netherlands," August 3, 1646. In "The Jogues Papers," trans. by John Gilmay Shea in *Collections of The New-York Historical Society,* second series, vol. 3, part 1 (New York: D. Appleton & Co., 1857), pp. 215–16.
4. Robert Juet, "The Third Voyage of Master Henry Hudson," in J. Franklin Jameson, *Narratives of New Netherland, 1609–1664* (1909; reprint ed., New York: Barnes & Noble, 1959), p. 18.
5. Adriaen van der Donck, *A Description of the New Netherlands,* Thomas F. O'Donnell, ed. (Syracuse, NY: Syracuse University Press, 1968), p. 2; originally published in Amsterdam, 1655.
6. Evert Nieuwenhof in ibid., p. x.
7. See Alice P. Kenney, *Stubborn for Liberty: The Dutch in New York* (Syracuse, NY: Syracuse University Press, 1975), pp. 31–32.
8. See Milton W. Hamilton, *Henry Hudson and the Dutch in New York* (Albany: University of the State of New York, 1964), pp. 46–47.
9. Van der Donck, pp. 7–8.
10. For more about Dutch settlement along the Delaware, see Henri and Barbara van der Zee, *A Sweet and Alien Land: The Story of Dutch New York* (New York: Viking Press, 1978), pp. 61–62 and passim.
11. David Pietersz de Vries, "Short Historical and Journal Notes of Several Voyages in the Four Parts of the World," in *Collections of The New-York Historical Society,* second series, vol. 3, part 1 (New York: D. Appleton & Co., 1857), p. 89.
12. Van der Zee, p. 78.
13. Van der Donck, p. 129.
14. Ibid., p. 19.
15. Ibid., pp. 29–30.
16. Ibid., p. 20.
17. Ibid., p. 45.
18. De Vries, p. 89.
19. See, for example, A. Leon Higginbotham, Jr., *In the Matter of Color: Race and the American Legal Process: The Colonial Period* (New York: Oxford University Press, 1978), pp. 100–5.
20. Ibid., pp. 105–9.
21. Adriaen van der Donck, et al., "The Representation of New Netherland," in Jameson, pp. 329–30. In defense of the West India Company's handling of the matter, company official Cornelis van Tienhoven wrote to the Dutch government, "At present there are only three of these children [of half-freed slaves] who do any service. One of them is at the House of Hope [a trading post on the present site of Hartford, Connecticut], one at the Company's bouwery, and one with Martin Crigier, who has brought the girl up well, as everybody knows." See Jameson, pp. 364–65.
22. Michael G. Kammen, *Colonial New York: A History* (New York: Charles Scribner's Sons, 1975), pp. 17–19.
23. De Vries, p. 94.
24. Van der Donck, pp. 20–22.
25. See Kenney 1975, pp. 25–31.
26. Van der Donck, p. 71.
27. Ibid., p. 94.
28. See Hamilton, p. 54.
29. Letter from the Rev. Samuel Drisius to the Classis of Amsterdam, September 15, 1664, in Jameson, pp. 414–15.
30. See Higginbotham, pp. 114–23.
31. Jasper Danckaerts and Peter Sluyter, "Journal of a Voyage to New York and a Tour in Several of the American Colonies in 1679–1680," in *Memoirs of The Long Island Historical Society,* vol. 1 (Brooklyn, 1867), p. 136.
32. See Higginbotham, pp. 116, 122.
33. Kammen, pp. 91, 145.
34. Governor Dongan's Report to the Committee of Trade on the Province of New York, February 22, 1687. In Edmund Bailey O'Callaghan, ed., *The Documentary History of the State of New York,* vol. 1 (Albany: Weed, Parsons & Co., 1849–51), pp. 161–62.
35. Ibid.
36. From a letter by Lodwick to two members of the Royal Society in London, in *Collections of The New-York Historical Society,* second series, vol. 2 (New York: D. Appleton & Co., 1849), pp. 243–50.
37. Sarah Kemble Knight, *The Journal of Madame Knight,* introductory note by Malcolm Freiberg (Boston: David R. Godine, 1972), pp. 30–31.
38. Peter Kalm, *The America of 1750: Peter Kalm's Travels in North America,* Adolph B. Benson, ed. (New York: Wilson-Erickson, 1937), vol. 1, p. 343.
39. Ibid., p. 345.
40. Ibid., pp. 344, 346.
41. Ibid., p. 346.
42. Kammen, p. 81.
43. Kalm, vol. 1, p. 143.
44. Ibid., p. 346.
45. Danckaerts and Sluyter, pp. 119–20.
46. Kalm, vol. 2, pp. 611–13.
47. Kalm, vol. 1, pp. 346–47.
48. Kalm, vol. 2, pp. 602–3.
49. Kenney 1975, p. 134.
50. The Reverend William Edward Schenck, "Account of my trips to Holmdel, N.J. & to Flatlands, L.I.," unpublished journal, The Brooklyn Museum Library Collection, 1891, pp. 13–14.
51. For an extensive analysis of the relationship between the Dutch language and the Dutch Reformed Church, see Gerald F. de Jong, *The Dutch Reformed Church in the American Colonies* (Grand Rapids, MI: Wm. B. Eerdmans, 1978), pp. 211–27.
52. Kenney 1975, p. 133.
53. Charles Gehring, "The Dutch Language in Decline and Its Relationship to Social Change," Ph.D. dissertation, Indiana University, 1973, p. 12. De Jong, p. 219, points out that there were other reasons, in addition to the change in language, for the transfer of membership away from the Dutch church.
54. Benjamin F. Thompson, *History of Long Island* (New York: E. French, 1839), p. 498.

55. Gehring, pp. 4–5.
56. Gertrude Lefferts Vanderbilt, *The Social History of Flatbush* (New York: D. Appleton & Co., 1881), p. 252.
57. Gehring, pp. 101, 106.
58. Ibid., p. 24. This orthographic divergence is more complicated than it might appear and could be due to one or more of several causes.
59. Ibid., p. 57.
60. Alexander Hamilton, *Hamilton's Itinerarium being a Narrative of a Journey from Annapolis, Maryland through Delaware, Pennsylvania, New York, New Jersey, Connecticut, Rhode Island, Massachusetts and New Hampshire from May to September, 1774*, Albert Bushnell Hart, ed. (St. Louis: W. K. Bixby, 1907), p. 86.
61. De Jong, p. 217.
62. Kalm, vol. 2, pp. 626–27.
63. Gehring, p. 114.
64. This was pointed out to me by Lee Roberts.
65. Gehring, p. 17; Alice P. Kenney, "The Albany Dutch: Loyalists and Patriots," *New York History*, no. 42 (October 1961), p. 344.
66. Henry R. Stiles, *History of the City of Brooklyn* (Brooklyn: published by subscription, 1867), vol. 1, p. 243.
67. Ibid., p. 244.
68. Henry R. Stiles, *The Civil, Political, Professional and Ecclesiastical History and Commercial and Industrial Record of the County of Kings and the City of Brooklyn, N.Y. from 1683 to 1884* (New York and Brooklyn: W. W. Munsell & Co., 1884), vol. 1, p. 72.
69. See Kenney 1975, pp. 135–72, for activities of the Dutch during the Revolution.
70. Stiles 1884, vol. 1, p. 73.
71. Nicholas Schenck Papers, Manuscript Division, New-York Historical Society.
72. Maud Esther Dilliard, *Old Dutch Houses of Brooklyn* (New York: Richard R. Smith, 1945), unpaged.
73. Stiles 1867, vol. 1, pp. 299–300.
74. Dilliard; Rosalie Fellows Bailey, *Pre-Revolutionary Dutch Houses and Families in Northern New Jersey and Southern New York* (1936; reprint ed., New York: Dover, 1968), p. 69.
75. Thompson, p. 449.
76. Nicholas Schenck Papers, Manuscript Division, New-York Historical Society.
77. See David W. McCullough, *Brooklyn . . . and How It Got That Way* (New York: Dial Press, 1983), p. 9.
78. See Margaret Latimer, ed., *Brooklyn Almanac* (Brooklyn: Brooklyn Educational and Cultural Alliance, 1984), p. 24; see also McCullough, p. 17.
79. Jabez D. Hammond, *History of Political Parties in the State of New York* (Albany: Van Benthuysen, 1842), vol. 1, p. 581.
80. Higginbotham, p. 143.
81. U.S. Census, Flatlands, Kings County, New York, 1790, p. 98; 1810, vol. 3, p. 658.
82. Higginbotham, p. 143.
83. Nicholas Schenck Papers, Manuscript Division, New-York Historical Society.
84. Higginbotham, p. 147.
85. Nicholas Schenck Papers, Manuscript Division, New-York Historical Society.
86. Original bills in The New-York Historical Society Manuscript Division and The Brooklyn Museum Department of Decorative Arts (accession number 42.367). See also Robert E. P. Hendrick, "Refurbishing the Nicholas Schenck House," *The Brooklyn Museum Annual*, vol. 9 (1967–68), p. 103.
87. Original bill in The New-York Historical Society Manuscript Division.
88. Thompson, p. 450.
89. Jane Schenck (Malbone), "Journal," manuscript in The Brooklyn Museum Library Collection, 1812–16, unpaged.
90. See Vanderbilt, pp. 149–51.
91. Jane Schenck (Malbone).
92. Ibid.
93. Ibid.
94. See Stiles 1867, vol. 1, pp. 396–410.
95. Jane Schenck (Malbone).
96. Ibid.
97. Ibid.
98. Nicholas Schenck Papers, Manuscript Division, New-York Historical Society.
99. Stiles 1884, vol. 1, p. 49.
100. See Alice P. Kenney, "Neglected Heritage: Hudson River Valley Dutch National Culture," *Winterthur Portfolio*, vol. 20, no. 1 (Spring 1985), pp. 51–53.

CHAPTER FOUR:
A NEW IDENTITY,
A NEW STYLE

1. In a letter of November 11, 1797, the Kings County surveyor Jeremiah Lott requested the assistance of Nicholas Schenck in the preparation of the map illustrated here. "I have already made considerable Progress in the protraction of my Maps," he wrote, "which has induced me to request the favour of you, to complete the Observations which we omitted in our Survey in order to find the Distance from your house to Bergen's Island." The letter is now at The New-York Historical Society.
2. Maud Esther Dilliard, *Old Dutch Houses of Brooklyn* (New York: Richard R. Smith, 1945), unpaged.
3. Rosalie Fellows Bailey, *Pre-Revolutionary Dutch Houses and Families in Northern New Jersey and Southern New York* (1936; reprint ed., New York: Dover, 1968), p. 69.
4. See Chapter 1, note 29.
5. Henry R. Stiles, *The Civil, Political, Professional and Ecclesiastical History and Commercial and Industrial Record of the County of Kings and the City of Brooklyn, N.Y. from 1683 to 1884* (New York and Brooklyn: W. W. Munsell & Co., 1884), vol. 2, p. 1344.
6. See Henry C. Mercer, *The Bible in Iron* (Doylestown, PA: Bucks County Historical Society, 1914), pp. 121–22.
7. Henry Gardner Seaver, letter to *The New York Times*, December 16, 1924; printed in *The New York Times*, January 2, 1925, p. 14.
8. Bailey, p. 69; Stiles, vol. 1, p. 69.
9. Stiles, vol. 2, p. 1344.
10. For recent scholarship reflecting this view, see Barbaralee Diamonstein, *The Landmarks of New York* (New York: Harry N. Abrams, Inc., 1988), p. 22.
11. See, for example, Bailey, p. 91.
12. Dilliard.
13. Examination by Henk J. Zantkuyl, August 1986.
14. Bailey, p. 20.
15. Thomas Jefferson Wertenbaker, *The Founding of American Civilization: The Middle Colonies* (New York: Cooper Square, 1963), pp. 66–74.
16. Alan Gowans, *Images of American Living: Four Centuries of Architecture and Furniture as Cultural Expression* (Philadelphia and New York: J. B. Lippincott, 1964), p. 59.
17. Virginia and Lee McAlester, *A Field Guide to American Houses* (New York: Alfred A. Knopf, 1984), p. 116.
18. Hugh Morrison, *Early American Architecture from the First Colonial Settlement to the National Period* (New York: Oxford University Press, 1951), p. 123.
19. Arum Hartunian, "The Dutch-American Vernacular Style

of Architecture," in *The Dutch and America* (Los Angeles: UCLA Press, 1982), pp. 9–19.
20. David Steven Cohen, "Defining the Dutch-American Farmhouse," unpublished manuscript, New Jersey Historical Commission, Trenton, 1986, pp. 7–12.
21. Ibid., pp. 12–13.
22. Above the second floor, high under the rafters, was another storage loft. It was accessible through the large gable opening referred to earlier.
23. Nicholas Schenck Papers, Manuscript Division, New-York Historical Society.
24. Journals at The Brooklyn Historical Society. Details provided by Lee Roberts.
25. Michel-Guillaume-St. Jean de Crèvecoeur, *Sketches of Eighteenth-Century America: More Letters from an American Farmer* (New Haven: Yale University Press, 1925), p. 141.
26. Ibid.
27. John Fitchen, *The New World Dutch Barn* (Syracuse, NY: Syracuse University Press, 1968), p. 82.
28. Crèvecoeur, p. 141.
29. Peter Kalm, *The America of 1750: Peter Kalm's Travels in North America*, Adolph B. Benson, ed. (New York: Wilson-Erickson, 1937), vol. 1, pp. 118–19.
30. A copy of Nicholas Schenck, Sr.'s will is included among the Nicholas Schenck Papers at The New-York Historical Society. The will reads in part, "I give Devise and bequeath unto my son Nicholas Schenck all that messuage dwelling house, Barn tract or parcel of Land Situate Lying and being in the township of Flatlands aforesaid, in the neck so called...to have and to hold...unto him my said son Nicholas Schenck, and to his heir & assigns forever."
31. A copy of Nicholas Schenck, Jr.'s will may also be found at The New-York Historical Society. It reads in part, "I give and bequeath unto my two sons James & Stephen Schenck all that Messuage dwelling house, barn and tract of land called the homestead including that part purchased from Johannes Ditmars Situate lying and being in the township of Flatlands aforesaid in the homestead or neck so called . . .to have and to hold the said messuage dwelling house barn tract or parcel of land meadow and woodland unto them my said sons James and Stephen and to their heirs and assigns forever."
32. Letter from Lillian Tyler Pelham Bantz to Marvin Schwartz, April 10, 1964, in the files of The Brooklyn Museum Department of Decorative Arts.
33. Dilliard.
34. See note 32 above.
35. Although the house remained essentially unchanged during the Whittakers' tenancy, minor alterations were made about 1880. The old Dutch front door, as noted earlier, was cut down to make room for a transom, and transoms were added to interior bedroom doors as well.
36. This information is in the files of the New York City Parks Department. It was gathered by Ralph L. Walter for a paper that he wrote in 1976 for a course at Columbia University. A copy of the paper is now in the files of The Brooklyn Museum Department of Decorative Arts.
37. "Saving Oldest Brooklyn House," *The New York Times*, December 7, 1924, section 9, p. 7.
38. Ibid., December 16, 1924, p. 24.
39. Ibid., January 2, 1925, p. 14.
40. Dianne H. Pilgrim, "Introduction," in Donald Peirce and Hope Alswang, *American Interiors: New England and the South* (Brooklyn: The Brooklyn Museum, 1983), p. 2.
41. William Henry Fox, "Memoirs of Dr. William Henry Fox, 1858–1952," undated manuscript, The Brooklyn Museum Library Collection, vol. 2, pp. 731–32.
42. See note 36 above.
43. Telephone conversation between Robert G. Kron and Ralph L. Walter, 1976.

Chapter Five:
Consumer Goods and Family Heirlooms, or The Morn of Independence

1. Nicholas Schenck Papers, Manuscript Division, New-York Historical Society.
2. Brown is the only paint besides white mentioned with regard to the Schenck House in Elizabeth Haynes, *A Guide to The American Rooms of The Brooklyn Museum* (Brooklyn: The Brooklyn Museum, 1936). Though Haynes does not identify the dark color used on the mantelpiece, she says brown paint was used in the hallway.
3. See Robert E. P. Hendrick, "Refurbishing the Nicholas Schenck House," *The Brooklyn Museum Annual*, vol. 9 (1967–68), pp. 99–112.
4. Richard C. Nylander, *Wallpaper for Historic Buildings* (Washington, DC: The Preservation Press, 1983), p. 17; Catherine Lynn, *Wallpaper in America from the Seventeenth Century to World War I* (New York: W. W. Norton & Company, 1980), p. 279.
5. *Mercantile Advertiser*, as quoted in Rita Susswein Gottesman, *The Arts & Crafts in New York, 1800–1804* (New York: New-York Historical Society, 1965), p. 166.
6. *New York Gazette and General Advertiser*, as quoted in Gottesman, p. 167.
7. *Republican Watch-Tower*, as quoted in Gottesman, p. 168.
8. Inventories, vol. 1, 1832–1836, Film 879.630, Genealogy Department of the Church of Jesus Christ of Latter-Day Saints. Under Kings County, New York Surrogates Court Inventory of Estates, 1830–1865.
9. Manuscript Division, New-York Historical Society.
10. See Nina Fletcher Little, *Floor Coverings in New England Before 1850* (Old Sturbridge Village, MA: Old Sturbridge Village, 1967), pp. 26–28; Anthony Landreau, *America Underfoot* (Washington, DC: Smithsonian Institution, 1976), p. 36; Helene Von Rosenstiel, *American Rugs and Carpets* (New York: William Morrow & Co., 1978), p. 103.
11. See Josephine H. Peirce, *Fire on the Hearth* (Springfield, MA: Pond-Ekberg Co., 1951), pp. 49–52.
12. See note 8 above.
13. Charles R. Hummel, *With Hammer in Hand, The Dominy Craftsmen of East Hampton, New York* (Charlottesville, VA: The University Press of Virginia, 1968), pp. 343–44.
14. *Weekly Museum*, February 28, 1801; also January 30, 1802, and April 2, 1803; as quoted in Gottesman, p. 136.
15. See John Tarrant Kenney, *The Hitchcock Chair* (New York: Clarkson N. Potter, 1971).
16. Arum Hartunian, "The Dutch-American Vernacular Style of Architecture," in *The Dutch and America* (Los Angeles: UCLA Press, 1982), p. 13.
17. Inventory of the estate of James Schenck. Appraised December 14, 1885; entered January 20, 1886. Copy in the files of The Brooklyn Museum Department of Decorative Arts.
18. Luke Vincent Lockwood, *Colonial Furniture in America* (New York: Charles Scribner's Sons, 1913), vol. 1, p. 227, fig. 249.
19. The label reads as follows:

M. ALLISON,
CABINETMAKER,
NO. 46 & 48 VESEY STREET,

Grateful to his friends and the public for past favours, and relying on the superior quality of his work, for fashion and durability, takes this method to inform them, that he has currently on hand and constantly making

NOTES

CABINET FURNITURE

IN ALL ITS VARIETY
SOFAS, MAHOGANY AND ROSEWOOD CHAIRS

Of all descriptions, faithfully made of the best materials, which he will dispose of as Cheap as any Regular Cabinet Maker in this City. Knowing the deception of work made for Auction, he trusts that if people would examine for themselves, and compare the work and the price, that the business, so destructive to all good work and deceptive to the public would have an end.

All orders faithfully executed and punctually attended to.

New York, November, 1825

20. Roderic H. Blackburn, "Dutch Arts & Culture in Colonial America," *Antiques*, vol. 130, no. 1 (July 1986), p. 143.
21. See note 8 above.
22. *The Housekeeping Book of Susanna Whatman, 1776–1800*. Introduction by Christine Hardyment (London: Century, 1987), p. 37. Fuller's earth was a fine dull-green clay (hydrous silicate of alumina) used by fullers in the cloth-making industry and prized for its cleaning properties.
23. Dean F. Failey, *Long Island Is My Nation* (Setauket, NY: Society for the Preservation of Long Island Antiquities, 1976), pp. 204–5.
24. Hartunian, p. 13.
25. Original bill in The Brooklyn Museum Department of Decorative Arts, accession number 42.367.
26. *The Workwoman's Guide*, 2nd ed. (London: Simptain, Marshall & Co.; Birmingham: Thomas Evans, 1840), p. 192. Quoted in Jane Nylander, *Fabrics for Historic Buildings*, 2nd ed. (Washington, DC: The Preservation Press, 1980), p. 31.
27. Quoted in Florence Montgomery, *Printed Textiles: English and American Cottons and Linens, 1700–1850* (New York: The Viking Press, 1970), p. 63.
28. Abbott Lowell Cummings, *Bed Hangings* (Boston: Society for the Preservation of New England Antiquities, 1961), p. 45, fig. 31. See also Jane Nylander, "Bed Hangings, Part I: High Post Beds," *Early American Life*, vol. 15, no. 3 (June 1984), pp. 46–48.
29. Jane Nylander 1980, p. 32. See also Montgomery, p. 330.
30. See Failey, p. 123.
31. See Hummel, p. 276.
32. Joseph B. Felt, *The Customs of New England* (Boston: T. R. Martin, 1853), pp. 20–21.
33. General Jeremiah Johnson was a fourth-generation descendant of a carpenter named Jan Barentse van Driest who immigrated to America in 1657 or 1658 from Zutphen in Gelderland. Apparently, Johnson's great-grandfather, who in the Dutch fashion had been given the patronymic Janse, dropped the van Driest and adopted Johnson as his family name. See Teunis G. Bergen, *Early Settlers of Kings County* (New York: S. W. Green's Son, 1881), pp. 329–30. See also Henry R. Stiles, *History of the City of Brooklyn* (Brooklyn: published by subscription, 1867), vol. 2, p. 255.
34. Letter from Lillian Tyler Pelham Bantz to Marvin Schwartz, April 10, 1964, in the files of The Brooklyn Museum Department of Decorative Arts.
35. See Edgar deN. Mayhew and Minor Myers, Jr., *A Documentary History of American Interiors* (New York: Charles Scribner's Sons, 1980), p. 122.
36. Donald C. Peirce, "New York Furniture at The Brooklyn Museum," *Antiques*, vol. 115, no. 5 (May 1979), p. 994.
37. See note 8 above.
38. Gertrude Lefferts Vanderbilt, *The Social History of Flatbush* (New York: D. Appleton and Co., 1881), pp. 86–87.
39. See Simon Jervis, *Printed Furniture Designs Before 1650* (Leeds: Maney & Son Ltd., for The Furniture History Society, 1974), pp. 41 and 294. The complete title of de Passe's volume, published in Latin, was *Oficina Arcularia In Qua Sunt Ad Spectantia Diversa Eximia Exempla Ex Varius Autoribus Collecta*.
40. Failey, pp. 104–5.
41. For the older view, see Huyler Held, "Long Island Dutch Splat Backs," *Antiques*, vol. 30, no. 4 (October 1936), pp. 168–70; for more recent research, see Failey, pp. 81–84.
42. Hummel, pp. 246–52.
43. See note 8 above.
44. Vanderbilt, p. 92.
45. The Museum itself has three religious books with a history of ownership in the Schenck family. One, a Dutch Psalter entitled *De Cl. Psalmen des Propheten Davids* (accession number 60.75), was published in Amsterdam in 1671 and is inscribed with the date 1679 and the words "Johannes Schenck/Zyn Bock." Another, a Dutch New Testament published in Amsterdam in 1728 (accession number 67.15.2), is inscribed for an Abraham Schenck, while the third, a Bible printed in English and dated 1800 (accession number 67.15.3), is inscribed for a Jacob Schenck.
46. This and the preceding information about John Barrett's Bible were provided by Lee Roberts.
47. Jane Schenck (Malbone), "Journal," manuscript in The Brooklyn Museum Library Collection, 1812–16, unpaged.

APPENDIX

In his 1964 book *The Jan Martense Schenck House*, Marvin D. Schwartz published an appendix devoted to an extensive analysis of the Schenck House structure. That appendix is reprinted here in full.

The purpose of the appendix is to summarize the findings made in examining the structural details of the house. The decisions for many aspects of the restoration were based on two kinds of evidence: documentation and examination of the structural elements in the process of dismantling and reconstructing the house. A field book compiled during the reconstruction by Ian Smith, a collaborating architect, contains sketches of the pertinent details and is available in the office of the Department of Decorative Arts.

Examination of the framework made it clear that the L-shaped plan was the product of two building periods. The original section of the house was twelve posts long. These posts have Roman numerals on them and today eleven of the original posts, numbered consecutively, are to be found on the west side of the house. The post at the south end was replaced in about 1800 during stage 3. [Schwartz identified five stages in the construction of the house: circa 1675, the original building; circa 1730, the removal of the western aisle; circa 1800, the addition of the kitchen wing; circa 1830–50, the addition of the porch; late 1800s, the division of the attic into rooms.] On the east side, the four posts at the south end were replaced in stage 3, and parts of numbers III, IV, and V had to be replaced during the reconstruction. The posts of the kitchen wing, in contrast to the others, were unfinished on the outer or covered sides and had curved corner edges on the inner or room sides. The original posts had first been stained a walnut red while the others had a grey blue first coat. In the rafters the change was equally obvious. At the north end, the rafters had been cut to accommodate the slope of the kitchen roof. Number I had been removed, II was cut very close to the plate. The rest of the eight rafters have been well preserved and are now stored in the attic. At the south gable end the notches for the purlins were numbered, as were the purlins. The alterations to the south end involved cutting the plate out and substituting new studs chamfered into the collar beam on top and mortised into the replacement beam inserted at the attic floor level. The pair of rafters number V come into the center with the chimney opening and trimmer above the break in the plate where the dormer comes and joining IV and VI.

The center section of the beams had obvious changes. The beams at posts VI and VIII had been covered by walls in about 1800. Cross beams that surrounded the original fireplaces and joined VI and VIII had been changed and replaced.

Evidence of one seventeenth-century window was found in east post V where the mortise holes for the horizontal members of the window were uncovered. In the attic, the south gable mortise holes in the collar beam have been interpreted in the same way. To put in the 1730 window frames on the west façade it was necessary to cut out parts of the posts where they were to go. The south room east window was similar, but the posts had been changed and by 1952 the upper sash had been replaced. The kitchen wing windows differed in detail and dimension. The nineteenth-century dormers did not match the downstairs windows.

East post III had evidence of mortise holes for the seventeenth-century door. The door in the west façade has a fine walnut frame with details of 1730–50. Matching it was one in the east façade that had been covered with shingles to serve as the frame of a late nineteenth-century makeshift window pane inserted into it. Probably to place it, the cross beam or trimmer between VI and VII, under the dormer, had to be removed. Neither door nor window in the south wall had survived in 1952. There were, however, two horizontal members found in the wall, that could be interpreted as the upper parts of doors or windows, and one door sill. This resulted in making one opening a door and the other a window. The door used had come from another Brooklyn house and dates about 1750. All eleven original posts on the west façade had mortise holes on the outside which were made to hold down-slanting elements. These have been interpreted as being the frame of the overhang which was the roof of a shelter that could have been used for animals. Markings on the beams that might have served as indications of early walls or bed-boxes were never consistent. The north room could have had a wall dividing it about five feet from the door, if the mark on several of the beams had been followed. There was not quite enough evidence, however.

Before dismantling the house, only the heavy beams with their knee braces and projecting posts confirmed the seventeenth-century date of the house suggested by documents and family tradition. With the exception of the eighteenth-century windows, the early details had been concealed. The fireplace in the south room, although papered over, did have a molding related to those common between 1760 and 1800, and was probably put in during the remodeling of 1800. The shelf was much later. The beams and post had been painted frequently and were an enamel white in 1952. While removing the paint a number of colors were encountered, with the obsequious grey blue just above the stain.

The kitchen wing was not restored because it was not a part of the seventeenth-century phase of the house. In connecting the wing and the main section, the roof lines were distorted and some significant evidence of the earlier phase would have been sacrificed. Actually, the wing had architectural integrity, and the fireplace wall is distinctive. During the demolition, the small oven opening was uncovered, and the lines of a handsome kitchen fireplace revealed. These may very well be used at a later date.

In restoring the seventeenth-century fireplaces, it was decided to seek models for two handsome mantels. Although one finds mantels omitted in some contemporary Dutch houses of both this continent and Europe, it was reasoned that in the New York area, where fine furniture and ceramics were so commonly mentioned in inventories, fine architectural details would not be omitted. The two models selected were from houses in the Hudson River Valley. The simpler of the two came from the Jean Hasbrouck house in New Paltz. The other, from the de Windt house in Tappan, is now a part of an eighteenth-century panelled wall. The fireplace has been enclosed and side pilasters moved forward, but originally it looked as it does in the reconstruction.